CONTENTS

ISBN 0 85147 320 2

First Edition 1970

Second Edition, fully revised 1972

Printed in Brighton England for Autopress Ltd by G Beard & Son Ltd

FIAT 500 1957-72 AUTOBOOK

Workshop Manual for
Fiat 500 (110) 1957-60
Fiat 500D (110D) 1960-65
Fiat Giardiniera (120) 1960-68
Fiat 'New 500' (110F) 1965-72
Fiat 500L (110F/L) 1969-72
Fiat Autobianchi Giardiniera 1968-72

by

Kenneth Ball G I Mech E

and the

Autopress team of Technical Writers

AUTOPRESS LTD GOLDEN LANE BRIGHTON BN1 2QJ ENGLAND

The AUTOBOOK series of Workshop Manuals covers the majority of British and Continental motor cars.

For a full list see the back of this manual.

ACKNOWLEDGEMENT

My thanks are due to Fiat (England) Ltd. for their unstinted co-operation and also for supplying data and illustrations.

I am also grateful to a considerable number of owners who have discussed their cars at length and many of whose suggestions have been included in this manual.

Kenneth Ball G I Mech E
Associate Member Guild of Motoring Writers
Ditchling Sussex England.

INTRODUCTION

This do-it-yourself Workshop Manual has been specially written for the owner who wishes to maintain his car in first class condition and to carry out his own servicing and repairs. Considerable savings on garage charges can be made, and one can drive in safety and confidence knowing the work has been done properly.

Comprehensive step-by-step instructions and illustrations are given on all dismantling, overhauling and assembling operations. Certain assemblies require the use of expensive special tools, the purchase of which would be unjustified. In these cases information is included but the reader is recommended to hand the unit to the agent for attention.

Throughout the Manual hints and tips are included which will be found invaluable, and there is an easy to follow fault diagnosis at the end of each chapter.

Whilst every care has been taken to ensure correctness of information it is obviously not possible to guarantee complete freedom from errors or to accept liability arising from such errors or omissions.

Instructions may refer to the righthand or lefthand sides of the vehicle or the components. These are the same as the righthand or lefthand of an observer standing behind the car and looking forward.

CHAPTER 1

THE ENGINE

1:1 Description

The 'New 500' two-cylinder aircooled engine operates on the four-stroke 'Otto Cycle' and is fitted directly to the transmission unit which incorporates the rear drive assembly as shown in **FIG 1:1** and **FIG 1:2**.

With the power unit fitted at the rear several advantages are obtained including better load distribution to the wheels when the vehicle is loaded, elimination of propeller shaft reducing the size of centre tunnel and better use of available space.

The cylinder block comprises two cast iron cylinder barrels with cooling fins. The bottom of the cylinders fit into machined seats in the aluminium crankcase.

The aluminium crankcase carries eight studs on which are located the two cylinder barrels with the aluminium cylinder head on the top.

A two bush crankshaft of special cast iron is fitted into the lower half of the crankcase. The centre of which is provided with a counterweight and is hollow to allow for lubrication.

The steel connecting rods have thin wall bearing halves on the big-end, and bronze bushes in the small-end. The offset piston pin is of steel and retained in the piston by two circlips.

Light alloy pistons are used and are of the taper-oval-shaped type with a maximum diameter at the base of the skirt, along an axis perpendicular to the piston pin. Pistons are fitted with four rings as follows, one compression at the top, two standard oil scraper rings and one side slotted oil scraper ring.

The one-piece aluminium cylinder head is finned to provide a larger cooling surface and carries the inlet and exhaust manifolds.

The inlet manifolds merge into a single centralized flange onto which is mounted the carburetter. The exhaust manifolds run almost parallel to the axis of the engine.

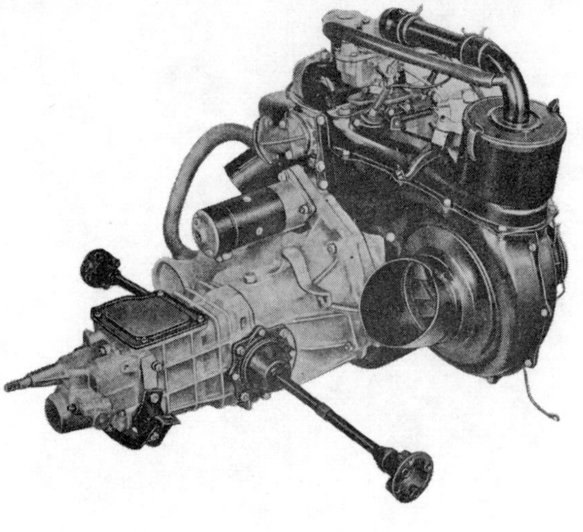

FIG 1:1 Left side view of the power plant to suit 500 Sedan

Mounted on the top of the cylinder head is the overhead valve rocker mechanism that is operated by a chain driven camshaft through tappets and vertical pushrods.

The carburetter is of the downdraft type fitted with a starting device that is controlled by a lever on the central floor tunnel. A pleated paper element air cleaner and silencer is fitted to the carburetter air intake. A mechanical diaphragm type fuel pump operated from the camshaft by a pushrod, supplies petrol to the carburetter from a fuel tank located at the front of the vehicle.

Engine lubrication is provided by a gear pump driven from the camshaft and mounted within the timing cover drawing oil from the engine sump. The oil is cleaned by a centrifugal pump situated at the rear end of the crankshaft and pressure is controlled by a valve mounted on the pump body. Crankcase ventilation is provided for through a rubber hose connected to the top of the rocker cover.

The engine is cooled by air from a centrifugal blower mounted on the generator shaft and is housed in a specially designed cowling conveying air to and around the engine. The air temperature is governed by a special thermostat fitted in the engine cowling.

FIG 1:2 Right side rear three-quarter view of the power plant for 500 Station Wagon

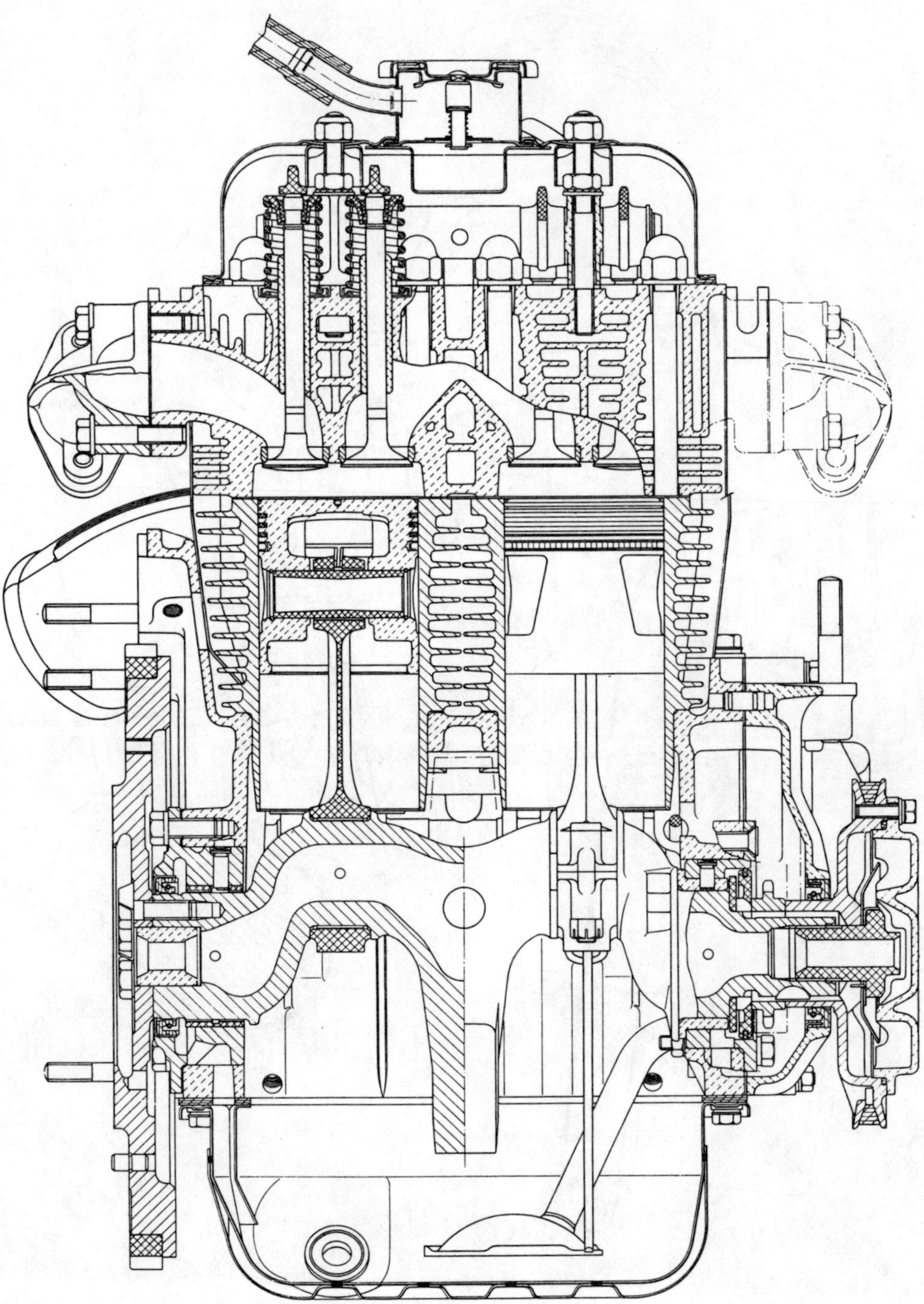

FIG 1:3 Engine section through crankshaft, pistons and valves

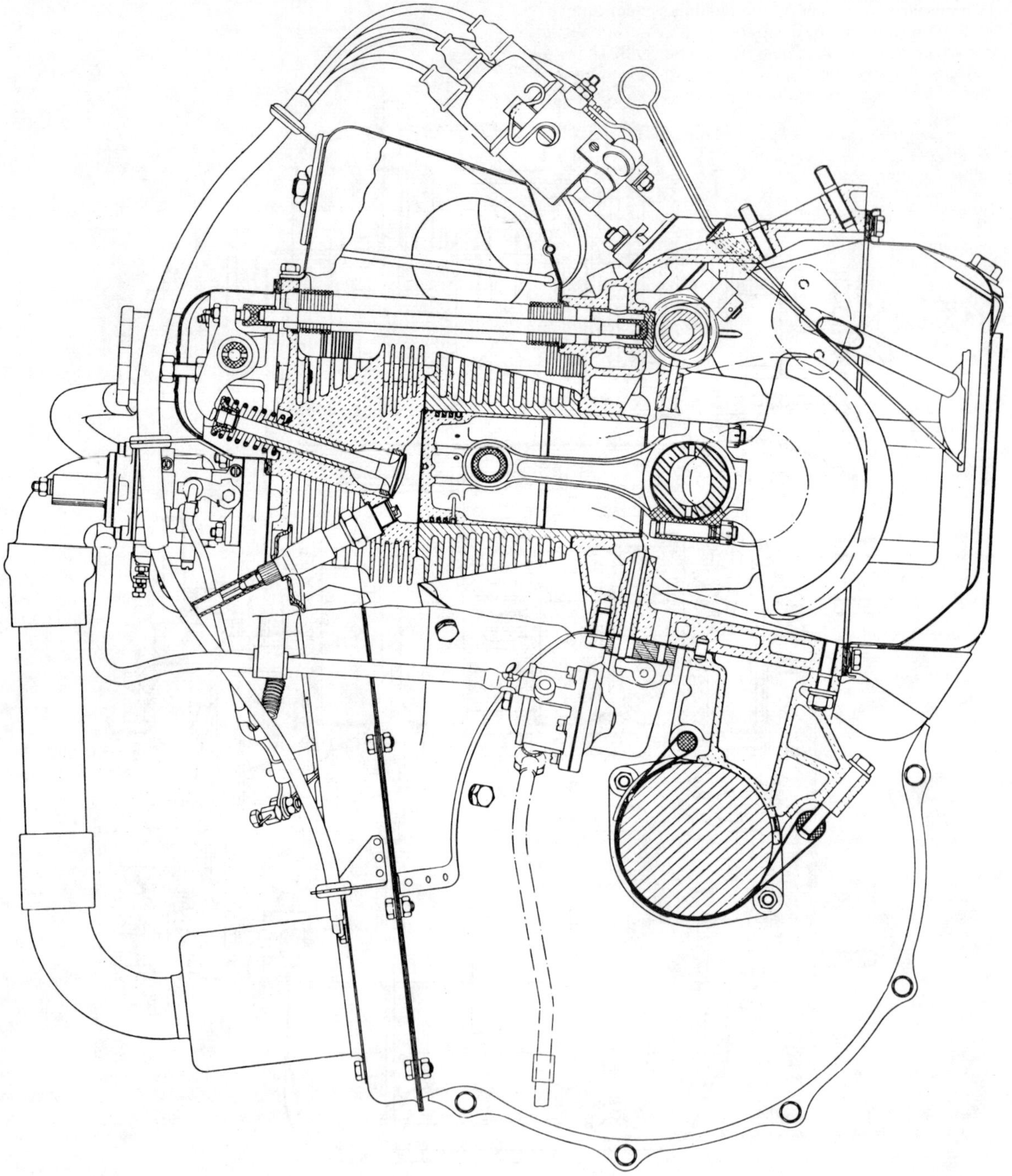

FIG 1:4 Engine cross-section through a cylinder

The interior of the car can be heated by the engine warmed air being ducted into the front compartment and is controlled by a lever on the heating system tunnel.

Engine ignition is by a battery, ignition coil and distributor which is driven by a gear on the camshaft. The engine is started by an electric starter motor which is mounted on the gearbox casing and is controlled by a lever located behind the gearchange lever.

The complete power unit is mounted by a spring support at the centre of the rear body crossmember and by two rubber pads mounted laterally to the gearbox.

1:2 Engine removal (sedan—all versions)

To remove the engine from the car proceed as follows:

1 Raise the rear of the car and place on firmly based stands placed under suitable brackets on the underside of the body.

2 Disconnect the battery positive terminal clamp from the battery terminal post. Release the clip securing the main petrol pipe to the tank sender unit and ease the pipe from the unit. Drain the oil from the engine sump into a suitably sized container.

3 Disconnect the rear number plate light wire (see **FIG 1:6**). Release the engine compartment lid, check strap from its slot and separate the lid from the body by sliding the hinge apart.

4 Remove the cables attached to the ignition coil, also to the generator and the starter motor. Remove the starter motor control tie rod. Release the oil pressure indicator cable, the main petrol pipeline at the pump, the accelerator and starting device controls.

5 Remove the two hoses of the heating and cooling system which are the input hose to the blower and the hose for the car heating system. Release and lift out the engine apron. Remove the starter motor mounting bolts and carefully lift away the motor.

6 Using a garage hydraulic jack with suitable cradle (see **FIG 1:7**) or a rope sling relieve the engine weight from its mountings. Remove the nuts securing the gearbox to the engine and the flywheel protection apron.

7 Remove the bolts fixing the elastic support to the crossmember. Remove the rear crossmember mounting nuts noting that the engine earth cable is held by one mounting nut and lift away the crossmember.

8 Carefully ease the engine away from the gearbox ensuring that there is no strain placed on the clutch shaft. Lower the engine to the floor taking care that no weight is allowed on any of the attachments.

1:3 Engine removal (station wagon)

To remove the engine from the station wagon proceed as follows:

1 Raise the rear of the vehicle and place on firmly based stands placed under suitable brackets on the underside of the body.

2 Disconnect the battery positive terminal clamp from the battery terminal post. Release the clip securing the main petrol pipe to the tank sender unit and ease the pipe from the unit. Drain the oil from the engine sump into a clean dry container of suitable size.

3 Hold the rear door open and secure using string to stop it swinging to the closed position. Secure the luggage compartment floor panel in its upright position.

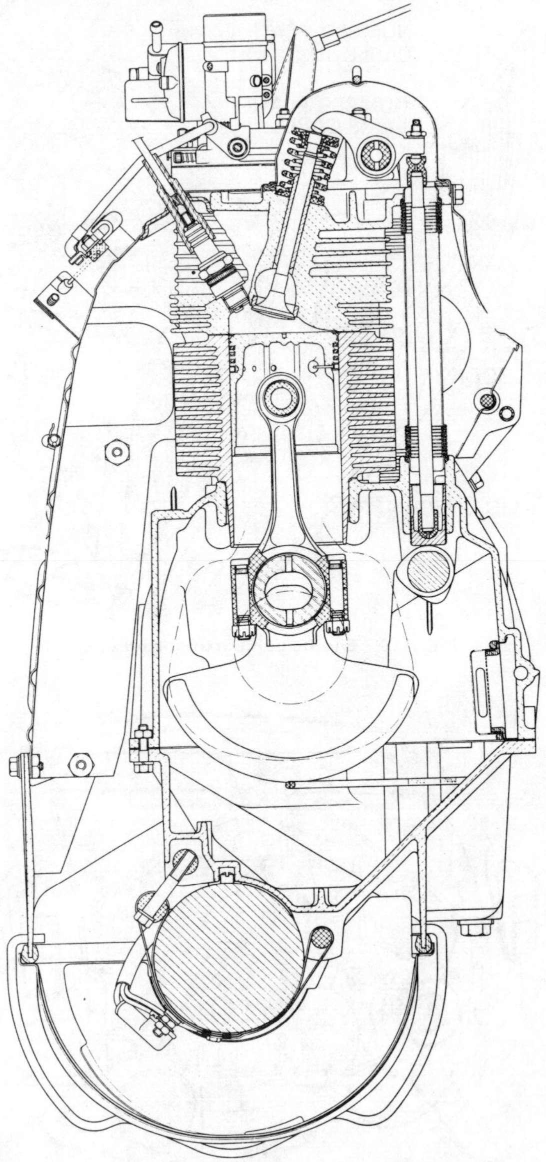

FIG 1:5 120.000 engine assembly: cross-section view through a cylinder

4 Remove the cables attached to the ignition coil, also to the generator and starter motor. Remove the starter motor control tie rod. Release the oil pressure indicator cable, the main petrol pipeline at the pump, the accelerator and starting device controls. Disconnect the air filter housing.

5 Remove the hose connecting the car heating system to the engine cowling. Disconnect the clip holding the air pipe to the blower and carefully disconnect the pipe from the blower cowling. Remove the starter motor mounting bolts and carefully lift away the motor.

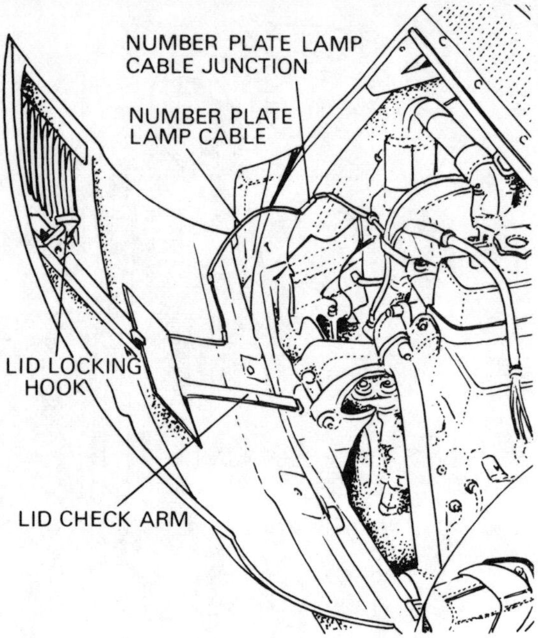

FIG 1:6 Engine compartment lid open

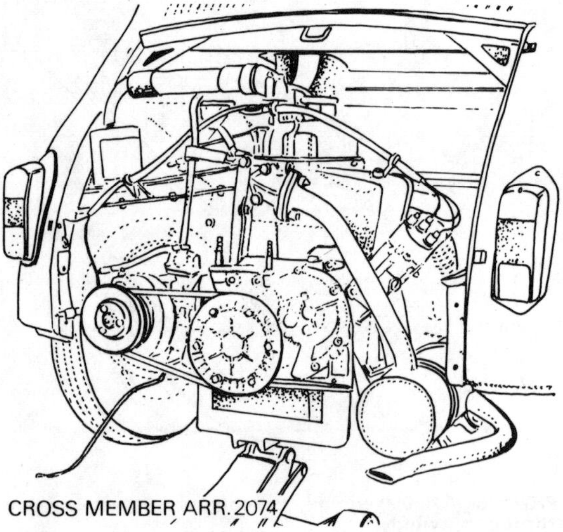

FIG 1:7 Engine removal using the jack with cross-member Arr.2074

6 Using a garage hydraulic jack with a suitable cradle relieve the engine weight from its mountings. Remove the nuts securing the gearbox to the engine.
7 Remove the nuts securing the rear bumper blade and panel to the body. Note that the engine earth cable is held by one mounting nut. Carefully dismantle the engine elastic mounting or release the bracket from the engine rear cover by removing the two nuts and washers. Lift away the rear panel assembly carefully making sure that rear air ducting panels are not strained or the mating faces damaged.
8 Carefully ease the engine away from the gearbox ensuring that there is no strain placed on the clutch shaft. Lower the engine to the floor taking care that no weight is allowed on any of the attachments.

1:4 Engine disassembly (sedan—all versions)

To dismantle the engine proceed as follows:

1 Remove the exhaust silencer by releasing the two collars for attachment to the engine and the two connections for the exhaust pipe. It will be noted that there is one exhaust pipe connection on either side of the cylinder head.
2 Place the engine on a firm wooden top bench. Remove the two tappet cover retaining nuts and washers and lift away the cover. Remove the connection for cooling air delivery to the sump cooling ducts at the side of the sump.
3 Remove the air cleaner after first releasing the two bolts on the air cowling and the two nuts for the air elbow connection to the carburetter.
4 Remove the generator drive belt by releasing the three nuts so splitting the semi-pulley. Lift away the drive belt.
5 Remove all the bolts securing the air conveyor ducting to the cylinder head, to the crankcase and also to the engine cowling assembly opposite to the air conveyor. Release the accelerator control tie rod and carefully lift away the air conveyor assembly complete with the generator after first removing the clamp fixing the generator to the crankcase.

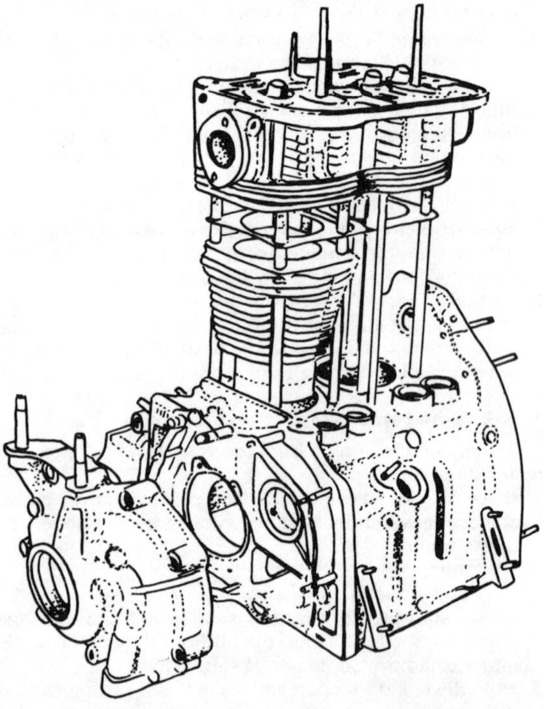

FIG 1:8 Engine components: crankcase, cylinder head, timing sprockets cover

6 Release the ignition distributor support retaining nut and lift away the distributor together with its support.

7 Remove all the mounting bolts of the engine cooling cowling and lift away the assembly. Release the two carburetter retaining nuts and carefully remove the carburetter together with its drip tray.

8 Lift away the valve rocker assembly having first released the two retaining nuts together with the plain washers and lock washers. Carefully lift out the valve rocker pushrods noting their relevant positions.

9 Slacken the four central cylinder head cap nuts and the four conventional nuts in the order shown in **FIG 1:44**. Lift the cylinder head away from the barrels. If difficulty is experienced it is essential to use Fiat tool A.40014 or a similar drilled plate, otherwise serious damage could be caused if other means are used (see **FIG 1:9**).

10 Remove the four pushrod sleeves and the casing containing the oil ducting to the overhead valve gear.

11 Remove the fuel pump retaining nuts and washers and lift away the pump. Carefully pull out the pump control pushrod from the crankcase.

12 Remove the six screws holding the centrifugal oil filter pulley cover and lift away the cover. Remove the centrifugal filter mounting flange by unscrewing the crankshaft central bolt. Also remove the timing cover containing the oil pump gears and the oil pressure regulating valve. Note the position of the nuts, toothed and plain washers for correct reassembly.

13 Release the four camshaft sprocket retaining bolts and lift away the sprocket and timing chain. Using Fiat pulley A.46020 or a large universal two-leg puller as shown in **FIG 1:10** remove the crankshaft sprocket and its body.

14 Carefully lift out the rocker pushrod tappets making a note of their location and gently pull out the camshaft making sure the front bearing bore is not damaged by the cam lobes or distributor drive gear.

15 Mark the flywheel and crankshaft to ensure correct reassembly and release the six flywheel retaining bolts together with the lockwashers and lift away the flywheel.

16 Using Fiat tool A.60156 on the two central studs, lock the two cylinder barrels in place as shown in **FIG 1:11**.

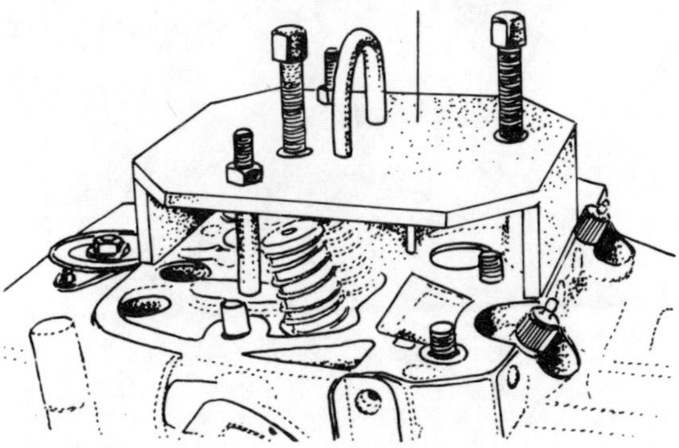

FIG 1:9 Tool A.40014 for cylinder head removal

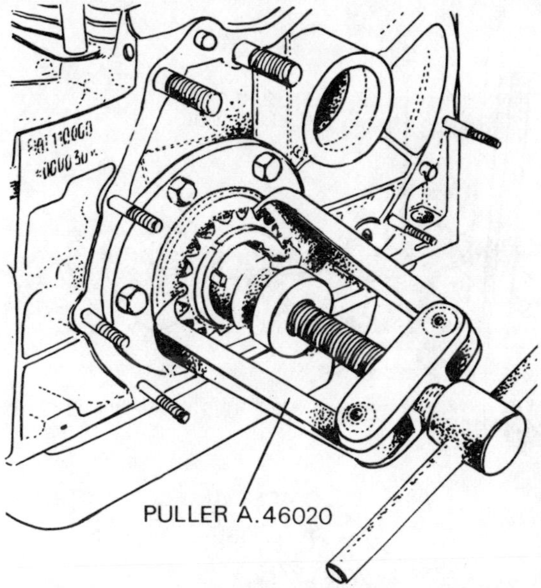

FIG 1:10 Removing crankshaft sprocket with puller A.46020

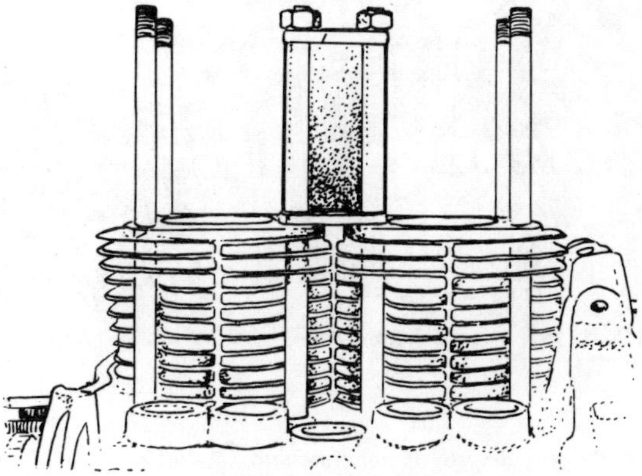

FIG 1:11 Cylinder hold-down tool A.60156

17 Turn the engine upside down ensuring that no weight is placed on the studs and remove the oil sump and the oil suction scoop.

18 Mark the connecting rods and end caps to ensure correct reassembly and remove the end caps. Place the engine on its side and remove the cylinder barrels clamp. Ensure that the studs are clean and carefully slide off the connecting rod-piston-cylinder assemblies from the crankcase.

19 Remove the six screws holding the rear main bearing housing to the crankcase and lift away the housing. Remove the six screws holding the front main bearing housing to the crankcase and lift away the housing.

20 Carefully ease the crankshaft from the crankcase moving it diagonally to assist withdrawal.

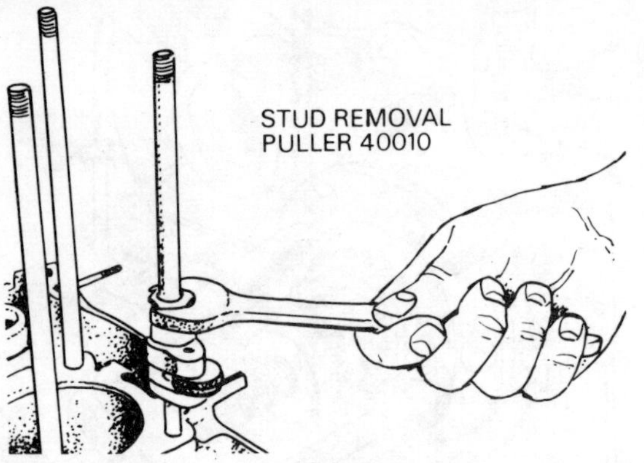

FIG 1:12 Removal of stud from crankcase by puller A.40010

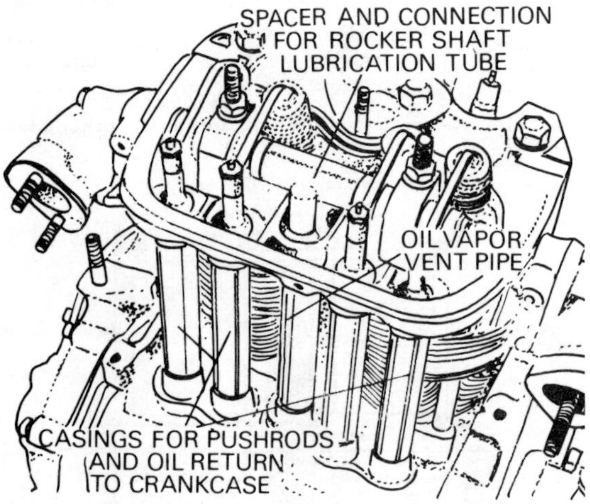

FIG 1:13 Engine without blower cowling and cylinder head cover

21 To ensure no damage occurs to the long cylinder barrel mounting studs these may be removed using Fiat puller A.40010 or a universal stud removal as shown in **FIG 1:12**.

1:5 Engine disassembly (station wagon)

To dismantle the engine proceed as follows:

1 Remove the exhaust silencer and manifold by releasing the four nuts holding the two flanges from the cylinder head. Also disconnect the two silencer mounting brackets and lift away the exhaust system (see **FIG 1:2**).

2 Place the engine on a firm wooden top bench. Release the clip holding the tappet cover and lift away together with the drip tray. Disconnect the fuel line and throttle linkage at the carburetter and carefully lift away the carburetter together with its insulator joint and gaskets.

3 Remove the generator drive belt by releasing the three nuts so splitting the semi-pulley. Lift away the drive belt.

4 Remove all the bolts securing the air conveyor ducting to the cylinder head and to the crankcase, carefully separate the panels and lift away the separate panels ensuring no damage is caused to the mating faces.

5 Release the ignition distributor retaining bolt and lift away the distributor.

6 Remove the fuel pump retaining bolts and also the three fuel pipe retaining clips and lift away the fuel pump assembly together with the insulator, gaskets and control rod.

7 Release the two valve rocker retaining nuts, note the order of assembly of washers and ease away the rocker shaft assembly from the top of the cylinder head. Carefully lift out the valve rocker pushrods noting their relevent positions for correct reassembly.

8 Slacken the four cylinder head cap nuts and the four conventional nuts in the order shown in **FIG 1:46**. Lift the cylinder head away from the barrels. If difficulty is experienced it is essential to use Fiat tool A.40014 or a similar drilled plate as shown in **FIG 1:9**, otherwise serious damage could be caused if other means are used.

9 Remove the four pushrod sleeves and the casing containing the oil ducting to the overhead valve gear.

10 Remove the six screws holding the centrifugal oil filter pulley cover and lift away the cover. Remove the centrifugal filter mounting flange by unscrewing the crankshaft central bolt. Also remove the timing cover from the rear of the crankcase. Note carefully the position of the nuts, toothed and plain washers for correct reassembly.

11 Release the four crankshaft sprocket retaining bolts and lift away the sprocket and timing chain. Using Fiat puller A.46020 or a large universal two-leg puller as shown in **FIG 1:10** remove the crankshaft sprocket and its key.

12 Carefully lift out the rocker pushrod tappets making a note of their location and gently pull out the camshaft making sure that the front bearing bore is not damaged by the cam lobes.

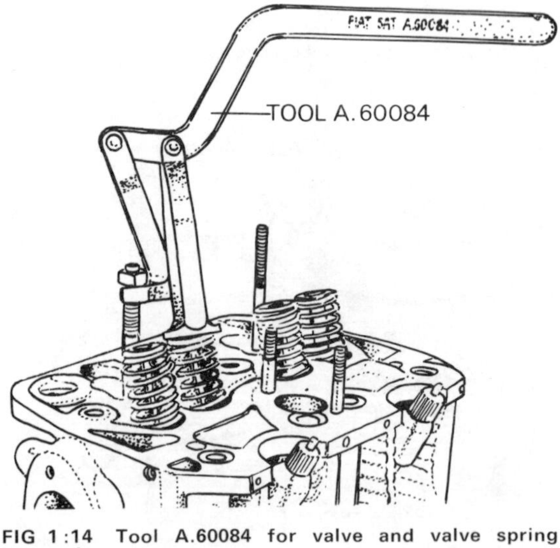

FIG 1:14 Tool A.60084 for valve and valve spring removal

13 Remove all the bolts and washers joining the sump casting to the crankcase making a special note of the location of bolts of different lengths.
14 Mark the flywheel and crankshaft to ensure correct reassembly and release the six flywheel retaining bolts together with the lockwashers and lift away the flywheel.
15 Using Fiat tool A.60156 on the two central studs, lock the two cylinder barrels in place (see **FIG 1:11**).
16 Turn the engine upside down ensuring that no weight is placed on the studs.
17 Mark the connecting rods and end caps to ensure correct reassembly and remove the end caps. Place the engine on its side and remove the cylinder barrels clamp. Ensure that the studs are clean and carefully slide off the connecting rod-piston-cylinder assemblies from the crankcase.
18 Remove the six screws holding the rear bearing housing to the crankcase and lift away the housing. Remove the six screws holding the front main bearing housing to the crankcase and lift away its housing.
19 Carefully ease the crankshaft from the crankcase moving it diagonally to assist withdrawal.
20 To ensure no damage occurs to the long cylinder barrel mounting studs these may be removed using Fiat puller A.40010 or a universal stud remover as shown in **FIG 1:12**.

1:6 Cylinder head removal, servicing and replacement

Description:

The aluminium cylinder head is finned to increase the cooling surface. Through bolts secure the head and the two cylinders to the crankcase. The valves are controlled by a camshaft through tappets, pushrods and rockers. The connection between the head and the crankcase is via five sleeves mounted directly between the head and crankcase, and these accommodate the pushrods, lubricating oil and passage for the crankcase gases. The cylinder head has been modified for the 110 F.000 and 120.000 engines as they now incorporate a heater safety device as described in **Section 4:4**.

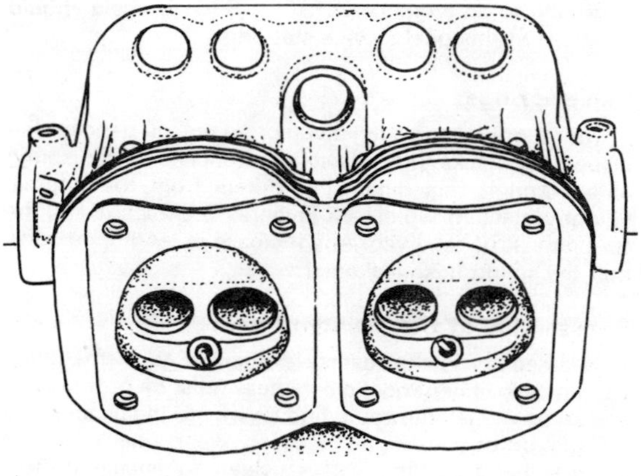

FIG 1:15 Cylinder head on surface plate

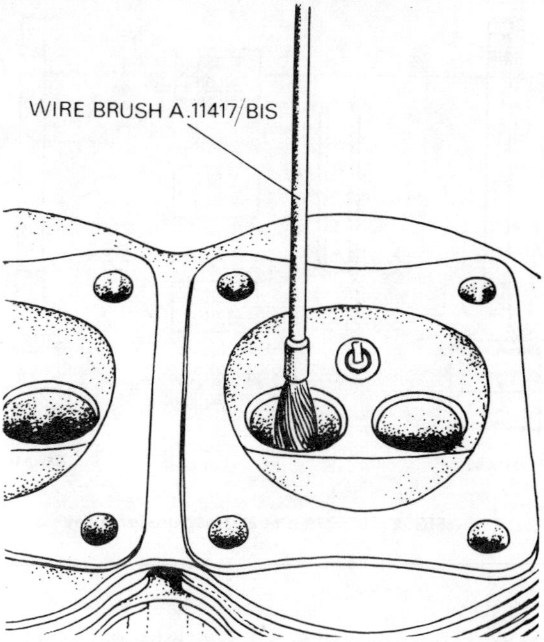

FIG 1:16 Cleaning valve guides

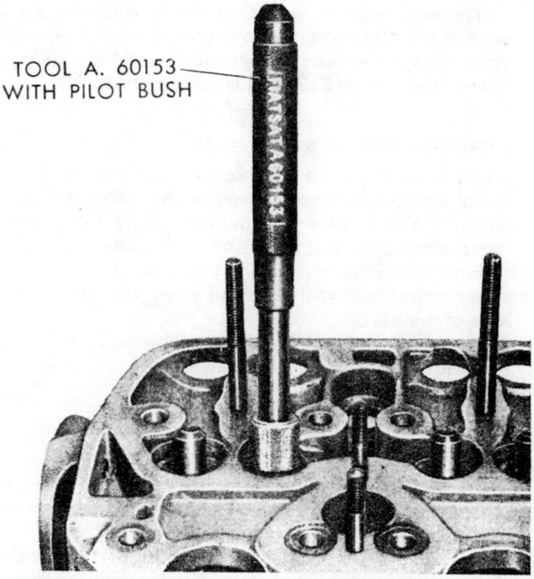

FIG 1:17 Installing a valve guide using Tool A.60153 provided with pilot bush

Removal of cylinder head:

The cylinder head should be removed whenever the valves require attention or the engine to be decarbonized. To remove the cylinder head proceed as follows:

1 Remove the air cleaner, carburetter, rocker cover and the screws securing the blower conveyor to the cylinder

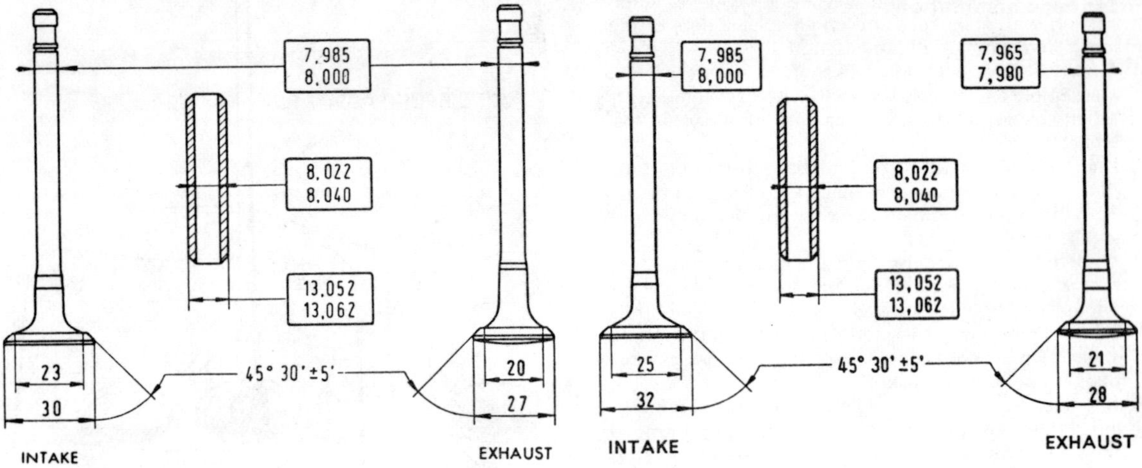

FIG 1:18 Main specifications of intake and exhaust valves and valves guides (dimensions in mm)

head. Disconnect the two side exhaust manifolds. Note the spark plug HT cables locations and disconnect from spark plugs.

2 Remove the rocker shaft pedestal and lift away the rocker gear. Extract the pushrods, making a careful note of their location. Remove the cylinder head hold down nuts in the order shown in **FIG 1:44** and using a puller as shown in **FIG 1:9** lift off the head.

Dismantling the cylinder head:

1 Using Fiat valve spring compressor A.60084 or a universal spring compressor depress the valve spring as shown in **FIG 1:14** and lift out the cotters. Release the compressor and withdraw the lock cone, oil shield (inlet valve only) upper spring cup, valve spring and lower spring cup. Withdraw the valve from the underside of the head.

2 Dismantle the remaining three valve assemblies as detailed above ensuring that all parts are kept in sets for correct reassembly.

Inspection and servicing of the cylinder head:

1 Remove all carbon deposits from the combustion chambers and valve ports using a rotary wire brush or a set of scrapers.

2 Thoroughly clean the cylinder head and to test for distortion lightly coat the machined faces with 'Engineers Blue' or lamp black and place the cylinder head on a surface plate (see **FIG 1:15**). Carefully slide to and fro and any streaks left behind will indicate a distorted surface. Carefully file any high spots and retest as detailed above. Only the least possible amount of material should be removed. Upon completion thoroughly clean to ensure no traces of abrasive material are left behind.

3 Carefully clean the valve guides as shown in **FIG 1:16** using Fiat guide brush A.11417 bis. Should the guides be worn then they should be removed using a press and a suitable sized drift. The guides are press fitted with a pinch fit of .00134 to .00244 inch. To install the guides use Fiat tool A.60153 as shown in **FIG 1:17**. As the guides have no stop ring during the press fitting, the depth of insertion is determined by the Fiat tool. If the tool is not available take the necessary depth measurements before the old guides are removed. The normal fit clearance between valve stem and guide is .00087 to .00217 inch with a maximum wear limit of .0059 inch. To check this see **FIG 1:18**.

4 The valve seats should always be reconditioned after decarbonization. It is suggested that this operation be left to a local service station with valve seat cutting equipment. The valve seat angle for both inlet and exhaust valves is 45° ± 5'.

5 Inspect the valves for soundness or distortion and if the clearance between guide and stem is within the manufacturers wear tolerance of .0049 inch the valve may be cleaned using a wire brush and the seating face ground to an angle of 45°30' ± 5'. This again should be left to the local service station.

Valve springs:

Thoroughly clean the valve springs of oil deposit and inspect for cracks. It is advisable to check the free spring height and if this dimension differs from the original height, details of which are given in Technical Data, the spring must be renewed. Any increase in length indicates that the spring has weakened.

Reassembly of the cylinder head:

Reassembly is the reverse procedure to dismantling. During assembly utmost cleanliness must be observed as any abrasive material could find its way to the pistons and cylinder bores causing unnecessary wear. Check that the cylinder barrel mating face is clean to ensure correct gasket sealing.

Cylinder head installation:

To refit the cylinder head proceed as follows:

1 Place a new cylinder head joint on the cleaned faces of the cylinder barrels. Insert the rocker pushrod and lubrication pipe sleeves together with the relevant gaskets and rings.
2 Fit the washers and nuts to the studs and tighten to fingertight.
3 Tighten the nuts in the order shown in **FIG 1:44** and **FIG 1:46** to a torque wrench setting of 18.1 lb ft. Reset the torque wrench to a new setting of 23.9 lb ft and tighten the nuts once more in the recommended order. Replace the pushrods in the correct order.
4 Refit the rocker shaft ensuring correct location of the lubrication tube to the rocker shaft and replace the plain and lockwashers. Tighten the nuts to a torque wrench setting of 15.2 lb ft. Reset the tappet to rocker clearance adjustment.
5 Connect the two exhaust side manifolds to the cylinder head. Using new gasket refit the spark plugs and HT cables. Replace the rocker cover fitted with a new cork gasket and blower conveyor to the cylinder head securing screws. Refit the carburetter and reconnect its fuel line and controls. Refit the air cleaner and elbow and connect the rocker cover breather pipe (if fitted).

1:7 Timing gear overhaul

Camshaft:

The cast iron camshaft is located in the crankcase and is supported at either end in sets machined directly in the crankcase. No bushes are used. The camshaft is driven by a chain from the crankshaft at half engine speed and operates the overhead valves through tappets, pushrods and rockers (see **FIG 1:20**).

During engine overhaul the camshaft journals and cam faces should be free of score marks or signs of seizure and have a bright mirror finish. Should any slight indentations be found then these may be removed by using a very fine oil stone.

The distributor drive gear should be inspected for tooth wear which if excessive means that the camshaft must be replaced.

Tappets:

The tappets should be inspected for signs of seizure or excessive wear. The end surface that is in contact with the camshaft should be smooth without signs of excessive wear. Any slight scratches or indentations may be removed using a very fine oil stone.

Pushrods and sleeves:

The pushrods operated in special axially restant sleeves that are compressed on assembly between the cylinder head and the crankcase. It is through these sleeves that the engine sump is vented also through which the oil returning from the cylinder head passes.

Two rubber O-ring seals are fitted to each sleeve to ensure an oil tight seal between the cylinder head and crankcase. The sleeves should be checked for distortion and exact equal length and when refitting new seals must always be fitted.

The pushrods should be checked for straightness and the two ends that contact the rocker setscrew and the

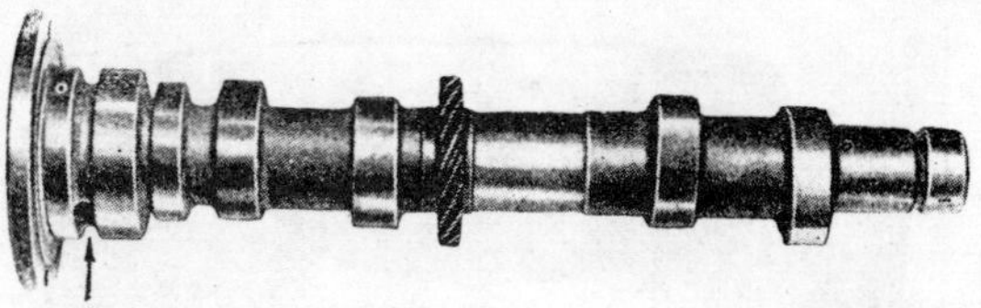

FIG 1:19 Camshaft. The arrow points to the lube oil outlet port

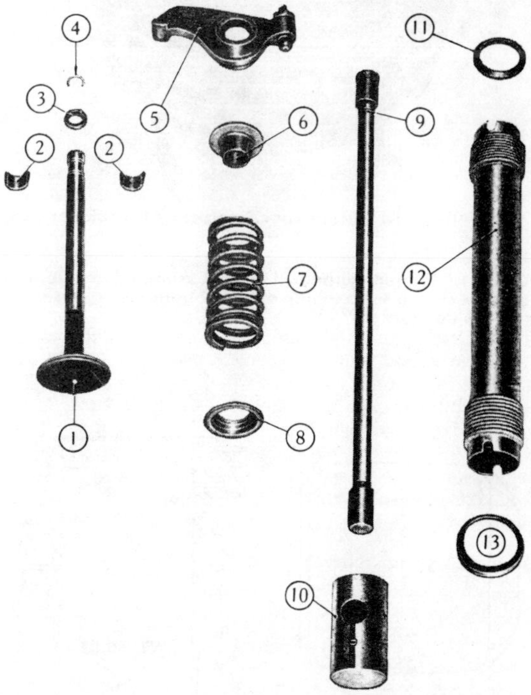

FIG 1:20 Valve, pushrod and tappet assembly

Key to Fig 1:20 1 Intake valve 2 Upper cup lock 3 Oil shield (for intake valves only) 4 Snap ring 5 Rocker 6 Upper spring cup 7 Valve spring 8 Lower spring cup 9 Pushrod 10 Tappet 11 Oil seal ring 12 Pushrod sleeve 13 Seal ring

tappet seat must not show any signs of roughness or excessive wear which if evident must be renewed.

Rocker and rocker shaft:

During valve gear overhauls the clearance between the rocker shaft bore and the rocker must be checked. The maximum permissable wear between these two parts is .0059 inch. It is recommended that the part which is most worn be renewed, or in extreme cases both parts.

1:8 Crankcase and cylinders

The crankcase is an aluminium casting suitably ribbed to ensure correct air cooling. The main bearing and camshaft bearing bores are directly cast as also are the tappet

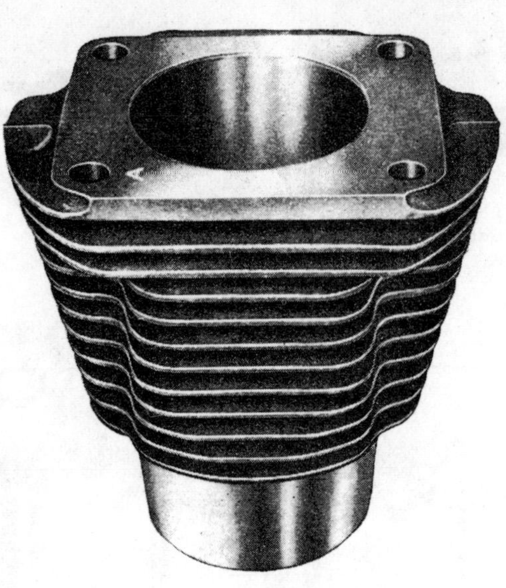

FIG 1:21 Finned cylinder. Letter A stamped on cylinder indicates the class to which cylinder belongs, as referred to its inside diameter

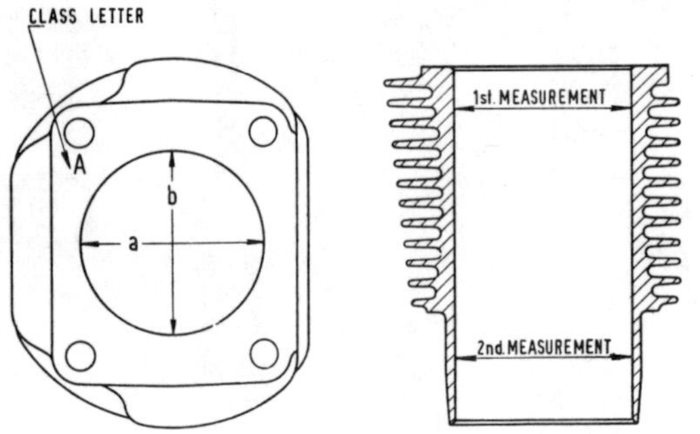

FIG 1:22 Cylinder measurement points

seats, gearbox companion flange and timing gear cover mounting flange.

The cast iron cylinders are finned radially to increase the cooling air surface and are located symmetrically on the crankcase, each being held by four studs. The cylinders are installed by sliding into the crankcase bores and finally held in place of the cylinder head (see **FIGS 1:8** and **1:21**).

Once the engine has been dismantled, the crankcase and cylinders must be thoroughly cleaned both internally and externally. Ensure that all the oil galleries are free from sediment.

Inspect the cylinder bores for score marks which may be removed if not too deep. The clearance between the piston maximum diameter and the cylinder bore should be checked to ensure that it is within the maximum wear limit of .0059 inch.

It is essential that the diameter measurements are taken at two different heights in the cylinder bore along both the longitudinal and transverse axles as shown in **FIG 1:22**. It is recommended that to zero the internal micrometer Fiat ring gauge C.672 is used (see **FIG 1:23**).

If bore wear or ovality is between .0059 and .0079 inch the cylinder bore may be honed. Should however the wear limit of .0079 inch be exceeded then the bores must be recut.

Honing or reboring cylinder bores:

This operation should bring the bore size to correspond to the oversize piston sizes in order to obtain the correct clearance between the piston and cylinder. These limits are given in Technical Data. It will be observed that the cylinders are divided into three classes depending on the bore diameter. The classes are identified by the letters 'A', 'B' and 'C', one of which will be stamped on the mating face with the cylinder head as shown in **FIG 1:21**. Pistons are divided into three classes to correspond with the cylinder bore sizes. Naturally the piston and bore must belong to the same class. The maximum permissable limit in relation to piston sizes is .0236 inch.

Pistons and rings for the Model 500 sports engine are not available in oversize dimensions so if the cylinder bore diameter is above the maximum wear limit new parts must be fitted.

Checking cylinder height:

The cylinder height must be checked between the seating face on the crankcase and the top surface and this dimension should be $3.5433 \pm .0006$ inch.

If this dimension is less than specified the cylinder must be renewed to prevent possible carbon deposits on the piston crown and underside of combustion chamber causing the piston to strike the cylinder head (see **FIG 1:24**).

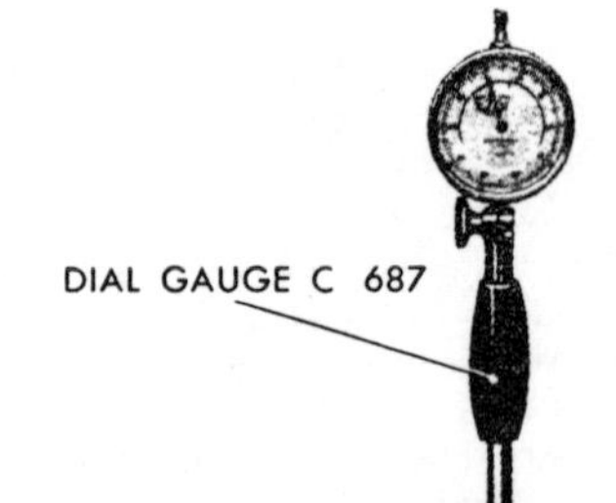

FIG 1:23 Checking cylinder diameter by dial gauge C.687 brought to zero with ring gauge C.672

Insert a .0079 ± .00197 inch thick oil paper gasket between the crankcase and cylinder bottom face and a .0236 to .0275 inch thick graphitized asbestos gasket between the cylinder and cylinder head. The compression of the gaskets on assembly will eliminate any very small differences between the two mating surfaces.

Inspection of tappet seats:

The tappet seats should be checked for scoring and correct clearance which must not exceed .00315 inch. Should the clearance be greater than the maximum specified the seating may be reamed to oversize dimensions as detailed in Technical Data. Tappets are available in .00197 and .00394 inch diameter oversize.

1:9 Piston assembly

Inspection:

Before inspection the pistons must be thoroughly cleaned and the ring grooves and piston head decarbonized. Check for deep score marks and signs of distortion or fracture especially around the skirt and piston pin areas. Using a feeler gauge ensure that the piston clearances in the bore do not exceed a maximum of .0059 inch for the Model 500 engine and .0079 inch for the Model 500 sports engine (see **FIG 1:25**). The measurements should be taken at the bottom of the skirt and square to the piston pin axis.

Should the clearance be greater than the maximum permissable, the cylinders may be rebored and oversize pistons fitted (Model 500 only). Pistons are supplied in the following oversizes, .0079, .0157 and .0236 inch. It should be noted that oversize pistons and rings are not available for the Model 500 sports engine so if the piston to cylinder wall clearance is greater than the permissable maximum limit the cylinder and piston assembly must be renewed.

The piston ring to groove clearance must be checked as shown in **FIGS 1:26** and **1:27**. In both cases the readings should be compared with the piston data. Piston rings are available in the same oversizes classes as the pistons. When installing piston rings the gap should be placed opposite to the piston expansion stops. Ensure that the ring gaps are scattered and not in a line.

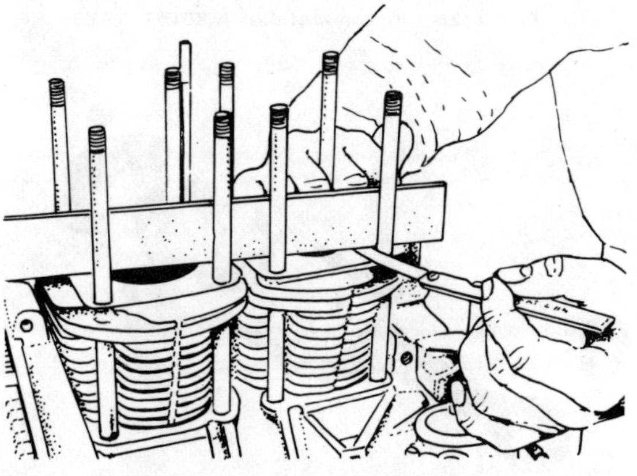

FIG 1:24 Checking cylinder head mating face for level. Out-of-true should not exceed .00315 inch

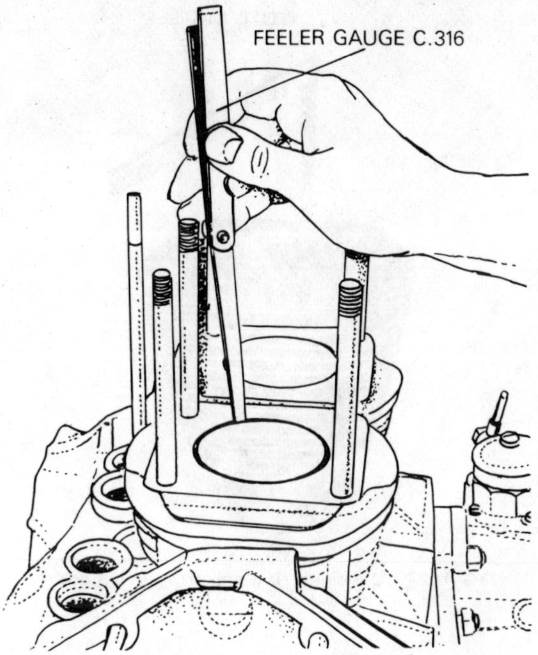

FIG 1:25 Using feeler gauge C.316 to check piston-to-cylinder wall clearance

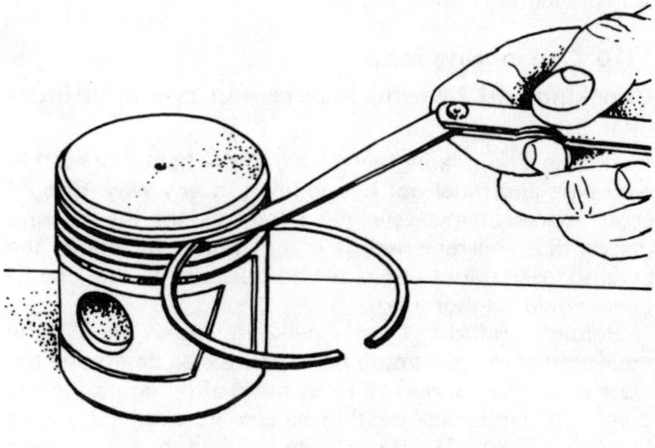

FIG 1:26 Checking piston ring-to-land clearance

Check that the fit between the piston pin and boss is a pinch fit. If excessive clearance is found the boss may be reamed and a .0079 inch diameter oversize piston pin fitted. The pin to bore pinch fit must be between .0000 to .0039 inch. At all times the pins should be installed only after the piston has been heated in hot water to a temperature of 80°C. Upon reassembly of the piston to the engine the expansion slot must be placed facing the camshaft.

Reassembly of piston:

The installation of the piston and connecting rod should be carried out on a clean workbench as shown in

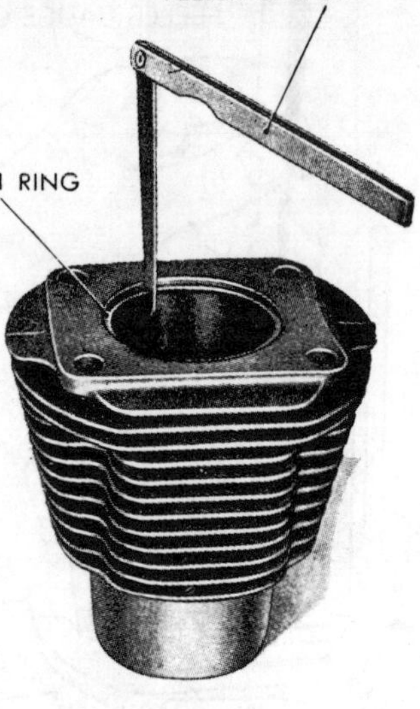

FIG 1:27 Checking ring gap (ring in cylinder)

FIG 1:28. A universal piston ring compressor should be used to keep the rings tight in their grooves. The correct matching of the piston and connecting rod is described in a later section of this chapter.

1:10 Connecting rods

Checking rod bearing inserts and crankpin journals:

The big-end bearing halves are of the babbit lined thin wall type and must not be modified in any way. Should score marks or excessive wear be evident the bearing inserts must be renewed. It is recommended that if the bearing inserts are to be renewed due to wear the crankpins should be reground.

Before regrinding the crankpins they should be measured at the maximum point of wear to determine the class of bearing undersize to be fitted after regrinding the crankpins. Undersize bearing halves are available in the following sizes .01, .02, .03 and .04 inch. The correct bearing half to crankpin is .00043 to .00240 inch and must be checked as detailed in the following section.

Checking rod bearing insert to crankpin journal clearance:

Before the crankshaft is installed into the engine after overhaul the clearance must be checked to ensure that it is within the manufacturers recommended limits. To check the clearance proceed as follows:

1 Lubricate the crankpin and bearing inserts and install the connecting rod together with its bearing halves on the crankpin. Tighten the cap nuts to a torque wrench setting of 23.9 lb ft.
2 Rotate the connecting rod around the crankshaft journal several times to seat the bearing insert correctly. Remove the bearing end cap and carefully wipe away all traces of the lubricant.
3 Place a piece of 'Plastigage type PG-1' along the full width of the bearing insert along the crankshaft longitudinal axis (see **FIG 1:30**). Refit the bearing cap and tighten the nuts to a torque wrench setting of 23.9 lb ft. Remove the bearing cap and upon inspection the 'Plastigage' will be found to have adhered to either the crankpin or bearing insert and will have developed a rectangular section. To determine the actual clearance between the crankpin and bearing insert compare the width of the flattened 'Plastigage' at its widest point with the graduations on the envelope as shown in **FIG 1:31**.
4 If the clearance indicated is within the recommended

FIG 1:28 Piston installer A.60154

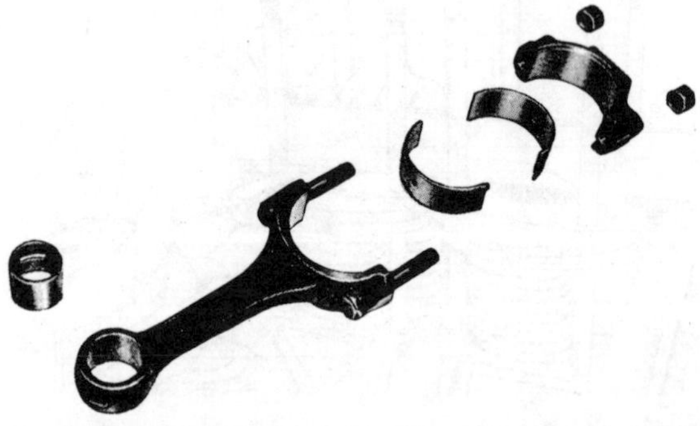

FIG 1:29 Connecting rod components

tolerance range of .00043 to .00240 inch or less than .0059 inch the bearing inserts may be used again without any need for regrinding. Should however the clearance be greater than .0059 inch the inserts must be renewed by undersize inserts after the crankpin journals have been reground.

5 It should be observed that 'Plastigage PG-1' is suitable for measuring clearances up to .0030 inch so that if during operation 3 above produces no flattening of the 'Plastigage' the procedure must be repeated using 'Plastigage PR-1' which enables clearances up to .0060 inch to be measured if it is not greater than the .0059 limit.

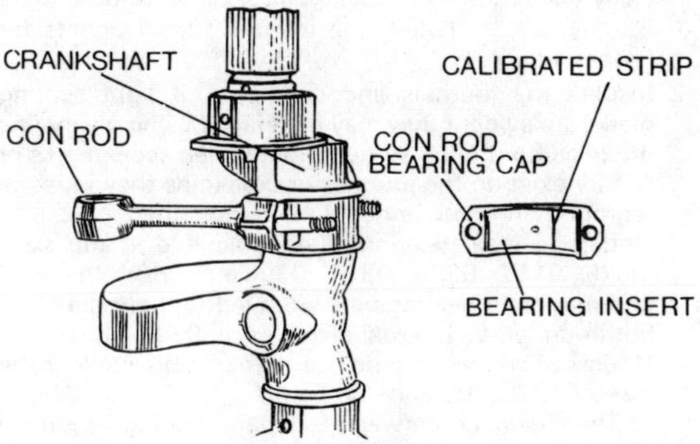

FIG 1:30 'Plastigage' position for bearing insert-to-crankpin journal clearance inspection

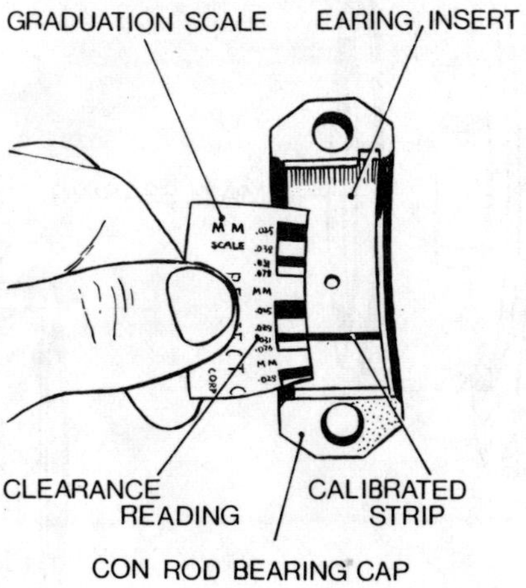

FIG 1:31 Checking bearing insert-to-crankpin journal clearance by comparing width of flattened 'Plastigage'

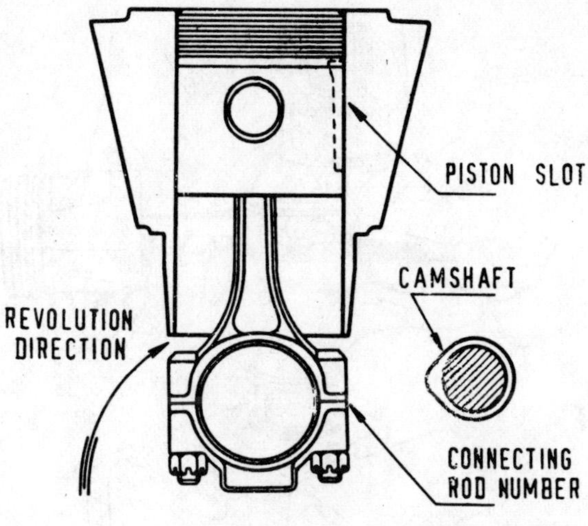

FIG 1:32 Connecting rod-piston assembly installation on engine

Installation of connecting rod bearing inserts:

During reassembly of the big-end bearing inserts the parts must be thoroughly cleaned and then to reassemble proceed as follows:

1 Ensure the bearing half to connecting rod surfaces are perfectly smooth and free of score marks. Under no circumstances may the bearing surface be reworked.
2 Check the bearing half location lug is radially free in its seat otherwise the crankshaft may be firmly but carefully pushed to the bearing insert so ensuring correct bearing surface contact.
3 As the circumference of the bearing half is greater than the seats in connecting rod and cap the bearing must be fitted so that the projection at each end of the bearing half is equal.
4 Thoroughly lubricate all parts and tighten the end cap nuts to a torque wrench setting of 23.9 lb ft.

Little end bushing:

The small end bush must be a firm fitting in the connecting rod and show no signs of deep scoring, scuffing, ovality or excessive wear.

Should it be considered necessary, the bush may be reamed using a Fiat expanding reamer U.0307 so that the bush internal diameter permits an oversize piston pin to be fitted with a clearance of .00020 to .00063 inch.

To fit a replacement bush proceed as follows:

1 Firmly hold the connecting rod between soft faces in a vice in such a way that it will not bend when working on the small-end and using a suitably sized drift, remove the old bush.
2 Use Fiat tool A.60155 or a suitably sized drift and carefully install the new bush which must be an interference fit of between .0011 to .0036 inch.
3 A small slot must be cut in the bush to correspond with the groove machined at the top of the connecting rod so ensuring good lubrication between the bush and piston pin.

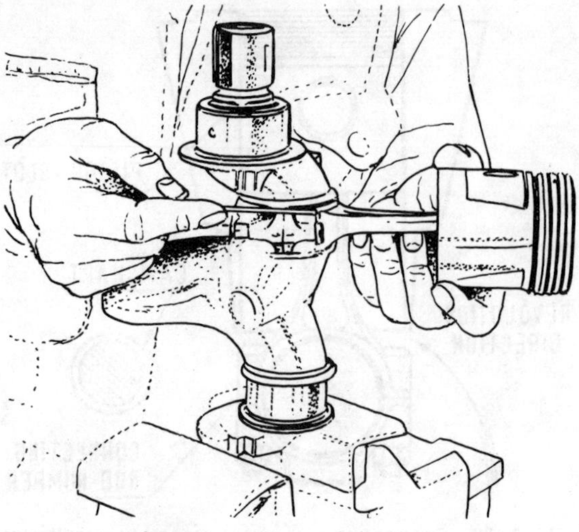

FIG 1:33 Checking crankshaft land-to-connecting rod shoulder clearance

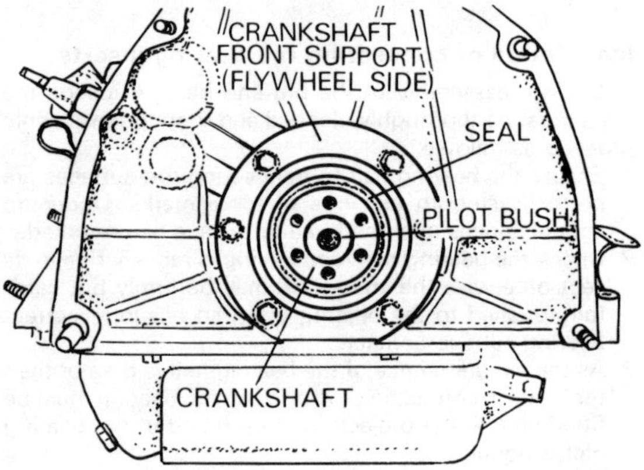

FIG 1:34 Engine front end without flywheel

4 Using an expanding reamer or Fiat reamer U.0307 ease out the internal diameter of the bush to between .7874 to .7876 inch so that a standard piston may be fitted.

Piston-connecting rod assembly:

To assemble the piston to the connecting rod fit the connecting rod to the piston so that the cylinder identification number which is stamped on the connecting rod stem and cap faces the expansion slot side in the piston as shown in **FIG 1:32**.

Lubricate the piston with engine oil, compress the piston rings into their grooves and insert the piston connecting rod assembly into the cylinder barrel with the identification numbers facing to the side opposite to the camshaft as shown in **FIG 1:32**.

If one or both connecting rods have been renewed the new connecting rod cap and body must be stamped with the cylinder identification number. The figures should be stamped as shown in **FIG 1:33**.

Upon reassembly the connecting rod cap nuts must be tightened to a torque wrench setting of 23.9 lb ft.

1:11 Crankshaft and main bearings

The special cast iron crankshaft is hollow to allow for the passage of lubrication oil. It is supported at its ends and is provided with two cranks and a central counterweight. The crankshaft plays an important part in the operation of the lubrication system as its cavity provides a passage for the oil flowing from the centrifugal filter.

Before inspecting the crankshaft thoroughly clean the internal passage and drillings as well as the exterior and then proceed as follows:

1 Carefully inspect the crankshaft for minute cracks especially where there is a change in section. Should there be any doubt always consult the official agents for further advice.

2 Inspect the journals and crankpins. If light scoring marks are evident they may be refaced using a very fine grade carborundum stone. Should deep score marks or ovality exist on the journals or crankpins they must be reground and new undersize bearings fitted.
Undersize main bearings are obtainable in the sizes .0079, .0157, .0236, .0314, .0394 inch. Both the front and rear main bearings are supplied without supports but in undersize internal diameter of .0394 inch.
Undersize connecting rod bearings are obtainable in the sizes .01, .02, .03 and .04 inch.
The clearance between the main bearing to journal should be .00079 to .00256 inch and the connecting rod bearing half to crankpin between .00043 to .0024 inch.

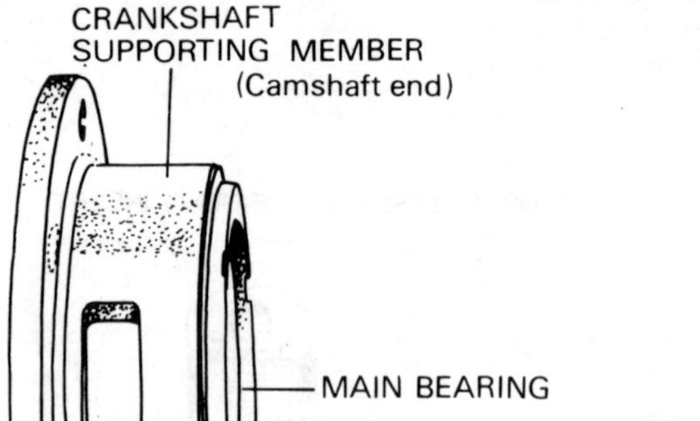

FIG 1:35 Camshaft end crankshaft supporting member and bearing assembly, and spare main bearing

After the crankshaft has been reground it is important that all traces of swarf are removed by constant washing and then drying with a non-fluffy rag.

3 The clearance between the main bearings and journals must be checked before installing the crankshaft in the engine. It should also serve as a recheck after the crankshaft has been reground.

Measure the maximum main bearing internal diameter and the minimum journal diameter using accurate measuring equipment. The clearance must not exceed .0039 inch otherwise the journals must be reground and undersize bearings fitted.

Undersize bearings with .0394 inch stock on the internal diameter are also supplied as spares but the diameter of this type of bearing must be adapted to the corresponding crankpin undersize and then press fitted support. The recommended interference fit is .00039 to .00197 inch.

After fitting drill in the bearings a hole in line with the location dowel seat in the support and finish using Fiat reamer U.0334 or an applicable expanding reamer. Press fit in the location dowels noting that the hollow dowel must be placed on the flywheel end support.

It is recommended that after press fitting the bearing and dowels the assembly be heated in an oven or engine oil bath for a period of one hour at a temperature of 150°C (302°F).

When the assembly is at normal room temperature ream the bearing to its recommended finished size.

Crankshaft oil seals:

Two inner spring rubber oil seals are located, one in a special seat in the timing gear cover and the other in the flywheel end of the crankshaft support and provide oil tightness. These seals are shown in **FIGS 1 : 3** and **1 : 34**.

Whenever the engine is dismantled for overhaul these seals should be carefully inspected for correct seating and that the inner seal surface is not worn and that the contact area is perfect both on the crankshaft and on the fan and generator drive pulley hub.

Clutch shaft pilot bushing:

A self-lubricating bronze bush is fitted in the end of the crankshaft as shown in **FIG 1 : 34** and provides a bearing for the clutch shaft. Should the bush be worn use Fiat pulley A.40006/1/2 to remove the worn bush. A new bush should be fitted using a suitably sized drift.

1 :12 Flywheel and starter ring gear

The flywheel should be inspected for wear at the clutch driven plate contact area. It should be flat and have a mirror finish.

The ring gear teeth should be checked for damage which if evident, the ring gear must be replaced. To facilitate the fitting of a new ring gear on the flywheel, the new ring gear should be heated in an oil bath to a temperature of 80°C (176°F). Using a press gently ease the expanded ring gear over the flywheel and press fully home.

1 :13 The oil pump

Sedan:

A helical-spur gear type oil pump is driven by the camshaft through a front dog drive coupling. The gears are

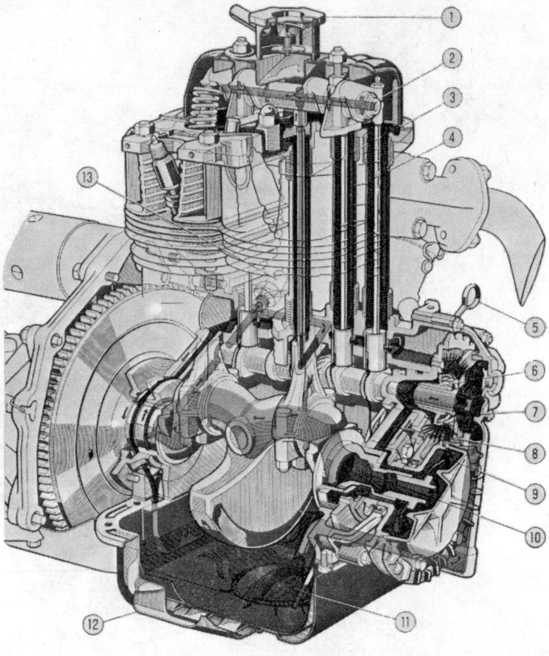

FIG 1 : 36 Engine lubrication diagram

Key to Fig 1 : 36 1 Oil filler with steam vent valve 2 Rocker shaft 3 Line, oil delivery to rocker shaft 4 Ducts, cylinder head oil drain 5 Level indicator rod 6 Oil pressure relief valve 7 Gear pump 8 Oil duct to centrifugal filter 9 Centrifugal oil filter 10 Crankshaft with central oil gallery 11 Oil pump intake screen filter 12 Sump cooling air conveyor 13 Low oil pressure indicator sending unit

located in a special housing in the timing gear cover and held in place by a cover plate. The oil pressure relief valve is mounted on the drive gear shaft guide.

A pump suction scoop fitted with a filter screen is secured in the crankcase and connects to a duct in the timing gear case as shown in **FIG 1 : 36**.

Pump removal and reassembly:

To remove the pump from the engine proceed as follows:

1 Remove the engine rear central support from the timing gear casing. Remove the filter cover pulley and lift away the drive belt.

2 Release the hollow screw attaching the slinger and the mounting flange of the filter on the crankshaft. Also release the nuts fixing the timing gear cover to the crankcase.

3 Remove the timing gear cover together with the oil pump assembly and the pressure relief valve.

4 Lift out the oil pump suction scoop with the filter screen attached from the sump.

5 Reassembly of the pump to the engine is the reverse procedure to dismantling.

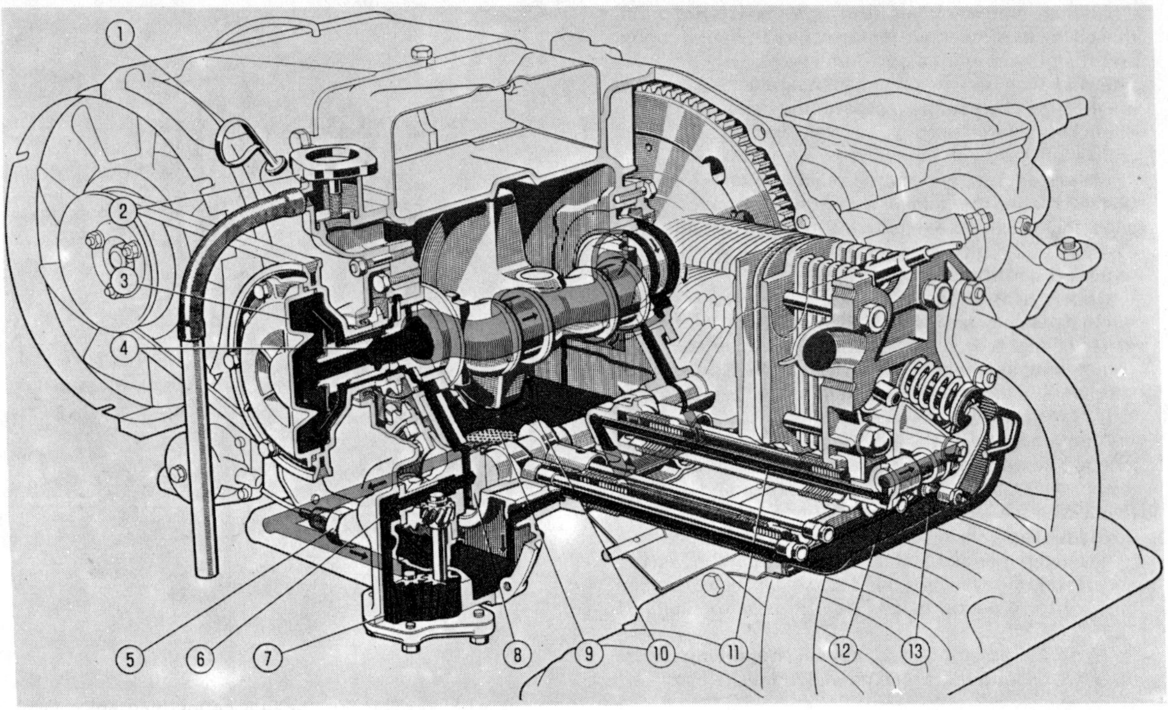

FIG 1:37 Lubrication diagram of engine 120.000

Key to Fig 1:37 1 Oil dipstick 2 Oil filler with vent valve 3 Centrifugal oil filter 4 Crankshaft, with central oil gallery 5 Low oil pressure indicator sending unit 6 Oil pressure relief valve 7 Gear pump 8 Camshaft, with central oil gallery 9 Oil suction filter from sump 10 Oil sump drain plug 11 Oil delivery line to rocker shaft 12 Rocker shaft 13 Head cover

Pump dismantling, inspection and reassembly:

1 Remove the lock ring and withdraw the pressure relief valve and spring. Remove the oil pump cover plate and ease out the gears and shaft.

2 Thoroughly clean all the parts and blow clean using a compressed air jet. Inspect the timing gear cover for cracks or distortion. Check that the inner duct for oil delivery to the pump is clear of obstruction. Use a compressed air jet to clean the passage.

3 Check the oil pump gear teeth for damage or excessive wear and fit new gears if necessary. The recommended backlash is .0059 inch with a maximum wear limit giving a backlash of .0079 inch. Check the clearance between the gear teeth and the housing walls in the timing gear cover. The recommended clearance is .0012 to .0035 inch with a maximum of .0047 inch. Ensure that the drive gear is firmly attached to its shaft. Upon assembly there is a pinch fit of .0016 to .0031 inch between the two parts.

4 The driven gear to shaft clearance upon assembly is .00079 to .00236 inch with a maximum wear limit of .0039 inch. Also check the width of the drive and driven gears which when new should be .3937 to .3928 inch with a minimum width of .3917. In service a spare drive gear is supplied complete with its shaft.

5 Inspect the filter screen on the end of the pump suction scoop and remove any obstruction. If the screen is damaged it must be renewed.

6 Check that the pump drive dog is a good fit on the camshaft and that the dogs are not badly worn so as to impair the pump operation.

7 Reassembly of the pump is the reverse procedure to dismantling. Ensure that the pump cover plate is correctly located by means of the dowel on the timing gear cover.

Station wagon:

A helical-spur gear type oil pump is driven from the lower end of the distributor drive spindle which is in mesh with the camshaft. The gears are located in a special housing in the bottom of the timing gear housing and are held in place by a cover plate. The oil pressure relief valve is located at the driven end of the camshaft.

A pump suction oil filter is fitted in the sump and this connects to a duct in the timing gear case so supplying oil to the pump (see **FIG 1:37**).

Pump gears removal, inspection and reassembly:

To remove the pump gears from the timing gear cover proceed as follows:

1 Drain the oil sump to ensure that the oil does not syphon out. Thoroughly clean the area around the pump body (see **FIG 1:37**).
2 Remove the end cover plate by releasing the retaining bolts and washers. Carefully ease the driven gear downwards followed by the driving gear and shaft
3 Clean all parts removed and blow clean using a compressed air jet. Inspect the timing gear cover pump area for cracks or distortion. Check that the inner duct for oil delivery to the pump is clear of obstruction. If in doubt remove the drain plug and filler cap and use a compressed air jet to clean the passage.
4 Check the gear teeth for damage or excessive wear, ensure that the drive gear is firmly attached to its spindle and that the end cover plate is not badly scored or pitted. Fit new parts as necessary.
5 Reassembly is the reverse procedure to dismantling, taking care that all parts are assembled clean and the end cover plate seating correctly with a new gasket.

1:14 Lubrication, oil filter, relief valve

Description:

The engine is pressure lubricated through a gear type pump which is incorporated in the timing gear cover and driven by the camshaft via front dog clutch. The lubrication circuits are shown in **FIGS 1:35** and **1:37**.

The pump draws oil from the sump through a suction horn fitted with a filter screen which is fixed to the crankcase by a duct in the timing gear cover. This supplies oil to the pump.

Oil passes from the camshaft rear seat onto the crankshaft rear support where it flows into an adjacent chamber. From here the oil flows through ducts in the crankshaft from end to the centrifugal oil filter. The centrifugal filter, which also acts as a pulley for the generator and blower drive, rotates with the crankshaft.

Oil from the filter enters a passage in the crankshaft, where it lubricates the main and connecting rod bearings and passes from a special groove in the front main bearing and ducting in the crankcase into which is inserted the oil pressure warning sender unit, and also the delivery pipe for oil to the overhead valve gear.

The pushrod sleeves provide the return path for the oil from the cylinder head and delivers oil to the tappet gear and the camshaft cams. The tappets are suitably drilled to allow correct circulation of the oil. The tappets are located in two casting cavities, one of which communicates with the timing gear housing and the other one to the crankshaft front drain support drain.

The oil pressure is regulated by a pressure relief valve 5 (see **FIG 1:38**) mounted at the rear end of the camshaft. It comprises a hubbed disc which slides on a guide 6 of the oil pump drive shaft 7. Under spring load 9 the valve disc circumferentially closes an annular chamber which communicates with the lubrication circuit. Excessive oil pressure causes the disc to uncover the chamber.

Centrifugal oil filter:

The oil filter is of the centrifugal type comprising of two flanges and an oil slinger. The filter is attached to the rear end of the crankshaft as shown in **FIG 1:38**. The outside diameter of the oil slinger (see **FIG 1:39**) is smaller in diameter than that of the flanges but of such a

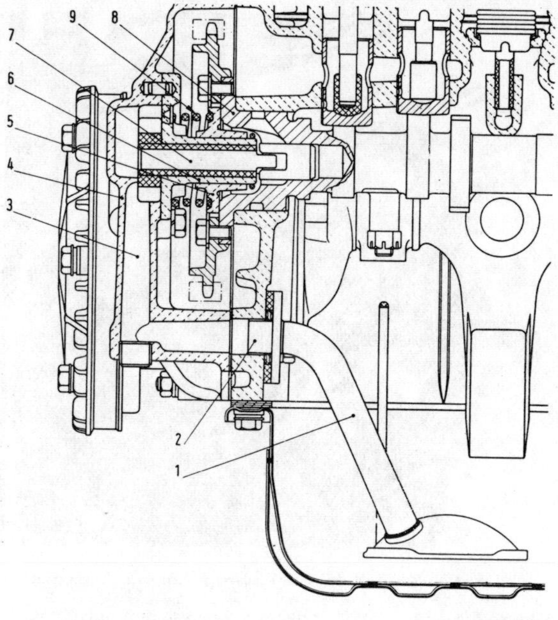

FIG 1:38 Engine longitudinal section through oil pump

Key to Fig 1:38 Suction scoop 2 Hole in crankcase 3 Duct in timing sprocket cover 4 Timing sprocket cover 5 Oil pressure relief valve 6 Drive shaft guide and oil pump cover 7 Oil pump driving gear shaft 8 Camshaft 9 Oil pressure relief valve spring

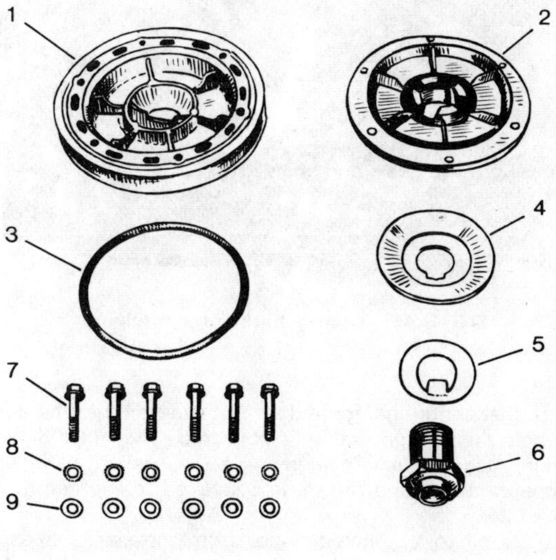

FIG 1:39 Centrifugal oil filter components

Key to Fig 1:39 1 Drive pulley 2 Rotor hub 3 Seal ring 4 Oil slinger 5 Lockplate 6 Hub-to-crankshaft hollow screw 7, 8, 9 Pulley-to-hub mounting screws, toothed washers and plain washers

FIG 1:40 **Engine detail showing lube oil passages**

Key to Fig 1:40 1 Splines in crankshaft for oil passage to filter 2 Oil inlet into circuit from filter 3 Hole for oil passage to main bearing

FIG 1:41 **Timing marks on sprockets**

size that centrifugal force does not sling oil into the area where the foreign matter is collected. The outer flange inner face has radial vanes on its face which retain the foreign matter and the oil is conveyed to the centre of the filter.

The oil to be filtered issues from the side splines 1 (see **FIG 1:40**) of the crankshaft and is forced by the slinger to the periphery of the filter where it is cleaned and returns to the centre of the filter and into the crankshaft drilling 2. The inner flange or hub and the slinger are secured to the crankshaft by a special hollow screw 6 as shown in **FIG 1:39**, the outer flange is attached to the hub by six screws.

A groove is machined on the outer flange periphery to form a pulley for the generator and blower drive belt.

Cleaning and inspection:

To ensure a reliable lubrication system there must be no oil leaks from the gasket between the outer and inner flanges. Every time the engine is overhauled the filter must be dismantled, cleaned and new gaskets fitted. To clean the filter, remove the six screws and washers and separate the drive pulley and hub. Carefully scrape the inner surfaces to remove all sludge.

Upon reassembly the filter to crankshaft hollow mounting screws must be tightened to a torque wrench setting of 108.5 lb ft. The cover to mounting flange screws must be tightened to a torque wrench setting of 5.8 lb ft.

Oil pressure indicator sender unit:

The oil pressure indicator sender unit is located on the righthand side of the cylinder block and is connected to an indicator light in the instrument cluster on the dashboard.

The red indicator lights only when the ignition is switched on and goes out when oil pressure has built up to between 8.5 and 14 lb/sq in.

Should an accidental shortcircuit occur in the oil pressure indicator circuit, the sender unit may be damaged so the cause must be traced and rectified before the unit is renewed.

1:15 Valve timing

If the camshaft has been disconnected from the crankshaft for any service operation the valve gear will have to be retimed and to do this proceed as follows:

1 Turn the crankshaft until the reference line on its sprocket is pointing towards the camshaft as shown in **FIG 1:41**.
2 Turn the camshaft until the reference dot on its sprocket registers with the crankshaft sprocket. Leave the gears undisturbed and carefully mount the chain. Should it be necessary to check the valve timing and sprocket marks, proceed as follows:

1 Fit Fiat C.673 tool as shown in **FIG 1:42**.
2 Temporarily adjust the valve stem-to-rocker arm clearance of cylinder No. 1 at .0177 inch for the inlet valve and .0150 inch for the exhaust valve (Model 500 engine) or at .0154 inch for both valves (Model 500 sports).
3 Rotate the crankshaft and set the flywheel timing mark at 'O' on the graduated sector. Check that the sprocket marks are correctly lined up in this position.
If the engine is being assembled to install the driven gear, proceed as follows:

1 Set the timing mark on the drive sprocket towards the centre of the camshaft.
2 Position the driven sprocket on the camshaft mounting flange with four screw holes in line and tighten two mounting screws only.
3 Rotate the camshaft until the driven sprocket mark registers with the reference line on the drive sprocket.
4 Remove the driven sprocket without moving the camshaft. Install the timing chain and replace the driven sprocket. Tighten the four screws to a torque wrench setting of 6.5 lb ft.

5 Using the graduated sector check that all the advance and retard angles are as detailed in Technical Data. Readjust the valve stem to rocker arm clearance to the correct setting.

1:16 Valve tappet-to-rocker clearance adjustment

It is important that the clearance between the valve stem and rocker is kept within the recommended clearance of .0059 inch to be measured when the engine is cold.

If the clearance is excessive operating noise will occur and if less than recommended the valves will stay open too long which will result in damage to the valve face and its seating.

Inspect the contacting surfaces for scoring or pitting which, if excessive, new parts must be fitted. Also check the condition of the rocker-to-valve and rocker ball head-to-pushrod contact surfaces are free from wear or pitting. The faces must have a mirror finish.

The oilway in the rockers and shaft must be thoroughly inspected and free from sludge, otherwise lubrication failure will occur.

The assembly clearance between the rocker arm and shaft should be .00063 to .00217 inch and the clearance between the rocker shaft and the shaft support should be .00020 to .00138 inch with a maximum wear limit of .0039 inch.

1:17 Engine assembly (sedan—all versions)

To reassemble the engine proceed as follows:

1 Thoroughly clean and dry all the parts, ensure that all drillings are free from dirt or sludge and place on a clean dry surface.

2 Carefully install the cylinder-piston-connecting rod assemblies with new paper gaskets between the cylinders and crankcase seats.

3 Refit the big-end bearing shells to the connecting rods, ensuring that they are free from any dirt or metallic particles. Carefully ease the crankshaft into the crankcase, lubricate the main journals with clean engine oil, place a new paper gasket between the supporting member and the flywheel end of the crankcase. Install the supporting member and bearing assemblies. Secure the supporting members with the screws and special toothed washers.

4 Locate the connecting rod big-end half onto the crankpin journals, liberally lubricate the journals with fresh engine oil, fit the remaining shell half, matching bearing end cap and tighten the bearing cap nuts to a torque wrench setting of 23.9 lb ft.

5 Inspect the camshaft bearing bores and remove any burrs with a hand scraper wetted with oil. Carefully slide in the camshaft ensuring the cam lobes or gear teeth do not score the front bearing bore.

6 Fit a new timing gear cover paper gasket held in place with a little grease. Install the outer thrust ring, inner thrust ring, shoulder washer and slide on the camshaft drive sprocket, locking it with the Woodruff key. Assemble the timing chain and driven sprocket, ensuring that the timing marks on the sprocket are indexing as shown in **FIG 1:41**. Secure the driven sprocket with six screws and lockplates and carefully bend down the lockplates.

FIG 1:42 Graduated sector C.673 for valve gear timing

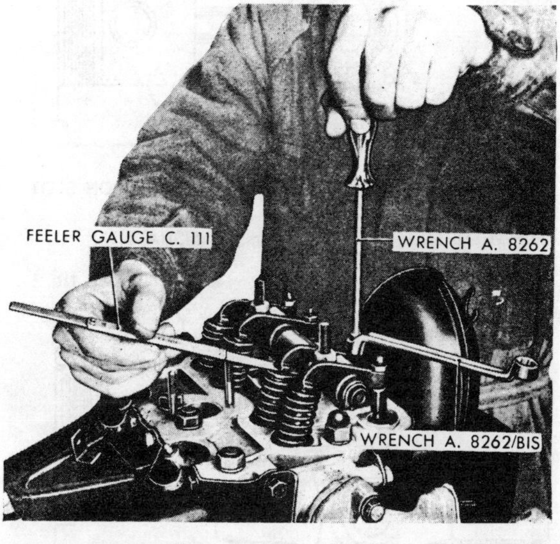

FIG 1:43 Adjusting rocker clearance by wrenches A.8262, A.8262/bis and feeler gauge C.110 (.0059 inch) or C.111 (.0039 inch)

7 Install the timing gear cover, the oil pump, oil pressure relief valve and seal assembly. Secure with nuts, special toothed washers and plain washers located in the same manner as was noted on dismantling. Locate the oil pump suction horn and secure with the nuts and toothed washers.

8 Install the flywheel in the same relative position to the crankshaft as was noted on dismantling. Replace the

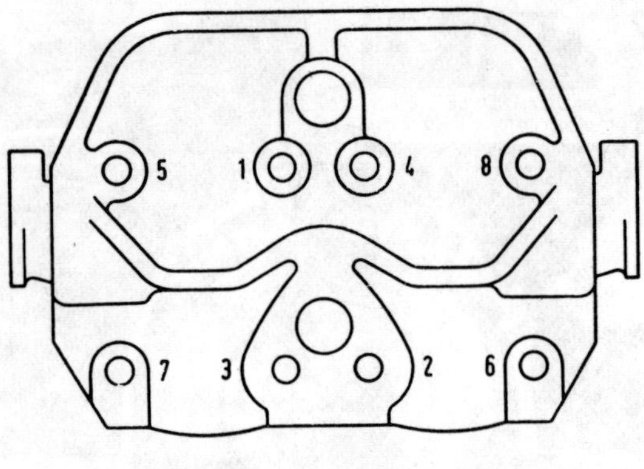

FIG 1:44 Cylinder head hold-down nuts tightening sequence. 500 Sedan

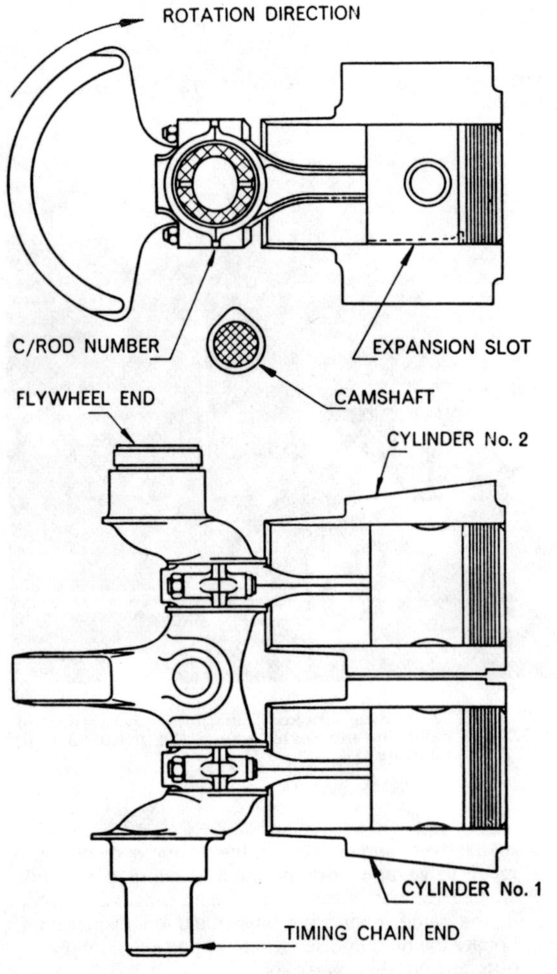

FIG 1:45 The correct position of connecting rod-piston assembly on engine 120.000

screws and together with new lockplates tighten to a torque wrench setting of 23.1 lb ft. Bend down the lockplates.

9 Slide the centrifugal oil filter mounting flange, the oil slinger and the mounting screw together with its lockplates onto the crankshaft and tighten the screw to a torque wrench setting of 108.5 lb ft. Bend down the lockplate.

10 Assemble the clutch assembly to the flywheel and using Fiat pilot A.62023 centralize the driven plate to the pressure plate assembly. Secure the pressure plate assembly using screws and toothed washers.

11 Fit new oil pan cork gasket, if necessary using a little grease to hold in position and carefully fit the oil pan securing with screws, toothed washers and lockplates. Bend down the lockplates onto the screws heads.

12 Fit the oil cooling air conveyor on the oil pan and secure with screws and toothed washers.

13 Carefully turn the engine over and fit the centrifugal filter mounting flange rubber seal. Fit the oil filter cover and secure with screws together with plain and toothed washers to a torque wrench setting of 5.8 lb ft.

14 Ensure the faces of the cylinder head and cylinders are free from dirt and oil and carefully slide the cylinder head gasket over the studs ensuring that it is the correct way up. Insert the tappets in the same order to removal together with the sleeves, pushrods, oil delivery line to the rocker arm shaft and the casing with its seal ring.

15 Thoroughly inspect the cylinder head to ensure that it has been correctly reassembled, carefully slide it over the studs and secure using the four cap nuts internally and four standard nuts and plain washers externally. Tighten the nuts in the order as shown in **FIG 1:44** to a torque wrench setting of 23.9 lb ft.

16 Fit the rocker arm shaft and arm assembly together with the two supports. Tighten the supports using screws, plain and toothed washers to a torque wrench setting of 15.2 lb ft. Adjust the tappet-to-rocker clearance as detailed in **Section 1:16**.

17 Temporarily plug the intake duct hole to ensure that no foreign matter finds its way into the engine. Install the spark plugs having ensured that they are clean and correctly adjusted.

18 Reassemble the engine cowling and air exhaust throttle valve assembly which should be secured on the top side using two nuts, two plain washers and two toothed washers and on the underside with two screws and two toothed washers. The valve assembly should be located centrally using one screw and one spring washer.

19 Fit the toothed washers on the end of the spark plug electrode and tighten the terminals together with the special rubber boots.

20 Refit the fan, generator and ground cable assembly and secure the crankcase, also the warmed air intake shrouding. Finally tighten the generator to fan nuts.

21 Fit both lower exhaust silencer mounting brackets onto the crankcase but do not tighten fully. Fit the air conveyor and secure to the engine cowling using six screws, six toothed washers and one nut together with a toothed washer. Join together the two

sections of the air conveyor securing with seven screws, six toothed washers and vie nuts.

22 Slide the fuel pump control rod into its seating, assemble the insulator between oil wetted graphite gaskets and fit the pump to the crankcase using nuts and toothed washers.

23 Fit the air conveyor cover complete with the accelerator control relay lever and rod. Secure using eight mounting screws, eight toothed washers, eight plain washers and eight nuts. Fit the fuel line retaining clip which is secured by one of the air conveyor upper screws. Install the generator and fan drive pulley having first placed four adjusting rings between the pulley halves and the thrust ring on the outside. Secure the pulley to generator shaft using three screws and three toothed washers. Fit the generator fan drive belt.

24 Refit the carburetter having first positioned the bakelite heat shield between the two oil moistened graphite gaskets. Secure the carburetter using two copper washers and two self-locking nuts. Fit the exhaust silencer and secure to the exhaust manifolds with nuts and spring washers. Place the two graphite gaskets between the manifold joints. Fit both exhaust silencer upper mounting brackets and secure them on the top side to the brackets already in place with nuts and toothed washers on the bottom side with screws and toothed washers.

25 Carefully position the distributor at a 10 deg. advance setting and secure with a nut, plain washer and spring washer. Fit the fuel pump to carburetter line complete with mounting bracket rubber lining and secure the line with two clamps. If difficulty is experienced in positioning the fuel line into the pump or carburetter funnels it is suggested that the line ends should be heated in hot water and thoroughly dried before installing.

26 Install the air cleaner elbow and rubber hose assembly on the top of the carburetter using a graphite gasket in between and secure with nuts, plain washers and spring washers. Carefully position the air cleaner, line and hose assembly and connect it to the elbow. Secure the cleaner to air conveyor cover using screws and toothed washers.

27 Fit the spark plug cables complete with the rubber grommet for cable mounting bracket on engine cowling and connect the cables to the distributor and spark plugs. Fit the oil pressure gauge sender unit together with its sealing washer.

28 Install the cylinder head cover and oil breather pipe assembly with a cork gasket inserted between. Secure with self-locking nuts and fibre washers. Connect the accelerator control relay lever rod to the carburetter and secure with the clip.

29 Fill the oil pan with the correct grade and quantity of oil, insert the dipstick and the engine is ready for refitting.

1:18 Engine assembly (station wagon)

Reassembly of this engine is straightforward as it is the reverse procedure to dismantling. It is recommended that **Sections 1:5** and **1:17** are studied as the assembly technique is similar for both the horizontal and vertical cylinder engines. The following points should however be noted:

1 Refer to **FIG 1:45** for the correct positioning of the connecting rod-piston assembly on the 120.000 engine.

2 The sequence of tightening the cylinder head nuts is different, the new order being given in **FIG 1:46**.

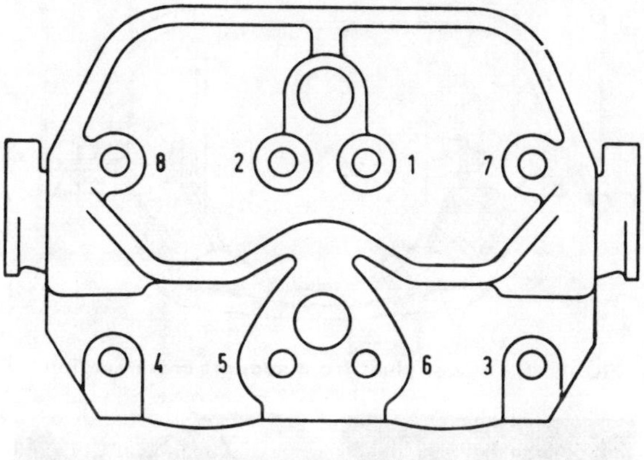

FIG 1:46 Cylinder head stud nut tightening sequence. 500 Sedan and Station Wagon

FIG 1:47 Power plant rear suspension

Key to Fig 1:47 1 Suspension arm 2 Screw, rubber pad to bracket 3 Bracket-to-engine nut 4 Nut, arm to bracket 5 Arm bracket 6 Spring 7 Arm pin-to-support nut 8 Screws, pin to support 9 Pin arm to support

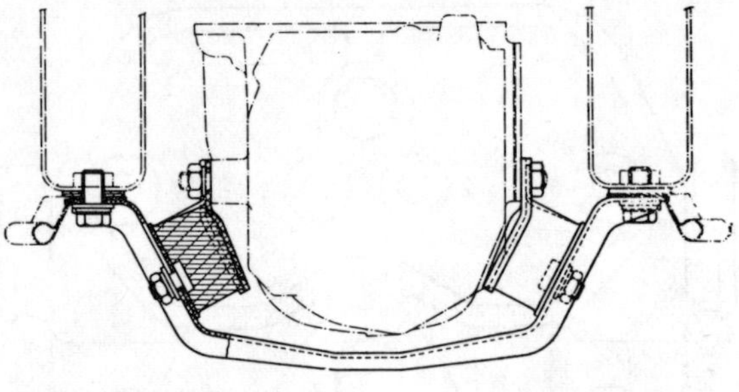

FIG 1:48 Power plant front support cross-section

FIG 1:41 Checking the generator and blower drive belt tension

Key to Fig 1:49 A Normal give-in: about $\frac{13}{32}$ inch under a 22 lb pressure B Nuts securing the pulley halves with spacer rings

1:19 Power plant mountings

The combined power and transmission unit is elastically mounted on two supports.

The front of the unit rests on a crossmember which is secured under the car floor through two rubber block mountings that are bolted to the gearbox casing as shown in **FIG 1:48**. The position of the rubber blocks on the crossmember is adjustable so that the assembly can be correctly aligned.

With the rear of the unit the engine crankcase is sprung to the body rear crossmember through an articulated swinging arm that compresses a coil spring as shown in **FIGS 1:47** and **1:49**. A rubber bump pad is mounted inside the spring to give a progressive action.

Whenever the power and transmission unit is being serviced the condition of the mountings should be checked and any worn or damaged parts renewed.

1:20 Adjustment of generator and fan drive belt

The centrifugal oil filter cover/pulley on the crankshaft transmits the drive through a V-belt to the generator and centrifugal fan pulley.

When the V-belt has been correctly adjusted the belt should sag $\frac{13}{32}$ inch under a hand pressure of about 22 lb as shown in **FIG 1:49.**

Should the belt be too slack the generator and centrifugal fan will not operate at the correct speed causing overheating and a discharged battery. Also the belt will slip causing rapid wear of the belt. Conversely if the belt is too tight excessive loading will be placed on the generator bearings causing excessive bearing wear and noisy operation.

To adjust the belt tension proceed as follows:

1 Remove the three nuts 'B' (see **FIG 1:49**) on the generator pulley and this will split the pulley into two parts between which are spacer rings.
2 The tension of the belt is increased or decreased by either reducing or increasing the number of spacers.
3 Place the spacer rings removed from between the pulley halves on the pulley outer face so that the rings may be re-inserted when fitting a new belt.
4 Tighten the three nuts to a torque wrench setting of 14.5 lb ft.

1:21 Modifications

Since its introduction the Fiat new 500 models have been continually developed. The main modifications that have been made are as follows:

1 Heating system safety device
2 Recirculation device for the blow-by gases
3 Cylinder head modified to incorporate item 1
4 Double valve springs fitted
5 Cylinder barrels modified to incorporate item 1
6 Flywheel modified to incorporate new type diaphragm spring clutch mounting
7 Larger air cleaner container.

Details of these modifications are to be found in the relevant sections if they necessitate a change in service overhaul procedure. Other information is to be found in Technical Data.

1:22 Fault diagnosis

(a) Engine will not start

1 Defective coil
2 Faulty distributor capacitor (condener)
3 Dirty, pitted or incorrectly set contact breaker points
4 Ignition wires loose or insulation faulty
5 Water on sparking plug leads
6 Corrosion of battery terminals or battery discharged
7 Faulty or jammed starter
8 Sparking plug leads wrongly connected
9 Vapour lock in fuel pipes
10 Defective fuel pump
11 Overchoking
12 Underchoking
13 Blocked petrol filter or carburetter jets
14 Leaking valves
15 Sticking valves
16 Valve timing incorrect
17 Ignition timing incorrect

(b) Engine stalls

1 Check 1, 2, 3, 4, 10, 11, 12, 13, 14 and 15 in (a)
2 Sparking plugs defective or gaps incorrect
3 Retarded ignition

4 Mixture too weak
5 Water in fuel system
6 Petrol tank vent blocked
7 Incorrect valve clearance

(c) Engine idles badly

1 Check 1 and 6 in (b)
2 Air leak at manifold joints
3 Slow-running jet blocked or out of adjustment
4 Air leak in carburetter
5 Over-rich mixture
6 Worn piston rings
7 Worn valve stems or guides
8 Weak exhaust valve springs

(d) Engine misfires

1 Check 1, 2, 3, 4, 5, 8, 10, 13, 14, 15, 16, 17 in (a); 2, 3, 4 and 7 in (b)
2 Weak or broken valve springs

(e) Engine overheats

1 Generator and fan drive belt too loose
2 Shutter or thermostat seized in closed position

(f) Compression low

1 Check 14 and 15 in (a), 6 and 7 in (c) and 2 in (d)
2 Worn piston ring grooves
3 Scored or worn cylinder bores

(g) Engine lacks power

1 Check 3, 10, 11, 13, 14, 15, 16 and 17 in (a), 2, 3, 4 and 7 in (b) 6 and 7 in (c) and 2 in (d). Also check (e) and (f)
2 Leaking joint washers
3 Fouled sparking plugs
4 Automatic centrifugal advance not operating

(h) Burnt valves or seats

1 Check 14 and 15 in (a), 7 in (b) and 2 in (d). Also check (e)
2 Excessive carbon around valve seat and head

(j) Sticking valves

1 Check 2 in (d)
2 Bent valve stem
3 Scored valve stem or guide
4 Incorrect valve clearance

(k) Excessive cylinder wear

1 Check 11 in (a) and see Chapter 4
2 Lack of oil
3 Dirty oil
4 Piston rings gummed up or broken
5 Badly fitting piston rings
6 Connecting rods bent

(l) Excessive oil consumption

1 Check 6 and 7 in (c) and check (k)
2 Ring gaps too wide
3 Oil return holes in piston choked with carbon
4 Scored cylinders
5 Oil level too high
6 External oil leaks
7 Ineffective valve stem oil seals

(m) Crankshaft and connecting rod bearing failure

1 Check 2 in (k)
2 Restricted oilways
3 Worn journals or crank pins
4 Loose bearing caps
5 Extremely low oil pressure
6 Bent connecting rod

(n) High fuel consumption (see Chapter 2)

(o) Engine vibration

1 Loose generator bolts
2 Blower blade assembly out-of-balance
3 Incorrect clearance for rear engine mounting rubber

CHAPTER 2

THE FUEL SYSTEM

2:1 Description

All the new 500 models use a mechanical diaphragm fuel feed pump as shown in **FIG 2:1**. Four types of carburetter are fitted depending on the model to which the engine is installed. Each carburetter operation and adjustment is fully described, together with details of the recirculation device for blow-by gases and oil vapours.

2:2 Fuel pump operating principles

Refer to **FIG 2:2**. An eccentric on the rotating camshaft actuates the operating rocker 21 via a pushrod 25 which depresses the diaphragm 14 and so creates a depression in the pumping chamber located in upper body 5. Under atmospheric pressure, petrol passes through the pipeline connection and inlet valve into the pumping chamber. The return spring 15 then raises the diaphragm, expelling the petrol through the outlet valve and pipeline to the carburetter float chamber.

When the float chamber is full, the pressure in the pipeline and pumping chamber holds the diaphragm depressed against the tension of the return spring.

2:3 Routine maintenance

A poor delivery of fuel to the carburetter may be due to a fault in the fuel pump or related lines. Periodically the pump body screws 19 (see **FIG 2:2**) and upper cover screw 1 should be checked for tightness. The fuel pump lines should be disconnected and checked for freedom of restriction, chafing and loose connections. The fuel pump filter should be removed and cleaned periodically.

2:4 Pump removal, dismantling and examination

The pump is located on the carburetter side of the engine crankcase (sedan) or under the generator at the front of the crankcase (station wagon).

Removal:

1 Disconnect the fuel pipe from the tank to stop petrol syphoning out of the tank and then release the fuel inlet and outlet pipes from the pump body.
2 Remove the two nuts and washers holding pump to crankcase.
3 Carefully lift away the pump, gaskets and insulating pad from the crankcase (see **FIG 2:3**).

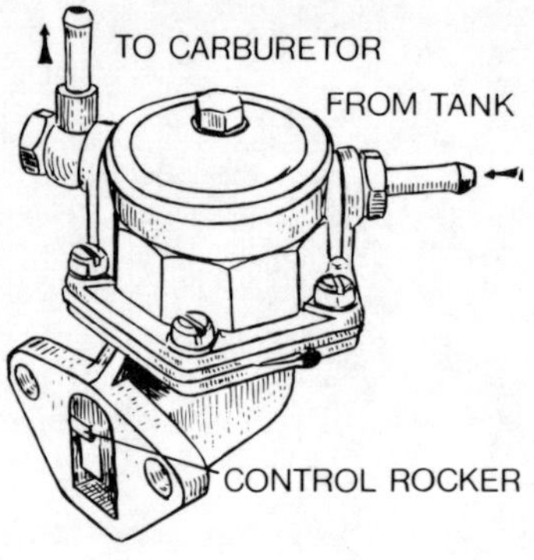

FIG 2:1 **Fuel pump. Arrows point to fuel inlet and outlet**

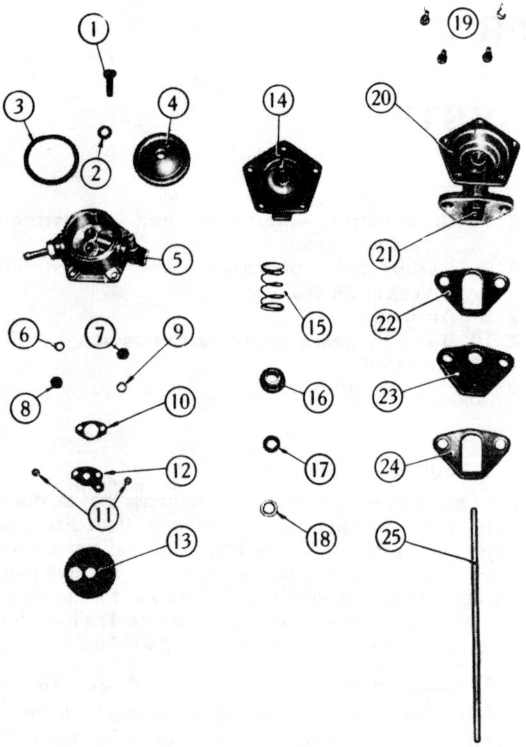

FIG 2:2 **Fuel pump components**

Key to Fig 2:2 1 Cover screw 2 Screw gasket 3 Cover gasket 4 Cover 5 Upper body 6 Spring for inlet valve 7 Inlet valve 8 Outlet valve 9 Spring for outlet valve 10 Plate gasket 11 Plate screws 12 Valve retaining plate complete with tie rod 13 Filter gauze 14 Diaphragm, thrust cup 15 Return spring 16 Spring 17 Felt 18 Washer for felt 19 Connection screws 20 Lower body 21 Rocker 22, 24 Gaskets 23 Insulating pad 25 Pump control pushrod

Dismantling:

1 Refer to **FIG 2:2** and remove the cover mounting screw 1 and washer 2. Lift off cover 4 and filter 13. Mark the relative position of the two halves of the pump body. Remove the pump bodies interlocking screws 19 and separate the upper half from the lower half of the body.

2 Push down the centre of the diaphragm assembly 14 and rotate through 90 deg. to release diaphragm from the rocker 21. Lift out diaphragm and spring 15.

3 Release the two valve assemblies in the upper body by removing the valve retaining plate locking screws 11, and lifting out the plate 12, gasket 10, valve springs 6 and 9, and valves 7 and 8.

4 Using a pin punch remove the rocker pivot pin together with the two washers and carefully lift away rocker and reaction spring.

5 Thoroughly wash all components in petrol and blow dry with compressed air or a foot pump. Inspect the valves 7 and 8 for evidence of damage and valve springs 6 and 9 for weakness or cracks. Check to see that the diaphragm reaction spring and rocker are not distorted or unserviceable. Generally inspect all parts for cracks, distortion and the diaphragm for stiffness and also the rocker and pin for wear.

2:5 Reassembly, installation and adjustment

Ensure that all parts are clean and dry. Assembling is the reverse procedure of dismantling. Lubricate the rocker lever and pin before placing them in the lower body.

Installation:

Carefully slide the pump control pushrod into the crankcase, assemble the two gaskets with the insulating pad in between and slide over the pump retaining studs. Ease the pump towards the crankcase ensuring the pushrod locates correctly in the rocker end. Finally tighten the two retaining nuts and spring washers.

2:6 Carburetter operation and adjustment, Weber 26.IMB.1 and 26.IMB.3

The new 500 sedan engine is fitted with the Weber 26.IMB.1 carburetter, whilst the new 500 sports engine is fitted with the Weber 26.IMB.3 carburetter. In both cases the carburetter is of a downdraft single body design with

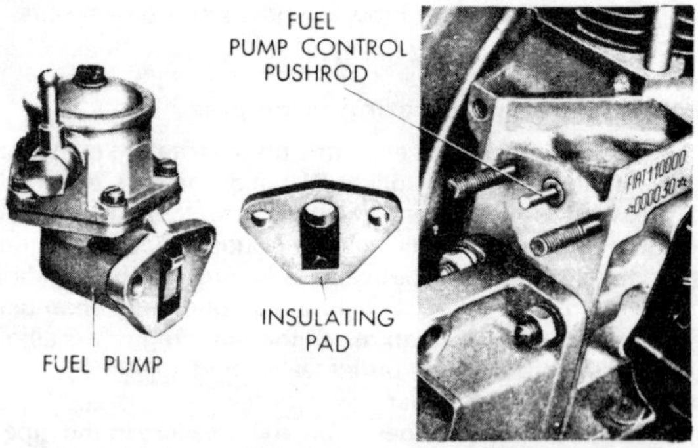

FIG 2:3 **Fuel pump and control pushrod**

a 1.0236 inch diameter throat measured at the height of the throttle shaft. The amount of charge passing to the manifold is controlled by a throttle butterfly valve from an accelerator pedal operating a lever secured to the throttle valve shaft via a cable. The carburetter is fitted with a progressive action starting device which enables the driver to suit the mixture richness to the most arduous of starting conditions, and will enable the engine to run evenly until it reaches its normal operating temperature.

A dampened needle valve ensures a smooth running engine as it is not affected by engine vibrations and therefore giving a constant fuel level in the carburetter bowl. A secondary venturi is incorporated in the single casting of the carburetter body and this has a diameter of 0.8268 inch.

Carburetter operation:

Filtered air flows through the venturi 24 (see **FIG 2:4**) where it mixes with fuel flowing from the nozzle 25 and the charge is then conveyed to the cylinders through the primary venturi 21 and throat, where the throttle butterfly 19 controls the amount of charge.

Petrol flows from the main fuel line to the bowl 16 through a gauze filter 7 and needle valve 10, where the float 12 pivoting at point 11, controls the opening of the needle 10 so maintaining a constant fuel level. From the bowl 16 fuel reaches the emulsion well 23 via the metered main jet 15 where, after having been mixed with the air coming from the metered air corrector screw 1, through the emulsion orifices 22 and spray nozzle 25, it finally reaches the venturis where it mixes with the air stream

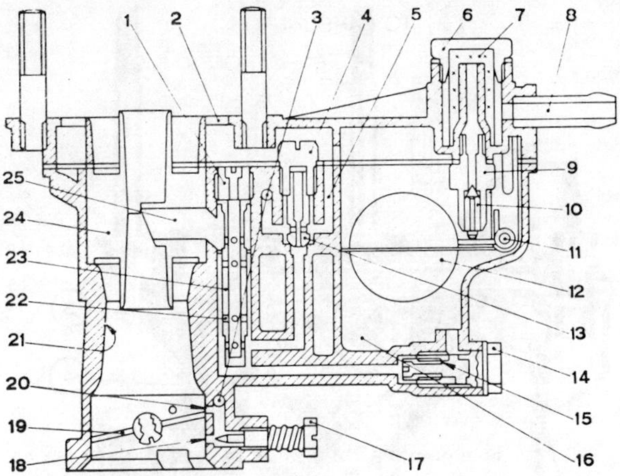

FIG 2:4 Diagrammatic section of Weber 26.IMB1 carburetter

Key to Fig 2:4 1 Air corrector jet 2 Air inlet 3 Idle speed mixture duct 4 Idle speed jet holder 5 Idle speed air orifice 6 Filter cover 7 Filter 8 Fuel inlet connection 9 Needle valve seat 10 Needle 11 Float pivot 12 Float 13 Idle speed jet 14 Main jet holder 15 Main jet 16 Bowl 17 Idle speed mixture adjustment screw 18 Idle speed mixture orifice 19 Throttle 20 Transition hole 21 Primary venturi (not interchangeable) 22 Emulsion orifices 23 Emulsion well 24 Secondary venturi (not interchangeable) 25 Main nozzle

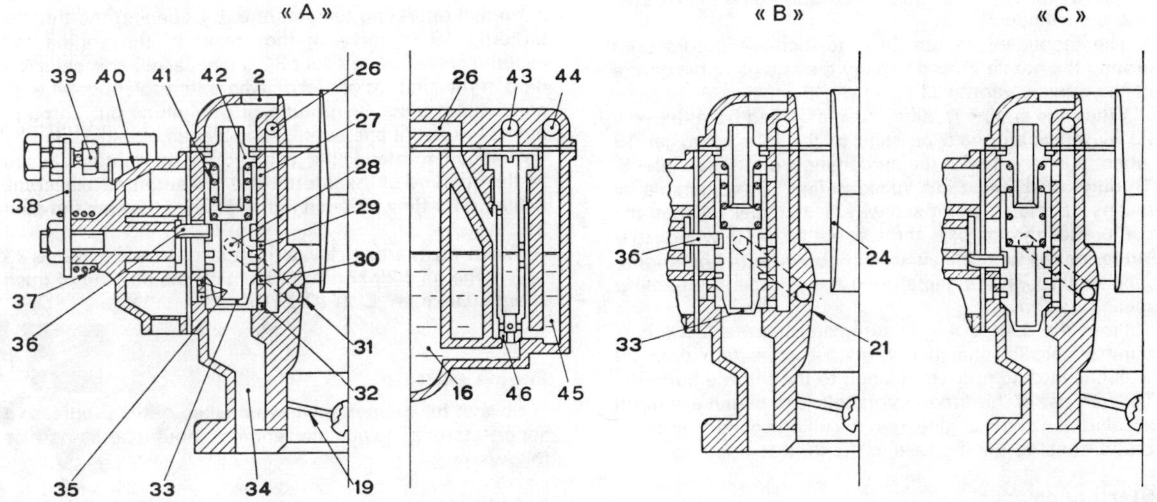

FIG 2:5 Starting device (choke) diagrammatic section

Key to Fig 2:5 A Device fully inserted B Device partially inserted C Device disinserted 2 Air inlet 16 Bowl 19 Throttle 21 Primary venturi 24 Secondary venturi 26 Mixture duct 27 Mixture leaning air orifice 28 Transition duct 29 Transition mixture orifice 30 Starting mixture orifice 31 Transition orifice 32 Starting mixture orifice 33 Starting valve 34 Mixture duct 35 Starting device air orifices 36 Rocker 37 Lever return spring 38 Starting device control lever 39 Control wire screw 40 Cover with support for starting device control bowden 41 Starting valve spring 42 Spring casing. 43 Starting jet emulsion air orifice 44 Air emulsion reserve well orifice 45 Starting reserve well 46 Starting jet

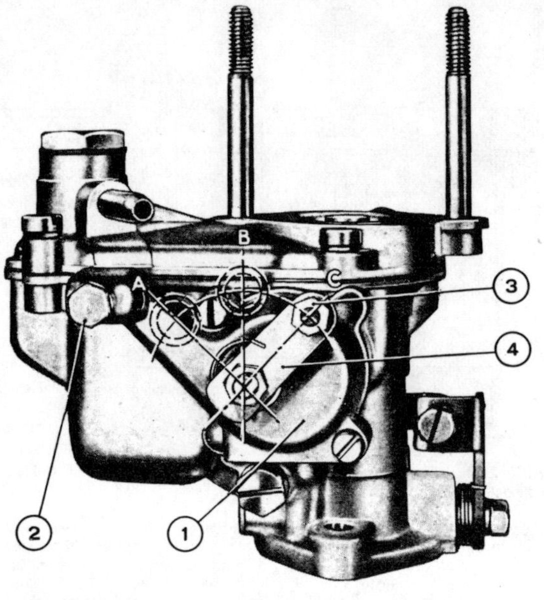

FIG 2:6 Weber 26.IMB.1 carburetter starting device (choke) end

Key to Fig 2:6 1 Choke device cover 2 Bowden mounting screw 3 Nut and screw, choke bowden wire 4 Choke control lever A Position of lever 4 for 'fully inserted' choke B 'Partially inserted' choke C 'Disinserted' choke

caused by the engine suction and the charge is then drawn into the cylinders.

The secondary venturi 24 is to increase the vacuum around the nozzle 25 and to carry the charge to the centre of the primary venturi 21.

When the engine is idling, fuel is carried from the well 23 via an appropriate passage to the idle speed jet 13 where it is mixed with the air coming from the air inlet 5. Through duct 3 and idle speed orifice 18 (adjustable by means of a taper point screw 17), the fuel reaches the carburetter throat, past throttle butterfly 19 where it is further mixed with the air stream drawn in by the engine vacuum through the gap around the throttle in the idling speed position.

From the duct 3 the mixture can also reach the carburetter throttle chamber through a transition hole 20 which is located in exact relation to the throttle butterfly. The purpose of this progression hole is to permit a smooth acceleration of the engine from the idling speed, this being proportional to the increase in the throttle opening.

Starting device:

This enables the engine to be started when it is cold under the most arduous of weather conditions. It is controlled by means of a lever placed behind the gearshift lever and must be progressively adjusted to its normal rest position as the engine reaches the normal operating temperature. The starting device comprises a valve 33 (see **FIG 2:5**) actuated by the lug of the rocker 36 which is connected to the control lever 38 by a suitable shaft. By pulling the device control fully across through lever 38 and rocker 36, the valve 33 is lifted from its seating and brought into the 'fully open' position. Refer to diagram 'A' (**FIG 2:5**). Under these conditions the valve 33 closes the air hole 27 and the mixture hole 29 and uncovers mixture orifices 30 and 32 which also communicate with the starting jet 46 through a duct 26 and air holes 35. With the valve 33 partially open the hole 29 may communicate with the carburetter throat through the valve central slot, duct 28 and the hole 31 drilled in the venturi 21 corresponding with the venturi restriction.

When the throttle is set at the idling speed position, the engine vacuum caused by the operation of the starter enables the fuel contained in the recess of jet 46, in the jet and in the reserve well 45 to be mixed with the air coming from holes 43 and 44. The mixture arrives through the duct 26 and holes 30 and 32, at the same time as air passing from the holes 35, past the throttle through duct 34 so permitting easy starting of the engine.

After the engine has fired initially, the device will deliver a charge with a rich petrol/air ratio so as to permit regular running of the engine whilst it is cold. As soon as the engine has warmed up to normal operating temperature this charge would obviously be too rich and therefore it is necessary to gradually ease off the operation of the starting device as the engine reaches its normal operating temperature. During this adjustment the valve 43 slowly uncovers the hole 27 which will permit a greater amount of air to enter through the spring guide hole 42 so weakening the mixture at the same time as closing the progression holes 30 and 32 and air holes 35 the amount of mixture is also reduced. See diagram 'B' (**FIG 2:5**).

The hole 29, the duct 28 and the hole 31, which are drilled in the venturi 21 permit a regular progression of acceleration whilst the engine is cold as well as when it is at normal operating temperature. By opening the throttle butterfly 19 to increase the speed of the engine the vacuum acting on the duct 34 is decreased. This causes a drop in the amount of fuel delivered through duct 34 with consequent irregular running of the engine but, through hole 31, duct 28 and hole 29 some charge is sucked in by the vacuum formed in the restriction of the venturi, caused by the opening of the throttle and this automatically compensates for the reduction in the delivery through the duct 34.

When the starting device is not in operation, valve 33 covers the hole 29 and so preventing the passing of fresh charge. Diagram 'C' (**FIG 2:5**).

Engine starting:

So that full advantage may be taken of the progressive action starting device the engine should be started as follows:

1 Cold starts:

The starting device should be moved across the position 'A', (**FIG 2:6**). Once the engine has fired push the control in partially.

2 Warm starts:

Only partially move the starting device as shown in position 'B' (**FIG 2:6**).

3 Engine warm-up:

As the engine begins to warm up to its normal operating temperature, gradually push home the starting device lever so as only to supply the engine with the richened charge enabling the cold engine operation to be smooth and regular. Position 'B' (**FIG 2:6**).

4 Normal car driving:

Once the engine has reached its normal operating temperature the starting device should be completely brought out of operation by bringing the control lever to the position 'C' (**FIG 2:6**).

Idle speed adjustment:

The idling speed of the engine is adjusted by means of a throttle setscrew and the mixture setscrew, the position of which are shown in **FIG 2:7**. The throttle screw allows for the adjustment of the throttle butterfly opening, the conical mixture setscrew meters the amount of charge issuing from the idling speed passage which causes the mixture to blend with the air flowing past the throttle that leaves a gap between its edges and the throat walls. This ensures a correct petrol/air mixture ratio best suited to the engine requirements giving smooth operation.

The engine idling speed must always be adjusted when the engine is at its normal operating temperature and then setting the throttle butterfly position to its minimum opening position by adjusting the throttle setscrew so giving a steady engine speed. Turn the mixture screw in or out so as to set the mixture richness to the most suitable ratio for the selected throttle opening. This will accomplish a fast but steady idling. Reduce the minimum throttle opening slightly by adjusting the throttle setscrew until the best idling speed is obtained.

Adjustment of fuel level in float chamber:

The needle valve, seating and float are easily accessible for inspection by removing the carburetter top cover. Before checking the petrol level in the float chamber, ensure that the needle valve seat is screwed well home and that the gasket is in place. Also check that the calibrated orifice in the valve seat is unobstructed and not worn and finally check that the needle slides freely in its guide. Should the valve and seating be leaking, then the valve assembly must be renewed. Check that the float is not distorted or punctured and that it moves on its pivot without resistance or excessive play. Again renew the float assembly if there is any doubt. To check the level proceed as follows:

1. Check that the needle valve 3 (see **FIG 2:8**) is screwed tight on its seat.
2. Keep the carburetter cover 1 upright or else the weight of the float 9 will lower the ball 8 fitted on the needle 4. Check that with the cover held in the vertical position and the float arm 6 in slight contact with the ball 8 of the needle 4, the float is $\frac{5}{16}$ inch away from the cover with its gasket 2 fitted flat against the cover face.
3. Check that the float travel is $\frac{5}{16}$ inch and if necessary bend the lug 5 to give the required settings.
4. If the float 9 is not correctly positioned, bend the float arms 7 until the correct adjustment is obtained. Ensure that the arm 6 is perpendicular to the needle axis and does not show any rough spots or indentations which might impair free movement of the needle. Check that the float 9 freely moves about its pivot pin.

Every time a new float or needle valve assembly is fitted the above detailed adjustment operations must be completed to ensure correct fuel levels.

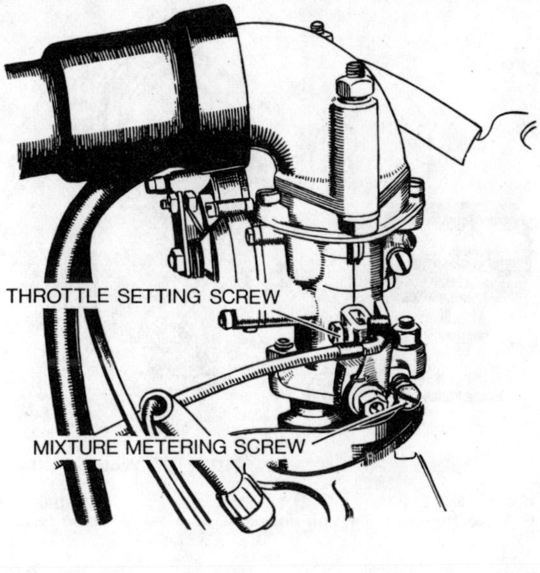

FIG 2:7 Weber 26.IMB.1 carburetter in place on engine. Idle speed is adjusted by working respectively on throttle setting screw and mixture metering screw

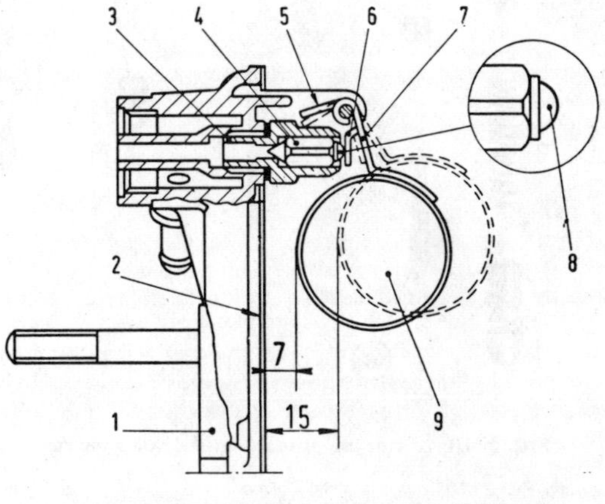

FIG 2:8 Float adjustment data

Key to Fig 2:8 1 Carburetter cover 2 Cover gasket 3 Needle valve seat 4 Needle 5 Lug 6, 7 Arms 8 Needle ball 9 Float 7 .2756 inch 15 .5906 inch

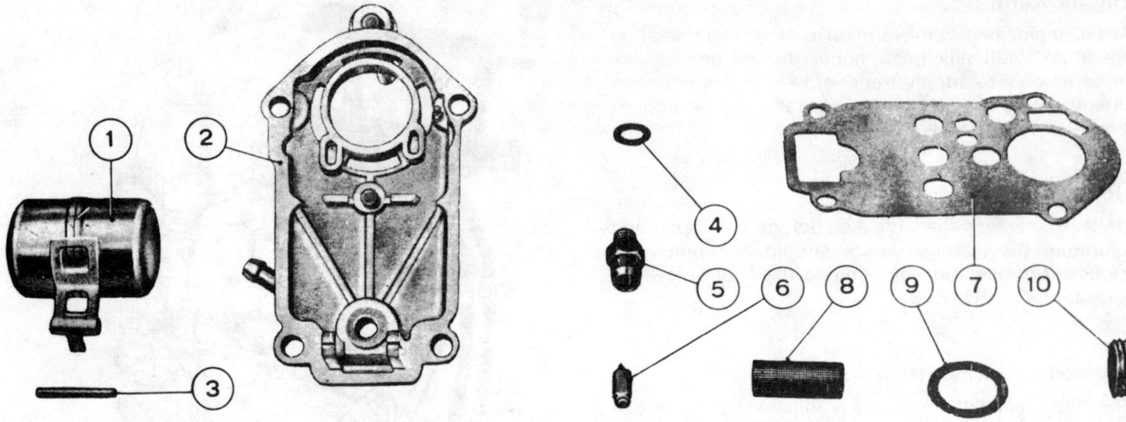

FIG 2:9 Weber 26.IMB.1 carburetter cover components

Key to Fig 2:9 1 Float 2 Caburetter cover 3 Float pivot 4 Needle valve for gasket 5, 6 Needle valve seat and needle valve 7 Cover gasket 8 Filter strainer 9 Gasket 10 Filter inspection plug

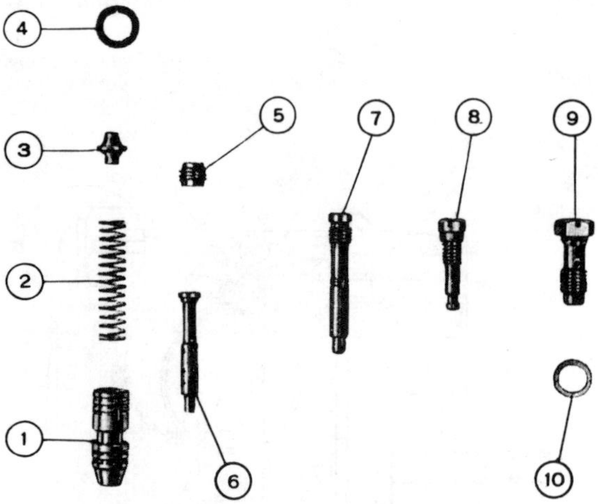

FIG 2:10 Jets, jet holders and choke valve

Key to Fig 2:10 1 Choke valve 2 Spring 3 Spring retainer and guide 4 Lock ring 5 Air bleed jet 6 Emulsion well 7 Choke jet 8 Idling jet holder and jet 9 Main jet holder and jet 10 Main jet holder gasket

Throttle valve components:

The throttle valve shaft should rotate freely in its guides and this should be checked when the engine is at its normal operating temperature. Any excessive clearance caused by wear or the throttle valve butterfly distorted are liable to cause irregular engine operation which will be more pronounced at idling speed. Should the above conditions be evident then the throttle valve butterfly and the shaft assembly together with its sealing rings must be renewed.

Carburetter cleaning:

To thoroughly clean the carburetter proceed as follows:

1 **Passages.** All fuel passages have a diameter that are specially calibrated to ensure best operating conditions. It is therefore essential that any dirt or scale that has been deposited by petrol must be removed. Thoroughly clean with petrol and blow dry using a compressed air jet directed through all the passages in the castings. It is essential that no drills or other metal objects be passed through the jets or the passages otherwise these could alter the finely calibrated diameters.

2 **Calibrated parts.** Idling and main jet holders, and the relevant bayonet coupled jets are easily removed by using a suitably sized wrench or screwdriver. To clean the different calibrated parts, thoroughly wash in petrol and blow dry using a compressed air jet. Do not use any fine drills or metallic points as these may alter the fine calibration of the orifices. Should it be necessary to dismantle the carburetter adjustment components for inspection always ensure that after reassembly of the parts that they are seated correctly to avoid possible operating troubles in the future.

3 **Filter.** To clean the filter unscrew and remove its plug 10 (see **FIG 2:9**) located on the top of the carburetter cover and then gently ease out the filter. Wash the filter carefully in petrol, also ensure that the filter seat is clean and then blow dry using a compressed air jet.

2:7 Carburetter operation and adjustment, Weber 26.IMB.4

The new 500.D sedan engine is fitted with the Weber 26.IMB.4 carburetter which is of single downdraft design. This carburetter is fitted with a progressive action starting device which enables the driver to adjust the mixture richness to the most arduous of starting conditions, and will enable the engine to run evenly until it reaches its normal operating temperature.

A dampened needle valve ensures a smooth running engine as it is not affected by engine vibrations therefore giving a constant fuel level in the carburetter bowl. A secondary venturi is incorporated in the single casting of the carburetter body.

The diagrammatic view in **FIG 2:11** clearly shows the operation of the carburetter which is basically the same as the Weber 26.IMB.1 as described in **Section 2:6**.

Starting device:

A progressive action starting device is fitted and has the function of ensuring that the engine may be easily started when cold. It is controlled by a lever which is placed behind the gearshift lever and this must be gradually returned to its normal rest position as the engine reaches its normal operating temperature.

The starting device is shown in **FIG 2:12** and comprises a valve 33 operated by the lug of a rocker 36 which is connected through a shaft to the control lever 38. By operating the starting device control lever to the end of its stroke, lever 38 and rocker 36 together with the valve 33 is lifted from its seating and brought to the 'fully open' position as shown in 'A' (**FIG 2:12**). Under these conditions the valve 33 closes the air hole 27 and the mixture hole 29 and uncovers the mixture orifices 30 and 32, these communicating with the starting jet 46 also through the duct 26 and the air holes 35.

It should be noted that with the valve 33 partially opened, the hole 29 may communicate with the carburetter throat through the valve central slot, duct 28 and the hole 31 which is drilled in the venturi 21 opposite the restrictions.

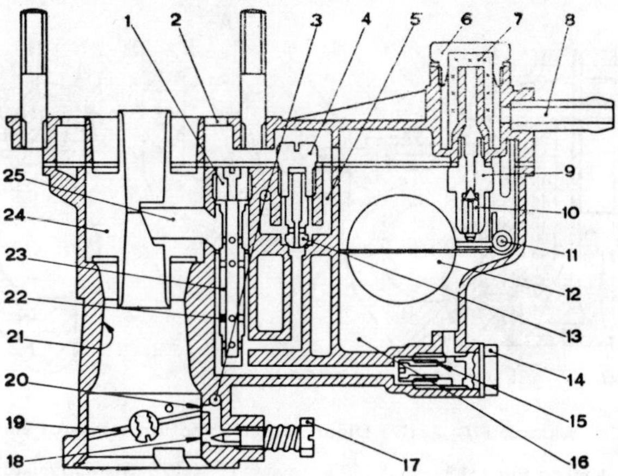

FIG 2:11 Diagrammatic section view of Weber 26.IMB.4 carburetter

Key to Fig 2:11 1 Air corrector jet 2 Air inlet 3 Idle speed mixture duct 4 Idle speed jet holder 5 Idle speed air orifice 6 Filter cover 7 Filter 8 Fuel inlet connection 9 Needle valve seat 10 Needle 11 Float pivot 12 Float 13 Idle speed jet 14 Main jet holder 15 Main jet 16 Bowl 17 Idle speed mixture adjustment screw 18 Idle speed mixture orifice 19 Throttle 20 Transition hole 21 Primary venturi (not interchangeable) 22 Emulsion orifices 23 Emulsion well 24 Secondary venturi (not interchangeable) 25 Main nozzle

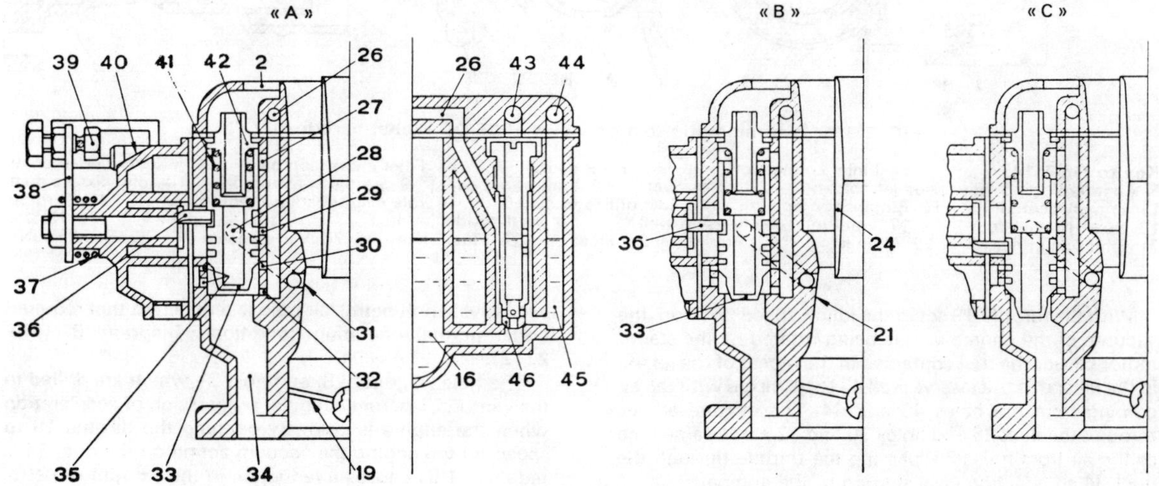

FIG 2:12 Diagrammatic section views of 26.IMB.4 Weber carburetter starting device

Key to Fig 2:12 2 Air inlet 16 Bowl 19 Throttle 21 Primary venturi 24 Secondary venturi 26 Mixture duct 27 Mixture leaning air orifice 28 Transition duct 29 Transition mixture orifice 30 Starting mixture orifice 31 Transition orifice 32 Starting mixture orifice 33 Starting valve 34 Mixture duct 35 Starting device air orifices 36 Rocker 37 Lever return spring 38 Starting device control lever 39 Control wire screw 40 Cover with support for starting device control bowden 41 Starting valve spring 42 Spring casing 43 Starting jet emulsion air orifice 44 Air emulsion reserve well orifice 45 Starting reserve well 46 Starting jet A Choke fully inserted B Choke partially inserted C Choke disengaged

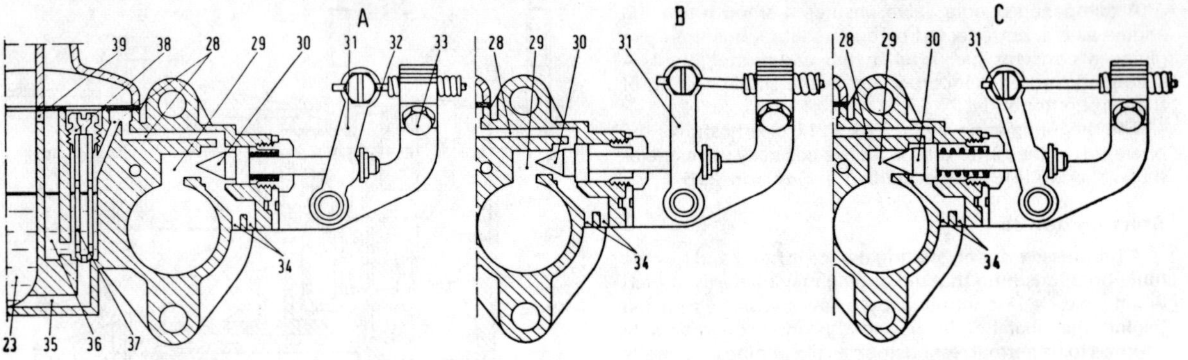

FIG 2:13 Diagrammatic section views of 26.OC Weber carburetter through the starting device

Key to Fig 2:13 23 Bowl 28 Starting mixture duct 29 Starting mixture duct 30 Starting valve 31 Starting device control lever 32 Starting device control wire 33 Bowden fixing screw 34 Emulsion air orifices 35 Bowl-to-starting jet duct 36 Starting reserve well 37 Starting jet 38 Starting air corrector screw 39 Reserve well emulsion air slot A Choke fully inserted B Choke partially inserted C Choke disengaged

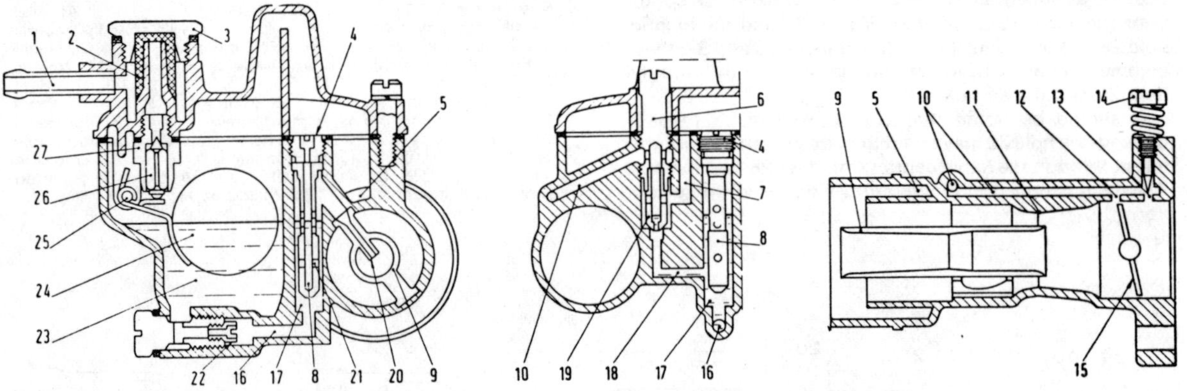

FIG 2:14 Diagrammatic section views of 26.OC Weber carburetter

Key to Fig 2:14 1 Fuel inlet connection 2 Filter gauze 3 Filter inspection plug 4 Air corrector jet 5 Air intake 6 Idle speed jet holder 7 Idle air duct 8 Emulsion tube 9 Secondary venturi 10 Idle mixture duct 11 Primary venturi 12 Progression hole 13 Idle orifice to duct 14 Idle mixture adjustment screw 15 Throttle 16 Bowl-to-well duct 17 Emulsion tube housing well 18 Well-to-idle jet duct 19 Idle speed jet 20 Nozzle 21 Emulsion orifices 22 Main jet 23 Bowl 24 Float 25 Float pivot 26 Valve needle 27 Needle valve

With the throttle 19 set in the idling speed position, the vacuum of the engine as it is being rotated by the starter motor causes the fuel contained in the recess of the jet 46, in the jet and in the reserve well 45 to be mixed with the air coming from the holes 43 and 44. The mixture arrives through the duct 26 and holes 30 and 32 at the same time as the air from holes 35, passing the throttle through the duct 34 so enabling easy starting of the engine.

Once the engine has fired the starting device delivers a charge whose petrol/air ratio is such that the engine will run evenly whilst it is cold. As the engine operating temperature increases obviously this charge would be excessively rich as it is necessary to gradually weaken off the starting device which occurs by the valve 33 slowly uncovering the hole 27 permitting a greater amount of air to enter through the spring guide holes 42 whilst gradually closing holes 30 and 32 and the air holes 35 the excessively rich petrol/air ratio is reduced to that required under normal operating conditions. Diagram 'B' (**FIG 2:12**).

The hole 29, duct 28, and hole 31 which are drilled in the venturi 21 permit a regular progression of acceleration when the engine is cold. By opening the throttle 19 to speed up the engine the vacuum acting on the duct 34 is reduced. This causes a reduction in the amount of petrol delivered through the duct 34 giving irregular running of the engine, but some charge is sucked in through hole 31, duct 28 and hole 29 by vacuum created in the restriction of the venturi caused by the opening of the throttle and this will compensate for the reduction in delivery through the duct 34.

When the starting device is not in use, the valve 33 also covers hole 29 so preventing the admittance of petrol/air as shown in diagram 'C' (**FIG 2:12**).

Engine starting:

The same procedure should be used as described for the Weber 26.IMB.1 carburetter as detailed in **Section 2:6**.

Idle speed adjustment:

Refer to **Section 2:6** for full details on how this adjustment should be completed.

Fuel lever in float chamber:

See **Section 2:6** for full details of this check and adjustment.

Throttle valve components:

See **Section 2:6** for full check details.

Carburetter cleaning:

For full instructions refer to **Section 2:6**.

2:8 Carburetter operation and adjustment, Weber 26.OC

The new 500 station wagon is fitted with the Weber 26.OC carburetter which is of a horizontal draft design to suit the engine which is fitted in the horizontal position. The carburetter is fitted with a progressive action starting device which enables the driver to adjust the mixture richness to the most arduous of starting conditions, and will enable the engine to run evenly until it reaches normal operating temperature.

A dampened needle valve ensures a smooth running engine as it is not affected by engine vibrations and therefore giving a constant fuel level in the carburetter bowls. A secondary venturi is incorporated in the single casting of the carburetter body.

Carburetter operation, starting device:

The petrol from bowl 23 (see **FIG 2:13**) reaches the starting jet 37 through the duct 35. By operating the choke lever 31 to the end of its stroke, the valve 30 is lifted from its seat and brought to the 'fully open' position as shown in diagram 'A' (**FIG 2:13**). Under these conditions the valve 30 uncovers both the starting mixture ducts 28 and 29. With the throttle set in the idling speed position the engine vacuum created by the operation of the starter motor causes the fuel contained in the recess of jet 37 in the jet and the reserve well 36 to be mixed with the air coming from the air jet 38.

The mixture arrives through the ducts 28 and 29 at the same time as air from holes 34, past the throttle so permitting easy starting of the engine.

Once the engine has initially fired the starting device will deliver a mixture whose petrol/air ratio is such that the engine will run regularly even though it is cold. As soon as the engine warms up this rich charge would be excessive and therefore it becomes necessary to gradually ease back the operation of the starting device. As this is occurring, the valve 30 gradually covers up the mixture duct orifice 28 so as to weaken the mixture while by closing the duct 29 gradually. It also reduces the amount of mixture delivered by the carburetter as shown in diagram 'B' (**FIG 2:13**).

When the starting device is not in operation valve 30 covers the hole 29 so preventing the passage of mixture as shown in diagram 'C' (**FIG 2:13**).

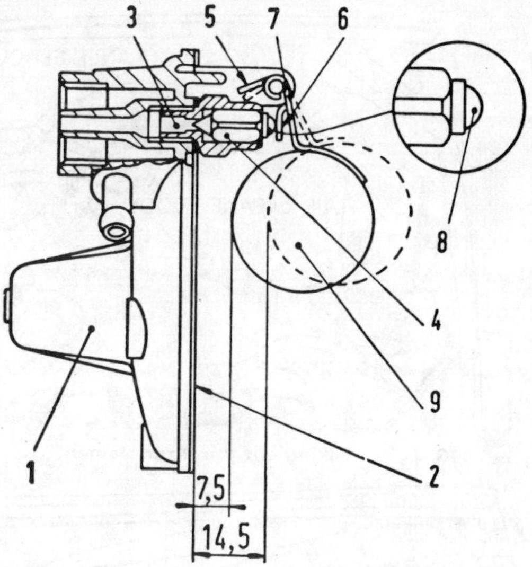

FIG 2:15 Float level setting diagram Weber carburetter type 26.OC

7,5=.29 inch 14,5=.57 inch

Key to Fig 2 : 16 Carburetter cover 2 Cover gasket 3 Needle valve 4 Valve needle 5 Lug 6, 7 Arms 8 Needle ball 9 Float

Engine starting:

So that full advantage may be taken of the progressive action starting device the engine should be started as follows:

1 **Cold starts.** The starting device should be moved across to position 'A' as shown in **FIG 2:13**. Once the engine has fired push the control in partially.
2 **Warm starts.** Only partially move the starting device to position 'B' as shown in **FIG 2:13**.
3 **Engine warm-up.** As the engine begins to warm up to its normal operating temperature. Gradually push home the starting device lever so as only to supply the engine with the richened charge enabling the cold engine operation to be smooth and regular. Position 'B' shown in **FIG 2:13**.
4 **Normal car driving.** Once the engine has reached its normal operating temperature the starting device should be completely brought out of operation by bringing the control lever to the position 'C' shown in **FIG 2:13**.

Idle speed adjustment:

The idling speed is adjusted by movement of the throttle setscrew and the mixture setscrew. The throttle screw allows for the adjustment of the throttle opening whereas the conical mixture setscrew has the purpose of metering the amount of charge issuing from the idling speed passage, which will then mix with the air flowing past the throttle which when correctly set for normal idling speed should leave a gap between its edges and the throat walls. This ensures a correct petrol/air ratio best suited to the engine requirements and smooth operation.

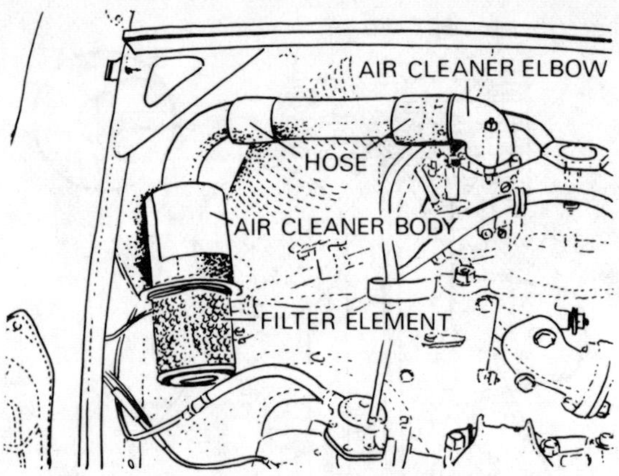

FIG 2:16 Taking out the filter element

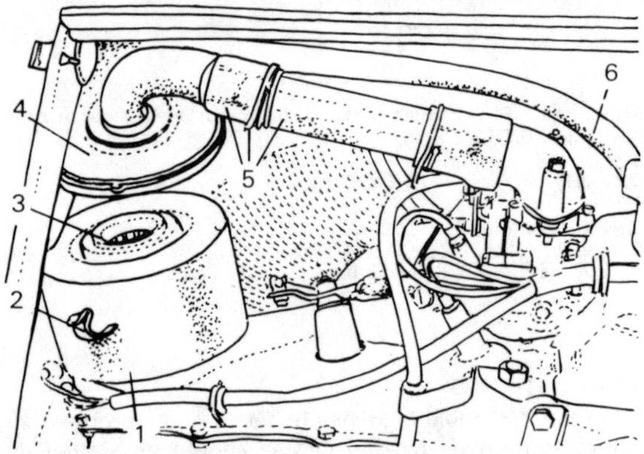

FIG 2:17 Removing the air cleaner

Key to Fig 2:17 1 Filter housing 2 Spring hooks 3 Filter element 4 Cover 5 Air suction pipe, hoses and clamps 6 Re-circulation pipe for blow-by gases and oil vapours

The idling speed should always be adjusted with the engine running and at its normal operating temperature by first setting the throttle to its maximum opening by turning the throttle setscrew so enabling an accurate adjustment to be made. Then slowly turn the mixture setscrew either in or out so as to adjust the mixture petrol/air ratio to the most suitable for the throttle opening, this will accomplish a fast and steady idling speed which should be then reduced by closing the throttle opening slightly by easing back the throttle setscrew. This adjustment should continue until the best idling speed is obtained.

Adjustment of fuel level in float chamber:

To check and adjust the level of fuel in the carburetter float chamber proceed as follows:

1 Check that the needle valve 3 (see **FIG 2:15**) is screwed tight on its seat.

2 Keep the carburetter cover 1 upright or else the weight of the float 9 will lower the ball 8 fitted on the needle 4. Check that with the cover held in the vertical position and the float arm 6 in slight contact with the ball 8 of the needle 4, the float is .2953 inch away from the cover with its gasket 2 fitted flat against the cover face.

3 Check that the float level is .5709 inch from the cover face and if necessary bend the lug 5 to give the required setting.

4 If the float 9 is not correctly positioned bend the float arm 7 until the correct adjustment is obtained. Ensure that the arm 6 is perpendicular to the needle axis and does not show any rough spots or indentations which might impair free movement of the needle. Check that the float 9 moves about its pivot pin.

Every time a new float or needle valve is fitted the above detailed adjustment operations must be completed to ensure correct fuel levels.

Throttle valve components:

See **Section 2:6** for full check details.

Carburetter cleaning:

For full instruction refer to **Section 2:6**.

2:9 Air cleaner (sedan)

The pleated paper air cleaner element is contained in a casing housed in a recess of one of the silencing chambers provided in the blower conveyor as shown in **FIG 2:16**. The air cleaner is connected to the carburetter by means of a specially shaped hose. The silencing chamber is designed to dampen the air intake noise and the carburetter venturi hiss and is so located in the blower conveyor system so that only clean dry air is drawn into the induction system.

To ensure complete protection of the engine it is recommended that the air filter element be replaced every 6000 miles or even earlier if the vehicle is operating in dusty conditions.

It should be noted that an oversize air cleaner may be obtained if the vehicle is to be operated in very dusty areas.

Air cleaner—engine 110 F.000:

To remove the air cleaner element, disengage both the spring hooks 2 as shown in **FIG 2:17** and lift away the cover 4 by turning it inwards together with the hose 5.

Air cleaner—station wagon:

A pleated paper air cleaner element is housed in a special air intake chamber connected to the front of the engine air cooling cowling (see **FIG 4:2**). To remove the will be seen located towards the rear of the power unit compartment. Remove the retaining wing nut, lift off the lid and the element can be withdrawn by lifting upwards.

2:10 Blow-by-gases recirculation device

Engine 110 F.000

All the oil vapours and blow-by-gases that are formed in the engine crankcase are drawn to the cylinder head cover recess 1 (see **FIG 2:18**). From here they travel into the pipe 5 via a breather valve 2 which is firmly attached to the oil filler cap 3 and the strainer 4 located in the filler neck. The oil vapours and gases are then drawn back into the duct 9 from the pipe 5 which connects the air cleaner 6 to the carburetter 7. This ensures a complete closed circuit circulation.

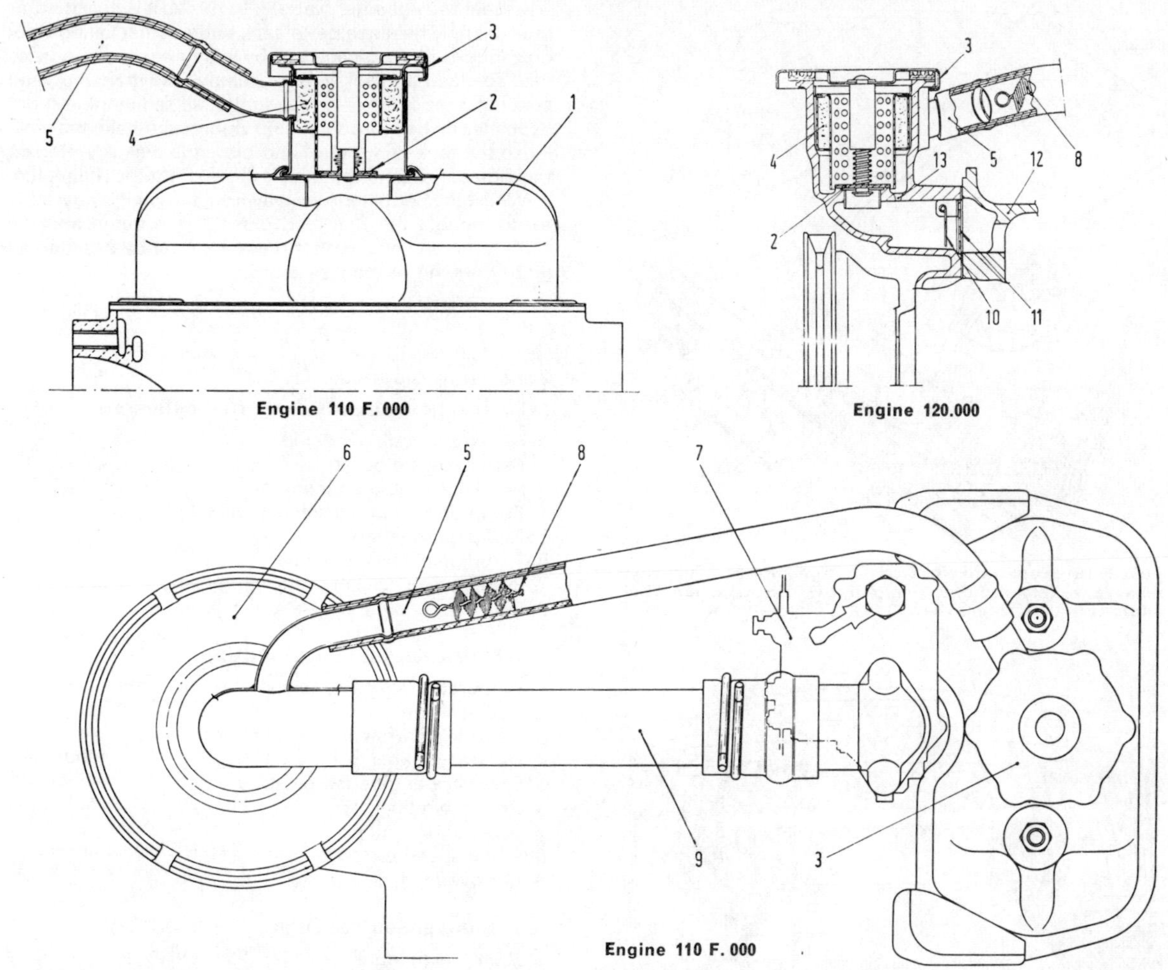

FIG 2:18 Diagram of blow-by gases re-circulation device

Key to Fig 2:18 1 Head cover 2 Blow-by gases and oil vapours breather valve 3 Oil filler cap 4 Strainer 5 Pipe 6 Air cleaner 7 Carburetter 8 Flame trap 9 Air suction pipe, air cleaner to carburetter 10 Movable partition 11 Filter gauze 12 Crankcase 13 Exhaust duct

Engine 120.000:

From engine No. 288156 the oil vapours and blow-by-gases instead of being exhausted to the atmosphere are conveyed to the air cleaner and from here they are drawn back into the combustion chambers. To ensure that an excessive of oil vapour does not pass along the piping with the blow-by-gases a diaphragm is fitted in the duct in front of the breather valve 2 (see **FIG 2:18**), the diaphragm comprising a filter gauze 11 and moveable partition 10.

It should be noted that the oil vapour strainer 4 (see **FIG 2:18**) and the flame trap 8 can easily be removed from their seating for cleaning or renewal.

2:11 Fuel tank

The fuel tank is located in the front compartment as shown in **FIG 2:19**, it comprises a filler union fitted with a cap, a fuel reserve supply indicator sender unit and a connection incorporating a filter for the main fuel supply pipes. To remove the tank proceed as follows:

1 Remove the contents of the front compartment including the spare wheel and tool bag.
2 Disconnect the main fuel line at the sender unit and also disconnect the cable to the fuel reserve supply indicator.
3 Remove the four screws together with the clips that fix the tank to the body and carefully lift away the fuel tank.
4 Carefully drain the contents of the tank into a clean dry container of a suitable capacity.

Fuel tank—sedan (110 F.) and station wagon (120):

The fuel tank is arranged in the front compartment as shown in **FIG 2:20**. To remove the fuel tank proceed as follows:

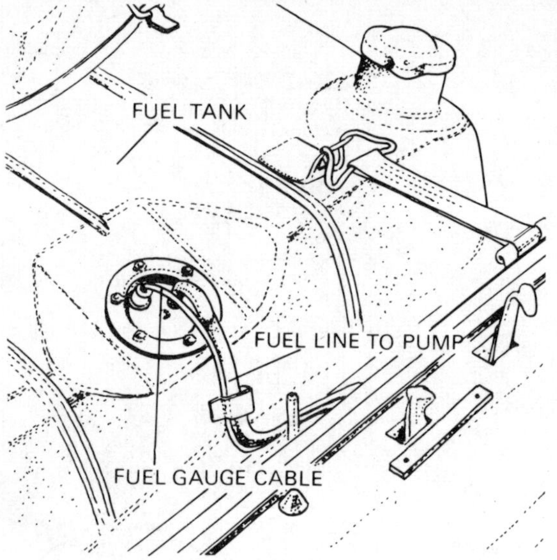

FIG 2:19 Fuel tank in front compartment. The fuel reserve supply indicator (red light) glows when fuel amount in tank is less than .8 to 1.1 Imp galls. or 5 litre

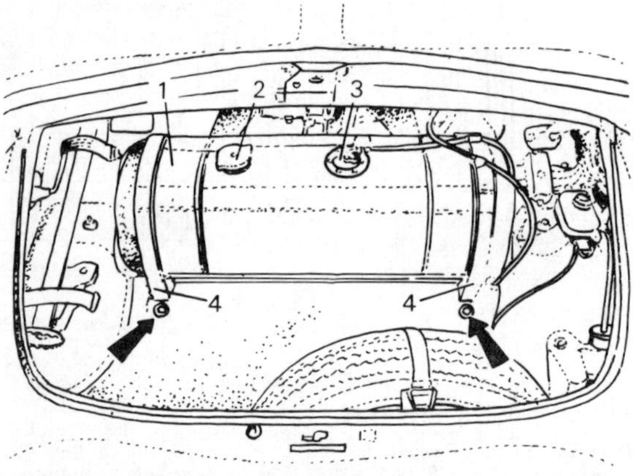

FIG 2:20 Location of the fuel tank in Sedan front compartment

Key to Fig 2:20 1 Fuel tank 2 Filler cap with vent valve 3 Fuel suction pipe and reserve supply indicator tank unit 4 Tank clamping bands
Note Arrows point to fuel tank clamping band screws

1 Remove both screws which secure the front ends of the clamping bands to the dash panel. The screws are shown by arrows in **FIG 2:20**.

Petrol tank cleaning:

The tank must be thoroughly checked for leaks especially at the joint seams. Should a leak be found it is advisable for a garage to attend to this as it is very dangerous to apply heat to a petrol tank without first taking strict precautions and a garage will be in a better position to do this. To clean the tank interior, remove the drain plug and spray in a jet of air or petrol so that all sediment and dirt deposits can be loosened. Then vigorously shake the tank. Flush the tank with petrol and blow the tank dry. Repeat this procedure until the tank is clean. Refit the drain plug.

Whilst the petrol tank is away from the car it is advisable to disconnect the fuel feed pipes at the pump and the carburetter and ensure that these are clear by using an air jet to one end of the pipe.

2:12 Fault diagnosis

(a) Leakage or insufficient fuel delivered

1 Air vent in tank restricted
2 Petrol pipes blocked
3 Air leaks at pipe connections
4 Pump or carburetter filters blocked
5 Pump gaskets faulty
6 Pump diaphragm defective
7 Pump valves sticking or seating badly
8 Fuel vapourizing in pipelines due to heat

(b) Excessive fuel consumption

1 Carburetter needs adjusting
2 Fuel leakage
3 Sticking controls or choke device
4 Dirty air cleaner
5 Excessive engine temperature
6 Brakes binding
7 Tyres under-inflated
8 Idling speed too high
9 Car overloaded

(c) Idling speed too high

1 Rich fuel mixture
2 Carburetter controls sticking
3 Slow-running screws incorrectly adjusted
4 Worn carburetter butterfly valve

(d) Noisy fuel pump

1 Loose mountings
2 Air leaks on suction side and at diaphragm
3 Obstruction in fuel pipe
4 Clogged pump filter

(e) No fuel delivery

1 Float needle stuck
2 Vent in tank blocked
3 Pipeline obstructed
4 Pump diaphragm stiff or damaged
5 Inlet valve in pump stuck open
6 Bad air leak on suction side of pump

CHAPTER 3

THE IGNITION SYSTEM

3:1 Description

The ignition system fitted to all the models covered by this manual consists of an ignition coil, ignition distributor fitted with contact breaker points, a centrifugal automatic advance system, condenser, low- and high-tension wiring, spark plugs and a power supply provided by a generator and battery. The wiring diagram is shown in **FIG 3:1**.

1 The low-tension circuit which is sometimes called the primary circuit includes the power supply, contact breaker points, condenser and ignition coil primary winding.

2 The high-tension circuit which is sometimes called the secondary circuit includes the ignition coil primary winding, distributor rotor, distributor cap with terminals and the central brush, high-tension cables and the spark plugs.

3:2 Operation

The contact breaker points in the distributor interrupts the primary circuit by the points opening. The sudden stop in the flow of current in the primary winding, does not cause arcing at the contact breaker points because it discharges into the condenser connected in parallel with the contact breaker points. With the sudden collapse of the primary circuit, the indensity of the magnetic field drops causing an induced high-tension current in the ignition coil secondary winding. The high EMF is distributed to the sparking plugs by the ignition distributor rotor.

The automatic advance mechanism comprises a plate carrying two weights which are symmetrically pivoted on the plate at one end. Also attached to the weights at opposite ends to the pivots is the cam carrier shaft with special tension return springs. Under the action of centrifugal force as the rotational speed increases, the weights move outwards causing the cam carrier shaft to move angularly compared to the distributor drive shaft thus causing advancement of the ignition timing.

The contact breaker assembly comprises the cam on the drive shaft and two contact points, one of which is stationary while the other is under the influence of the cam, the action of which is transmitted by a rubbing block. The cam has two lobes to control the opening and closing of contact points. The stationary contact point is mounted on an adjustable support to enable the contact breaker point gap to be adjusted.

The HT current reaches the distributor cap central terminal, from the ignition coil and is distributed to each of the spark plugs at the correct time by the rotor arm.

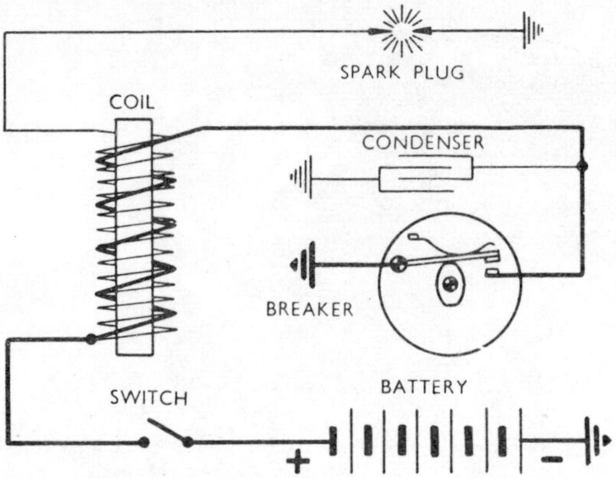

FIG 3:1 Ignition system wiring diagram

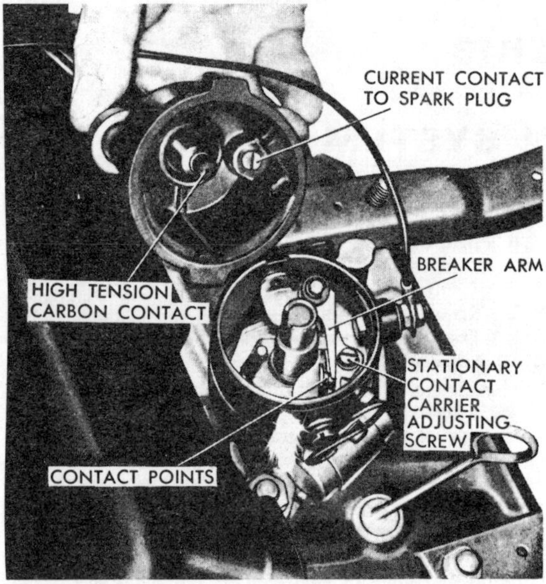

FIG 3:2 Ignition distributor in place on engine with cap lifted off

3:3 Routine maintenance

Refer to **FIG 3:2** and remove the distributor cap and lift off the rotor arm. Lubricate the cam spindle felt pad using Fiat VS oil. There is provision for the oil to make its way downwards. Squirt a few drops of oil into the distributor shaft lubrication fitting, the location being shown in **FIG 3:3**. Smear a little grease on the cam and a small drop of oil to the contact breaker point pivot.

Adjusting the contact breaker points:

Refer to **FIG 3:2** and slacken the stationary contact carrier adjusting screw. Slowly rotate the engine until one one of the two cams has opened the points to the fullest extent so that the gap is measured at the position of the maximum opening. Reset the gap to a correct clearance of .0185 to .0209 inch and tighten the contact carrier screw.

Cleaning the contact points:

If the contact points are dirty or pitted they must be cleaned by polishing them with a fine carborundum stone taking very great care to ensure that the contact faces are flat and square. Afterwards wipe away all dust with a cloth moistened in petrol. The contacts may be removed from the distributor body to assist refacing and cleaning referring to **Section 3:5**. If the moving contact is removed from its pivot, check that its operation is not sluggish. If it is tight, polish the pivot pin with a strip of fine emery cloth, clean off all dust and apply a tiny spot of oil to the top of the pivot pin. If a spring testing gauge is available the contact breaker spring should have a tension of 16.8±1.8 oz. measured at the points.

3:4 Ignition faults

If the engine runs unevenly set it to idle at a fast speed. Taking care not to touch any metal part of the sparking plug leads, pull up the insulator sleeve and short each plug in turn, using a screwdriver with an insulated handle. Connect the screwdriver blade between the plug top and the cylinder head. Shorting a plug which is firing properly will make the engine uneven running more pronounced. Shorting a plug in a cylinder which is not firing will make no difference.

Having located the faulty cylinder, stop the engine and remove the plug lead. Start the engine and hold the lead carefully to avoid shocks so that the metal end is about $\frac{3}{16}$ inch away from the cylinder head. A strong regular spark shows that the fault might be with the sparking plug. Remove and clean it according to the instructions in **Section 3:8**. Alternatively substitute it with a new plug.

If the spark is weak and irregular, check that the lead is not perished or cracked. If it appears to be defective, renew it and try another test. If there is no improvement, remove the distributor cap and wipe the inside clean and dry. Check the carbon brush located as shown in **FIG 3:2**. It should protrude from the cap moulding and be free to move against the pressure of the internal spring. Examine the surface inside the cap for signs of 'tracking' which can be seen as a thin black line between the electrodes or to some metal part in contact with the cap. This is caused by sparking, and the only cure is to fit a new cap.

Testing the low-tension circuit:

Before carrying out electrical tests, confirm that the contact breaker points are clean and correctly set, then proceed as follows:

1 Disconnect the black low-tension cable from the ignition coil and from the side of the distributor. Connect a test lamp between the two terminals. Turn the engine over slowly. If the lamp lights when the contacts close and goes out when they open, the low-tension circuit is in order. If the lamp fails to light the contacts are dirty or there is a break or loose connection in the low-tension wiring.

2 If the fault lies in the low-tension circuit, switch on the ignition and turn the crankshaft until the contact breaker points are fully open. Refer to the wiring diagram in Technical Data and check the circuit with

an 0–20 voltmeter. If the circuit is in order the meter should read approximately 12-volts.

3 **Battery to fuse box terminal 30.** Connect the voltmeter between the terminal 30 and earth. No reading indicates a faulty cable or loose connection.

4 **Fuse box.** Connect the voltmeter between the other auxiliary terminal 30 and earth. No reading indicates a broken or loose connection.

5 **Fuse box auxiliary terminal 30 to terminal number 30 on ignition switch.** Connect the meter between terminal number 30 on the ignition switch and earth. No reading indicates a damaged cable or loose connection.

6 **Ignition switch.** Connect the meter between terminal 15/54 and earth. Switch onto the ignition position, when no reading indicates a fault in the switch.

7 **Ignition switch to low-tension cable connection on the coil (blue cable).** Connect the meter between ignition coil terminal (blue cable) and earth. No reading indicates a damaged cable or loose connection.

8 **Ignition coil.** Disconnect the black low-tension cable connecting the coil to the distributor side terminal at the coil and connect the meter between this terminal and earth. No reading indicates a fault in the primary winding of the coil and a replacement coil must be fitted. If the reading is correct remake the connections to the coil.

9 **Ignition coil to distributor.** Disconnect the thin black low-tension cable at the side of the distributor and connect the meter between the end of this cable and earth. No reading indicates a damaged cable or loose connections.

10 **Contact breaker and capacitor.** Connect the meter across the contact breaker points. No reading indicates a faulty capacitor.

Capacitor:

The best method of testing a capacitor (condenser) is by substitution. Disconnect the original capacitor and connect a new one between the low-tension terminal on the side of the distributor and earth.

If a new capacitor is needed, fit a new one complete with bracket, but if necessary unsolder the original bracket and solder it onto the new capacitor using as little heat as possible. Capacitor capacity is .15–.20 microfarads.

3:5 Removing and dismantling distributor (sedan and sports)

To remove the distributor proceed as follows:

1 Rotate the engine slowly until the distributor rotor arm is opposite the brass segment in the distributor cap connected to No. 1 plug lead. This will provide a datum for replacement.

2 Disconnect the cable from the low-tension terminal on the side of the distributor body. Mark position of distributor on support. Release the distributor retaining nut and washer from the underside of the top flange of the distributor support and carefully lift away the distributor.

3 Pull off the rotor arm. Remove the insulated terminal assembly from the side of distributor body. Release the contact breaker carrier plate retaining screws and condenser flange screw from the outside of the distributor body. Carefully lift out the contact breaker plate assembly.

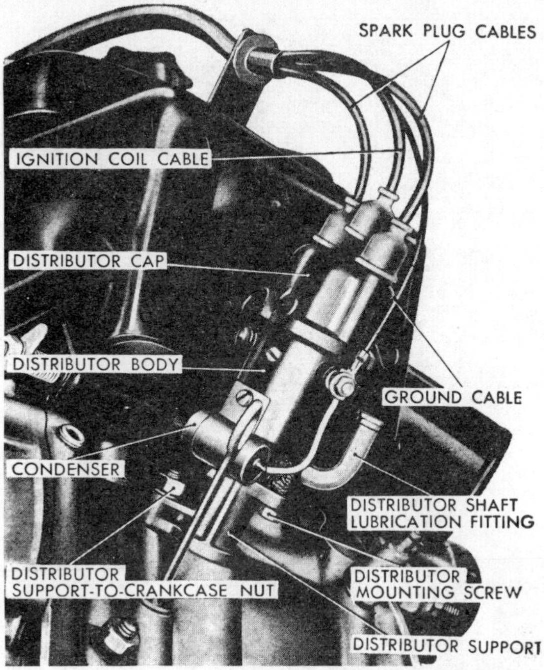

FIG 3:3 Ignition distributor in place on engine

4 Before further dismantling note the relative positions of the driving dog and the rotor arm driving slot at the top of the distributor cam spindle. The driving dog is offset and can only engage its driving spindle in one position. Then when the cam assembly is fitted to the centrifugal weights during reassembly the timing is not 80 deg. out.

5 Take out the cam lubrication felt pad recessed in the rotor arm housing on the end of the cam spindle. Remove the retaining screw, carefully disengage the springs and lift out the cam spindle. It should be noted that there is a small retaining ball and spring located in a drilling nearly at the top of the drive shaft spindle. Carefully lift away the weights.

6 Thoroughly clean all parts and inspect for excessive wear. The distributor cap must not be cracked or show signs of tracking. The cap terminals, rotor and contact breaker points can be cleaned with a very fine file. Emerypaper must not be used. If the clearance between the rotor and distributor cap segments exceeds .0118 inch both the rotor and distributor cap must be replaced. Inspect the contact breaker arm rubbing block for excessive wear and also the points for wear so that if the gap exceeds the last setting limit of .0209 inch and adjustment through the stationary contact carrier screw is no longer possible (see **FIG 3:2**), the contact breaker set must be renewed.

If the distributor drive shaft side or vertical movement is excessive the distributor must be renewed. Weak centrifugal weight springs or damaged weights must be renewed using original Fiat spares otherwise the automatic ignition advance characteristics could be altered.

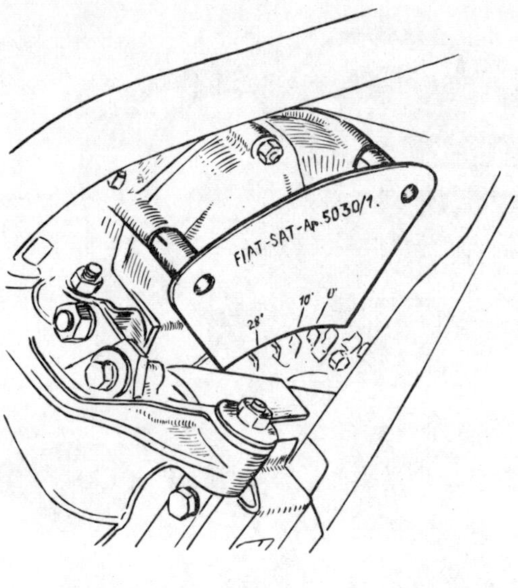

FIG 3:4 Use of fixture Ap.5030/1 to check ignition timing

Reassembly is the reverse procedure to dismantling but the following points should be noted:

1 Lubricate the parts of the centrifugal advance mechanism, the drive spindle and the part of the shaft which accepts the cam with Fiat VS oil.
2 Ensure that upon reassembly the slot in the rotor arm housing matches the distributor driving dog. Lubricate the felt pad in the rotor arm housing.
3 Fit the distributor back onto its support gently rotating the rotor arm so that the drive dog engages with the drive shaft mating flange. Provided the crankshaft has not been turned the rotor arm should finish up pointing to No. 1 cylinder segment in the distributor cap. Tighten the distributor retaining nut, refit the distributor cap and leads to the spark plugs and the LT lead to distributor body terminal.
4 Add a few drops of oil to the distributor shaft lubrication fitting (see **FIG 3:3**).

3:6 Removing and dismantling distributor (station wagon)

The distributor is located towards the top rear of the engine and is bolted direct onto the crankcase rear cover as shown in **FIG 1:2**. It is driven direct by a gear in mesh with a corresponding gear on the camshaft. The basic design of the distributor is the same as that for the sedan and sports engine, except that the distributor cap has been redesigned, there is a gear instead of the dog drive and no distributor support. To remove and dismantle the distributor proceed as previously described taking great care about marking the location of the distributor to rear cover and rotating the engine until No. 1 cylinder is on compression. This will ensure that reassembly is straightforward without loss of ignition timing.

3:7 Timing the ignition

It is necessary to retime the ignition should the distributor shaft or camshaft have been removed. To retime the ignition proceed as follows:

1 On the timing sprocket cover fit Fiat tool AP.5030/1 as shown in **FIG 3:4**. Ensure No. 1 cylinder is on the compression stroke with both valves closed. Rotate the crankshaft until the mark on the centrifugal filter cover lines up with the 10° mark on the fixture. This setting corresponds to a 10° static advance BTDC.
2 Remove the distributor cap and rotate the drive shaft by hand until the rotor points to the cap contact for No. 1 cylinder. Check the contact breaker points for a gap setting of .0185 to .0209 inch and adjust if necessary.
3 Without disturbing the distributor shaft, insert the lower coupling on its toothed end, install the support and tighten the locknut. Secure the distributor to the support using the mounting screw.

To check that the distributor is properly timed to the engine and the centrifugal automatic advance is operating correctly giving a total advance of 18° to 28° respectively proceed as follows:

1 Connect Fiat timing tester AP.5030 with a 220-volt-single-phase power outlet fitted with a good earth connection. It is important that the tester is earthed before it is allowed to operate. Also ensure that the tester earth terminal is connected to a bare metal part of the vehicle.
2 Remove No. 1 spark plug lead, insert the strobe light adapter and reconnect the spark plug lead. Using a piece of white chalk mark the TDC position on the centrifugal filter cover.
3 Start the engine and aim the strobe light beam towards the chalk mark drawn on the centrifugal filter cover. With the engine running slowly the mark on the centrifugal cover must correspond with the first white line on the fixture (10°). Slowly increase the speed of the engine so operating the automatic advance and the chalk mark should move counterclockwise until at maximum speed it reaches the second white mark on the fixture.

It should be noted that the ignition timing for the model 500 sports engine the static advance is 10°, an automatic advance of 12° giving a total advance at maximum engine speed of 22°.

Should Fiat fixture AP.5030/1 not be available the advance position may be set as follows:

1 Turn over the engine until No. 1 piston is on the compression stroke with both valves closed.
2 Rotate the crankshaft clockwise until the reference mark cast on the centrifugal filter cover is set .5118 to .5512 inch ahead of the arrow cast on the timing sprocket cover. This will give a static advance setting of 10° BTDC.
3 Proceed as directed for ignition distributor timing and mounting described earlier in this section.

3:8 Sparking plugs

The sparking plugs must be regularly inspected, cleaned and the electrode gap adjusted to a gap of .019 to .023 inch.

The inspection of the deposits on the electrodes is particularly useful because the colour and type of deposit indicates the condition inside the combustion chamber and may be used as a guide to engine tuning.

Before the spark plugs are removed blow away any loose dirt from the plug recesses using a compressed air jet or tyre pump. Store the plugs in the order of removal ready for inspection.

Examine the gaskets and if they are about half their thickness they may be used again otherwise they must be replaced.

Inspect the electrode end of the plugs and note the type and colour of the deposit. Normally it should be powdery and range from brown to a greyish tan in colour. There will also be slight wear of the electrodes and the general effect described is one which comes from mixed periods of high-speed and low-speed driving. Cleaning and resetting the gap is all that will be necessary.

If the deposits are white or yellowish they indicate long periods of constant-speed driving or much low-speed city driving. Again, the treatment is straightforward.

Dry, black, fluffy deposits are usually the result of running with too rich a mixture. Incomplete combustion of the petrol air charge may also be a cause and this might be traced to a defect in the ignition system or excessive idling.

Overheated sparking plugs have a white blistered look about the centre electrode and the side electrode may be badly eroded. This may be caused by poor cooling, wrong ignition timing or sustained high speeds under heavy load.

To clean the sparking plugs effectively they should be cleaned using an abrasive blasting machine and tested under pressure once the electrodes have been reset. File these until they are clean, bright and the faces parallel and set the gap to .019 to .023 inch. Do not try to bend the centre electrode.

Before replacing the plugs use a wire brush to clean the threads taking care that the electrodes are not touched. Thoroughly clean the spark plug in petrol, and dry using a compressed air jet or a tyre pump. If difficulty is found in screwing the plugs into the cylinder head by hand run a tap down the threads to clear away any carbon. If a tap is not available use an old sparking plug with crosscuts down the threads. Finally tighten the plugs to a torque wrench setting of 18 to 21 lb ft.

Sparking plug leads:

The spark plug leads and the lead from the coil to the distributor cap must be regularly checked for cracking of the insulation and also correct seating in the distributor cap and coil top. It is recommended that silicone grease is smeared around the sockets before the leads are replaced to ensure no moisture may enter causing difficult starting.

3:9 The distributor driving spindle (sedan and sports engine)

If for any reason, the driving spindle has been removed from its housing in the crankcase, it must be correctly meshed with the camshaft gear otherwise it will be impossible to set the ignition timing. This operation is covered fully in the reassembly of the engine section.

3:10 Fault diagnosis

(a) Engine will not fire

1 Battery discharged
2 Distributor contact points dirty, pitted or maladjusted
3 Distributor cap dirty, cracked or 'tracking'
4 Carbon brush inside distributor cap not touching rotor
5 Faulty cable or loose connection in low-tension circuit
6 Distributor rotor arm cracked
7 Faulty coil
8 Broken contact breaker spring
9 Contact points stuck open

(b) Engine misfires

1 Check 2, 3, 4, and 7 in (a)
2 Weak contact breaker spring
3 High-tension plug and coil leads cracked or perished
4 Sparking plug(s) loose
5 Sparking plug insulation cracked
6 Sparking plug gap incorrectly set
7 Ignition timing too far advanced

CHAPTER 4

THE COOLING SYSTEM

4:1 Description

Sedan:

All the Fiat new 500 models covered by this manual are aircooled by the forced air circulation system from a centrifugal blower which is mounted on the generator output shaft. The blower fan has fourteen veins which are arranged at various angles to reduce operating noise during high-speed operation. A specially designed cowling is shown in **FIGS 4:1** and **4:2** conveys the air from the blower and distributes it to the various parts of the exterior of the engines.

The main components of the air cooling system are as follows:

1 Air intake compartment at the rear end of the body.
2 An elbow pipe for the admittance of incoming air.
3 A flexible air pipe connecting the elbow pipe to the conveyor.
4 A spiral air conveyor which contains the centrifugal fan.
5 Distribution ducting for directing the air flow to various parts of the engine.
6 A bellows type thermostat is fitted to the cowling which operates a butterfly shutter controlling the air outlet from the engine which ensures control of the engine operating temperature.

When the shutter is in the open position, engine heated air is allowed to disperse to the outside of the engine cowling. With the shutter in its closed position, the air is recirculated in the engine cowling so ensuring a quick engine warm-up period.

It should be noted that by operating the heater lever which is located on the centre tunnel at the rear seat, warmed air flowing out from the engine cowling is passed to the inside of the car for heating and demisting purposes.

Station wagon:

Refer to **FIG 4:2** where it will be seen that as the engine is located on its side underneath the luggage compartment floor the ducting has been modified and the air intakes are located at the rear of the side windows. A linear blower is housed in the engine baffles and cowling and is attached to the drive end of the generator.

The thermostat 'C' (see **FIG 4:2**) is located on the righthand side of the engine cowling and should start opening the engine heated air outlet shutter 'D' when the temperature of the air rises to 178–185°F and the shutter should be wide open when the air is at a temperature of 196–207°F.

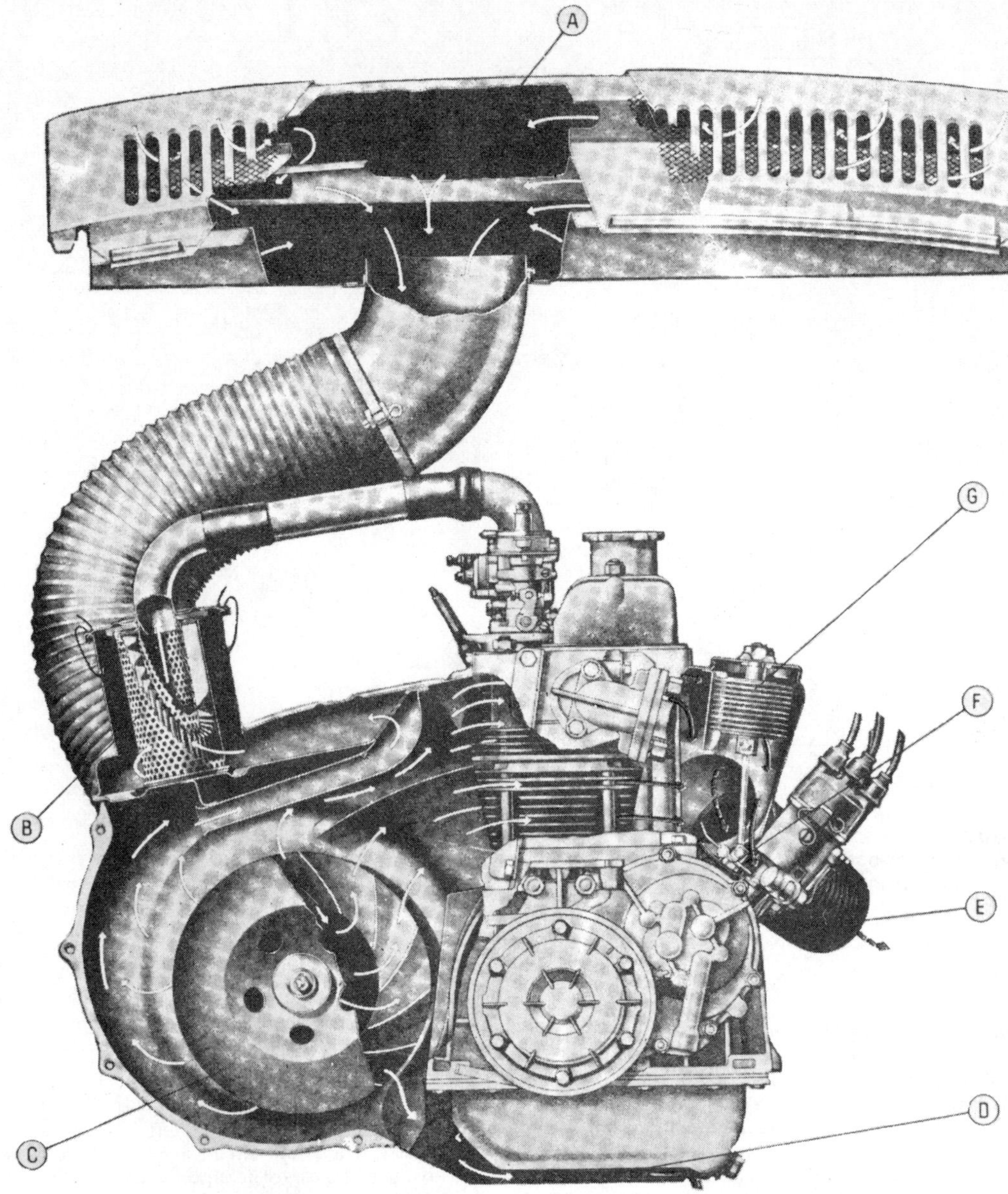

FIG 4:1 Engine cooling air circulation system

Key to Fig 4:1 **A** Engine cooling air intake **B** Carburetter air suction cleaner **C** Centrifugal fan and air conveyor **D** Oil pan cooling air passage **E** Warmed air admission hose to car interior **F** Engine air outlet control shutter, wide open position (at 178° to 189°F—81.° to 87° C) **G** Air outlet thermostat

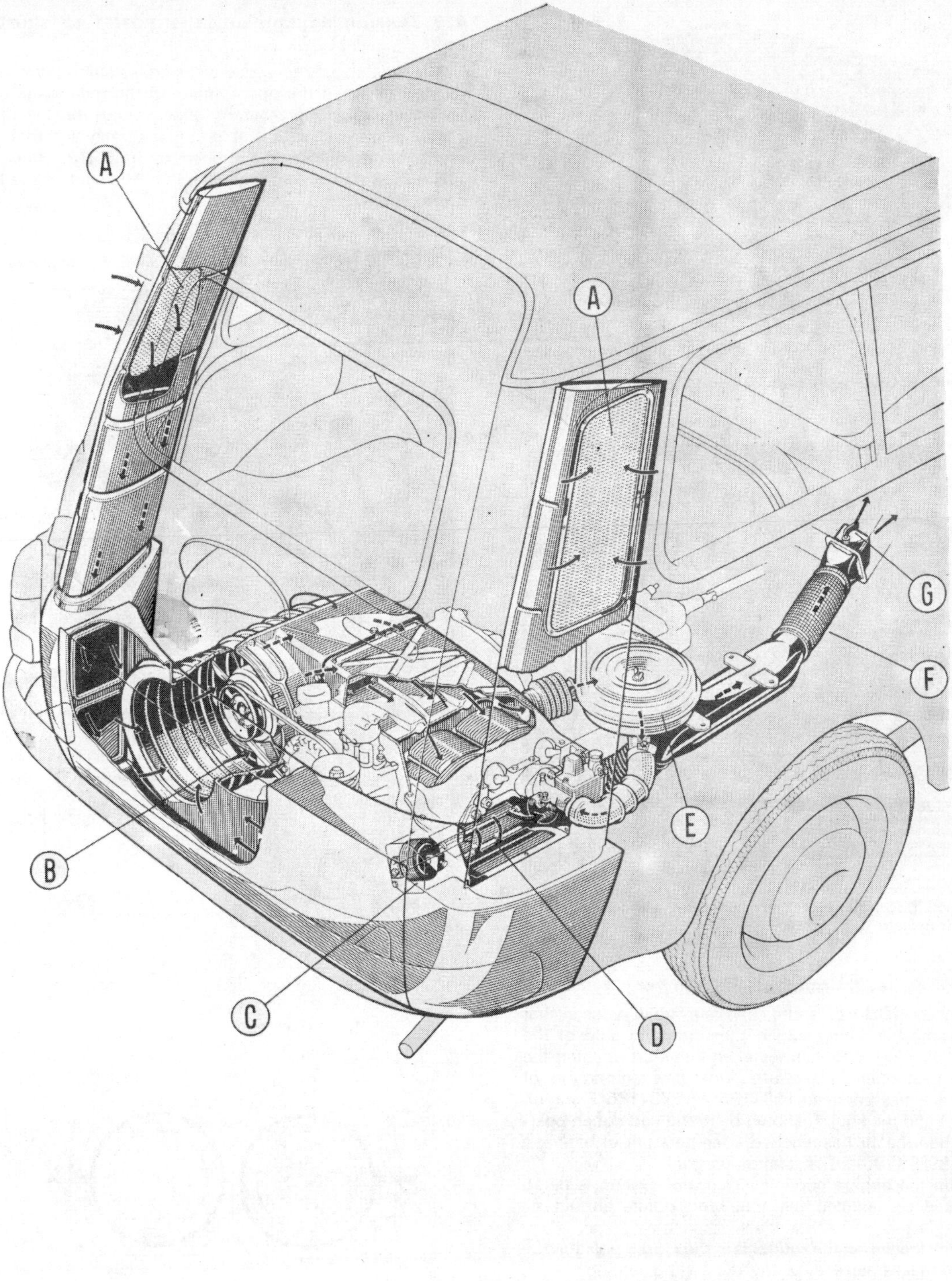

FIG 4:2 Cooling air circulation system of engine 120.000

Key to Fig 4:2 **A** Air intakes **B** Fan **C** Thermostat, engine air draft shutter control **D** Shutter, engine air draft **E** Carburetter air cleaner **F** Duct, warmed air-to-car interior **G** Lever, air-to-car interior valve control

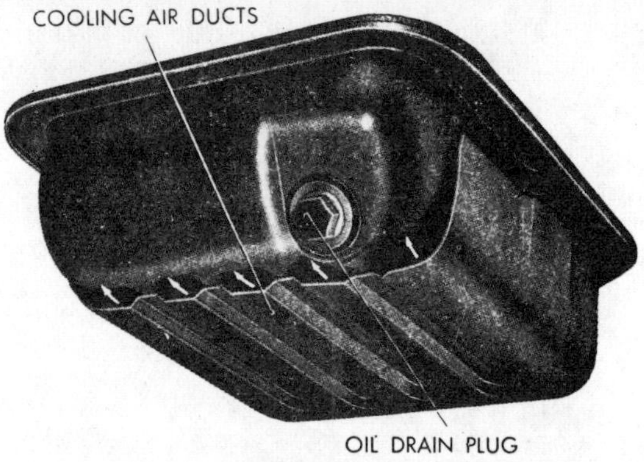

FIG 4:3 Oil sump with blower cowling. Arrows indicate air outlets

FIG 4:4 Cooling blower mounted on generator shaft extension

4:2 Air outlet thermostat and shutter

Refer to **FIGS 4:1** and **4:2** where it will be seen that the thermostat is located on the righthand side of the engine cowling. The thermostat should start opening the engine heated air outlet shutter when the temperature of the air reaches between 158–165°F (178–185°F station wagon) and the shutter should be in the wide open position when the air has reached a temperature of between 178–189°F (196–207°F station wagon).

When the engine cooling air control system is being inspected or serviced the following points should be noted:

1 Check that when the shutter is in the closed position the edge makes perfectly with the cowling seating.
2 Ensure that the shutter can swivel freely.
3 Check that the initial thermostat pulling power is between .0197 to .0394 inch.
4 Generally check the engine cowling for distortion, bad joint sealing or cracks.

4:3 Tension adjustment, thermostat to shutter link:

The tension may be varied by using the shims which are located between the upper shank of the thermostat and the cover shoulder washer. Before any adjustment is made ensure that the shutter is able to move freely and that the return spring has not stretched or fractured. Refer to **FIG 4:5** which shows the location of the shutter and the return spring.

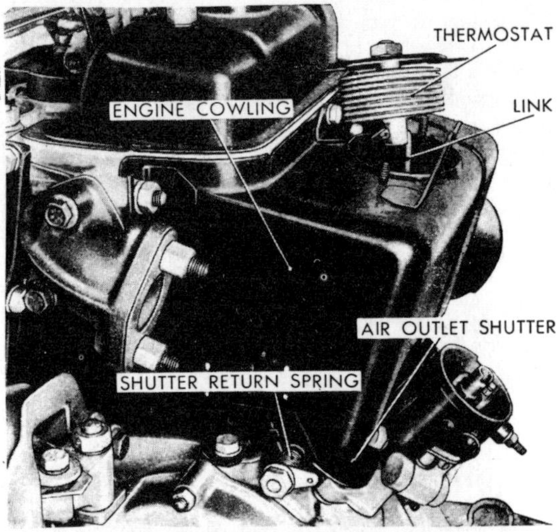

FIG 4:5 Location of cooling air outlet thermostat and shutter

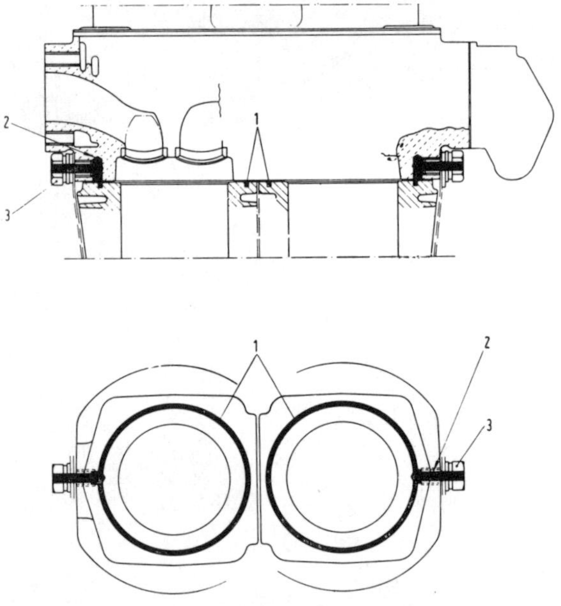

FIG 4:6 Diagram of the heating system safety device (sedan and station wagon)

Key to Fig 4:6 1 Circular seat in cylinders 2 Head ducts 3 Pierced screws

4:4 Heating system safety device

A special device has been fitted to the 110 F.000 and 120.000 engines so that if there is an accidental failure of the cylinder head gasket causing an exhaust gas leak into the heating system the safety device is fitted so that the exhaust gases will be expelled directly to the exterior of the cowling.

The safety device comprises a square section circular seat 1 (see **FIG 4:6**) which is formed in the upper face of the cylinder, a special duct in the cylinder head, a pierced screw 3 for each cylinder.

The system is so designed that the exhaust gases are released to the atmosphere from the circular seat in the cylinder via the duct 2 and the pierced screw 3. It should be noted that the screw 3 is also used for securing the conveyor.

4:5 Maintenance

Due to the simple design of the air cooling system maintenance has been kept to an absolute minimum and should consist of the following checks:

1 Inspect all the air conveyor system joints and ensure that all the joint nuts and bolts are tight and that there is no distortion between two joint faces.

2 Check that the tension of the generator and fan drive belt is correct which should be with a hand pressure of approximately 22 lb the belt should sag $\frac{13}{32}$ inch.

3 Ensure that the shutter can swivel freely and that the spring is in a serviceable condition.

4:6 Fault diagnosis

(a) Engine overheating

1 Generator and fan drive belt slipping
2 Shutter control thermostat defective
3 Shutter unable to swivel freely
4 Shutter return spring broken
5 Leaking joints in conveyor system

CHAPTER 5
THE CLUTCH

5:1 Description

New 500, 500D sedan and early station wagon:

The clutch is a single plate dry disc type operating on the inner face of the flywheel. **FIG 5:1** shows a longitudinal cross section of the clutch as it is assembled in the power unit.

A sheet metal clutch cover is attached to the flywheel by means of six screws and this encloses a clutch driven plate, the pressure plate and six springs. Three withdrawal levers are fitted so that the inner ends are attached to a carrier ring through which three springs hold the levers in place and the carrier ring in contact with the pressure plate, (see **FIG 5:1**). Release of the driven plate is obtained through a throw-out ring fitted with a central carbon thrust ring which acts on the withdrawal levers carrier ring. This is controlled by the clutch pedal through suitable linkage to the control fork.

When the clutch pedal is operated, the throw-out ring, together with the carbon thrust is pushed towards the flywheel and this exerts a pressure on the withdrawal levers carrier ring thereafter to the lever inner tips. The lever outer tips lift the pressure plate so disengaging the clutch.

Each of the three withdrawal levers is mounted on a bolt together with an adjustment nut which is inserted in the pressure plate. The levers are kept in their location by a guide which is formed in the pressure plate.

New 500, type 110.F, 110 sedan and late 500 station wagon:

A single plate dry type clutch is fitted with a diaphragm pressure spring. This design of clutch differs from the conventional clutch because the pressure coil springs and throw-out mechanism components are replaced by a single diaphragm spring.

The new system offers certain advantages which are as follows:

1 The load on the clutch pedal does not increase as the clutch disc lining wears but remains constant throughout the life of the clutch.

2 Due to the special shape and location of the diaphragm spring, which offers a constant force on the pressure plate throughout the clutch life, the clutch does not slip even though the driven plate linings may be excessively worn.

* Dimension to be obtained by adjusting the throwout lever.

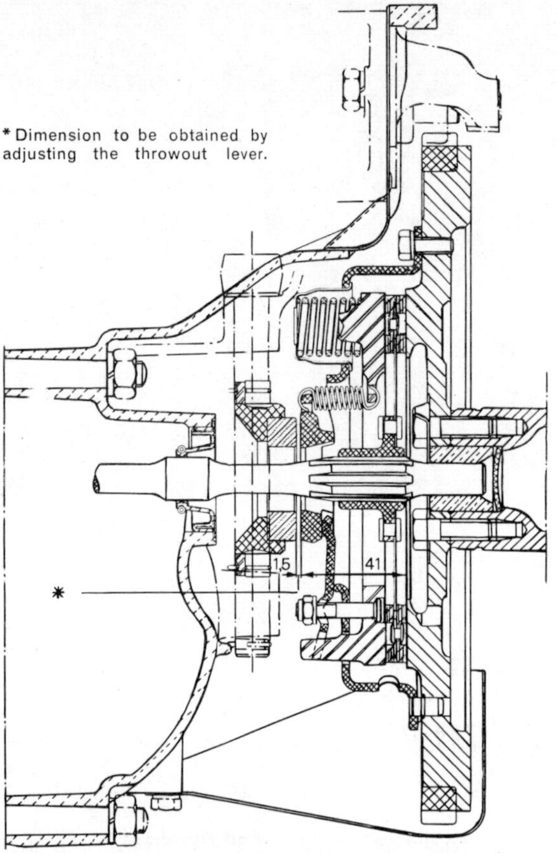

FIG 5:1 Clutch assembly longitudinal section (new 500, 500D sedan and early station wagon)

5:2 Removal and installation

To remove the clutch unit from the vehicle proceed as follows:

1 Remove the gearbox from the engine as described in **Chapter 6**.
2 Remove the six screws and washers that secure the clutch cover to the flywheel and gently ease the cover assembly from the location dowels in the flywheel and lift away. This will also free the driven plate.
3 Carefully clean the driven plate and clutch cover using a compressed air jet ready for inspection.
4 To refit the clutch cover assembly to the flywheel ensure that the driven plate is assembled the correct way round as shown in **FIG 5:1** and place the cover onto the flywheel using the locating dowels.
5 To ensure that the driven plate is correctly centred use Fiat pilot A.62023 (see **FIG 5:5**) or a suitably sized drift. Tighten the clutch mounting screws diagonally a turn at a time to ensure correct location of the cover onto the flywheel face. Finally tighten to a torque wrench setting of 5.8 to 7.2 lb ft.

5:3 Dismantling and inspection of clutch cover

New 500, 500D sedan and early 500 station wagon:

To dismantle the clutch cover assembly proceed as follows:

1 Place the clutch cover assembly on Fiat fixture A.62038 as shown in **FIG 5:6** and lock the cover using the three T-handles provided.
2 Release the withdrawal lever carrier ring springs and lift away the ring.
3 Unscrew the withdrawal lever fixing nuts on the bolts and lift out the levers and washers. Gradually slacken the three T-handles so relieving the pressure of the clutch springs. Remove the clutch cover, springs and lever mounting bolts. Carefully mark all the components to ensure that they are assembled correctly so ensuring that correct balance of the clutch unit is obtained.

Inspection:

Thoroughly clean all parts using a compressed air jet and proceed as follows:

1 Thoroughly check the springs for signs of overheating causing loss of tension and compare the effective length of the springs which when fitted new should have a length of .9646 inch under a load of not less than 43 lb. If the spring length is less than the recommended dimension fit a complete new set of springs.
2 The length of the withdrawal lever carrier ring retaining springs should be checked which under a normal clutch load should be .7677 inch whilst the length of the expanded spring under a load of 4.85 ± .44 lb should be 1.1811 inch. If the springs show sign of heating or weakening a new set should be fitted.
3 Check the withdrawal levers and their bolts for excessive wear and fit new parts as necessary.
4 Inspect the pressure plate for an excessively ridged surface or signs of cracking. If the ridges are not too severe the face may be refaced by turning on a centre lathe. Also inspect the flywheel friction surface which may also be refaced providing that the ridges are not too severe.
5 Whenever the clutch driven plate linings are worn a new driven plate should be fitted.
6 Inspect the clutch shaft splines and these should not have a lengthwise clearance in excess of .0039 inch and side clearance of .0118 inch with respect to the driven plate hub. Ensure that the driven plate slides easily on the clutch shaft protruding from the rear of the gearbox differential unit as any plate drag may be the cause of difficulty in gear selection.

5:4 Assembly and adjustment

New 500 sedan

To assemble the clutch cover assembly proceed as follows:

1 Place the pressure plate complete with carrier ring bolts and springs on Fiat fixture 62038 (see **FIG 5:2**).
2 Fit the six pressure springs in their respective seats on the pressure plate. Insert the cups on the springs and replace the cover.
3 Compress the clutch cover, continually checking that the withdrawal lever supporting bolts are properly guided into their holes in the cover. Onto the bolts, fit the three withdrawal levers with their relevant nuts and washers.
4 Replace the carrier ring on the levers and hook up the retaining springs.

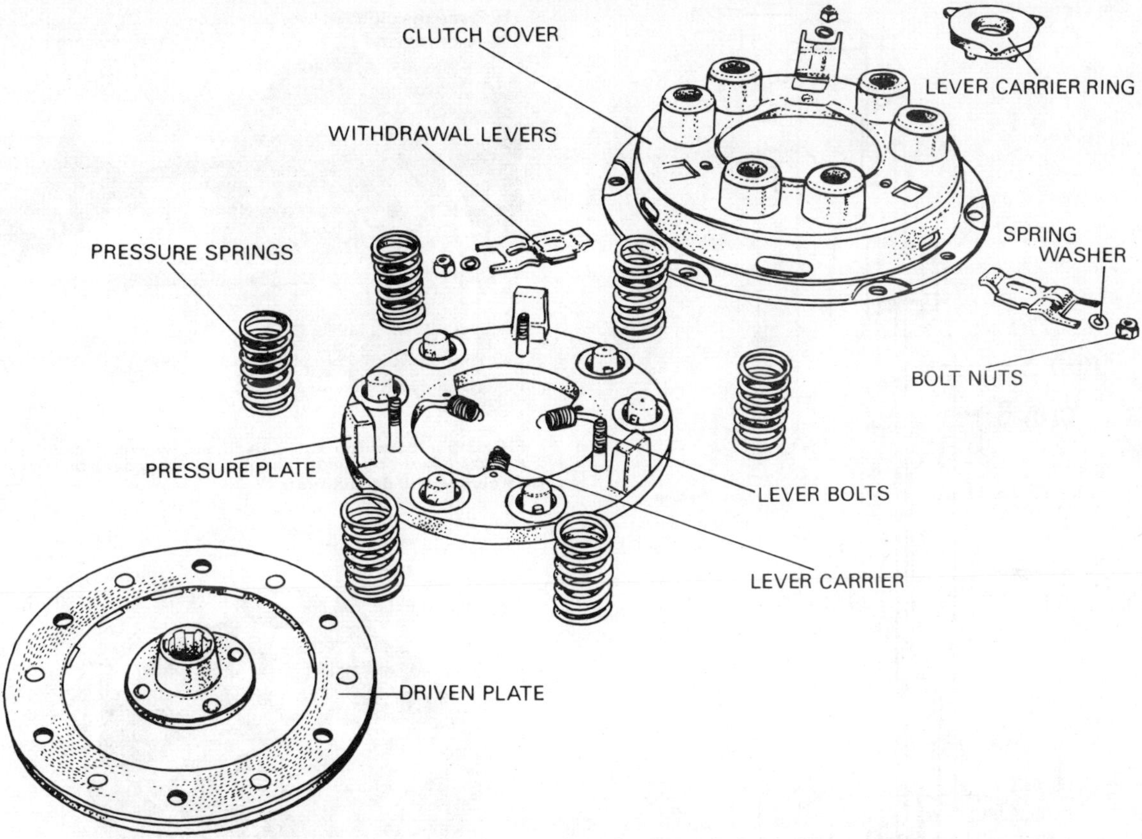

FIG 5:2 Clutch components (new 500, 500D sedan and early station wagon)

5 Finally tighten down the cover assembly using the three T-handles and adjust the clearance between the carrier ring and its central shoulder by means of the three adjustment nuts, setting the withdrawal levers stroke to .0039 inch. Check this adjustment using Fiat gauge C.110 and when correct lock the adjustment nuts by peining to the lever bolts.

500D sedan and early station wagon:

To assemble the clutch cover assembly proceed as described above but adjust the withdrawal levers as follows:

1 Secure the clutch cover assembly to Fiat fixture A.62038 with a ring .5413 to .5433 inch thick placed between the clutch cover plate and the pressure plate.
2 Adjust the height of the three withdrawal levers so that the lever tips are 1.9094 inch from the face of the Fiat supporting plate.

500 sedan (110.F) late 500 station wagon:

Inspection—diaphragm clutch:

To check the correct operation of the clutch cover

FIG 5:3 Clutch assembly installed on engine (new 500, 500D sedan and early station wagon)

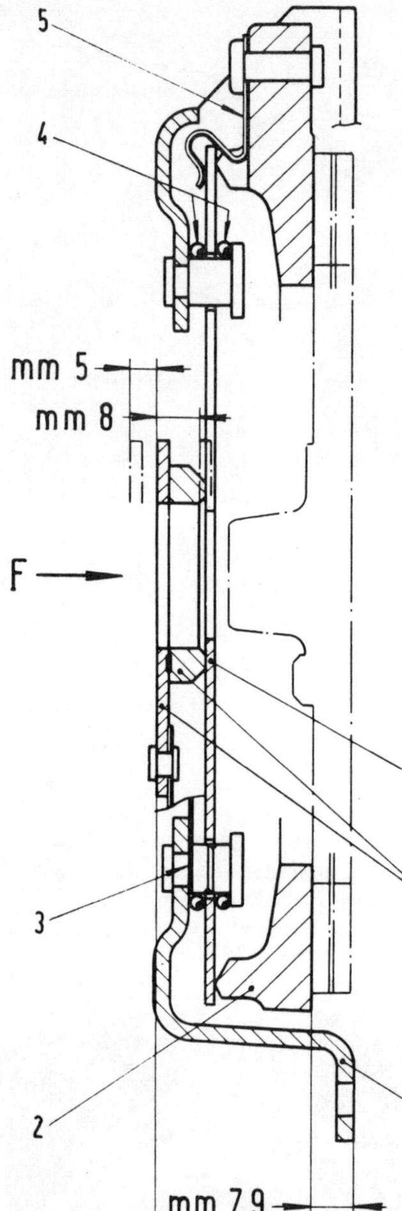

FIG 5:4 Clutch cover assembly inspection diagram (new 500)

Key to Fig 5:4 1 Clutch cover 2 Pressure plate 3 Clutch release flange plate 4 Diaphragm spring rings 5 Diaphragm spring retainer plate 6 Diaphragm spring 7 Clutch release flange
X = 1.463 ± .043 inches
F = direction of clutch release flange movement
8 mm = .315 inch = release travel
5 mm = .197 inch = maximum allowance for driven plate lining wear
7.9 mm = .311 inch

FIG 5:5 Installing the clutch on flywheel using pilot A.6203 (new 500, 500D sedan and early station wagon) to centre the driven plate

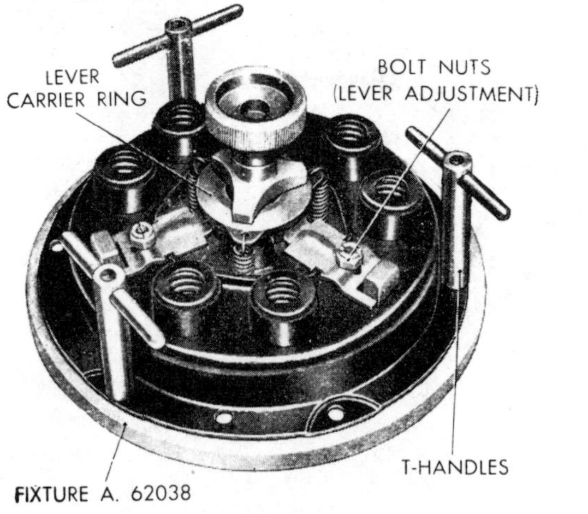

FIG 5:6 Fixture A.62038 for clutch disassembly, reassembly and adjustment (new 500, 500D sedan and early station wagon)

assembly proceed as follows:

1 Position the clutch cover assembly on Fiat fixture A.62038 with a spacer .311 inch thick between the cover and the plate.
2 Operate the clutch mechanism for four complete throw-out strokes by applying a load of at least 181 lb on the release flange as shown by the arrow 'F' in **FIG 5:4**.
3 Check that with a withdrawal travel of .315 inch the pressure plate is displaced .071 inch. Also check that the distance 'X' (see **FIG 5:4**) is 1.463 inch ± .043 inch. Should the results obtained not compare with the manufacturers recommended figures, then the clutch cover assembly should be renewed.

5:5 Installation of clutch on flywheel

Before assembling the clutch cover assembly and driven plate the following parts of the unit should be lubricated using Fiat Jota 3 grease.

1 Pressure plate—boss outer faces.
2 Clutch cover—withdrawal lever fulcrum.
3 Withdrawal lever stopnuts—contact face.
4 Withdrawal lever carrier ring—lever contact face.
5 Crankcase end pilot bushing lubricated with Fiat KG.15 grease.
6 Lubricate contact faces of driven plate and clutch shaft.

To install the clutch assembly proceed as follows:

1 Ensure that there is no grease or oil on the faces of the driven plate or flywheel face and position with the riased part of the hub towards the transmission unit.
2 Locate Fiat tool A.70085 (diaphragm clutch) or A.62023 (conventional spring clutch) or a suitably sized drift, through the driven plate hub and position in crankshaft pilot bushing. Gradually tighten the clutch unit mounting screws working diagonally and finally tighten to a torque wrench setting of 5.8 to 7.2 lb ft.

5:6 Pilot bushing

Whenever the clutch unit is being renewed or overhauled it is essential that the crankshaft pilot bush is checked for excessive wear or damage. Also check that

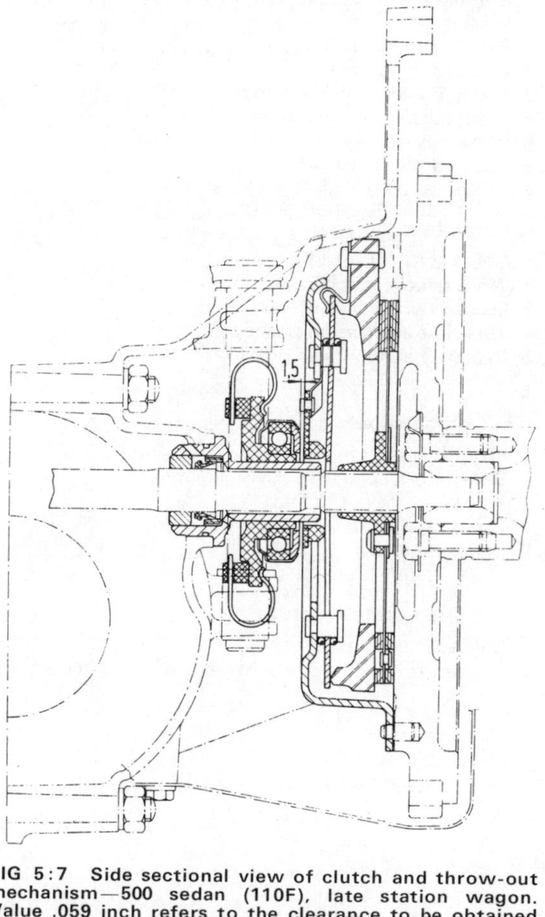

FIG 5:7 Side sectional view of clutch and throw-out mechanism—500 sedan (110F), late station wagon. Value .059 inch refers to the clearance to be obtained through the adjustment of clutch throw-out yoke rod

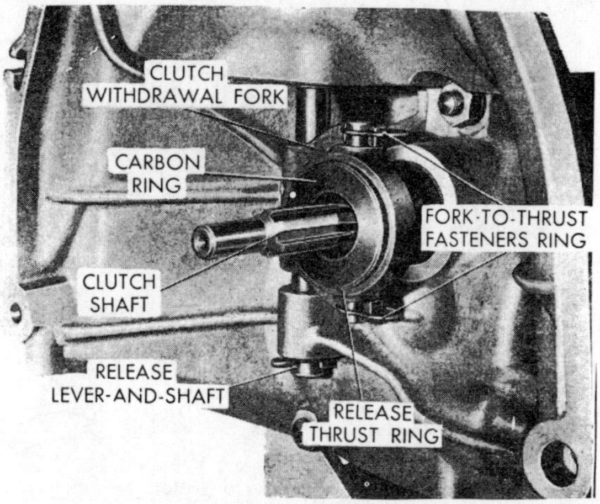

FIG 5:8 Clutch throw-out mechanism

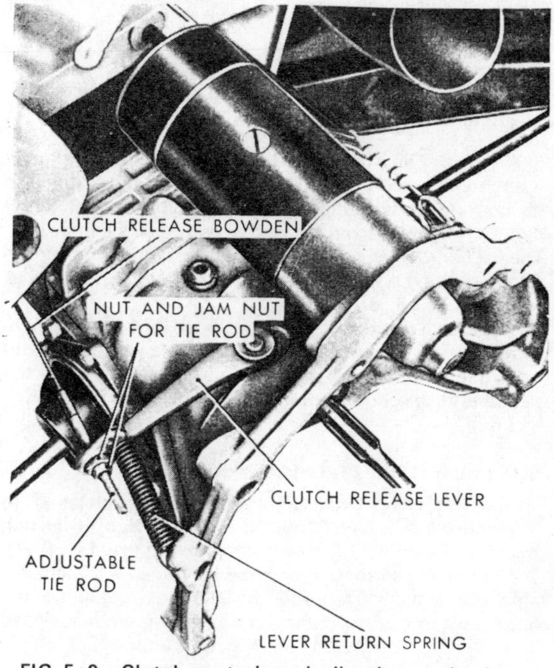

FIG 5:9 Clutch controls and adjusting mechanism

the spigot on the bush end is in a good serviceable condition. The maximum clearance between the clutch shaft spigot and the bush should not be greater than .0059 inch otherwise the pilot bush must be renewed. To remove the pilot bush use Fiat puller A.40006/1/2 or a small universal internal bush and bearing removal tool.

To fit a new bush use a suitably sized drift and drive the bush fully home and lubricate well with Fiat KG.15 grease.

5:7 Withdrawal mechanism

New 500 models:

The withdrawal mechanism comprises a forked lever (see **FIG 5:8**), which is located in the clutch housing and

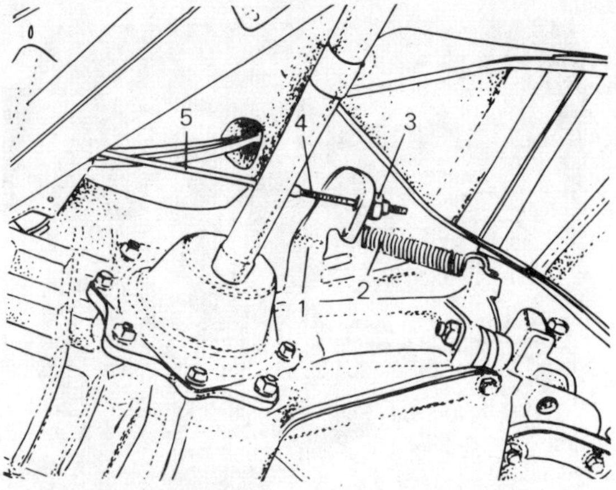

FIG 5:10 Clutch throw-out mechanism

Key to Fig 5:10 1 Clutch throw-out yoke 2 Yoke return spring 3 Rod nut and counternut 4 Adjustable rod 5 Clutch throw-out

onto this shaft the outer operating lever is attached by means of a key.

A return spring connected to the outer operating lever is anchored onto the gearbox casing. When the clutch is in its normal position the spring keeps the central thrust carbon ring away from the withdrawal levers carrier ring. The carbon ring is pressed against the carrier ring by the throw-out ring which is connected to the forked lever as shown in **FIG 5:8**.

The clutch pedal must have free travel of $1\frac{3}{8}$ to $1\frac{9}{16}$ inch. Should any adjustment be necessary release the locknut from the adjustable tie rod and adjust the position of the tie rod until the correct adjustment is obtained. Tighten the locknut.

500 sedan (110.F) late 500 station wagon):

The free travel of the clutch pedal should be $\frac{19}{32}$ to $1\frac{3}{16}$ inch which corresponds to a clearance of .059 inch between the throw-out sleeve and the ring (see **FIG 5:7**).

Should any correction be necessary release the adjustable rod locknut (see **FIG 5:10**), and reposition the adjustable rod using the rod nut until the recommended clutch pedal travel is obtained. Retighten the locknut.

5:8 Fault diagnosis

(a) Drag or spin

1 Oil or grease on driven plate lining
2 Misalignment between engine and gearbox first motion shaft
3 Driven plate hub binding on first motion shaft splines
4 Binding of first motion shaft spigot bearing
5 Distorted clutch plate
6 Warped or damaged pressure plate or clutch cover
7 Broken driven plate linings
8 Dirt or foreign matter in clutch

(b) Fierceness or snatch

1 Check 1, 2 and 3 in (a)
2 Worn clutch linings

(c) Slip

1 Check 1, 2 and 3 in (a)
2 Check 2 in (b)
3 Weak pressure springs or diaphragm spring

(d) Judder

1 Check 1, 2 and 3 in (a)
2 Pressure plate not parallel with flywheel face
3 Contact area of driven plate linings not evenly distributed
4 Bent first-motion shaft
5 Buckled driven plate
6 Faulty power unit mountings
7 Worn suspension mountings
8 Weak rear springs
9 Loose drive shafts

(e) Rattle

1 Check 3 in (c)
2 Worn release mechanism
3 Excessive backlash in transmission
4 Wear in transmission bearings
5 Release bearing loose on fork

(f) Tick or knock

1 Worn first motion shaft spigot or bearings
2 Badly worn splines in driven plate hub
3 Release plate out of line
4 Faulty Bendix drive on starter motor
5 Loose flywheel

(g) Driven plate fracture

1 Check 2 and 3 in (a)
2 Drag and distortion due to hanging gearbox in plate hub

CHAPTER 6

GEARBOX AND DIFFERENTIAL UNIT

6:1 Description

The gearbox and differential unit are housed in an aluminium alloy casing made up of two parts which split at the differential centre line. The output drive is transmitted by means of two half axle drive shafts coupled through wheel shafts and slip joints to the rear wheels (see **FIG 6:1**).

The gearbox provides four forward-speeds and a reverse, the fourth-speed being considered as an overdrive. All gears except first and reverse gears, which are straight toothed sliding gears, are in constant mesh and have helical teeth. No synchromesh is provided, gear engagement being completed by sliding shifter sleeves of the dog clutch type. The first-speed gear slides on the outside of the third and fourth shifter sleeve, whilst the reverse gear train moves on a fixed shaft. The clutch shaft is integral with the third, top and combined and first and second gear pinions, whilst the second gear pinion is splined at the front end. An internal splined coupling sleeve joins the clutch shaft and the input shaft and transmits the power from the engine to the gearbox. The mainshaft and differential drive pinion are combined together and besides carrying the constant mesh gears and the sliding first gear pinion, it also has attached the sliding sleeves and hubs.

The speedometer drive pinion is located at the front end.

The gearbox/differential casing is attached to the engine by six studs which locate in the crankcase. The front of the unit rests upon the rubber mounted support which is secured to the body floor.

The complete unit comprises three detachable parts made up as follows:

1 The support for the connection of the gearbox to the engine which also acts as part of the differential front end and clutch/flywheel housing at rear.
2 A central body which is divided into two compartments. The front compartment contains first, third, fourth and reverse gears with the primary shaft, layshaft and reverse shaft as well as the necessary gear selection striker rods and forks. The rear of this compartment also forms a half cover for the differential unit.
3 The gearbox casing cover, which contains the second-speed gears together with the relative fork, gear selection rod and speedometer drive gears.

The central part of the casing is provided with a top inspection cover. The primary shaft is coupled to the clutch shaft through an internally splined sleeve and two pins which are retained by rings. The primary shaft together with the first, third and fourth driving gears form a cluster.

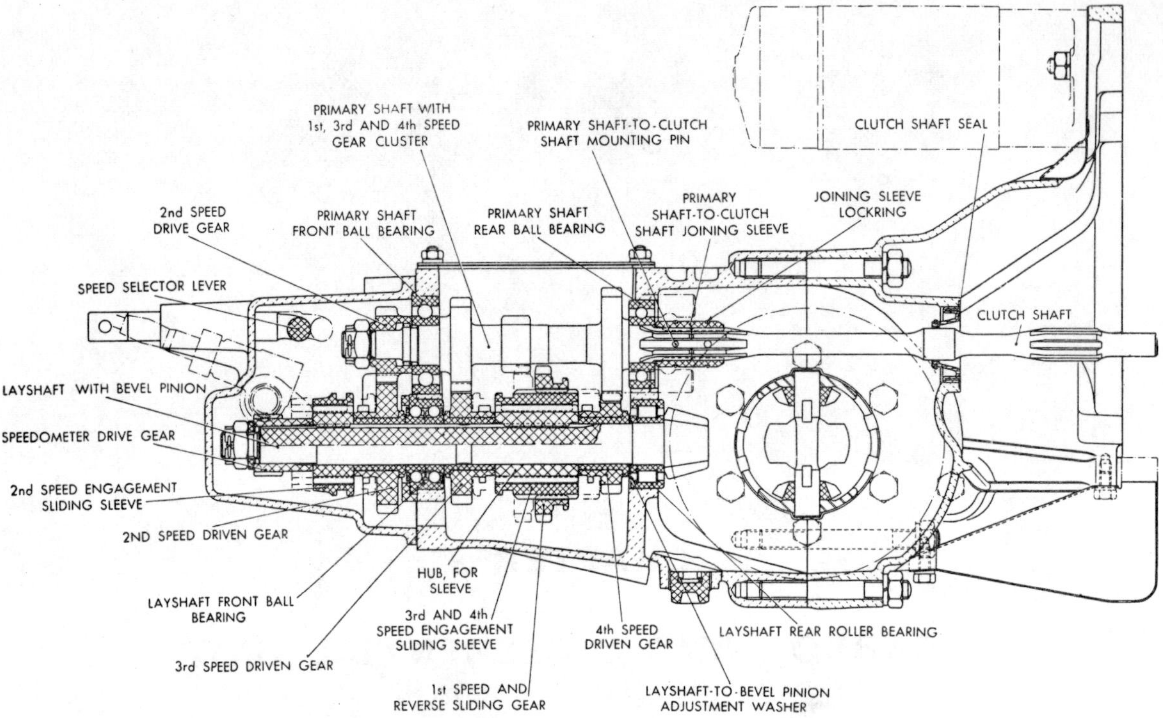

FIG 6:1 Gearbox-differential unit longitudinal section

On the primary shaft extension outside the main central body is mounted the second-speed driving gear. The primary shaft is supported at both ends by ballbearings whilst the clutch shaft rotates in a bronze spigot bush which is press fitted into the end of the crankshaft. An oil seal is fitted in the clutch shaft passage seat in the connection support. The layshaft, together with the drive pinion of the differential unit is supported at the front by a ballbearing race. The layshaft carries the pinion adjustment shim, the fourth-speed driven gear and its bushing, the hub and relevant engagement sleeve for the third- and fourth-speed with first-speed and reverse-speed, the third-speed gear and bushing and, outside the casing the second gear and bushing, the hub with relevant second-speed engagement sleeve and the speedometer drive gear.

The gears are operated by a gear selection lever mounted on the tunnel situated between the two front seats. This operates through a rod actuating the selector and shifting mechanism which is housed in the gearbox casing cover. Refer to **FIG 6:3** where it will be seen that the positioning of the striker rods is ensured by a spring-loaded ball-bearing. The risk of engaging two gears at the same time is eliminated by three rollers which slide in suitable slots machined in the rod (see **FIG 6:4**).

The differential unit and the final drive gear train are housed in the two semi-covers which have previously been described, the final drive pinion being integral with the layshaft. The differential casing may be split into two halves. The bevel gear is fitted on one of the halves and 8s secured by the same screws joining the two halves together. The differential side gears are internally splined into which are located the splined axle shaft ends which are able to slide by means of a specially designed slip joint. Two specially shaped rubber oil boots are inserted on the swing axle shafts and fit over the side gear extensions to ensure that there is no loss of lubricant or the ingress of dirt.

The transmission and differential unit to suit the station wagon differs from the sedan in that the transmission to engine mounting plate and the bellhousing are modified to suit the engine repositioned on its side.

6:2 Removal of gearbox/differential unit:

The complete unit may be removed whilst the engine remains in situ and to remove this unit proceed as follows:

1 Disconnect the battery positive cable and jack up the rear of the vehicle and place on firmly based stands.
2 Disconnect all control cables and wiring from the starter motor and the clutch lever. Remove the starter motor, the clutch lever reaction spring and the clutch cable support on the gearbox.
3 Remove the three bolts securing each of the driving shaft flanges to the flexible coupling at the wheel ends and carefully take out the inner spring.
4 Disconnect the shifter rod from the gearshift lever at the gearbox extension and also the speedometer drive cable. Remove also the flywheel undercover.

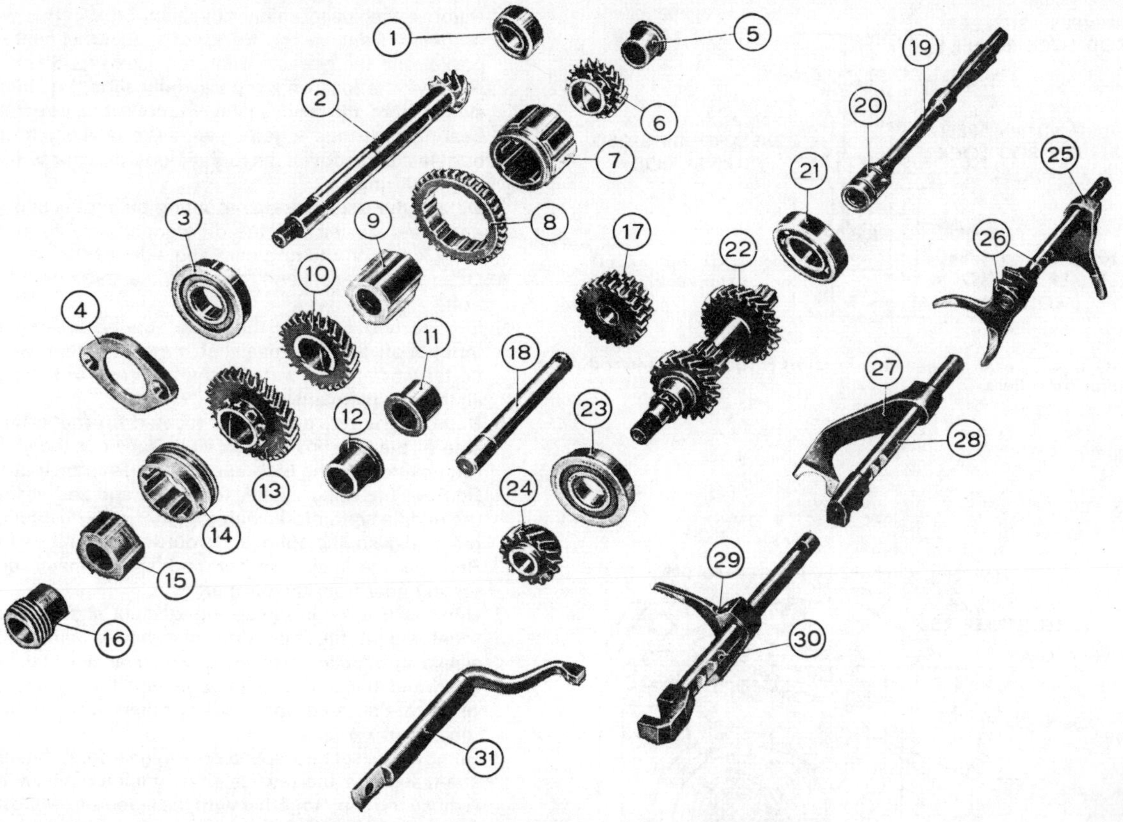

FIG 6:2 Gearbox gears, forks and striker rods

Key to Fig 6:2 1 Rear roller bearing 2 Layshaft with bevel pinion 3 Front ballbearing 4 Front bearing plate 5 Bushing 6 Fourth-speed driven gear 7 Third- and fourth-speed sliding sleeve 8 First and reverse sliding gear 9 Sliding sleeve hub 10 Third-speed driven gear 11 Bushing 12 Bushing 13 Second-speed driven gear 14 Second-speed sliding sleeve 15 Second-speed sliding sleeve hub 16 Speedo drive gear 17 Reverse sliding gear 18 Reverse sliding gear shaft 19 Clutch shaft 20 Clutch shaft-to-primary shaft sleeve 21 Primary shaft rear ballbearing 22 Primary shaft with first and reverse, third and fourth gear train 23 Primary shaft front ballbearing 24 Second-speed drive gear 25 First gear fork 26 First and second gear striker rod with second gear fork 27 Reverse gear fork 28 Reverse gear striker rod 29 Third and fourth gear fork 30 Third and fourth striker rod 31 Gear selector and engagement lever

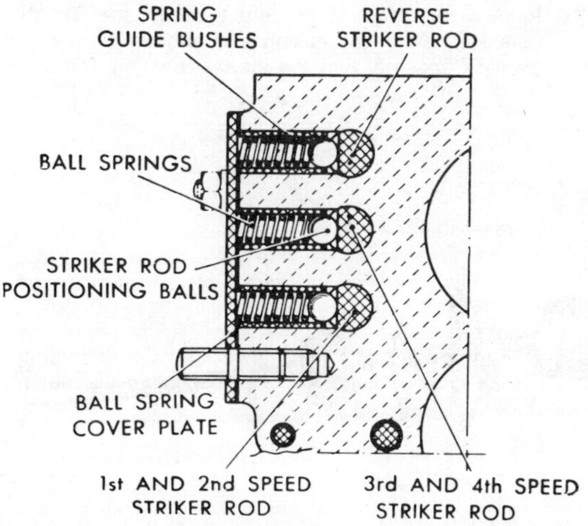

FIG 6:3 Detail of gearbox section through striker rod positioning ball springs

5 Using a garage type hydraulic jack fitted with Fiat support Arr.2076 carefully placed under the gearbox-differential unit take the weight of the unit from the front mounting. Carefully remove the nuts securing the transmission unit to the engine and also the nuts that secure the transmission front support to the body brackets.

6 Carefully draw the transmission forwards away from the engine taking very great care that no weight is allowed to act on the clutch shaft until the end of the clutch shaft is clear of the flywheel and clutch cover assembly. Carefully lower the transmission to the floor.

7 Remove the front support together with its rubbers, drain the oil from the transmission unit and thoroughly was the outside to remove all traces of dirt and grease and dry using a compressed air jet. The transmission is now ready for dismantling.

6:3 Dismantling—gearbox

Before dismantling the gearbox ensure that the exterior is thoroughly clean and then proceed as follows:

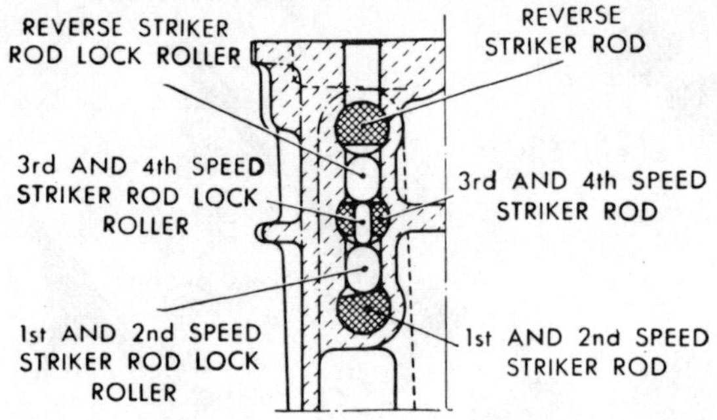

FIG 6:4 Detail of gearbox section through striker rod location rollers

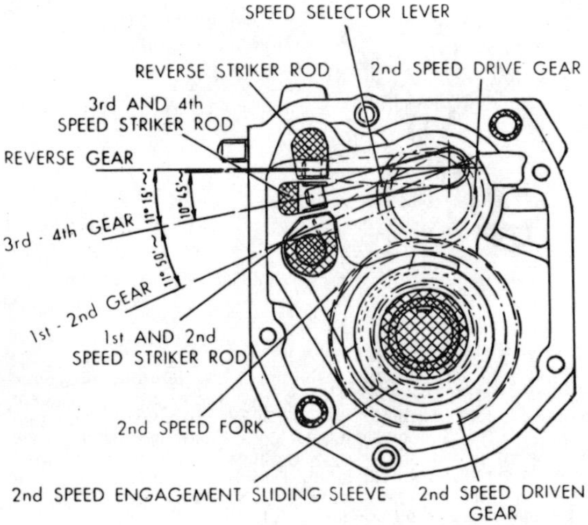

FIG 6:5 Cross section of gearbox through striker rods with the indication of the gear selector lever angular displacement

1 Remove the speedometer drive support together with its gears. Remove the front cover together with its gasket and the gear selection rod (see **FIG 6:2**).

2 Remove the lock ring and carefully slide the splined sleeve from the axle shafts. Remove the two roller bearing housings together with the relevent rubber boot fastening cover, the rubber boots and the adjuster ring lock rings.

3 Detach the transmission mounting on engine support and carefully remove the differential case assembly complete with the ring gear and axle shafts.

4 Open the fasteners and loosen all the shifter fork lock bolts.

5 Engage two gears at the same time so locking the input shaft and the mainshaft together. Remove the cotter pins and the nuts on the front end of the input shaft and the mainshaft.

6 Remove the retaining cover located on the lefthand side of the gearbox and carefully take out the shifter rod positioning the balls and springs from their bores. Remove the upper shifter fork shaft and shifter form, the middle shifter fork shaft together with its interlock pin and also the third and fourth gear shifter fork. Remove the plain washer and speedometer drive driving gear from the layshaft.

7 Remove the second gear engagement sliding sleeve together with the shifter fork, shifter fork shaft, sliding sleeve hub, second-speed driven gear with relevent bush and the first gear engagement fork. Take very great care not to drop the safety rollers whilst extracting the striker rods.

8 Remove the second-speed driving gear from the input shaft. Release the reverse shaft retaining screw and remove the shaft together with the reverse gear cluster. Remove the layshaft front bearing retaining plate.

9 Push the input shaft forwards until both ballbearing races are pressed from their seating and the coupling sleeve located between the input shaft and the clutch shaft can be reached from above. Carefully remove the retaining ring and a connection pin at the input shaft side of the coupling sleeve and carefully withdraw the clutch shaft and coupling sleeve.

10 Remove the input shaft front bearing race. Tilt the primary shaft in the casing and remove it from the gearbox housing. Remove the rear bearing. Carefully

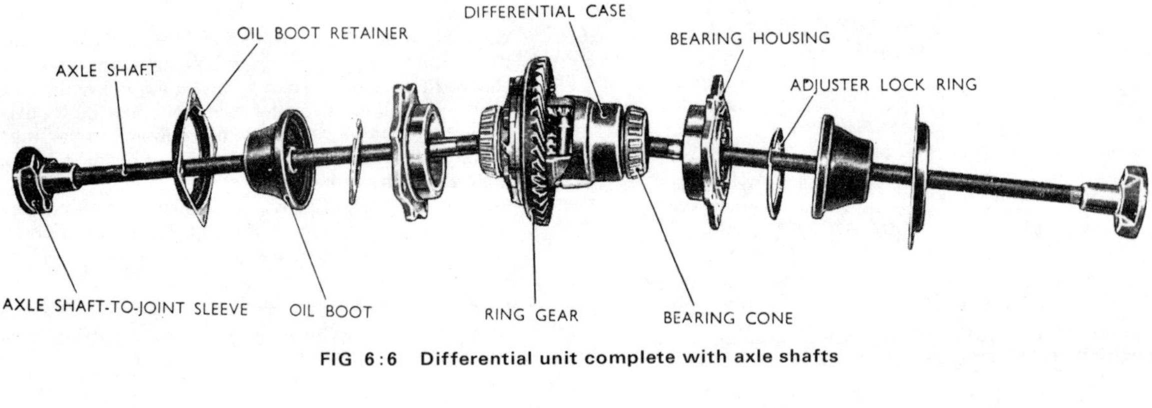

FIG 6:6 Differential unit complete with axle shafts

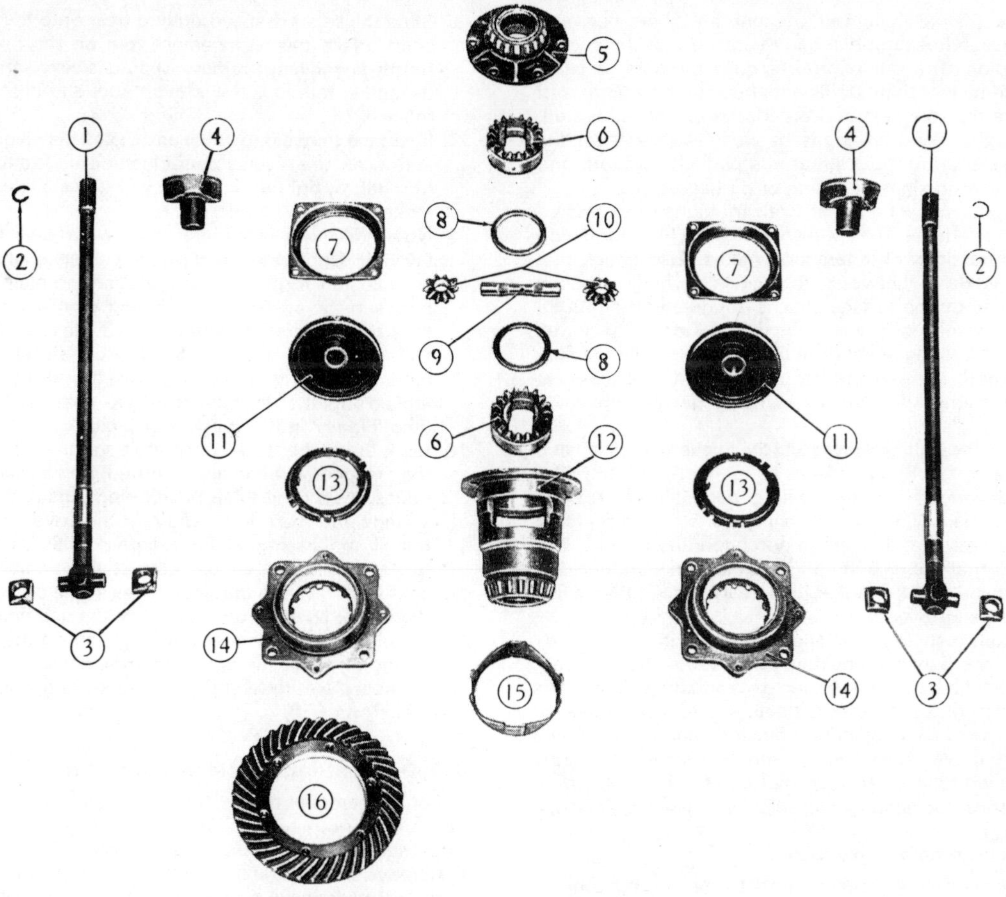

FIG 6:7 Differential components

Key to Fig 6:7 1 Axle shafts 2 Sleeve retainment lockrings 3 Slip joint casings 4 Axle shaft-to-wheel shaft coupling sleeve 5 Differential case cover with bearing inner race 6 Side gears 7 Oil boot retainment cover 8 Side gear thrust ring 9 Idle pinion shaft 10 Idle pinions 11 Oil boots 12 Differential case with bearing inner race 13 Adjuster retainment ring 14 Bearing housings with retaining nuts and outer races 15 Idle pinion shaft retainment cup 16 Bevel gear

withdraw the layshaft together with the final drive pinion and the roller bearing inner race from the rear.

11 From the inside of the gearbox casing carefully slide off the following parts from the mainshaft, the drive pinion adjustment shim, the third and fourth driven speed gears together with their bushes, the third- and fourth-speed hub and sliding sleeve, the first and reverse driven gear, and carefully drive out the front bearings and the bevel pinion rear bearing outer race.

12 Using a suitable press, drive out the drive pinion roller bearing inner race from the end of the mainshaft.

Inspection of components:

Before inspecting the various parts removed from the gearbox casing thoroughly wash all components and blow dry using a compressed air jet and then proceed as follows:

1 Thoroughly inspect the gearbox casing to ensure that it is not cracked and that the bearing seats are neither worn or damaged so allowing the bearing outer ring to rotate during the normal operation.

2 Thoroughly check the ballbearings to ensure that they are in perfect condition and that both radial ply and axial play is not excessive. The maximum permissible bearing play is as follows:

Front bearings of primary shaft layshaft:

(a) Sideways .002 inch
(b) Endwise .017 inch

Primary shaft rear bearing:

(a) Sideways .002 inch
(b) Endwise .016 inch

Hold the bearings firmly by the outer race and gently rock the inner race backwards and forwards. The sliding action produced should be free and silent. If any roughness is felt then the bearings must be renewed. Check the roller bearings by inspecting the condition of the rollers as well as the outer and inner races. Always fit new bearings if there is any doubt as to their efficiency.

3 Check the layshaft and the primary shaft between centres and using a dial gauge ensure that there is no distortion. The out of true reading for bearing seats should be less than .0008 inch. Inspect the splines and ensure that the side and outerfaces are not indented. Replace if there are signs of wear. Also inspect the reverse shaft to ensure that it is perfectly smooth and not showing signs of pitting or partial seizure.
4 Carefully inspect all gear teeth for signs of excessive wear or damage. The contact faces must be smooth and show no signs of indentation marks. Also check that the backlash between the gears, when correctly mounted on the surface plate is not greater than .0039 inch. The maximum wear limit is .0079 inch. Check that the quick engagement front teeth of the second-, third- and fourth-speed gears are not damaged or excessively worn. Renew if there are signs of gearchange lever misuse.
5 Inspect the sliding sleeves and the relevent hubs, ensure that all the working surfaces are perfectly smooth. The clearance between the mating parts should not be greater than .0059 inch. Also inspect the meshing teeth and ensure that they are in good condition.
6 Check that the gear shifting selector forks are not distorted and that the striker rods freely slide in their seats in the gearbox casing.
7 Carefully inspect that all the oil seals are in perfect condition and if there is any doubt they should be renewed.
8 Inspect the striker rod locking balls and the safety rollers and ensure that they slide freely in their seatings. Also check the ball load spring efficiency and if this shows signs of weakness then it should be renewed. Any faults with these items will cause difficulty in engaging gears or autodisengagement during engine acceleration.

6:4 Reassembly—gearbox

To reassemble the components to the gearbox ensure that all components are thoroughly clean and then proceed as follows:

1 Press the pinion rear roller bearing onto the layshaft. Install the layshaft in the casing, and at the same time fit the adjustment shim, the fourth-speed driven gear together with its bush, the sleeve and hub for third and fourth gear engagement, the first-speed and reverse driven gear and the third-speed driven gear with its hub.
2 Install the front layshaft ballbearing securing the bearing retainment plate with the screws and finally lock the screws in position.
3 Insert the primary shaft together with the first, third and fourth driving gear train in the gearbox housing slide the rear bearing onto the shaft. Push the input shaft forward to enable the clutch shaft coupling to be inserted in the rear and to be pulled up the primary shaft by means of the pin. Do not forget the retaining ring.
4 Slide the primary shaft backwards so pushing the rear bearing into its bore. Refit the front bearing onto the primary shaft.
5 On the layshaft insert the second-speed driven shaft and bush. The second gear sliding dog sleeve and the hub. Also insert the second-speed striker rod and the first-speed fork. Do not forget to fit the safety roller into its seating.
6 Slide the second-speed driving gear onto the primary shaft. Place the engagement fork on the third- and fourth-speed engagement sliding sleeve, and insert the striker rod, lock the relevent fork and fit the safety roller.
7 Insert the third safety roller and install the reverse shaft and insert the reverse gear cluster onto it and secure the shaft by tightening its block bolt. Install the reverse striker rod with its relevent fork.
8 Now refit the speedometer drive worm gear onto the layshaft. Tighten the nuts on the primary shaft and the layshaft not forgetting to interpose the plain washer between the speedometer driving worm and the nut to a torque wrench setting of 18.1 lb ft to 25.3 lb ft (primary shaft) and 28.9 to 36.2 lb ft (layshaft). It is recommended that the input shaft and layshaft are locked together by engaging two gears at the same time. Finally fit the split cotter pins.
10 Lock the shifter forks onto their shafts by tightening their respective bolts and bend up the special locking plates. Install the three positioning pins and relevent springs into their bores and refit the cover plate.
11 Install the casing cover together with its relevent gasket. This will enable correct positioning of the shift shaft lever so that it engages in the outer ends of the shifter shafts protruding from the gearbox casing.
12 Install the speedometer drive support on the gearbox casing and refit the upper gearbox cover.

For subsequent differential operations and adjustments see **Sections 6:6**.

6:5 Dismantling—differential and final drive

For the removal of the differential and final drive unit from the gearbox refer to **Section 6:3**. To dismantle the differential assembly proceed as follows:

1 Remove the retaining ring 2 (see **FIG 6:7**) retaining the splined sleeve 4 and slide the sleeve off the drive shaft.
2 Remove the retaining covers 7 and the oil boots all together with the bushes and seals, adjuster ring lock rings 13, adjuster rings housing 14, and bearing adjuster and roller bearing outer races.
3 Separate the differential housing halves by unscrewing and removing the six bolts that keep both the halves and the crownwheel together. It is advisable to mark the respective components to ensure correct matching upon reassembly.
4 Remove the differential pinion shaft retainer ring, also the differential pinions 10 by removing the shaft and withdrawing the two axle shafts 1.
5 Remove the differential side gears 6 and relevent thrust rings 8.
6 Using a press remove the differential bearing inner races from their seats on the carrier halves.
7 Thoroughly clean all parts and dry using a compressed air jet.

Inspection:

The components of the differential unit must be thoroughly inspected for correct operation and to determine the presence of any wear, damage or other irregularities. To check the items concerned proceed as follows:

1 Check thoroughly the idle pinion carrier shaft for signs

of wear, distorting or unevenness of the surfaces as this part is very heavily pressed when the vehicle is negotiating a corner. If the clearance to the idle pinions exceeds .0059 inch the shaft must be renewed.

2 Inspect the ring gear and pinion seat, the side gears and the idle pinions for correct meshing. This will be shown up by white marks on the sides of the gear teeth. Check that none of the teeth are broken, chipped or excessively worn and if any part is suspect then it must be renewed not forgetting that the ring gear and pinion come as a matched pair.

3 Inspect the condition of the ball and roller bearings, the rollers and balls and working faces must not show signs of pitting wear or cracking and if any part is suspect then the race must be renewed.

4 Check that there is not any undue wear on the faces of the thrust rings. Any slight indentations may be evened out using a fine oil stone but if the damage is excessive then new rings or oversize rings must be fitted as necessary. Thrust rings are supplied as service spares in the following thicknesses.

Standard	.0394 inch
Oversize	.0512–.0591 inch

6:6 Reassembly—differential unit

To reassemble the differential case proceed as follows:

1 Press onto the differential half housing which carries the ring gear one differential bearing inner race ensuring that it is pushed fully home onto its seating. Install the thrust ring and side gear (see **FIG 6:7**).

2 From the inside of the case insert the axle shaft complete with pivot and runners that form the slip joint. Also install the idle pinions and carrier shaft. Position the ring gear onto the housing half and install the differential pinion shaft retainer ring.

3 Press the other differential bearing inner race onto its seating on the left differential housing half and replace the left axle shaft complete with slip joint.

4 Join the two case halves together and tighten the retaining screws and also the retaining screws of the ring gear to a torque wrench setting of 23.1 lb ft. Secure all screws by bending up the lockplates.

5 Press the differential bearing outer races into their seatings in the bearing housings and also fit the oil seals. Also install the bearing housings over the driving shafts together with the adjuster rings.

6 Install the differential unit assembly into the final drive housing front half and bolt the rear half onto it. Tighten the six mounting nuts to a torque wrench setting of 27.5 lb ft. Finally place the bearing housings in their seats and tighten the mounting nuts to a torque wrench setting of 13 lb ft.

It should be noted that after the gearbox has been overhauled the complete differential unit should only be installed after the drive pinion depth adjustments has been carried out.

6:7 Final drive gear set adjustment

The installation and adjustment of the final drive gear set requires special care otherwise the unit may have to be dismantled again for further adjustment. So as to establish the correct mesh of the two gears, their relative position is accurately set during initial assembly at the factory.

FIG 6:8 Layshaft with final drive pinion. The arrow points to the number (14) for correct mating with ring gear and to the centesimal figure (—10) for accurate mating position of pinion and gear

Refer to **FIG 6:8** where it will be seen that two numbers are stamped on the pinion shaft near to the threaded end, the upper number is the matching number which should also appear on the crownwheel. The lower number indicates the positive or negative deviation from the theoretical distance between the centre line of the ring gear and the pinion face. It is this number which must be taken into account when calculating the adjusting shim thickness which has to be fitted between the rear roller bearing and the fourth-speed gear on the main shaft.

The formula from which the adjusting shim thickness can be calculated is as follows:

S=A—/B+C)

Where S=shim thickness.

A=distance between the front bearing inner race and the centre line of the ring gear.

B=distance of the drive pinion face to the ring gear centre line.

C=the total of the widths of the third-speed gear bush, third- and fourth-speed hub, fourth-speed gear bush and rear roller bearing inner race fitted onto the mainshaft.

It should be noted that 'A' is the total of half the diameter of the differential bearing housing seat which is in actual fact 41.00 mm, and the distance measured between the front bearing inner race and the differential bearing housing seat. The last dimension will have a minimum manufacturing limit of 150.54 mm. Any deviation from this value must be determined and considered when determining the total shim thickness 'S'.

A= 150.54 + 41.00 + a (deviation)

To determine deviation 'a' Fiat tool A.62036 should be assembled to the gearbox casing as shown in **FIG 6:9** and to take the reading proceed as follows:

1 Assemble the front ballbearing and its retainer into the gearbox housing and tighten the retainer bolts.

2 Hold the gearbox housing in the vertical position with the differential side upwards and insert Fiat tool A.62036 carefully from above into the bearing bore and lock it firmly by tightening the knurled nut.

3 Using Fiat dial gauge C.689 which has been previously screwed on a surface plate should next be mounted onto the top of Fiat tool A.62036 with its pointer resting on the lowest position of the differential bearing housing bore as shown in **FIG 6:10**. To obtain the lowest point move the pointer to both sides of the bottom dead centre position so as to obtain the maximum reading.

The distance 'B' in the formula for calculating the shim thickness is designed to have a lower manufacturing limit of 75 mm. Any deviation 'b' is stamped on the drive pinion. Therefore to calculate the value of 'B'

B= 75 + b (deviation)

The distance 'C' in the formula for calculating the shim thickness is designed to have a lower manufacturing limit

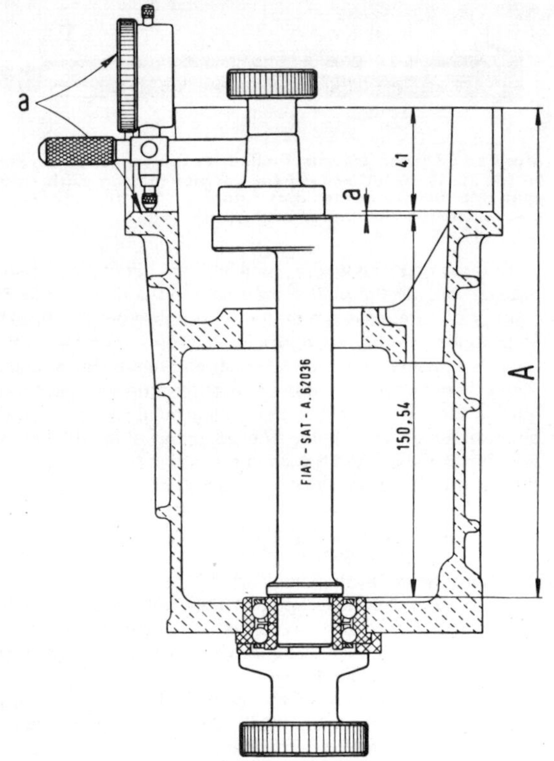

FIG 6:9 Graphic demonstration of values A and a

'A' Distance between pinion front bearing inner shoulder and the axis passing through the differential bearing housing centre
'a' Difference between the minimum value called out on drawing (5.9268 inches—150.54 mm) and actual machining value of the distance between pinion front bearing inner shoulder and differential bearing housings

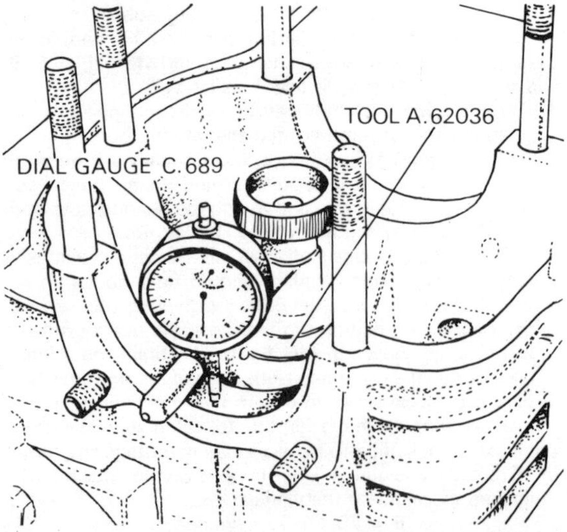

FIG 6:10 Reading value a on gauge C.689 to determine drive pinion shim thickness

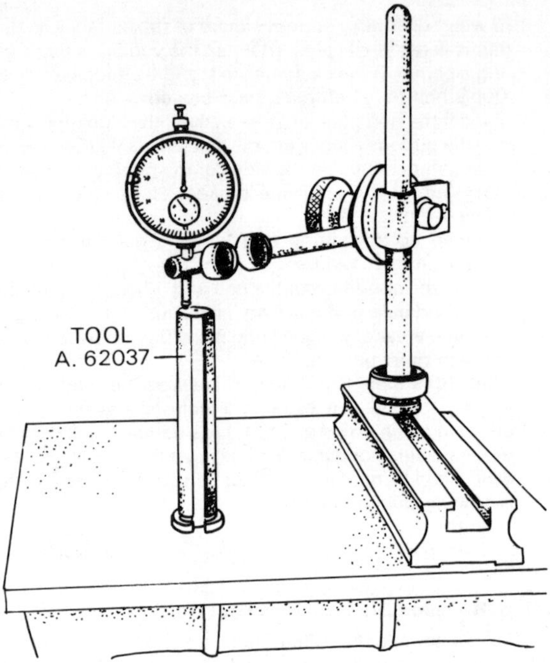

FIG 6:11 Setting dial indicator to zero on tool A.62037

of 115.64 mm. Fiat tool A.62037 as shown in **FIG 6:12** used in conjunction with the dial gauge can now be used to measure the deviation 'c' from the lower manufacturing limit as follows:

1 Place the dial gauge on a stand on the surface plate and place Fiat tool A.62037 on the plate as shown in the **FIG 6:11**.
2 Carefully slide onto the Fiat tool the following items, third-speed driven bush, third- and fourth-speed gear engagement sleeve, hub, fourth-speed driven gear bush and drive pinion roller bearing inner race. Set the dial gauge to zero using Fiat tool A.62037 as the datum and then rest the dial gauge plunger on the roller bearing inner race and take a reading at the dial as shown in **FIG 6:11**. This reading will represent 'c' which can now be used in the formula.

$$C = 115.64 + c \quad \text{(deviation)}$$

Once the values of 'A', 'B' and 'C' have been found as detailed above we can now insert the values into the basic formula S A (B C) which will now give us:

$$S = 150.54 + 41.00 + a - (75 + b + 115.64 + c)$$

which can be simplified by using algebra to give us the following formula:

$$S = 0.90 + a - (b + c)$$

Shims are supplied in the following thicknesses, .0039 inch and .0059 inch. One or more shims should be used to make up the required shim thickness.

Adjusting final drive gear set (500D, and 500F sedan and early station wagon):

The procedure for adjustment of the final drive gear set is exactly the same as for the new 500 model except

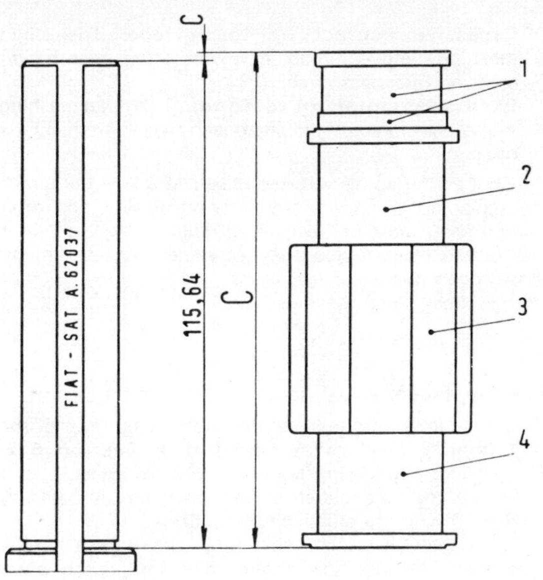

FIG 6:12 **Graphic demonstration of C and c**

Key to Fig 6:12 1 Bevel pinion rear roller bearing inner race 2 Bush, fourth-speed driven gear 3 Hub, third- and fourth-speed engagement sleeve 4 Bush, third-speed driven gear
'C' Total height of items 1, 2, 3 and 4 which must be mounted on final drive pinion
'c' Difference between actual height 'C' and the minimum drawing call-out 4.5527 inch represented by tool A.62037

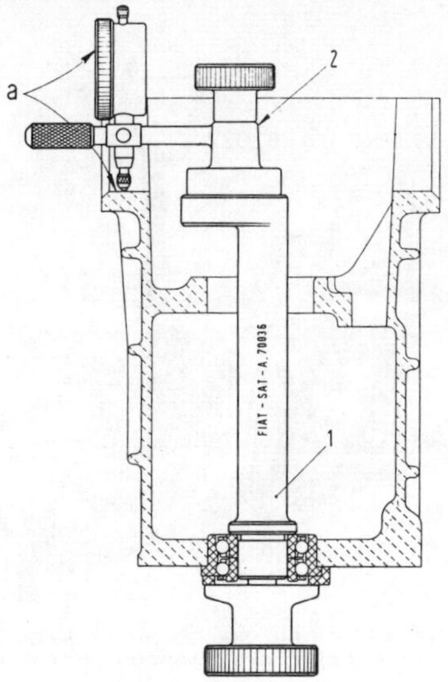

FIG 6:13 **Diagram showing the position of tools for determining the value of a**

Key to Fig 6:13 1 Dummy pinion, tool A.70036 2 Support with dial gauge, tool A.95690

that the new Fiat tools are used to determine shim thickness as detailed below:

$S = 0.90 + a - (b + c)$

Where S = shim thickness
0.90 = standard coefficient
a = value of reading on the dial indicator A.95690 applied to fixture A.70036 as shown in **FIG 6:13**.
b = value stamped on pinion stem as shown in **FIG 6:8**.
c = value read on the dial indicator corresponding to the difference between height of Tool A.70037 as shown in **FIG 6:14**, and the sum of the thicknesses of the items to be installed in pinion and included between front bearing inner shoulder and rear bearing outer shoulder.

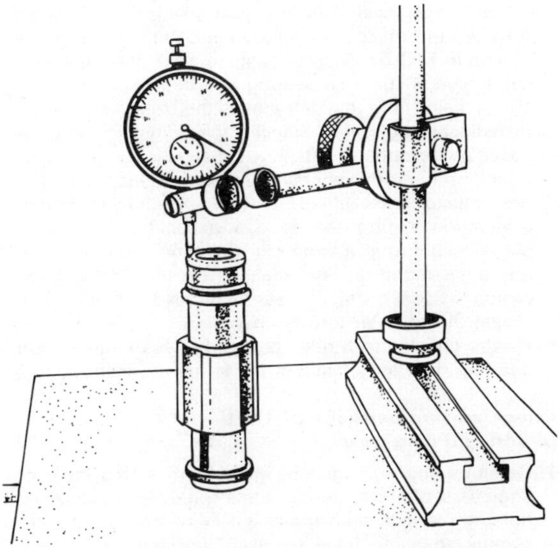

FIG 6:14 **Reading value c on dial indicator**

Ring gear clearance and differential bearing preload:

To enable the correct ring gear tooth clearance to be ascertained use Fiat tool A.62039 together with a dial gauge. The support for dial gauge should be fixed into the two lower bolt holes of the flywheel housing and the pointer of the dial gauge adjusted so that it is located through the clutch shaft hole in the final drive housing so resting on a ring gear tooth (see **FIG 6:15**). Then proceed as follows:

1 During reassembly the differential bearing nuts should not have been screwed fully home to the differential bearing outer races when installing into the final drive unit. These should now be carefully screwed in until they are in gentle contact with the bearing races.

2 Slide Fiat tool A.62040 over one of the drive shafts and using Fiat tool A.62041 lock the drive shaft to the differential housing thus preventing the drive pinion from rotating.

3 Gently turn the drive shaft which should now be locked to the ring gear and note the movement of the dial gauge indicator. This will show the tooth clearance. When the clearance is correctly adjusted the

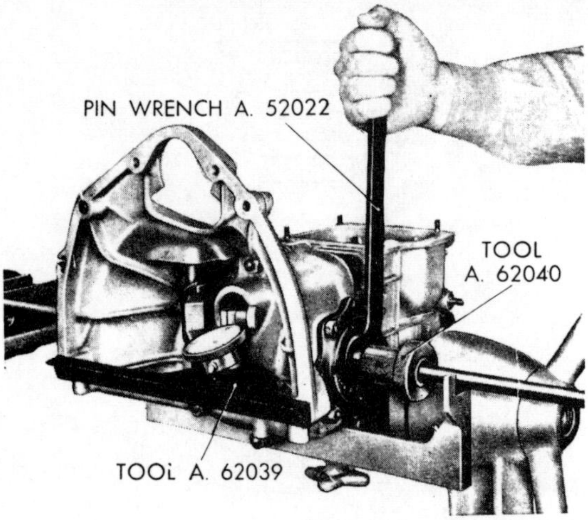

FIG 6:15 Adjusting ring gear-to-pinion backlash and differential bearing play, using special wrench A.52022

reading on the dial gauge should be between .0031 to .0047 inch. The actual clearance is adjusted by screwing in one adjusting nut and screwing out the other by the equivalent amount using Fiat spanner A.52022 as shown in **FIG 6:15**.

4 Remove Fiat tool A.62041 and using Fiat support A.62040 mount the special dynamometer A.95697 as shown in **FIG 6:15** on the axle shaft. Rotate the axle shaft several turns so seating the bearings and then check using the dynamometer the rotation torque. If necessary tighten or slacken the adjusters until the specified torque of 1.01 ± .07 lb ft is obtained. This operation must be very carefully carried out because if one adjuster is set differently with respect to the other, a variation in ring gear to pinion backlash may take place, resulting in a variation of rotation torque. After any adjustments always recheck on the ring gear to pinion backlash and if necessary readjust and then repeat the rotation torque check.

6 Finally check the tooth contact between the pinion and ring gear as detailed in the following instructions:

Check and adjustment of tooth contact between pinion and ring gear:

1 Carefully apply to the ring gear teeth a thin layer of engineers' blue and gently rotate the differential whilst holding the axle shaft firmly but allowing them to slip slightly so as to have the unit working under load conditions.

2 A contact impression will be left on the ring gear teeth and the contact will be correct when the drive pinion tooth contact pattern is evenly distributed on the ring gear teeth as shown in **FIG 6:16**. Should the tooth contact be incorrect the following observations should be noted.

Excessive contact on tooth flank. Too deep meshing—move pinion out from ring gear by reducing thickness of shim.

Excessive contact on tooth heel. Too slight meshing—move pinion in towards ring gear by increasing thickness of shim.

Excessive contact on tooth face. Too slight meshing—move pinion in towards ring gear by increasing thickness of shim.

Excessive contact of tooth toe. Too deep meshing—move pinion out from ring gear by reducing thickness of shim.

With all the above detailed cases, to adjust the pinion by replacing the shim, the differential unit and drive pinion shaft must be dismantled. This means that when the unit is reassembled after the necessary adjustments have been made, the backlash and bearing rotation torque must be repeated.

6:8 Replacement of gearbox—differential unit

Installation is the reverse procedure to removal of the unit from the vehicle as described in **Section 6:2**. However, the following points should be noted:

1 Ensure that the clutch driven disc hub is correctly aligned with the clutch shaft pilot bush.

2 The complete transmission unit should be carefully pushed towards the engine and the clutch shaft inserted into the driven disc hub splines and finally home into the pilot bush. Extreme care must be taken to ensure that no weight is placed on the clutch shaft otherwise distortion may take place.

3 Carefully connect the gearbox rear housing to the engine crankcase by using the studs, two of which have special location dowels fitted. Screw home finger tight the gearbox/differential to body to front support mounting screws inserting the fibre washers. Lower the hydraulic garage jack and pull it away from underneath the vehicle. Screw in the four lower mounting nuts and tighten to a torque wrench setting of between 18.1 to 21.7 lb ft. Finally tighten the front support screws.

4 Reconnect the gear shift control rod and the speedometer drive cable. Insert the springs between the axle shafts and wheel drive shaft and tighten the three mounting screws of each splined sleeve on the flexible joint to a torque wrench setting of 20.3 lb ft.

5 Refit the flywheel housing cover. Replace the starter motor together with its relevant cover and tighten the two mounting nuts to a torque wrench setting of 18.1 to 21.7 lb ft. Reconnect the starter control rod, the two starter cables, the clutch control tie rod and hook up the return spring and secure the clutch control cable retainer bracket to the gearbox casings. Reconnect the cable to the battery positive terminal post.

6 Lower the vehicle to the floor gently and then give a thorough road testing.

6:9 Swing axle shafts and slip joints

Description:

The two axle shafts are connected to the differential unit through specially designed slip joints which allow the shafts to swing and slide in the splined housing in the differential side gear. At the other end, the axle shafts are connected to the wheel drive shaft flexible joints using a sliding sleeve.

Correct tooth contact.

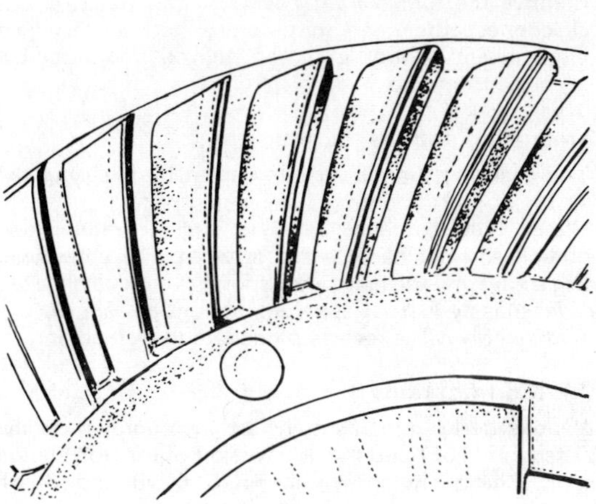

Excessive contact on tooth heel:

move pinion in towards ring gear by increasing thickness of shim.

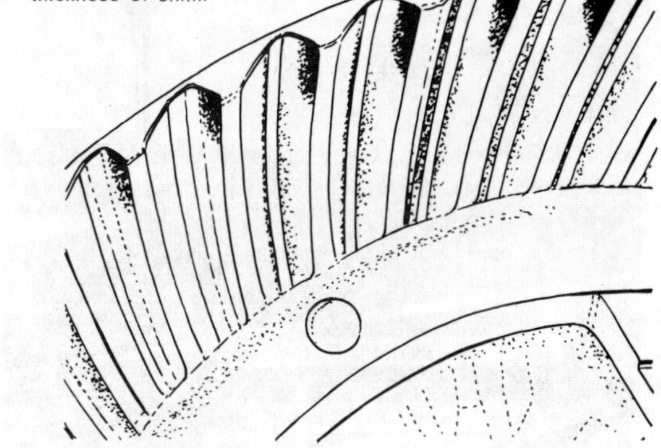

Excessive contact on tooth flank:

move pinion out from ring gear by reducing thickness of shim.

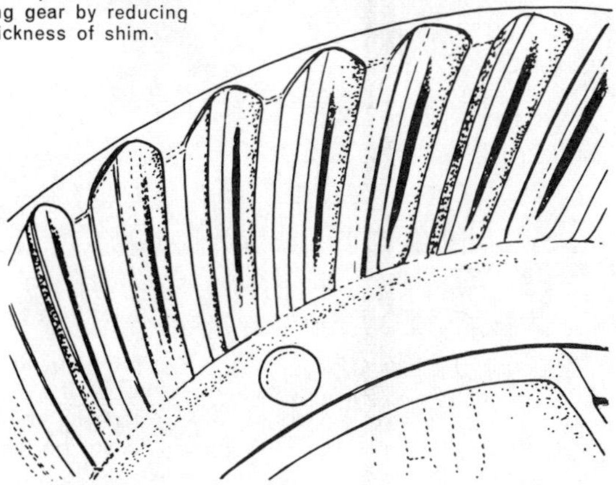

Excessive contact on tooth face:

move pinion in towards ring gear by increasing thickness of shim.

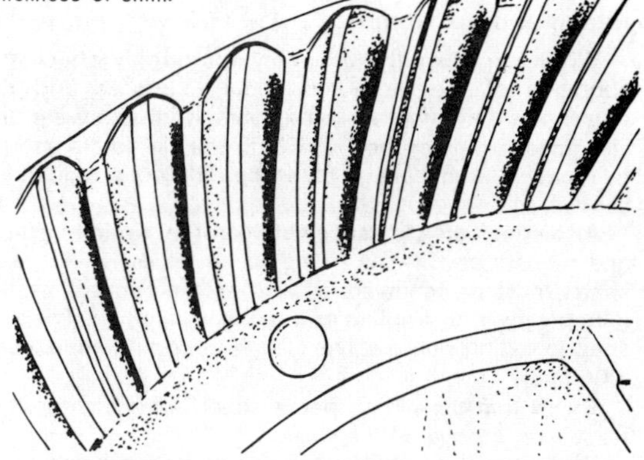

Excessive contact on tooth toe:

move pinion out from ring gear by reducing thickness of shim.

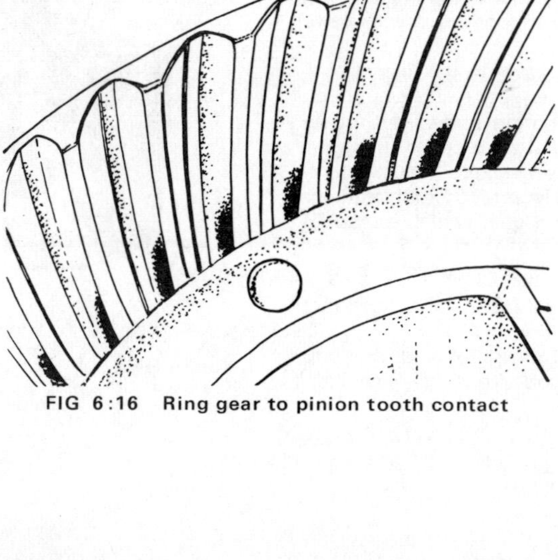

FIG 6:16 Ring gear to pinion tooth contact

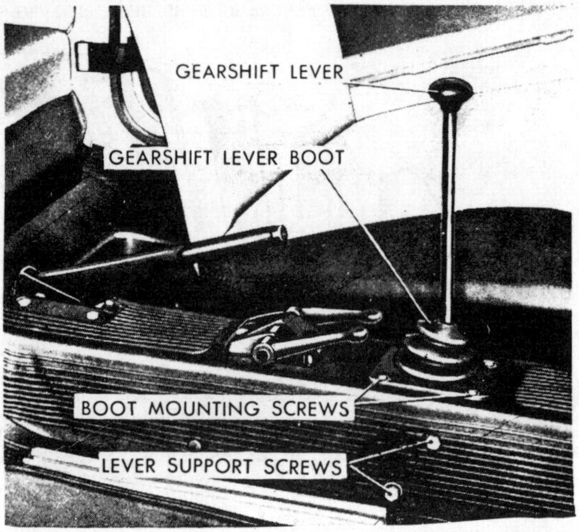

FIG 6:17 Location of gearshift lever on control passage tunnel

Repair and inspection:

Whilst servicing the assembly thoroughly check the condition of the slip joints sliding surfaces and the housing in the differential side gears. If, due to wear, the clearance is greater than .008 inch the slip joints should be renewed or in extreme cases the differential side gears as well.

Also check the clearance between the slip joint pivots and runners and if it is found to be excessive the axle shafts must be renewed as well as the runners as the joint pivot is not supplied as a service spare part. The axle shaft to sliding sleeve spline clearance should not exceed .006 inch.

Check that the sliding sleeve snap ring is a snug fit in its seating groove on the shaft.

Whenever the vehicle is being serviced the condition of the boots, bushings and oil seals should be checked and any damaged parts renewed.

6:10 Gear shift control mechanism

Should difficulty be experienced in obtaining correct gear selection then the gear shift control mechanism should be adjusted as follows:

1 Remove the screws fixing the cover to the tunnel and raise the cover to the top of the gear shift lever stem.
2 Slacken the lever support mounting screws and push the support forward if first- and third-speed engagement is incorrect or backwards if second-, fourth- and reverse-speed engagement are incorrect. Finally tighten the mounting screws. Refit the gear shift lever boot.

Removal:

To remove the gear shift control mechanism from the car proceed as follows:

1 Unscrew the gear shift control lever knob and the boot fixing screws and slide the boot from the gear shift lever.
2 Remove the screws fixing the assembly to the tunnel. Remove the tunnel front cover.
3 Disconnect the gear shift control rod at the gear engagement control lever and pull out the assembly from the front end.

Dismantling and inspection:

The gear shift handlever is removed by releasing the lever to support mounting self-locking nut.

Check that the lever ball and socket are in good condition and not badly pitted or worn. The inner lever return spring and the hand lever spring should be checked for weakness which, if apparent, should be renewed.

Reassembly is the reverse procedure to dismantling.

6:11 Modifications

Various design modifications are incorporated on the 500 sedan (110F) and the late version of the 500 station wagon. These are shown in **FIGS 6:19** and **6:20**,

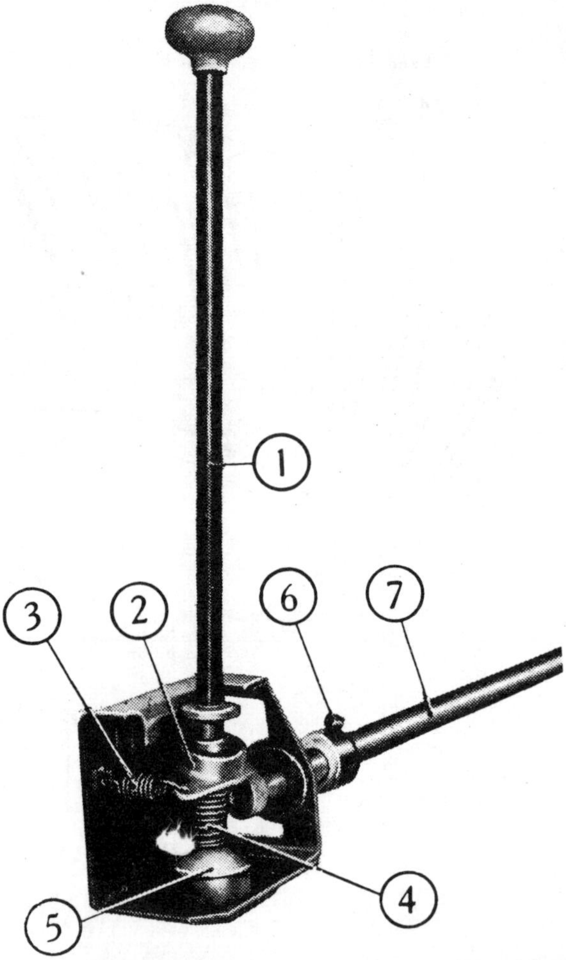

FIG 6:18 Gearshift control mechanism

Key to Fig 6:18 1 Hand lever 2 Inner lever 3 Lever return spring 4 Hand lever spring 5 Ball seat 6 Inner lever-to-rod mounting screw 7 Gearshift control rod

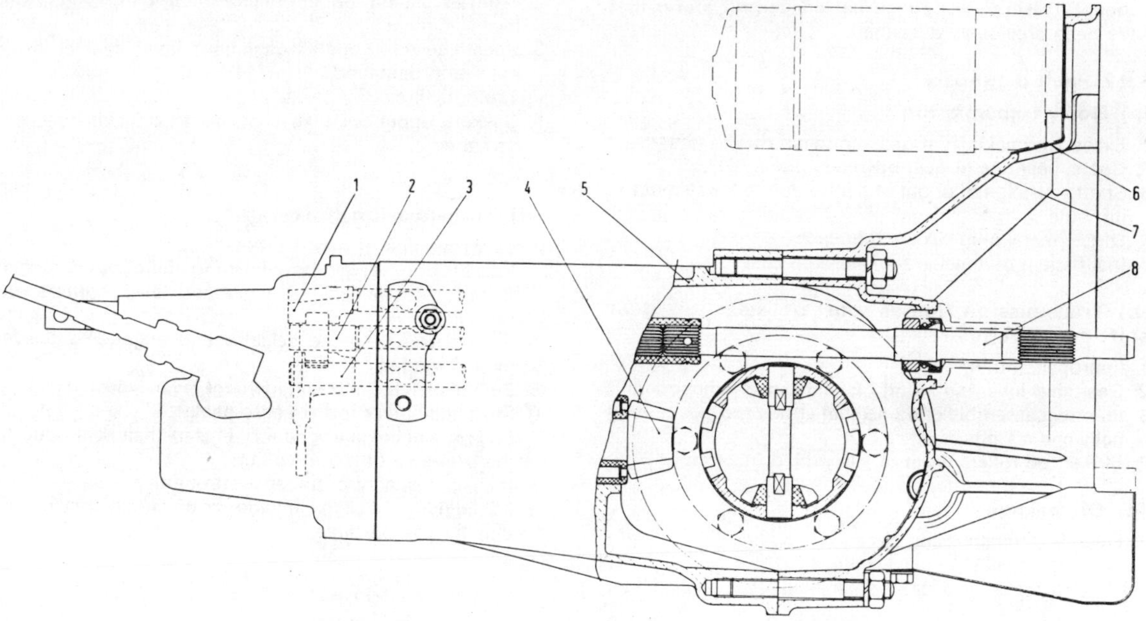

FIG 6:19 **Modified items in transmission-differential assembly**

Key to Fig 6:19 1 Reverse shifter shaft 2 Third and fourth shifter shaft 3 First and second shifter shaft 4 Countershaft pinion (and ring gear) 5–7 Transmission-differential case 6 Housing 8 Clutch shaft

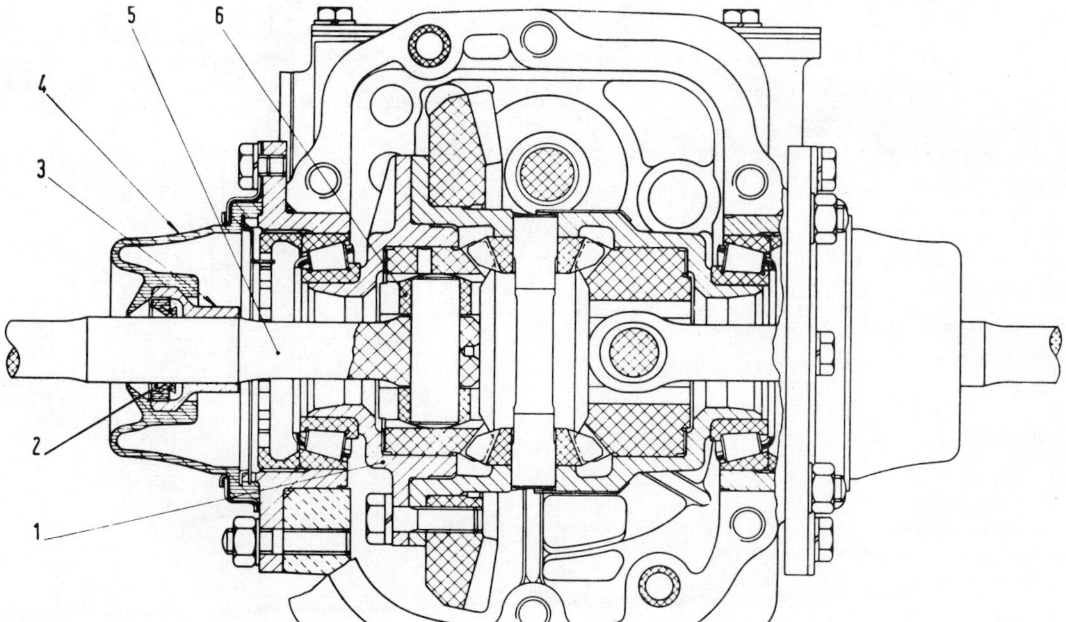

FIG 6:20 **End sectional view of transmission—differential assembly**

The items having undergone design modifications, besides those shown in **Fig 6:19** are the following: 1 Differential case and final drive gears 2 Seal 3 Bushing 4 Oil boot 5 Axle shaft 6 Joint casing although these do not affect the service procedures that have been previously described.

6:12 Fault diagnosis

(a) Noisy transmission

1 Excessive backlash of gears in mesh due to gear wear
2 Gears, bearings or gear bushings damaged
3 Shafts misaligned or out of centre due to loose mounting nuts
4 Dirt or metal chips in the lubricant
5 Insufficient oil level in transmission case

(b) Transmission jumps out of gear or gear shifting is irregular

1 Improper shifting
2 Gear shift lever mounting bracket out of adjustment
3 Incorrect assembly or damage of striker rod positioning balls and springs
4 Striker rod rollers worn or assembled incorrectly

(c) Oil leakage

1 Overfilled transmission case
2 Front extension, upper cover and clutch housing nuts loose
3 Speed selector and engagement lever seal at front extension damaged
4 Faulty bellhousing gasket
5 Gaskets, upper cover-to-case, front extension-to-case, damaged

(d) Transmission shifts hard

1 Defective link of gear shift lever to internal front lever
2 Internal front lever rubber bushing and plates damaged
3 Speed selector and engagement lever control rod twisted
4 Control rod-to-speed selector and engagement lever joint damaged
5 Speed selector and engagement lever worn
6 Stiffened striker rods in case ceats
7 Sliding sleeves and gears bound in their seats due to the presence of dirt in splines
8 Improper quality of transmission lubricant
9 Misadjusted clutch linkage and clutch make declutching impossible

CHAPTER 7

REAR SUSPENSION AND WHEELS

7:1 Description

The rear wheels are independently sprung by means of coil springs and V-shaped swinging arms acting on coil springs and telescopic double acting hydraulic shock absorbers. The swinging arms are mounted at their inner ends on 'estendblocks', the coil spring is fitted at the outer end of the swinging arm. At the wheel end of the suspension arm is attached a steel pressing to which the brake backplate and wheel bearing housing are bolted so forming a swinging unit to which is attached the road wheel.

The inner pivots are so located vertical wheel movements do not influence the drive shaft length which means that there is no need to fit a universal joint at the wheel end. Two taper roller bearings which are separated by a specially designed collapsible spacer are located in the rear wheel bearing housing and this carries the axle shaft. The outer end of the axle shaft is flanged and it is to this flange that the brake drum is bolted The splined inner end carries a rubber cushioned coupling to which the drive shaft flange is attached.

7:2 Removal of rear suspension assembly

1 Jack-up the vehicle and place on firmly based stands. Remove the road wheel on the side from which the suspension unit is to be removed.

2 Using a garage hydraulic jack support the swinging arm to facilitate the removal of the upper shock absorber mounting nut which is located inside the vehicle on the floor. To gain access to the nut remove the rear wheel housing linings.

3 Unhook the parking brake shoe control lever return spring.

4 Remove the three screws securing the drive shaft flange to the flexible coupling. Pull back the sleeve and remove the inner spring.

5 Remove the brake fluid reservoir cap, remove the filter and plug the delivery hole in the brake fluid reservoir and disconnect the flexible brake pipe from the bracket on the body floor.

6 Disconnect the parking brake control tie rod by first removing the cotter pin and removing the cable eye from the pin on the shoe control lever. Release the cable adjustment nuts and free the cable from the fairlead on the swinging arm.

7 Using the hydraulic jack carefully lower the swinging arm, fully retract the shock absorber by pushing in the outer cylinder and carefully pull out the coil spring together with its mounting rubber rings.

8 Remove the self-locking nut securing the swinging arm to the internal support welded on the floor. Extract the mounting pin and note the number and arrangement of shims between the bushings and the bracket. This will facilitate reassembly.

FIG 7:1 Rear suspension assembly

Key to Fig 7:1 1 Brake shoe control cable and sheath 2 Coil spring 3 Oil boot 4 Axle shaft 5 Bumper 6 Flexible joint 7 Swinging arm 8 Cable adjusting nut 9 Swinging arm-to-front bracket mounting pin 10 Swinging arm front bracket-to-underbody mounting screw 11 Engine front support crossmember 12 Swinging arm rear self-locking nut 13 Shock absorber-to-swinging arm lower nut 14 Sleeve screws 15 Axle shaft-to-flexible joint sleeve

9 Remove the three swinging external support fixing bolts securing the outer suspension arm bracket to the vehicle floor and remove the rear suspension assembly. Remove the special rubber pad located between the support bracket and the vehicle floor.

7:3 Servicing swing arms

Dismantling:

1 Remove the cotter pin and release the nut fixing the flexible joint to the wheel shaft. Remove the plain washer and the joint.

2 Using Fiat tool A.40005.1.9 or a universal two-leg puller, remove the wheel shaft and brake drum. Extract the two oil seals and both the outer and inner bearing inner rings, thrust ring of the joint and the resilient spacer.

3 Using Fiat tool A.6511, remove the two bearing outer rings.

4 Disconnect the brake hydraulic line at the wheel cylinder and remove the swinging external support. The bearing housing and brake housing flange may then be removed.

Inspection:

Thoroughly clean all the parts and install the swinging arm on Fiat fixture A.66064 as shown in **FIG 7:4**. If the swinging arm has not been distorted its installation on the fixture should be straightforward. Tighten the clamp screws 1 (see **FIG 7:3**) on the road wheel brake drum, connect the swinging arm inner member to the seating 2 on the fixture and finally fit the swinging arm external support holes on the fixture pins 3. Should difficulty be experienced in either one of these three operations then this is an indication that the swinging arm is distorted and should be straightened or a new assembly fitted. If this check is satisfactory proceed as follows:

1 Check that the 'estendblocks' are a snug fit in their respective seatings in the swinging arm and that the mounting pin slides in freely without excessive play. To renew the 'estendblocks' use Fiat tool A.66056 which is suitable for both their removal and installation.

2 Check that the inner and outer bearing outer rings have no play in their seatings and that the rollers and cages are not broken, cracked, show signs of overheating or are worn.

3 Ensure that the oil seals fit snugly on the wheel shaft, also on the joint spacer or shoulder ring and on the hub seats. If the oil seals should show any signs of wear then these should be renewed.

4 Inspect the resilient spacer for signs of hair line cracks, which if not evident the spacer may be used again as it is not permanently distorted during assembly. Should, however, new bearings or bearing housings be fitted it is considered good practice to fit a new spacer.

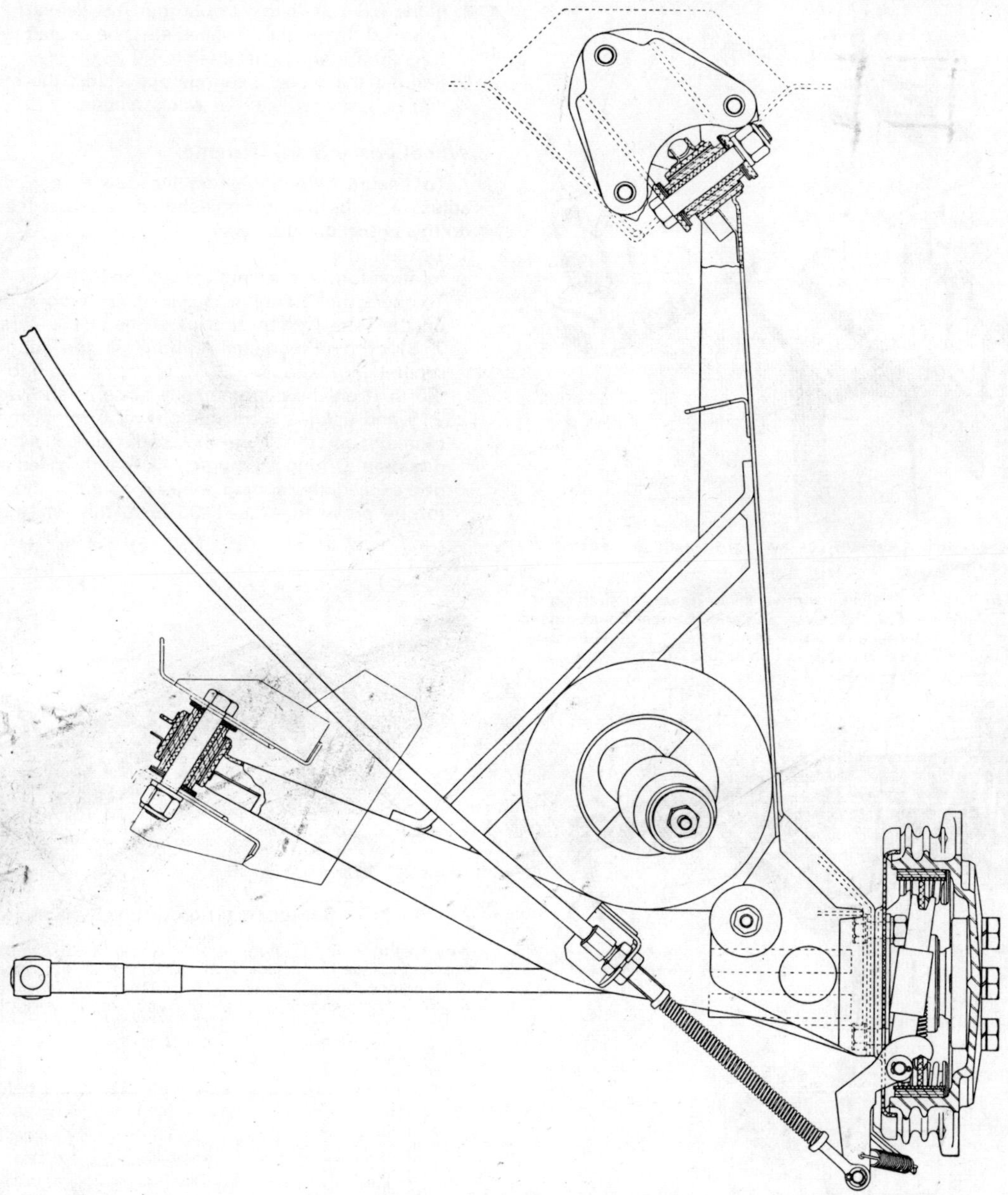

FIG 7:2 Right rear suspension assembly, sectioned through brake drum and arm mountings

5 Check the mating surface of the bearing inner rings on the wheel shaft and ensure that it is perfectly smooth. Also check that the shaft splines to flexible joint splines are not distorted or show signs of excess wear. The maximum permissible wear backlash is .0059 inch.
6 Ensure that the flexible joint is not damaged where the rubber is bonded to the metal. If signs of strain are indicated a new joint must be fitted.

Reassembly:

Reassembly of the swinging arm unit is the reverse procedure to dismantling. The following points should be noted:

1 Always use Fiat tool A.66056 to install 'estendblock' on the swing arm.
2 The mounting nuts for the bearing housing to the brake housing flange should always be tightened to a

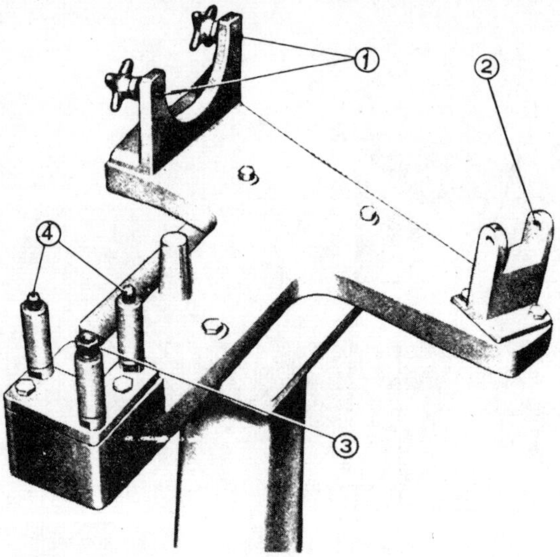

FIG 7:3 Fixture A.66064, for swinging arm inspection and adjustment

Key to Fig 7:3 1 Clamp screws, securing wheel shaft on fixture 2 Alignment bracket, swinging arm member check-up 3 Swinging arm external support centring pins 4 Nut, to secure swinging arm external support on fixture stud

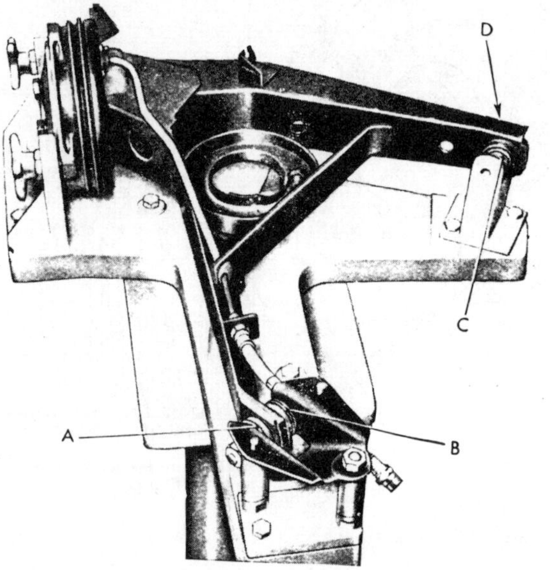

FIG 7:4 Adjusting right rear suspension swinging arm on fixture A.66064

Key to Fig 7:4 **A** and **B** Swinging arm external support adjustment shims **C** and **D** Swinging arm internal support adjustment shims

torque wrench setting of 43.4 lb/ft.

3 During assembly the bearings must be packed with Fiat MR grease, taking care not to overpack as this can result in early bearing failure.

4 If the axle shaft to flexible joint tie sleeve has been removed, the mating splines must be coated with Fiat B2G grease on re-installation.

5 Preload the wheel bearings and adjust the swinging arm as described later on in this section.

Wheel bearing adjustment:

To ensure a long bearing life due to correct initial adjustment the ballbearings should be preloaded and to do this proceed as follows:

1 Tighten the wheel shaft nut gradually so that the rotation torque does not exceed .36 lb/ft.

2 To check the rotation torque install Fiat tool A.95697/2 on the wheel drum and insert the shank 2 (see **FIG 7:5**) of dynomometer A.95697 in the support and securely hold the lever 3. Move the needle 5 to register .36 lb/ft on the dynomometer scale as shown in **FIG 7:5** and using the operating lever 6 rotate the dynomometer and the wheel shaft some turns in a clockwise direction. During rotation check that the needle 5 does not exceed the setting index 4. Should the rotation torque prove to exceed .36 lb/ft, this will indicate a

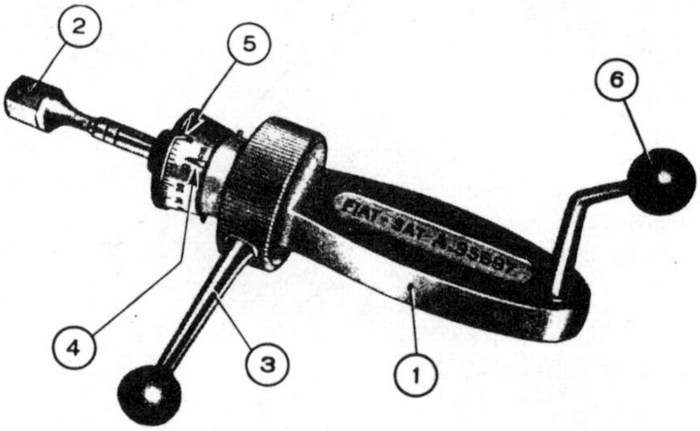

FIG 7:5 Bearing rotation torque dynamometer

Key to Fig 7:5 1 Dynamometer A.95697 2 Dynamometer shank to insert in item A.95697/2, fitted to wheel drum 3 Dynamometer grip lever 4 Rotation torque setting index 5 Adjustable needle 6 Dynamometer operating lever

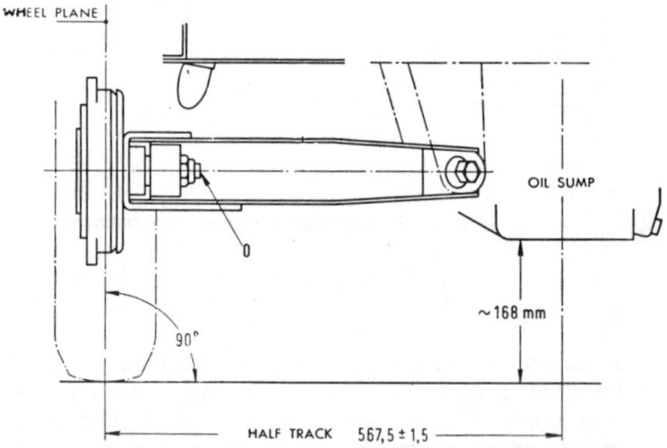

FIG 7:6 Position of rear suspension and of vehicle for rear wheel toe-in inspection and adjustment

Key to Fig 7:6 ~168 mm = 6.61 inch 567,5 ± 1,5 = 22.342 inch ± .059 inch high bearing preload. To reset remove the wheel shaft and fit a new resilient spacer. Repeat the rotation torque test.

Swinging arm adjustment:

To adjust the swinging arm use Fiat fixture A.66064 as shown in **FIG 7:3** and proceed as follows:

1 At points **A** and **B** as indicated in **FIG 7:4** between the 'estendblock' and the swinging arm to body front mounting bracket fit three shims on each side. To ensure that the shims are correctly centred use Fiat alignment bar A.66057.

2 Whilst removing the alignment bar, carefully slip in the mounting pin and screw on the nut. Once the rear wheel geometry adjustment has been completed this nut should be tightened to a torque wrench setting of 43.4 to 50.6 lb ft.

3 At points **C** and **D** (see **FIG 7:4**), insert the number of shims required to fill in the gap between the 'estendblock' and the two fixture shoulders. Having determined the number of shims required both at locations **C** and **D**, these must later be fitted between the 'estendblock' and the shoulders on the swinging arm to body mounting bracket.

7:4 Coil springs

The coil springs should be thoroughly cleaned and all traces of rust removed. Inspect the spring coils for hair line cracks, which if evident, a new pair of springs must be fitted to ensure correct vehicle height and stability. Check the free height and the height under loading of the coil springs and these must correspond to the figures quoted in **Technical Data.**

7:5 Installation of rear suspension assemblv

To replace the rear suspension assembly proceed as follows:

1 Insert the swinging arm inner end in the mounting bracket which is welded onto the body floor. Place between the 'estendblock' and bracket the number of adjustment shims as previously determined using Fiat fixture A.66064 as shown in **FIG 7:4.** Insert the Fiat alignment bar A.66057 through 'estendblock' and shims, aligning them with the holes in the mounting bracket. Firmly hold the entire assembly using a garage hydraulic jack if necessary, and carefully remove the alignment bar and at the same time ease in the mounting pin. Secure the nut which once the rear wheels geometry has been checked must be tightened to a torque wrench setting of 43.4 to 50.6 lb/ft.

2 Screw in finger tight the three swinging arm external bracket to body floor mounting screws together with the plain and spring washers. The screws will have to be tightened to a torque wrench setting of 28.9 to 36.2 lb/ft once the rear wheel geometry has been adjusted.

3 Carefully insert the coil spring, lower insulator ring onto the swinging arm, insert the spring on the shock absorber which should be previously secured to the arm and position the spring onto its seat on the arm. Place the upper insulator ring onto the spring, raise the suspension assembly using a garage hydraulic jack and insert the spring onto its seating under the body floor.

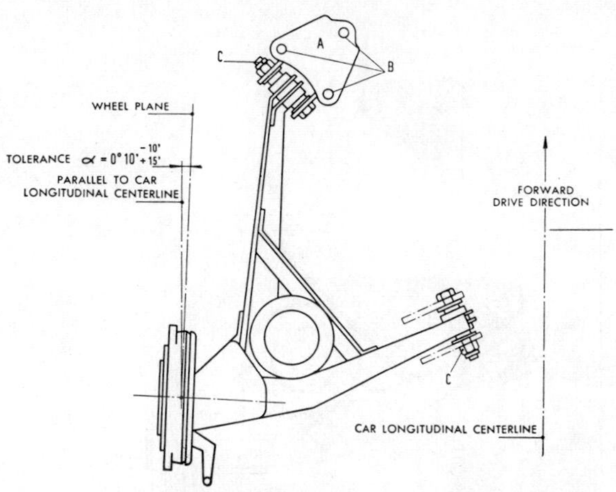

FIG 7:7 Adjusting rear wheel toe-in angle

Key to Fig 7:7 Rear wheel plane must be perpendicular to ground and parallel to car longitudinal centerline with a tolerance of 0° 10' $^{-10'}_{+15'}$ toe-in

To adjust rear wheel geometry, move suitably the swinging arm outer support. Slight movements are permitted by the play existing between the support holes A and the mounting screws. Screws B must be tightened to 28.9 to 36.2 lb ft (4000 to 5000 kg mm). Nuts C must be tightened to 43.4 to 50.6 lb ft (6000 to 7000 kgmm), after adjustment has been carried out. (These directions and specifications are also applicable to 500 Station Wagon).

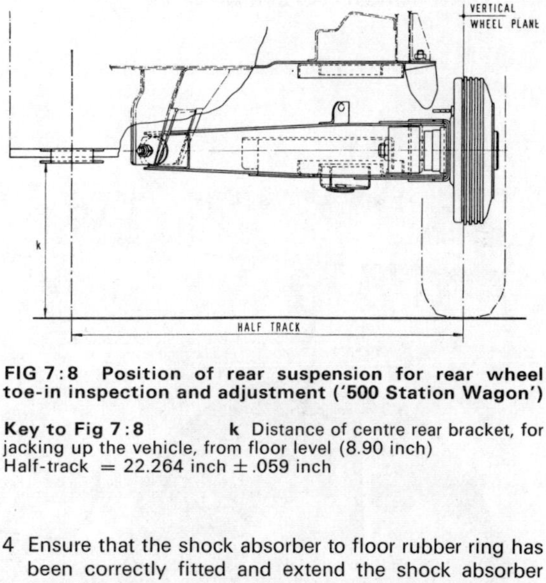

FIG 7:8 Position of rear suspension for rear wheel toe-in inspection and adjustment ('500 Station Wagon')

Key to Fig 7:8 **k** Distance of centre rear bracket, for jacking up the vehicle, from floor level (8.90 inch)
Half-track = 22.264 inch ± .059 inch

4 Ensure that the shock absorber to floor rubber ring has been correctly fitted and extend the shock absorber until its upper mounting pin protrudes into the vehicle through the hump in the floor panel. Secure the shock absorber by its mounting nut and lockwasher having first inserted the rubber ring and plain washer.

5 Refit the rear wheel housing in place, reconnect the brake line to the connection on body floor and remove the plug from the output hole in the brake fluid reservoir. Bleed the hydraulic brake system as described in **Chapter 10.**

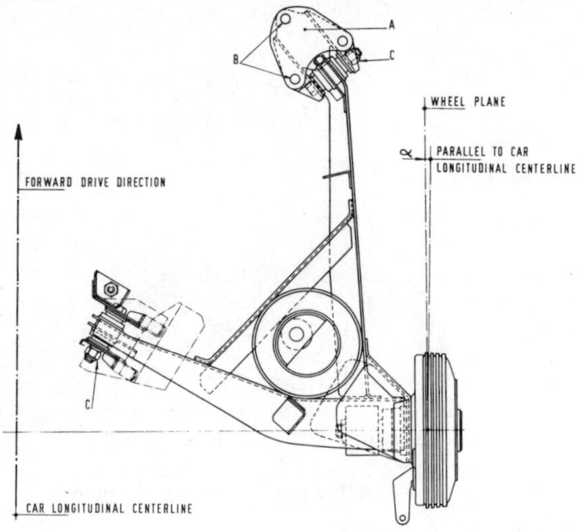

FIG 7:9 Adjusting rear wheel toe-in on '500 Station Wagon'

Key to Fig 7:9 **A** Front support **B** Screw holes for fixing support to underbody **C** Swinging arm pin nuts—α Wheel toe-in angle $(0° 10' {}^{-10'}_{+15'})$

NOTE—that the toe-in angle (α) will vary by 0° 10′ under a movement of some $\frac{7}{32}$ inch measured at 72.476 inch from wheel centre for Model 500D, and at 76.413 inch from wheel centre for 500 Station Wagon

6 Insert the inner spring between the axle shaft and the wheel shaft and couple the spline sleeve to the joint and tighten the screws to a torque wrench setting of 20.3 lb/ft.
7 Reconnect the parking brake tie rod and adjust the position of the cable using the two stretchers.
8 Refit the wheels and draw up the mounting screws to a torque wrench setting of 32.5 to 39.8 lb/ft. Carefully lower the vehicle to the floor.

7:6 Checking and adjusting rear wheel toe-in

This check should be carried out by a Fiat agent as special setting equipment is necessary. However, details of this check are given for reference purposes:

To check and adjust the rear wheel geometry proceed as follows:

1 Place the vehicle on firmly based stands and remove the front and rear wheels.
2 Install Fiat fixtures A.66062 as shown in **FIG 7:12** to enable correct spring compression and wheel location in the vertical position.
3 Lift the rear suspensions by compressing the coil springs and shock absorbers using garage hydraulic jacks. Screw on the fixture lower shank until the index registers with the mark 'Nuova 500' stamped on the bracket. In this position the wheel plane is vertical and the centre **O** (see **FIG 7:6**) of wheel shaft results at 5.00 inch from the buffer stop bracket.
4 Secure Fiat support C.696/3 to the wheel drum and connect gauge C.696 to the support. Tighten the two clamping screws as shown in **FIG 7:12.**
5 Apply at the front of Fiat gauge C.696 bracket numbered C.696/3 as shown in **FIG 7:11.**
6 Check that the pin mounted on the front end of the bracket C.696/3 is in touch with the front suspension swinging arm pin (see **FIG 7:11**). If these conditions are not complied with, proceed with item 7.

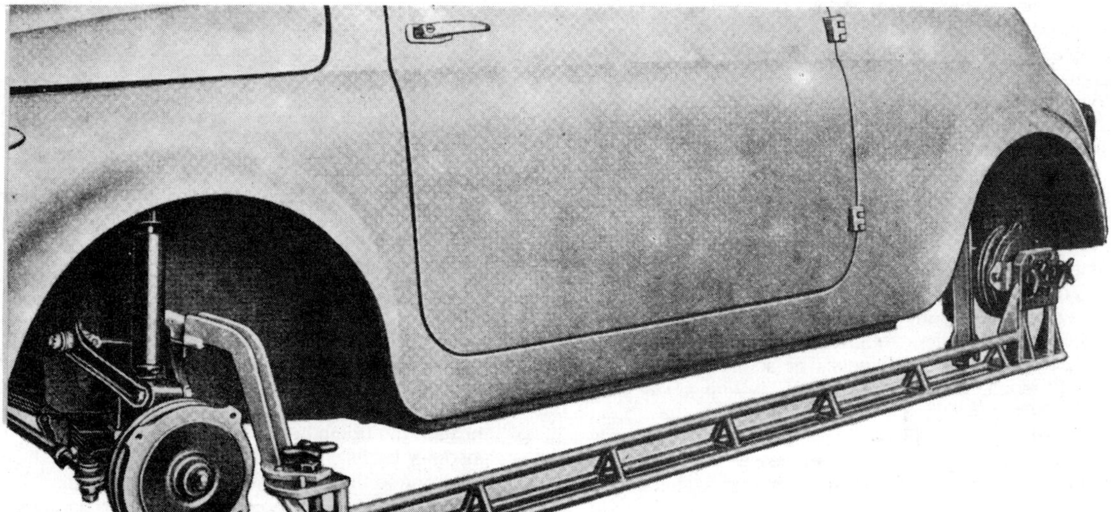

FIG 7:10 Checking left rear wheel toe-in

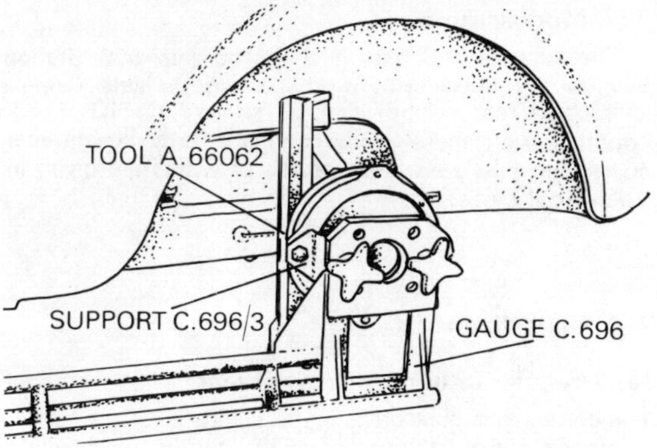

FIG 7:12 Checking left rear wheel toe-in

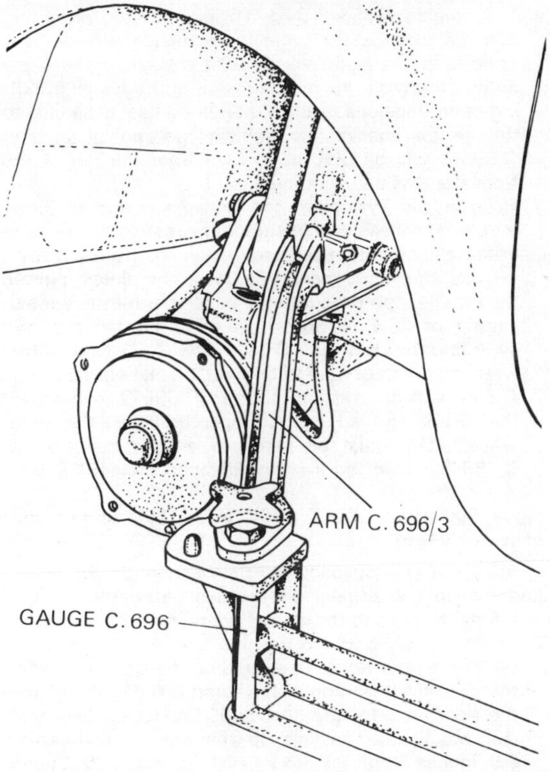

FIG 7:11 Checking left rear wheel toe-in

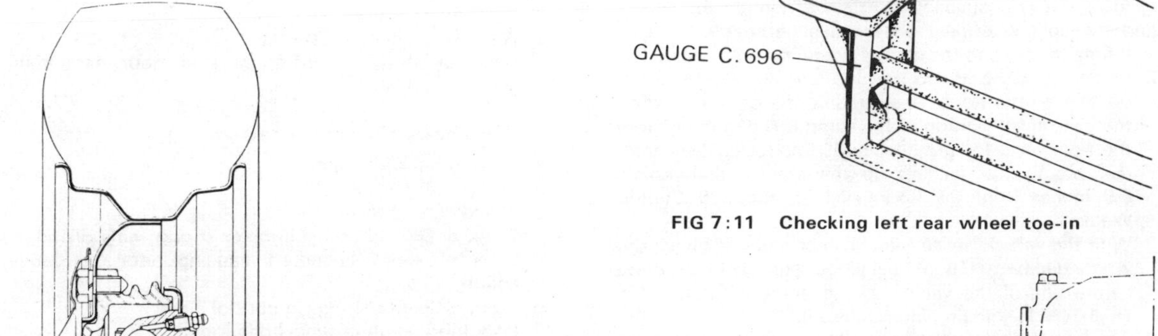

FIG 7:13 Sectional view of right side rear wheel and axle shaft

NOTE—This assembly differs from the early design in the following items: control arm, handbrake shoe actuating lever, flexible joint, axle shaft-to-flexible joint sleeve, sleeve snap ring, axle shaft and joint casing.

A tolerance of —10′ + 15′ is permitted providing that the value is the same for both rear wheels. It is important that both rear wheels are set to the same angle otherwise uneven tyre wear and adverse handling conditions will result. When the wheel is parallel to the centre line of the vehicle the pin of bracket C.696/3 will be .216 inch apart from the pin of the front suspension swinging arm.

7 Release the swinging arm outer support to body mounting screws and position arm in such a way as to obtain the condition as described in **Number 6** above.

After the adjustment has been completed tighten the outer support mounting screws to a torque wrench setting of 28.9 to 36.2 lb/ft. Also tighten the two swinging arm pin nuts **C** (see **FIG 7:7**) to a torque wrench setting of 43.4 to 50.6 lb/ft. Take off the gauge C.696 with bracket and support C.696/3, and repeat the check and adjustment operations on the other wheel. Care must be taken to ensure that bracket C.696/3 is reversed from the position previously used.

New 500 type 500D, 110F and 110L sedan and station wagon:

After the rear suspension has been replaced, check and, if necessary adjust the rear wheel geometry.

1 Inflate the tyres to the normal operating pressures.

2 Lower the car body so that the rear wheels are set at 90 deg. to the floor. This condition is obtained when the lowermost portion of the sump is 6.61 inches from the floor level for the new 500D model or the centre rear bracket for jacking up the rear of the vehicle 8.9 inches from the floor level for the 500 Station Wagon.

3 With the vehicle set to the above conditions check the wheel geometry. The wheel plane must be tilted to the centre line of the vehicle by an angle of 0 deg. 10′ (—10′, +15′) toeing in at the front.

4 The wheel plane must be 22.343 ± .059 inches from the centre line of the vehicle for the 500D model. Whereas for the 500 Station Wagon the distance must be 22.264 ± .059 inches.

5 To adjust the rear wheel toe-in adjust the positions of the mounting screws **A** and **B** as shown in **FIG 7:7.**

7:7 Modifications

The new 500 Sedan (110F) and late 500 Station Wagon are fitted with modified wheels side flexible joints and rear control arm as shown in **FIG 7:13.** Together with these modifications a new design rear coil spring has been fitted details of which are given in **Technical Data.**

7:8 Fault diagnosis

(a) Irregular or abnormal tyre wear

1 Incorrect tyre pressure
2 Wheels out of balance
3 Wheels off centre
4 Misadjusted brakes
5 Weak or broken coil springs
6 Excessive load
7 Incorrect wheel alignment

(b) Sag on one wheel

1 Incorrect tyre pressure
2 Weak or broken coil spring
3 Wear of shock absorber causing poor dampening action

(c) Squeaks, thumps or rattles

1 Wheels out of balance
2 Wheels off centre
3 Misadjusted brakes
4 Weak or broken coil springs or spring seats dislodged
5 Wear of shock absorbers causing poor dampening action
6 Worn rubber bushings in control arms
7 Poor lubrication of wheel bearings

(d) Pull to one side

1 Incorrect tyre pressure
2 Misadjusted brakes
3 Distorted suspension arm

CHAPTER 8

FRONT SUSPENSION AND HUBS

8:1 Description

The independent front suspension assembly fitted to the 'new 500' range comprises a transverse leaf spring which is anchored to the body through two rubber mountings and kingpins through 'estendblocks' as shown in **FIG 8:1.** The leaf spring also acts as an anti-roll bar which gives normal spring reaction even when the front road wheels encounter a rough road surface.

Special polyethylene insulating strips are fitted between the five springs leaves which are all clamped together by two rubber cushioned clamps.

Upper movement of the kingpins in the swinging arm is obtained by 'estendblocks'. The half arms are anchored to the body as shown in **FIG 8:3** and pivot on their pins through rubber bushes. Double acting hydraulic shock absorbers are fitted to the kingpin housings at the lower end and anchored at the top to the vehicle body. Two rubber buffers are secured to brackets mounted onto the body to limit the spring oscillations. The spring centre bolt is also fitted with a rubber pad.

8:2 Front suspension removal and dismantling

To remove the front suspension assembly proceed as follows:

1 Remove the hub caps and carefully slacken the road wheel retaining bolts. Using a garage hydraulic jack raise the front of the vehicle and place on firmly based stands. Remove the road wheels.
2 Disconnect the steering linkages from the pitman arm, the drag link and the steering knuckle arms.
3 Remove the shock absorber upper mounting nut from the body, lift away the half rubber bush and push down the outer cylinder.
4 Blank off the brake fluid reservoir outlet by inserting a suitable wooden peg through the reservoir filler opening and disconnect the brake hydraulic lines at the wheel cylinders.
5 Fit Fiat crossbeam Arr.2072 under the leaf spring and support this, using a garage hydraulic jack.
6 Remove the self-locking nut securing the leaf spring to the kingpin housing and ease out the spring mounting bolt taking care not to damage the thread. Also remove the nuts securing the swinging arm pin to studs on the body and remove the swinging arm assembly. Carefully lift out the adjusting shims and spacers from the studs making a careful note of the number of the shims and their locations.
7 Remove the nuts securing the leaf spring elastic mounting to the body (see **FIG 8:4**), and lower the

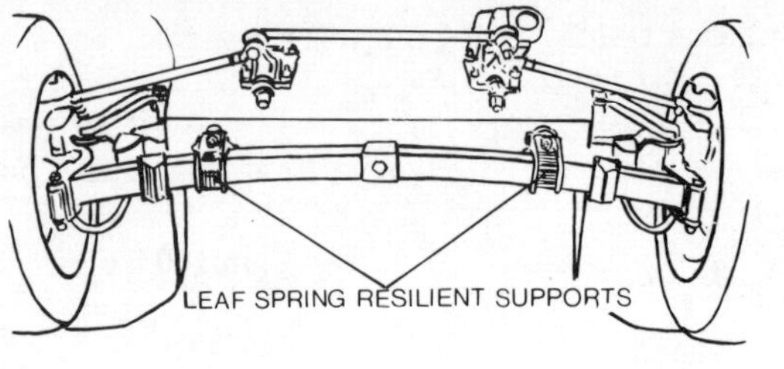

FIG 8:1 **Front suspension**

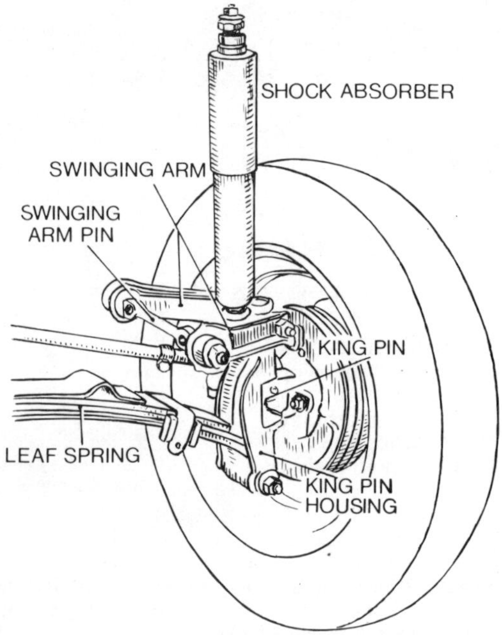

FIG 8:2 **Right front suspension**

hydraulic jack slowly so allowing the spring to be lowered from the underside of the vehicle.

8 Using Fiat wrench A.56030, disconnect the hydraulic shock absorber from the kingpin housing. Also remove the swinging arm pin mounting nuts and remove the pin.

9 Using Fiat drift A.66056 or a suitably sized drift remove the 'estenblock' from the kingpin housing. Using a suitably sized punch remove the block pin from the kingpin, remove the lower plug and take off the kingpin.

8:3 Leaf spring

Description:

The spring comprises a main leaf and four assister leaves. Specially shaped polyethylene insulation strips are fitted between the leaves which are held together by a centre bolt and two elastically mounted side clips as shown in **FIG 8:1.** The leaf spring is attached to the

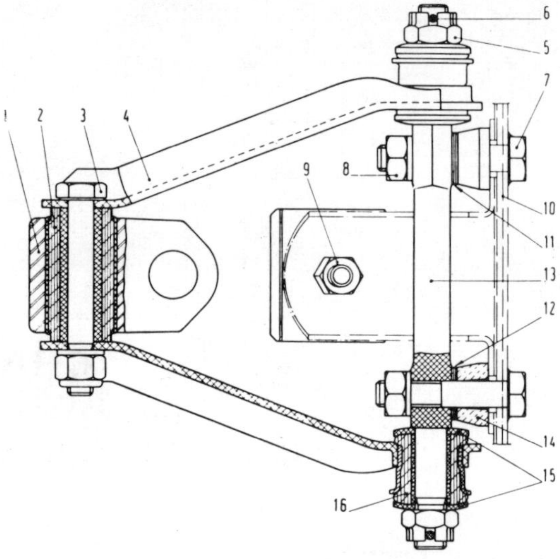

FIG 8:3 **Section through left swinging arm**

Key to Fig 8:3 1 Kingpin housing 2 Estendblock 3 Pin, swinging arm to kingpin housing 4 Half-arm 5 and 6 Nut and splitpin 7 Screw, welded on body 8 Nut, mounting, pin 13 to body 9 Rubber buffer mounting nut 10 Body panel 11 and 12 Camber and castor adjustment shims 13 Pin, swinging arm to body 14 Spacer 15 Cups, for rubber bush 16 Rubber bush

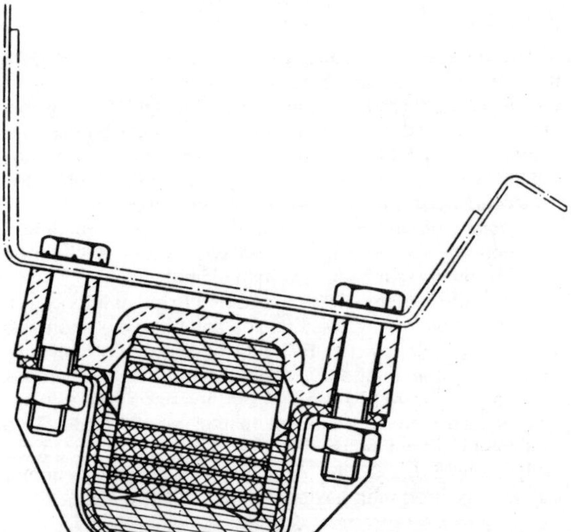

FIG 8:4 **Section through one spring mounting**

FRONT LEAF SPRING, LOADED AT CENTER

Position	Load P		Camber		Elastic give-in from pos. 2		Flexibility, between pos. 2 and pos. 3	
	lbs		in		in		in/100 lbs	
2	220.5		5.3936 ± .2362		—		2.23 ± .10	
3	440.9*		—		4.9212 ± .2362			

* When testing the spring never exceed 440.9 lbs load.

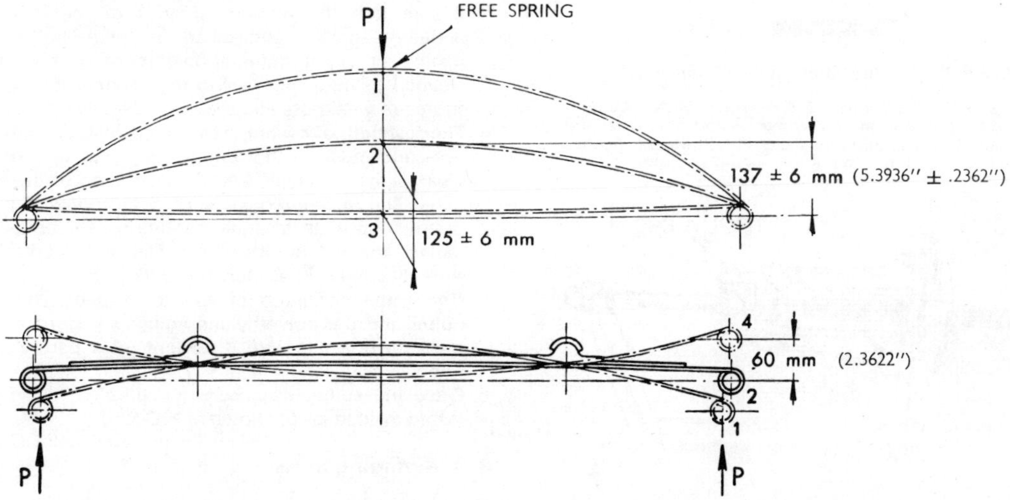

FRONT LEAF SPRING, INSTALLED ON CAR

Position		Load P		Camber		Elastic give-in from pos. 1		Flexibility between pos. 1 and pos. 3	
		lbs		in		in		in/100 lbs	
1	Initial load for flexibility check-up . .	220.5		—		—			
2	Static load	297.6		1.1023 ± .1181		—		1.55 ± .07	
3	Final load for flexibility check-up . .	330.7		—		1.7125 ± .0984			
4	Metal-to-metal deflection load	451.9		—		—			

Spring specifications are intended at assembly conditions, i. e., with pre-compressed rubber pads and without bumpers. Give-in check-up must be carried out by loading both eyes simultaneously.

FIG 8:5 Spring deflection test

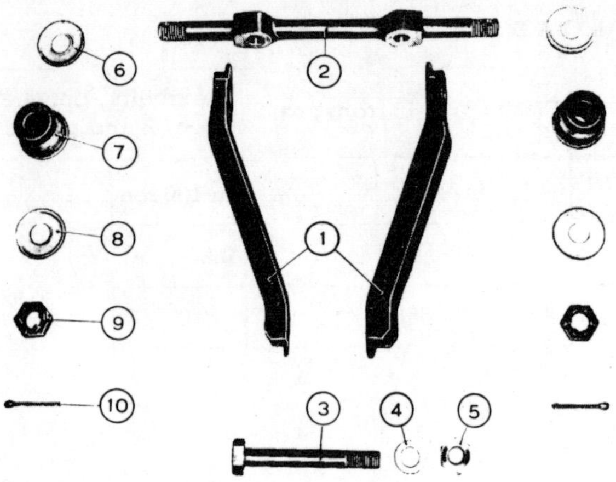

FIG 8:6 Swinging arm components

Key to Fig 8:6 1 Half-arms 2 Pin, arm to body mounting 3 Pin, arm to kingpin housing mounting 4 and 5 Washer and nut 6 and 8 Cups, rubber bushes 7 Rubber bushes 9 and 10 Splitpins and nuts, mounting, pin (2) to arms

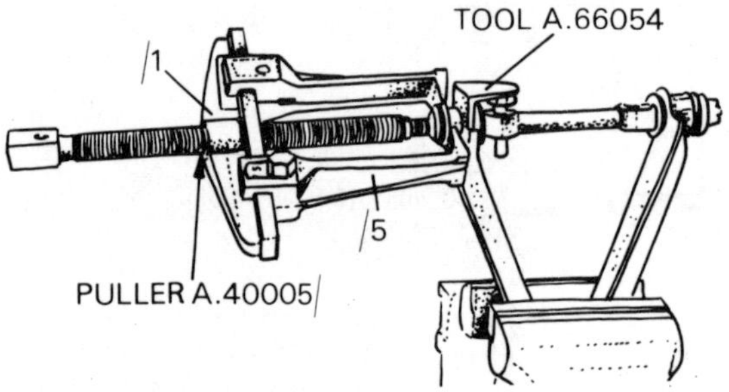

FIG 8:7 Removal of rubber bushes by universal puller A.40005 and arm retainer tool A.66054

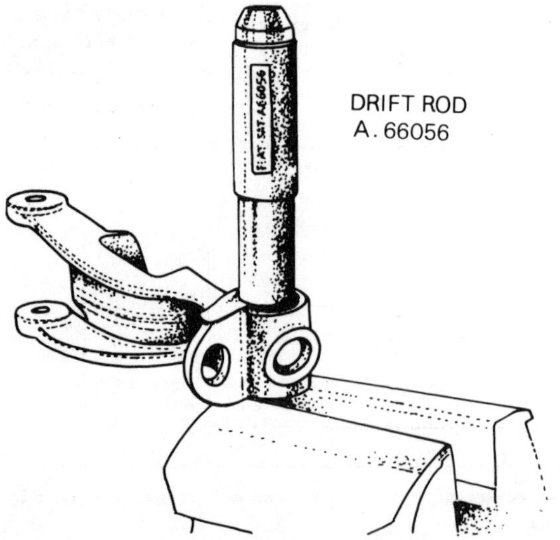

FIG 8:8 Drift rod A.66056 for kingpin housing 'Estendblock' removal and installation

kingpin housings by 'estendblocks' which are fitted in the main leaf eyes. A specially shaped rubber buffer is mounted on the spring centre bolt.

Leaf spring inspection and repair:

To dismantle the leaf spring assembly remove the two side clips and the centre bolt. Thoroughly wash all parts and to inspect proceed as follows:

1 Inspect carefully to check that the leaves are not broken or show signs of cracking which, if evident, the leaf must be renewed. It should be noted that the third spring leaf is not available as a service replacement part which means that if this leaf is damaged the whole spring must be renewed.
2 Check that there is no paint or underseal present between the leaves which, if evident, must be removed.
3 Ensure that the mating surfaces of the leaves are perfectly smooth and clean. If there are signs of rusting or slight indentations, these areas must be cleaned using a file. Any deep indentations will be a source of weakness and the leaf must be renewed.
4 The 'estendblocks' are press fitted into the main leaf eyes and must be thoroughly inspected for excessive wear, signs of seizure and dry operation of the rubber parts. The 'estendblocks' should be renewed if there is any doubt as to their condition. To remove and replace the 'estendblocks' use Fiat drift A.66056 or a suitably sized drift as shown in **FIG 8:8.**
5 Check the condition of all rubber pads, the centre buffer and the polyethylene linings for signs of wear, cracking or splits and, if evident, new parts must be fitted.
6 Once the spring has been reassembled it should be tested by loading as shown in **FIG 8:5.**

8:4 Swinging arms

Description:

The swinging arms comprise two pressed steel sheet half arms which are joined by two pins, one on the kingpin housing and the other on the body (see **FIG 8:6**). Rubber bushes ('flanblocks') are press fitted into the half arms for the attachment of the swinging arm pin to the body as shown in **FIG 8:6.**

Dismantling:

1 Clamp the swinging arm into a vice and fit Fiat tool A.66054 as shown in **FIG 8:7.** Remove the splitpin and nut securing the half arms onto their pin.
2 Using a universal two leg puller or Fiat puller A.40005 together with items **1** and **5** pull out the rubber bushes as shown in **FIG 8:7.** Remove tool A.66054 insert it on the other half arm and repeat the operation performed for the bush removal on the first arm.

Inspection:

Thoroughly clean the half arms and dry using a compressed air jet. Then proceed as follows:

1 Thoroughly inspect the half arms to ensure that they are not distorted or show signs of cracking which, if evident, should be renewed. Compare the two half arms to ensure that they have the same inclination and that the holes are not elongated but are true and properly aligned.

2 Check that the surface of the pin that is in contact with the camber and castor adjuster shims does not show any signs of indentation or roughness which could affect the accuracy of adjustment on reassembly. If there are any signs of rust or small markings these should be smoothed out using a file.
3 Inspect the condition of the half arm bushes, the inner surface of which must not show signs of seizure and the clearance of the bush to pin must not be greater than .0157 inch. Upon initial assembly the fit clearance is .00059 to .0059 inch. Ensure that the rubber parts of the bush are not torn, cracked or show signs of weakness which, if evident, must be renewed.
4 Use Fiat tool A.66058 or a suitably sized drift for refitting the rubber bushes into the swinging arms. Upon reassembly it should be observed that the tightening of the two swinging arms mounting nuts 5 (see **FIG 8:6**), must be carried out whilst keeping the axis of the swinging arm and the pin hole for the screws 7 on the same plane otherwise distortion can occur.

8:5 Kingpin housing

1 To remove and replace the 'estendblocks' use Fiat tool A.66056 as shown in **FIG 8:8.** Ensure that the 'estendblocks' is not worn and that there are no signs of seizure on its inner surface, or that the rubber has hardened. Renew if necessary.
2 Check that the kingpin to bush clearance is not greater than .0079 inch. The clearance when fitted new is .00063 to .00213 inch. If the clearance is excessive the two bushes must be renewed and also the kingpin if excessive wear is evident. To remove and refit the kingpin bushes use Fiat tool A.66016 and after reassembly the bushes must be accurately refaced using a reamer set to a diameter of .5912 to .5922 inch. If considered necessary use Fiat Fixture C.1004 to check that the kingpin housing has not been distorted which, if evident, the housing must be renewed.
3 Whilst the kingpin assembly is being inspected ensure that the lubrication hole is free to allow the passage of oil.
4 To prevent incorrect loading of the 'estendblocks' that is press fitted into the kingpin housing, the housing to swinging arm pin nut must be tightened with the parts so arranged that the angle between the swinging arm plane and the housing axis is approximately 95 deg. as shown in **FIG 8:14.**

8:6 Steering knuckle and wheel hub

Dismantling:

1 To remove the wheel hub cap use Fiat puller A.46023 as shown in **FIG 8:9.**
2 Using a universal two leg puller or Fiat puller A.40005 together with items **1** and **9** remove the wheel hub/drum assembly having first extracted the splitpin and released the hub retaining nut (see **FIG 8:10**).
3 Remove the outer roller bearing, the oil seal and the inner roller bearing outer race from the drum and pull out the steering knuckle inner roller bearing inner ring using Fiat puller A.46000
4 Release the two drum to steering knuckle mounting nuts and remove the complete brake housing flange.
5 To remove the steering knuckle from the kingpin housing, remove the 'estendblock' from the kingpin housing using Fiat drift A.66056 or a suitably sized drift as shown in **FIG 8:8.**
6 Using a suitably sized punch drive the lockpin from the kingpin, remove the lower plug and slide off the kingpin. The steering knuckle is then disengaged together with the snap ring, two thrust washers and a shoulder ring.

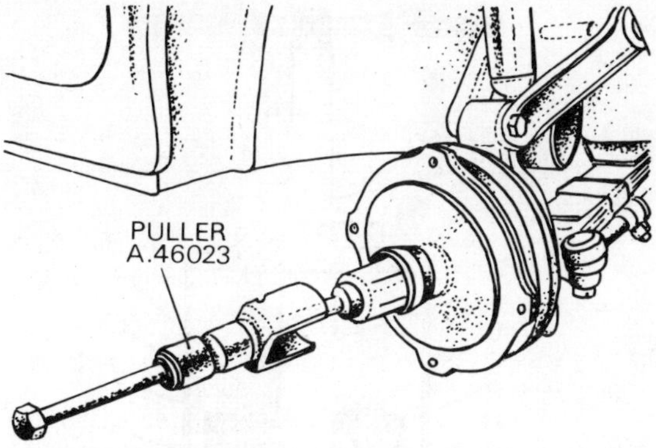

FIG 8:9 Removing right front wheel hub cap by remover A.46023

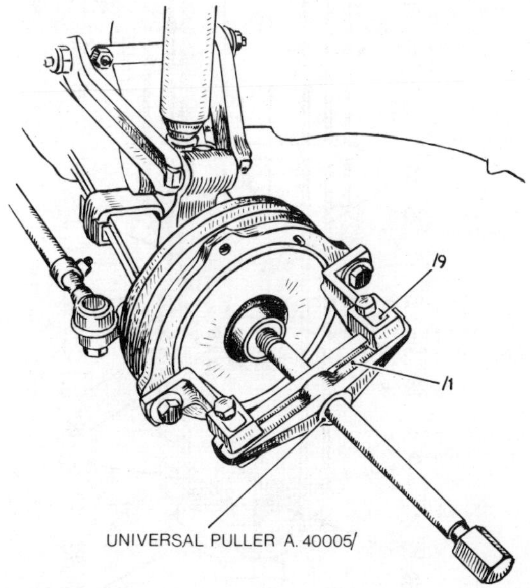

FIG 8:10 Removing left front wheel brake drum by puller A.40005

Inspection:

Thoroughly clean all parts and dry using a compressed air jet and to inspect proceed as follows:
1 Check that the steering knuckle and steering arm show

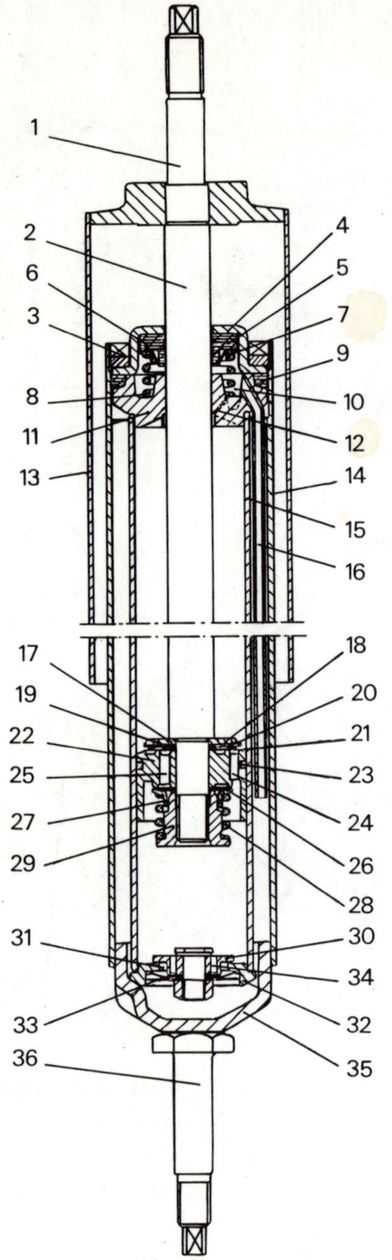

FIG 8:11 Sectional view of shock absorber

Key to Fig 8:11 1 Threaded shank, floor mounting 2 Rod 3 Cylinder upper blanking threaded ring 4 Seal housing 5 Rod seal 6 Tab spring 7 Spring cup 8 Gasket packing spring 9 Casing gasket 10 Vapour pocket drain and chamber 11 Rod guide bush 12 Vapour pocket drain capillary hole 13 Dust shield 14 Casing 15 Working cylinder 16 Vapour pocket drain passage 17 Valve lift limiting disc 18 Fluid passage orifice 19 Valve lift adjustment washer 20 Valve star-shaped spring 21 Inlet valve 22 Piston 23 Compression ring 24 Inlet valve holes in piston 25 Rebound valve holes in piston 26 Rebound valve 27 Valve guide cup 28 Rebound valve spring 29 Piston mounting plug 30 Compensating valve 31 Compensating valve annular passage 32 Compensating-and-compression valve carrier plug 33 Compression valve 34 Compression valve orifices 35 Lower plug 36 Threaded shank, lower mounting

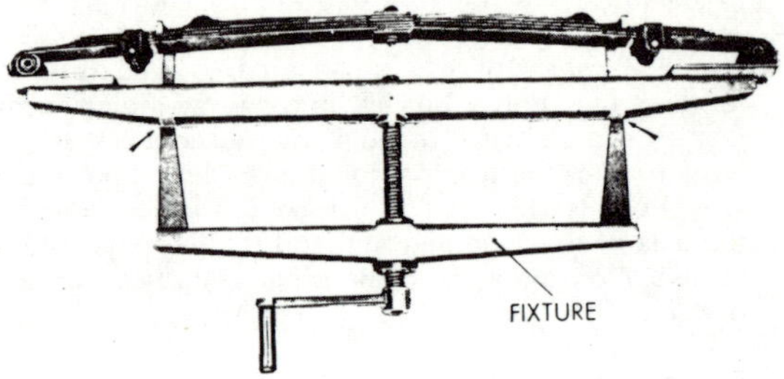

FIG 8:12 Leaf spring position under 'full static loads' on fixture A.66061 or A.74061

no signs of distortion or cracking which, if evident, new parts must be fitted.

2 Check the steering knuckle surfaces, that are in contact with the bearing inner races for any signs of scoring or seizure.

3 Inspect the condition of the two upper thrust rings and of the lower packing ring. Parts which show sign of excessive wear must be renewed. Lower packing rings are supplied in service in the thicknesses tabulated below.

	Stand.	Oversizes						Undersizes	
Ring	in.	.002	.004	.006	.008	.010	.012	.002	.004
Thkss	in. .0977	.0979	.1016	.1036	.1056	.1076	.1095	.0957	.0938
	in. .098	.100	.102	.104	.106	.108	.110	.096	.094

Once the items have been reassembled no appreciable clearance should be evident between the steering knuckle and the kingpin housing. This adjustment is obtained by installing the lower packing ring of suitable size.

4 Check that the seating on the drums for the roller bearing outer races are smooth as no clearance is allowable between the races and their seatings. Carefully inspect that the bearing cages and the rollers show no signs of chipping, breakage, or discolouration due to overheating.

5 Carefully inspect the seal which must not be torn and it should locate perfectly both on the drum and the steering knuckles.

Reassembly:

Reassembly is the reverse procedure to dismantling.

8:7 Hydraulic damper:

Description:

The front and rear shock absorbers are of the telescopic double acting type. Their dampening action takes place directly on the suspension without the use of any intermediate linkage. The shock absorber comprises a cylindrical body formed by to coaxial tubes 14 and 15 (see **FIG 8:11**), the inner tube acting as the working cylinder and the outer one as a casing. The fluid reservoir being located between the two sections. A third outer cylinder 13 shields the rod 2 from any road dirt.

On the top the cylinder body is enclosed by a bush 11, oil seals 5 and 9 and a housing 4. The rod 2 slides through the seals 5, the upper end is fixed into the vehicle body floor and its lower end carries the piston 22 on which rebound 26 and inlet valves 21 are arranged.

The bottom of the shock absorber is closed by a plug 35 with a threaded shank 36 for the shock absorber to be mounted onto the suspension unit. The cylinder 15 and carrier plug 32 is mounted with a compensation valve 30 and a compression valve 33. The piston is provided with two rows of orifices. The internal row is blanked underneath by the rebound valve which operates downwards. The external row is blanked by the inlet valve which opens upwards. Hydraulic shock absorbers fitted since March 1959 are provided with a vapour pocket bleeder from the cylinder exterior. The bleeder device comprises a capillary hole 12 interconnecting the inner cylinder 15 with the upper chamber 10 and also a passage tube 16 from the upper chamber to the fluid reservoir. Any vapour pockets in the pressure cylinder are excluded past the capillary hole 12 into the chamber 10 from which they flow downwards during shock absorber operation through the passage 16 in a light fluid stream and up to the top of the reservoir with the reservoir fluid.

Dismantling and inspection:

Normally during service if a shock absorber becomes weak in operation then a new unit should be fitted. Should however, it be necessary for the original unit to be overhauled proceed as follows:

1 Thoroughly clean the outer casing in petrol and blow dry using a compressed air jet.
2 Firmly clamp the lower shank of the shock absorber in a vice and telescope upwards the outer casing and using Fiat wrench A.56024 unscrew the upper threaded ring 3 (see **FIG 8:11**).
3 Remove the shock absorber from the vice and carefully remove the inner cylinder 15 using a screwdriver inserted in the cylinder bottom chamfer and remove the lower plug 32 which carries the compression and compensation valves.
4 Push the rod into the cylinder 15 and clamp the upper shank in a vice. Unscrew the plug 29, and carefully remove the piston 22 together with the inlet and rebound valves. Withdraw the rod 2 from the cylinder 15 and remove the seal gasket, the housing, and threaded ring. Thoroughly wash all parts in petrol and carefully blow dry using a compressed air jet. The following parts should be inspected as follows. Check that the inlet, rebound and compensation valve discs are not deformed or show signs of cracking.

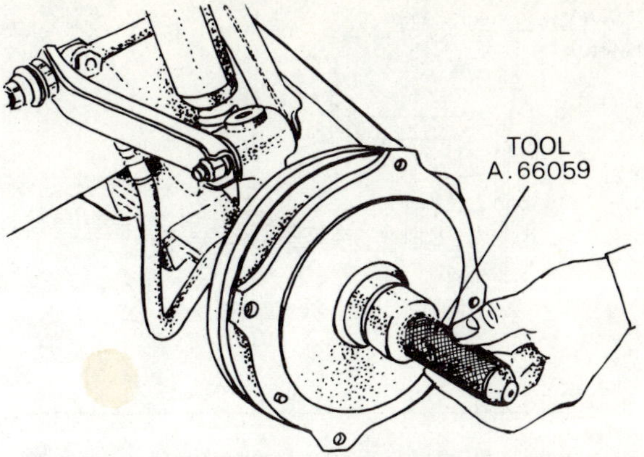

FIG 8:13 Installing right front wheel hub cap by tool **A.66059**

Inspect the surfaces of the piston, the seal ring and the compression valve to ensure that they are smooth and hydraulic fluid tight. Check that the rebound and compression valve springs and upper seal gasket springs are not broken or weak. Carefully inspect the two seal gaskets for damage or wear and it is recommended that they are renewed upon reassembly. Check that the rod and the cylinders show no sign of deformation and that the air pocket evacuating passage is not blocked. Also check that the capillary hole 12 is not blocked. Any parts which show signs of wear or damage must be renewed.

Reassembly:

Reassembly of the shock absorber is the reverse procedure to dismantling. Special care must be taken when refilling the shock absorber with Fiat SA1 oil otherwise its operating characteristics will be altered.

The hydraulic fluid capacity for the front shock absorbers is .112 imperial quarts.

The hydraulic capacity for the rear shock absorbers is .088 imperial quarts.

Only Fiat—SA1 oil must be used.

To insert the components into the shock absorber body proceed as follows:

1 Mount the piston on the rod, and insert the piston and rod assembly into the cylinder 15 (see **FIG 8:11**).
2 Push the piston against the bush 11 and then very carefully pour the correct amount of hydraulic fluid up to about $\frac{1}{2}$ inch from the edge.
3 Press fit the plug 32 and pour the remaining fluid into the casing 14.
4 Insert the cylinder 15 into the casing 14 and tighten the upper threaded ring 3.

8:8 Front suspension assembly and installation

1 Attach Fiat fixture A.66061 to the springs as shown in **FIG 8:12** and load it using the centre screw on the fixture until the index **'Nuova 500'** appears below the crossbeam lower edge. It is in this position the spring attains the full static load setting as on the

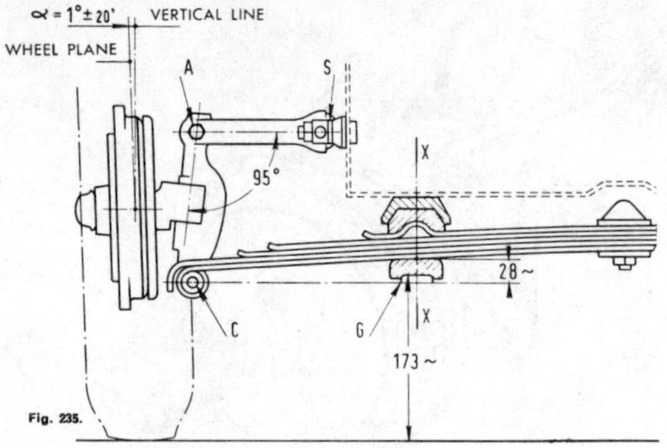

FIG 8:14 Swing arm setting

car. Ensure that the upper elastic supports on the studs projecting from the underside of the vehicle body are correctly located and insert the spring. Fit the two support lower caps with elastic pads and screw onto the stud nuts to a torque wrench setting of 28.9 lb/ft.

2 Assemble the brake housing flange onto the steering knuckle and tighten the nuts to a torque wrench setting of 14.5 lb/ft.

3 Assemble the roller bearings and seal onto the drum hub. Liberally pack the space between the two bearings with Fiat MR grease.

4 Replace the washer and nut securing the wheel hub to steering knuckle and tighten to a torque wrench setting of 21.7 lb/ft. Then slacken the nut by approximately 60 deg. and insert the cotter pin to steering knuckle opening. It should be noted that from vehicle number 043624 the right steering left steering knuckle is still threaded clockwise and identified by circular groove on the outside face. The steering knuckle nut is still threaded clockwise and has no identification mark. This modification was introduced as a preventative measure which already exists at lefthand steering knuckles to avoid the situation should the wheel bearings suddenly seize, the righthand steering knuckle nuts are dragged to lock the bearings and consequently the road wheels. This point should be noted when servicing front hubs so that the righthand steering knuckle nuts are not inadvertantly screwed outwards by counterclockwise rotation so causing excessive tightening of the nut.

4 Using Fiat tool A.66059 as shown in **FIG 8:13**, reassemble the cap to the hub. Also reassemble the steering knuckle to the kingpin housing replacing the two upper thrust rings, the snap ring and the lower packing ring whose thickness has already been selected as detailed in **Section 8:6** to take up any play between the knuckle and the kingpin housing. Secure the steering knuckle pin with the cotter.

5 Reconnect the swinging arm to the wheel assembly using the special nut and bolt. The nut must be screwed onto the bolt **A** (see **FIG 8:14**), by arranging the parts so that the angle between the arm plane and the kingpin housing is approximately 95 deg. as shown in **FIG 8:14.** Tighten the nut to a torque wrench setting of 39.8 lb/ft.

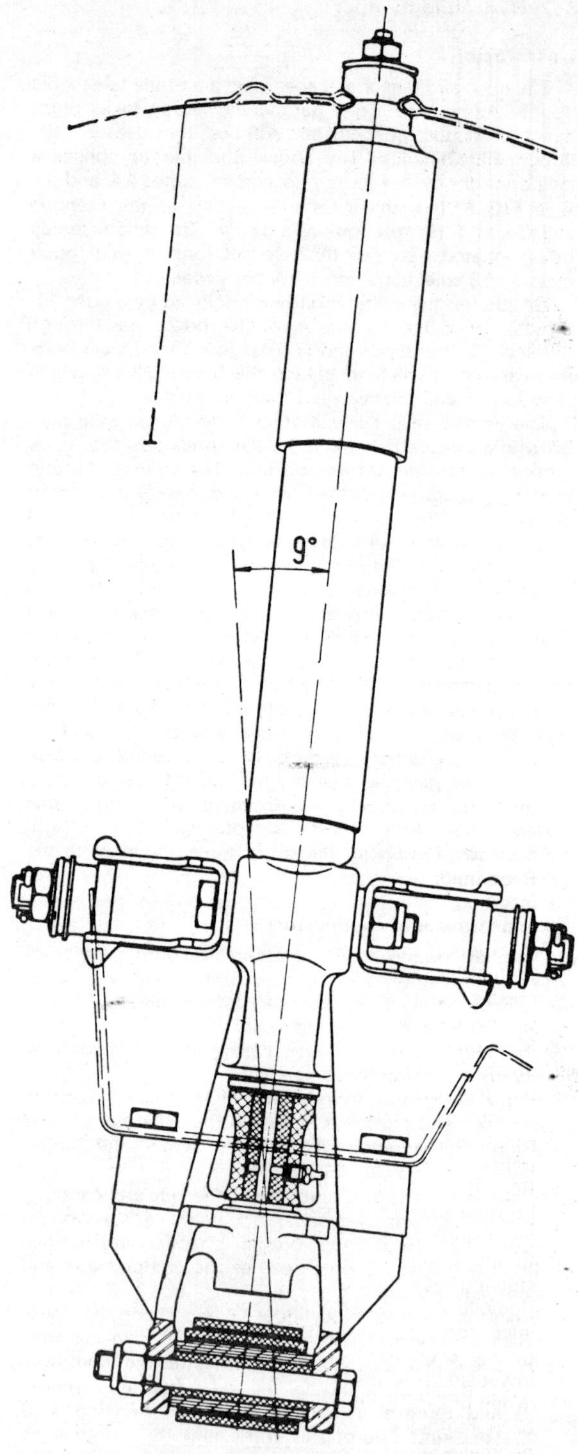

FIG 8:15 Section through steering knuckle and leaf spring mounting at kingpin

Key to Fig 8:15 (9° = Kingpin housing castor angle)

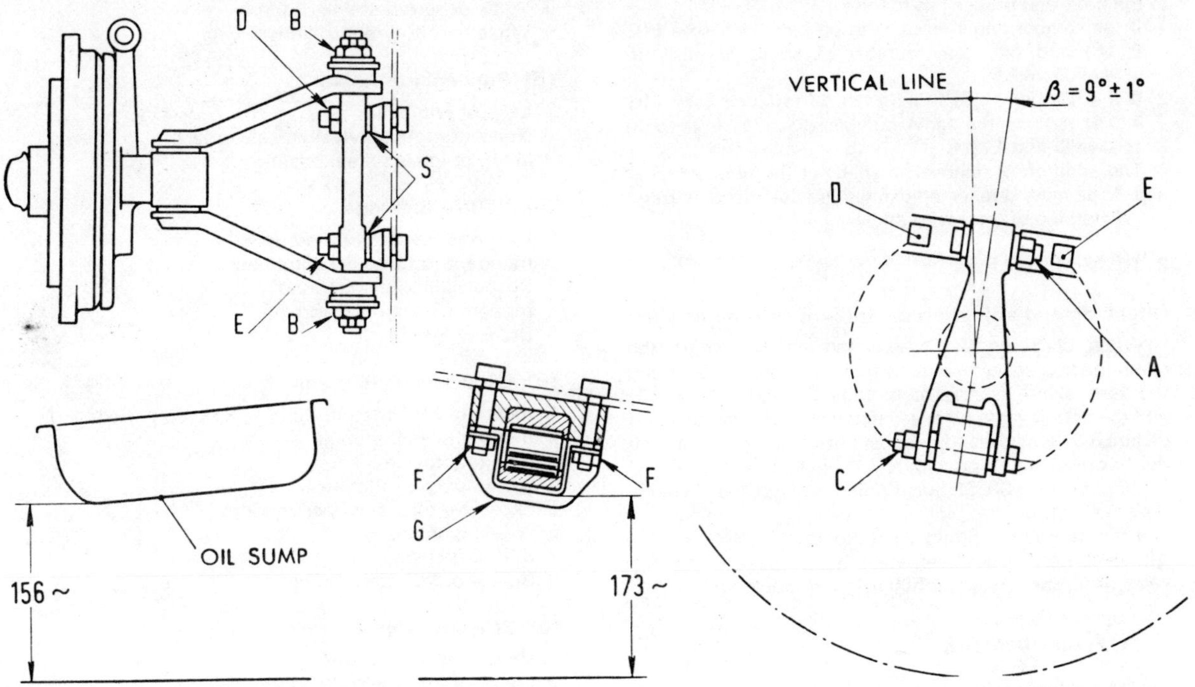

FIG 8:16 Castor, camber angles

6 Insert the swinging arm pin onto the two studs that are welded to the body sides so as to support the front suspension and wheel assembly.
7 Reconnect the kingpin housing to the spring eye by inserting the bolt and tightening the self-locking nut to a torque wrench setting of 28.9 lb/ft. It is important that during this operation the spring is always kept in the 'set' position by fixture A.66061 so as to ensure correct assembly and prevent excessive strain on the 'estendblocks'.
8 Slide off the swinging arm and insert the spacers and shims **S** (see **FIG 8:16**) onto the studs ensuring that the resulting thickness is the same as was found during dismantling. Reattach the swinging arm. Screw on the nuts securing the pin to the body and tighten to a torque wrench setting of 28.9 lb/ft.
9 Refit the shock absorber securing it to the kingpin housing and to the body inserting the plain washer between the rubber pad and the toothed washer.
10 Carefully remove Fiat fixture A.66061, connect the steering rods, hydraulic brake pipes and refit wheels. Remove the wooden plug from the brake fluid tank inlet opening. Carefully raise the vehicle using a garage hydraulic jack, remove the axle stands and lower slowly to the ground.
11 When both left- and righthand suspension units have been refitted to the vehicle the front end steering geometry must be checked and adjusted.

8:9 Steering geometry

Checking of the front wheel geometry is necessary if either excessive tyre wear or irregular steering performance is noticed or if the front suspension assembly has been dismantled for repair. The values for the front end setting under a normal static load normally considered to comprise four passengers should be as follows:

Camber angle — 1 deg. ± 20'
Castor angle — 9 deg. ± 1 deg.

The camber angle shown in **FIG 8:14** and the castor angle shown in **FIG 8:16** adjustments are performed by inserting shims **S** (see **FIG 8:16**) between the swinging arm pin and the spacers on the studs that are welded to the body at points **D** and **E** (see **FIG 8:16**). Shims .0197 inch thick are supplied in service to enable the castor and camber angles to be adjusted.

It is suggested that the castor and camber angles are checked at the local agents as specialised equipment is necessary for completion of these checks.

Adjustment of castor angle:

Slacken the two nuts securing the swinging arm pin to the body and proceed as follows:

1 If the castor angle requires to be increased (see **FIG 8:16**) move the shims **S** from the rear screw **E** to the front screw **D**.
2 If the castor angle requires to be reduced (see **FIG 8:16**) move the shims from the front screw **D** to the rear screw **E**.

Adjustment of camber angle:

Slacken the two nuts securing the swinging arm pin

to the body and proceed as follows:

1 If the camber angle requires to be increased (see **FIG 8:16**) add the same number of shims **S** on both screws **D** and **E.**
2 If the camber angle requires to be reduced (see **FIG 8:16**) remove the same number of shims from both screws **D** and **E.**

The addition or removal of shims at the two points **D** and **E** permits camber adjustment to be made without any disturbing of the castor angle.

8:10 Modifications

Checking and adjusting castor and camber angles:

When checking the castor and camber angle the static loading should be such that the distance between the semi-elliptic spring mountings **G** (see **FIG 8:16**) and the floor level to be approximately 6.81 inches, also a distance between the lowermost portion of the sump and the floor level of approximately 6.14 inch for the Model 500D. For the 500 Station Wagon version the distance between centre rear bracket for jacking-up the vehicle and the floor level should be approximately 8.90 inches. All other front wheel alignment specifications are the same as for the remaining 500 saloon models.

8:11 Fault diagnosis

(a) Wheel bounce

1 Tyre casing faulty
2 Uneven tyre pressures
3 Wheels out of balance
4 Semi-elliptic mounting spring worn
5 Weak or seized shock absorber
6 Wheel rim or tyre misaligned

(b) Suspension noise

1 Lack of lubrication
2 Noisy or inoperative shock absorbers
3 Worn or loose wheel bearings

(c) Pull to one side

1 Low or uneven tyre pressures
2 Incorrect front wheel alignment
3 Suspension arms distorted
4 Inoperative shock absorbers
5 Brakes binding

(d) Excessive tyre wear

1 Incorrect tyre rotation during servicing periods
2 Incorrect camber angle
3 Incorrect toe-in
4 Incorrect tyre inflation
5 Excessive play at wheel bearings
6 Wheel wobble
7 Stiff suspension arms
8 Brakes out of adjustment

(e) Wheel wobble

1 Uneven tyre pressures
2 Loose or worn wheel bearings
3 Inoperative shock absorbers
4 Loose steering knuckle or kingpin housing
5 Incorrect front wheel alignment
6 Control arm rubber bushings, or kingpin housing and semi-elliptic spring 'estendblock' worn

CHAPTER 9

THE STEERING SYSTEM

9:1 Description

The steering gear fitted to the new 500 range of vehicles is of the worm screw and sector type with a steering ratio of 1:13. The steering gearbox is located on the front lefthand side of the dash wall on the scuttle as shown in **FIG 9:1.** The steering gear comprises a pitman arm and relay lever pivoting on a pin supported on the body. A central track rod connects the pitman arm to the relay lever. Two track rods connect the pitman arm and relay lever to the knuckle arms.

9:2 Steering wheel removal and refitting

To remove the steering wheel proceed as follows:

1 Disconnect the battery positive terminal clamp and remove the horn control from the steering wheel.

2 Remove the cable from the push button seating and the cable insulation sleeve.

3 Using a suitably sized box spanner or Fiat wrench A.8279 unscrew the steering wheel to shaft nut as shown in **FIG 9:2.**

4 Using the palm of the hands against the back of the steering wheel rim gently tap the steering wheel forwards so releasing it from the inner shaft.

5 Reassembly is the reverse procedure to dismantling. Care should be taken to ensure that the front wheels are located in the straight ahead position when the steering wheel is being replaced otherwise the steering wheel spokes will not be correctly positioned.

9:3 Steering box removal and refitting

To remove the steering box from the vehicle proceed as follows:

1 From inside the vehicle remove the steering shaft worm screw mounting nut 8 (see **FIG 9:3**) and remove the lockwasher 7 and bolt 6.

2 From the underside of the vehicle remove the two tie rod locking nuts from the pitman arm and then using Fiat tool A.46006 or a suitable two leg puller withdraw the pins from the seats.

3 Remove the three nuts holding the steering box to the body panel. Ease out the worm screw from the steering shaft and lift away the steering box.

4 To refit the steering box is the reverse procedure to dismantling. The steering box to body mounting nuts should be tightened to a torque wrench setting of 14 lb/ft to 18 lb/ft.

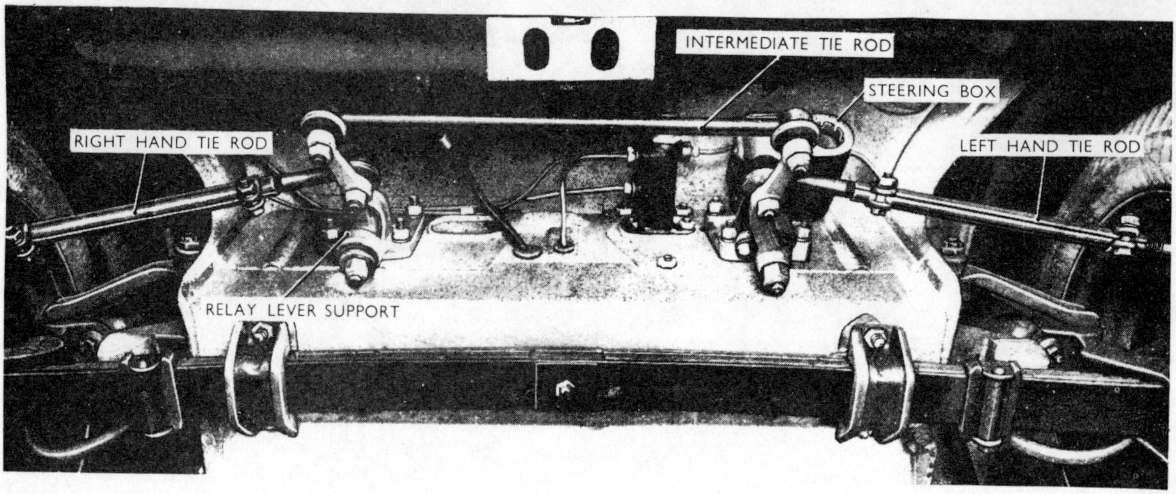

FIG 9 : 1 **Steering box, idler member and steering linkage arrangement on vehicle**

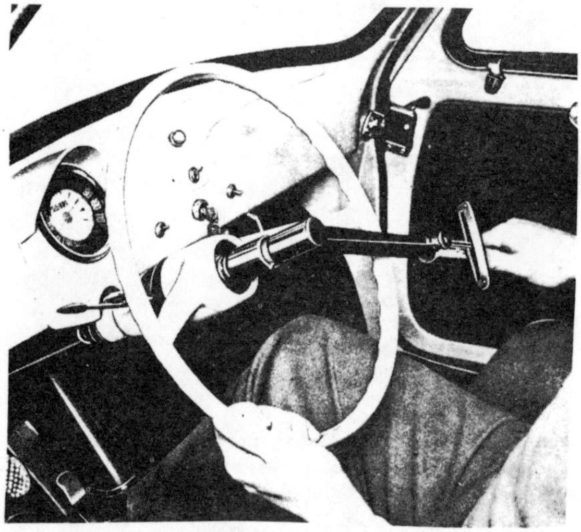

FIG 9 : 2 **Securing steering wheel mounting nut**

Key to Fig 9 : 2 (Tightening torque: 29 to 36 lb ft)

9 : 4 Steering box dismantling and reassembly

1 Remove the steering gear housing cover complete with the adjusting screw and locking nut and drain the oil from the unit.

2 Using Fiat puller A.4005.1.5 or a universal two leg puller remove the pitman arm.

3 Remove the cotter pin from the lower thrust bearing adjusting nut and unscrew this nut.

4 Remove the sealing ring at the sector shaft lower end and using Fiat tool A.8065 loosen the eccentric bush adjuster plate bolt and remove both the bolt and the adjusting plate. Also remove the upper sealing ring.

5 Lift out the sector together with the upper thrust washer and shims.

6 Remove the steering worm screw by pulling out from below. The two bearing inner rings will remain on the worm screw whilst the lower bearing outer ring will remain in the housing.

7 Remove the oil seal using Fiat tool A.10110 followed by the worm screw upper bearing outer ring using Fiat tool A.66040 or a suitably sized drift.

Inspection:

1 Carefully inspect the sector teeth and the worm screw threads to see that there are no signs of seizure, indentations or scoring. Check that the contact faces indicate that meshing between the two parts is taking place at the centre.

2 Check the clearance between the eccentric bush 5 (see **FIG 9 : 5**) and the worm sector 11 which must not exceed .0039 inch. These items have an initial assembly clearance of .00 to .0016 inch. It should be noted that if the eccentric bushing to sector shaft clearance exceeds .0039 inch a new bushing should be installed and its inner face reamed using Fiat reamer U.0360.20.

3 Ensure that the worm screw is not distorted. The permissible out of true is .0019 inch.

Adjustment:

1 If the backlash between the worm screw and the sector is excessive it should be adjusted by first disconnecting the pitman arm and its relevant seal. Remove the screw 7 (see **FIG 9 : 5**) fixing the abutment plate 6. Rotate the eccentric bush 5 by the adjustment plate and move the sector in towards the worm screw. The adjustment plate should be secured again using the second fixing hole.

Should the adjustment plate already be fixed in the second hole remove the plate from the bush and rotate one or more serrations and re-secure.

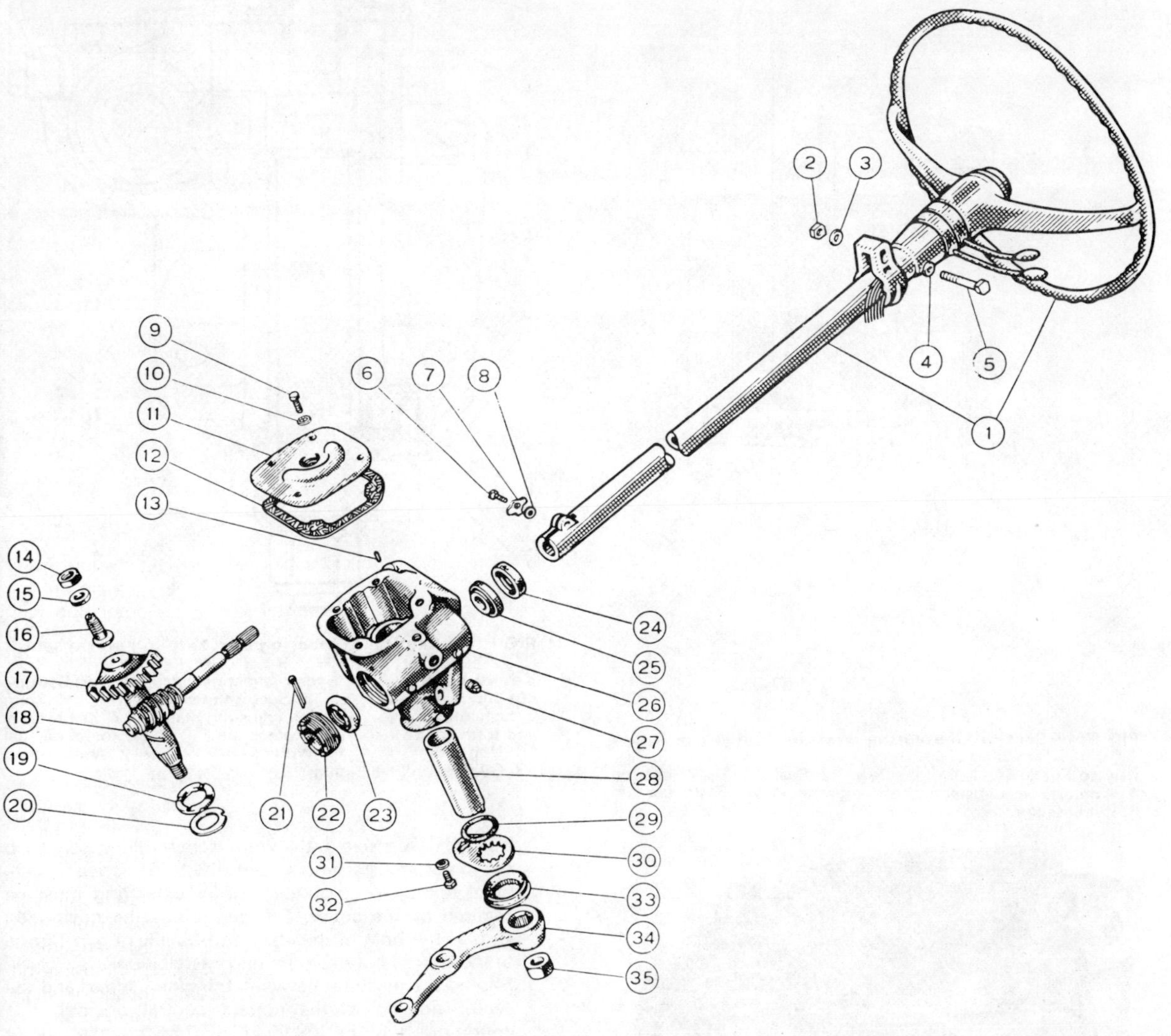

FIG 9 : 3 Layout of steering gear components

Key to Fig 9 : 3 1 Steering wheel and column assembly 2 Nut 3 Toothed washer 4 Plain washer 5 Steering column bracket-to-instrument panel screw 6 Steering column-to-worm screw locking screw 7 Lockplate 8 Plain washer 9 Cover screw 10 Toothed washer 11 Cover 12 Gasket 13 Pin 14 Nut 15 Plain washer 16 Worm sector adjusting screw 17 Worm sector and shaft assembly 18 Worm screw 19 Thrust washer 20 Shim 21 Splitpin 22 Lower sleeve, bearing retainer and worm screw adjuster 23 Roller bearing 24 Worm screw bearing upper seal 25 Roller bearing 26 Steering gear housing 27 Oil filling and draining plug 28 Eccentric bushing 29 Upper seal 30 Worm screw-to-sector lash adjusting plate 31 Toothed washer 32 Plate screw 33 Lower seal 34 Pitman arm 35 Self-locking nut

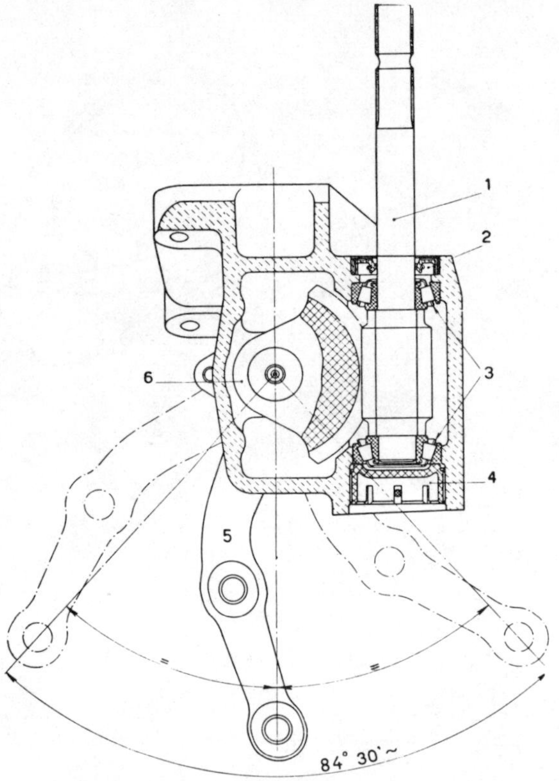

FIG 9:4 Section of steering box, through worm screw

Key to Fig 9:4 1 Worm screw 2 Seal 3 Roller bearing 4 Worm screw adjuster and bearing retainer 5 Pitman arm 6 Worm sector

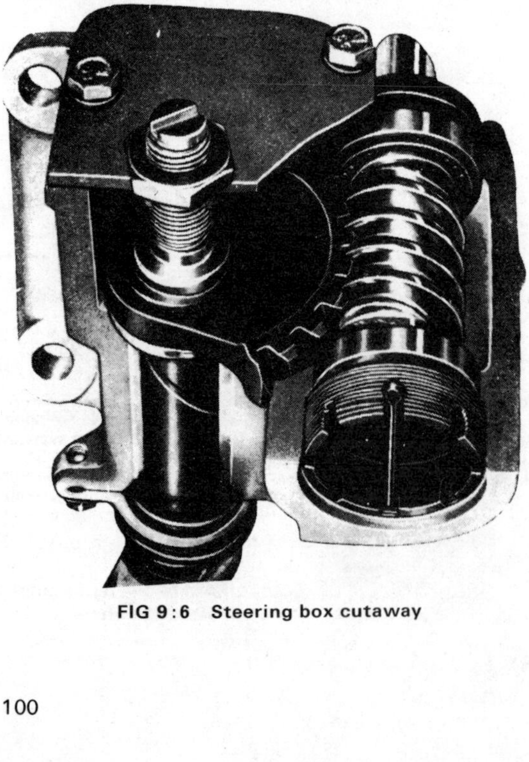

FIG 9:6 Steering box cutaway

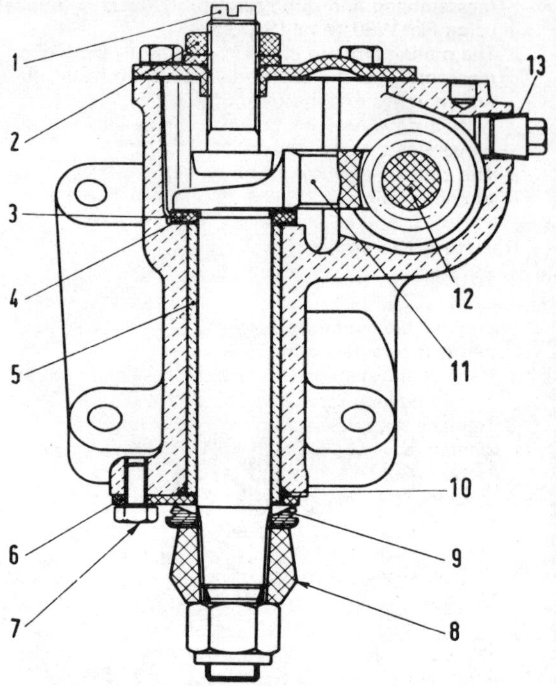

FIG 9:5 Section of steering box, through worm sector

Key to Fig 9:5 1 Sector adjustment screw 2 Locking nut and plain washer 3 Sector thrust washer 4 Shim 5 Eccentric bush 6 Bush adjusting plate 7 Plate screw and toothed washer 8 Pitman arm 9 Sector lower seal 10 Upper seal 11 Worm sector 12 Worm screw 13 Oil filler and level plug

2 If play is excessive in the worm screw rollers, screw up the lower adjuster ring 4 (see **FIG 9:5**). Once adjustment has been completed the adjuster ring must be secured by the cotter. The ring should be positioned so that the hole in the steering box lines up with one of the spaces between the ring castellations.

3 Should the meshing between the worm screw and the sector not be at the correct central position this condition may be rectified by moving the sector axially. To do this add or remove shims (see **FIG 9:5**) below the thrust ring of the worm sector. The final adjustment must be carried out by using the adjustment screw 1 (see **FIG 9:5**) on the cover and then locking the screw by nuts 2. In service shims are supplied .0039 inch thick.

The above described adjustments must eliminate any play and back lash in the steering gear without rendering the steering gear stiff to operate between the two locks.

4 During adjustment should any seal be found to be damaged then it should be renewed.

Reassembly:

Reassembly is the reverse procedure to dismantling but the following points should be noted:

1 All parts should be thoroughly cleaned before

reassembling and during assembly liberally lubricated using Fiat W90/M oil (SAE90 BP).

2 The pitman arm nut should be correctly positioned on reassembly to the sector shaft and both are marked with notches or a master tooth on the sector will mate with a double tooth on the pitman arm which will prevent incorrect reassembly.

3 The pitman arm nut must be tightened to a torque wrench setting of 72 lb/ft.

Refitting the steering box:

To refit the steering box to the vehicle proceed as follows:

1 Engage the worm screw from the steering shaft by gently manipulating the steering box.

2 Replace the steering box to body nuts and tighten to a torque wrench setting of 14 to 18 lb/ft.

3 Replace the two track rod pins in their seatings in the pitman arm and tighten the self-locking nuts to a torque wrench setting of 18 to 21 lb/ft.

4 Replace the steering shaft to worm screw mounting bolt, lock washer and nut.

9:5 Relay lever and support

The steering idler arm is secured to the body by means of a support bracket and a rubber bushed pivot bolt. This is shown in **FIG 9:7.** When this unit is being serviced the following points should be noted.

1 If there is excessive play between the pin and the bushes the bushes must be renewed. Also check the condition of the pin and if there are signs of excessive wear it must be renewed.

2 To eliminate torsional stresses in the rubber bushes during assembly the pin nut must be tightened to torque wrench setting of 39 to 43 lb/ft, once the front wheel toe-in has been correctly adjusted with the wheels set in the straight ahead position.

3 The relay lever support to body mounting nuts must be tightened to a torque wrench setting of 14 to 18 lb/ft.

9:6 Steering rods

The steering rod is connected to the idler arm and the drop arm by means of non-adjustable ball joints. The track rods are connected to the right and left steering arms by non-adjustable ball joints and comprise two sleeves which are split and having internally threaded ends. The ball joints are clamped to either end of the sleeves. To facilitate adjustment one ball joint end has a lefthand thread and the other a righthand thread. Adjustment is made by loosening both the clamping bolts and turning the central sleeve.

The intermediate steering rod is a single piece with a non-adjustable ball joint at either end.

To remove the steering rods from the pitman arm, the relay lever and knuckle arms Fiat pullers A.46006 and A.6473 or universal ball joint removers should be used.

If excessive play is evident in the ball joint linkage or the pin is damaged the complete ball joint assembly must be renewed.

Upon reassembly the tie rod to ball pin knuckle arm nuts must be tightened to a torque wrench setting of 18 to 21 lb/ft.

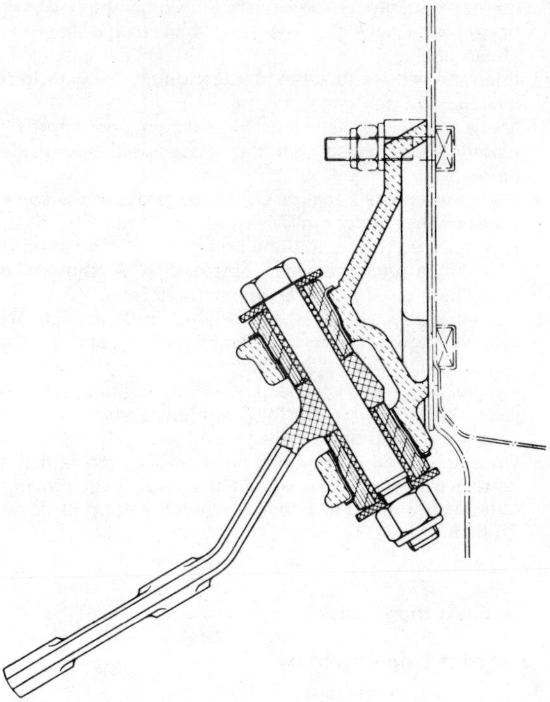

FIG 9:7 Relay lever support section

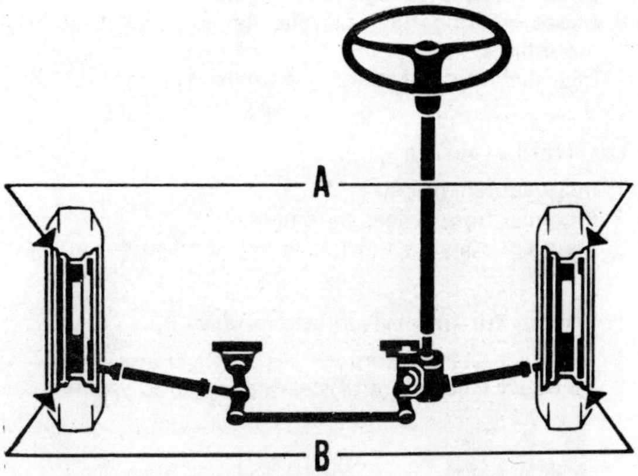

FIG 9:8 Front wheel toe-in checking diagram

Key to Fig 9:8 A—B =.000 inch to .079 inch

It is important that all steering linkages are thoroughly checked at regular intervals and if any parts are suspect then they must be renewed.

9:7 Front wheel toe-in

To check and adjust the front wheel toe-in proceed as follows:

1 Ensure that the tyres are inflated to the recommended pressures. Ensure that the steering wheel is in its

normal straight-ahead position with the spokes horizontal. Check that the wheels are in the straight-ahead position.

2 Load the vehicle to static load conditions or with four average size passengers.

3 Move the vehicle forwards for a distance of approximately six yards so that the suspension may settle correctly.

4 The toe-in measurements should be taken at the same point of the wheel rim. Measure at **A** (see **FIG 9:8**) then back up the car to bring points **A** to the position **B** and remeasure. The value obtained at **A** should be equal to or greater than **B** within .0079 inch.

5 As previously described the steering rods are adjustable in length. Loosen the clamps and screw in or out the adjusting sleeves and before tightening the clamp ensure that the sleeve slot registers with the clamp joint. With the clamp fully tightened there should always be a gap between the joint faces.

6 Once the steering gear has been re-installed and the correct front wheel toe-in set the relay lever pin nut must be tightened to a torque wrench setting of 78 to 85 lb/ft.

9:8 Fault diagnosis

(a) Front wheel shimmy

1 Incorrect tyre pressure
2 Incorrect front wheel alignment
3 Loose front wheel bearings
4 Wheels out of balance
5 Loose steering linkage connections
6 Loose steering gear or relay lever support at body mountings
7 Incorrect fitting of steering worm to worm sector

(b) Hard steering

1 Incorrect tyre pressure
2 Incorrect front wheel alignment
3 Incorrect adjustment of steering worm to worm sector

(c) Hard turning when stationary

1 Incorrect tyre pressure
2 Incorrect adjustment of steering worm to worm sector

(d) Pull to one side

1 Incorrect tyre pressure
2 Incorrect front wheel alignment
3 Incorrect front wheel bearing adjustment
4 Distorted kingpin housing or swinging arms
5 Unequal brake adjustment
6 Semi-elliptic spring weak or broken

(e) Rattles

1 Loose steering linkage connections
2 Loose steering gear or relay lever support at body mountings
3 Semi-elliptic spring weak or broken
4 Lack of lubrication

(f) Loose steering

1 Incorrect front wheel bearing adjustment
2 Loose steering linkage connections
3 Loose steering gear mountings
4 Incorrect adjustment of steering worm to worm sector

(g) Jerky steering

1 Incorrect front wheel alignment
2 Incorrect front wheel bearing adjustment
3 Wheels out of balance
4 Loose steering linkage connections
5 Loose or incorrect fitting of worm to sector

(h) Side-to-side wander

1 Incorrect tyre pressure
2 Incorrect front wheel alignment
3 Loose steering linkage connections
4 Loose steering gear or relay lever support at body mountings
5 Incorrect fitting of steering worm to worm sector
6 Distorted kingpin housing or swinging arm
7 Semi-elliptic spring weak or broken

(i) Tyre squeal on turns

1 Incorrect tyre pressure
2 Incorrect wheel alignment
3 Distorted kingpin housing or swinging arms

CHAPTER 10

THE BRAKING SYSTEM

10:1 Description

All four drum brake units are hydraulically operated by the brake pedal and the handbrake lever operates the rear brakes only through a mechanical linkage which normally requires no separate adjustment (see **FIG 10:1**).

The brake units are of the internal expanding type with one leading and one trailing shoe to each brake. A double ended wheel cylinder expands both shoes into contact with the drum under hydraulic pressure from the master cylinder. When the brake pedal pressure is released the shoes are retracted by means of springs.

The brake pedal is directly coupled to the hydraulic master cylinder where pressure on the fluid is generated. This is transmitted to the brakes by a system of metal and flexible pipes.

The braking units fitted to the new 500 Sedan models are equipped with a specially designed brake shoe clearance self-adjustment device which eliminates the need for manual adjustment of the brake shoe to drum clearance as is normal practice with a conventional braking system. Every time the brake pedal is depressed the self-adjustment device automatically takes up the excess clearance which may have developed between the lining and the drum due to normal service wear.

The brake units fitted to the 500 Station wagon model have a normal brake adjuster which should be used when the brake pedal travel becomes excessive. The adjuster is shown in **FIG 10:5**.

10:2 Maintenance

Brake adjustment (Station Wagon):

Jack each wheel in turn after first chocking the remaining three wheels and releasing the handbrake. Depress the brake pedal so as to force the brake shoes against the drum and keeping the shoes in this position turn the adjuster nuts until they contact the shoes and then back the nuts 20 deg. This will correctly set the shoe to drum clearance which should be checked for binding by releasing the brake pedal and ensuring that the road wheel revolves freely. The operation should then be repeated on the other wheel. This adjustment will automatically set the handbrake.

Preventative maintenance:

1 Thoroughly inspect the metal hydraulic fluid lines for rusting, cracking or flattening and that they are located away from any sharp edges which could cause a failure.

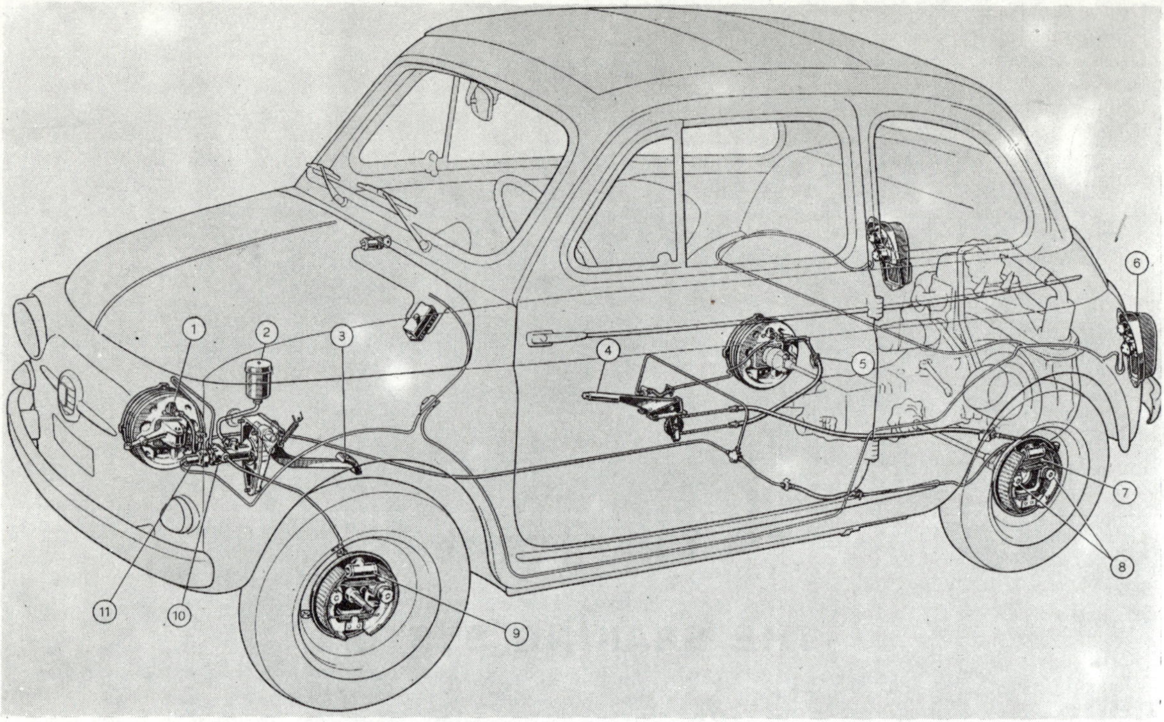

FIG 10:1 Diagrammatic view of service and rear wheel parking brake system

Key to Fig 10:1 1 Brake fluid reservoir 2 Bleeder connections 3 Service brake pedal 4 Hand lever, mechanical parking brake on rear wheels 5 Hand lever travel adjustment stretchers 6 Stop lamps 7 Mechanical brake operating lever, controlled from lever 4 8 Shoe clearance self-adjusting device 9 Wheel cylinders 10 Master cylinder 11 Stop light pressure-operated switch

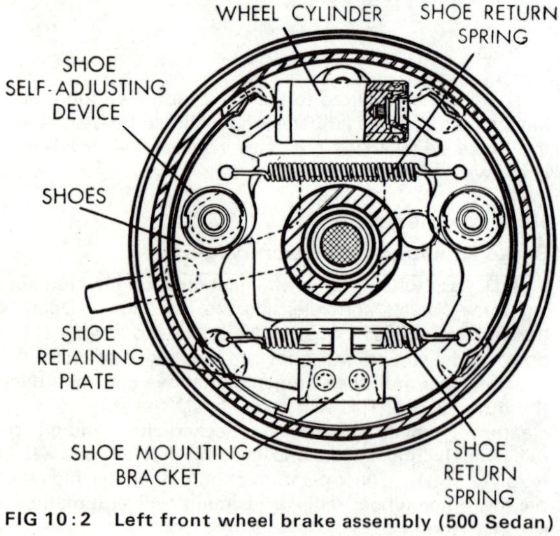

FIG 10:2 Left front wheel brake assembly (500 Sedan)

2 Check that the hydraulic flexible hoses are not contaminated with oil or grease which would destroy the rubber.
3 Ensure that all pipeline fastening clips are secure otherwise hydraulic line failure could occur due to cracking caused by excessive vibration.
4 Carefully clean all connections and inspect for hydraulic fluid leaks. Should any leaks be detected then the connections should be tightened taking very great care not to twist the pipes during this operation.
5 Ensure that the hydraulic fluid level in the reservoir is correctly filled up to the top of the filter using Fiat special 'Blue Label' brake fluid. Extra care must be taken to ensure that no fluid is spilled over the body paintwork, as this acts as a strong solvent.
6 Ensure that the play between the brake pedal pushrod and the master cylinder plunger is .019 inch. This will correspond to approximately .098 inch free pedal travel.

Never use any fluid but the recommended hydraulic fluid. Do not leave it in unsealed containers as it will absorb moisture which can be dangerous. It is best to discard fluid drained from the system or after a bleeding operation. Observe absolute cleanliness when working on all parts of the hydraulic system.

10:3 Front brakes

Front brake drum removal:

1 Remove the wheel trims and carefully slacken the road wheel retaining bolts. Using a garage hydraulic jack raise the front of the vehicle and place on firmly based stands. Remove the road wheels.

2 Using Fiat puller A.46023 as shown in **FIG 8:9** remove the wheel grease cap.
3 Using a universal two leg puller or Fiat puller A.40005 together with items 1 and 9 remove the wheel hub/drum assembly having first extracted the splitpin and released the hub retaining nut (see **FIG 8:10**).

Dismantling brake unit:

1 Using a compressed air jet thoroughly clean all components of the brake assembly.
2 Make a note of the location of the shoe return springs and gently ease the shoes away from the brake backplate (see **FIG 10:2**).
3 Disconnect the hydraulic line from the rear of the wheel cylinder and remove the two cylinder retaining bolts. Lift away the hydraulic cylinder.

Brake shoe lining:

Check the lining thickness and if found to be excessively reduced service replacement shoes must be fitted. The minimum allowable brake lining thickness is .059 inch.

Thoroughly check the linings for signs of oil or grease which, if evident, the shoes must be renewed and the drums and oil seals thoroughly inspected for the cause of oil ingress and the cause remedied before reassembly. Do not fit odd brake shoes and do not mix materials or unbalanced braking will result.

Do not allow grease, oil or paint to contact the friction linings.

Brake drums:

Whilst servicing the brakes, thoroughly inspect the drums for scoring, ovality or distortion as well as inspecting for minute hair line cracks. The drums may be refaced by using a centre lathe and finally finishing by lapping the drums to smooth out possible tool marks. The maximum permissible oversize beyond the nominal drum diameter of 6.702 to 6.712 inch is .039 inch. This limit must never be exceeded otherwise the strength of the drum will be impaired or a reduction in braking efficiency caused by the increase of shoe expansion travel and the consequent diminished contact pressure.

No brake adjustment will be required on the new 500 Saloon models after the drum has been reassembled as the self-adjusting device will accommodate for the shoe position to the new drum diameter during the first operation of the brake pedal.

Reassembly of front brakes:

This is the reverse procedure to dismantling. Ensure that the pull-off springs are correctly fitted to the holes in the webs of the brake shoes and that the shoes register correctly in the slotted ends of the pistons and the side mounting plate.

Upon assembly of the hub and brake drum assembly liberally pack the space between the two bearings with Fiat MR grease, replace the washer and nut securing the wheel hub to steering knuckle and tighten to a torque wrench setting of 21 lb ft. Then slacken the nut by approximately 60 deg. and insert the cotter pin to steering knuckle to opening.

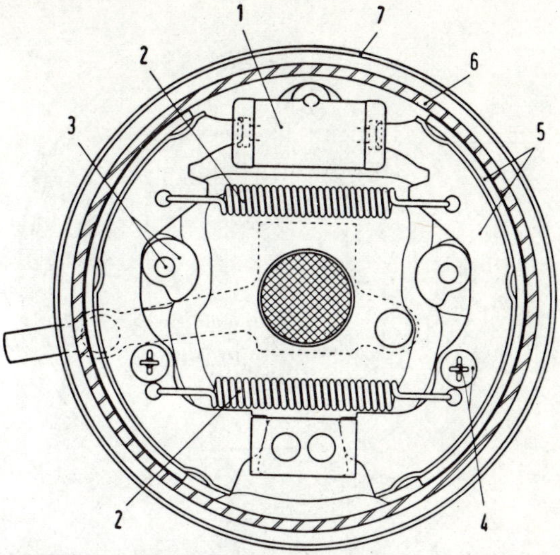

FIG 10:3 Section view of left side front brake assembly (500 Station Wagon)

Key to Fig 10:3 1 Wheel cylinder 2 Shoe return spring 3 Adjusting cams 4 Shoe guide pin 5 Shoe with lining 6 Drum 7 Housing flange

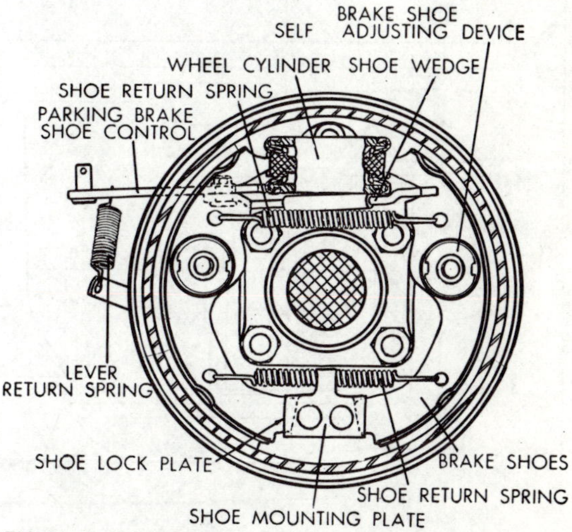

FIG 10:4 Right rear wheel brake assembly (500 Sedan)

10:4 Rear brakes

Rear brake drum removal:

1 Remove the wheel trims and carefully slacken the road wheel retaining bolts. Using a garage hydraulic jack raise the rear of the vehicle and place on firmly based stands. Remove the road wheels.
2 Remove the four drum to hub retaining bolts and spring washers and carefully withdraw the drum from the backplate assembly.

Dismantling brake unit:

1 Using a compressed air jet thoroughly clean all components of the brake assembly.

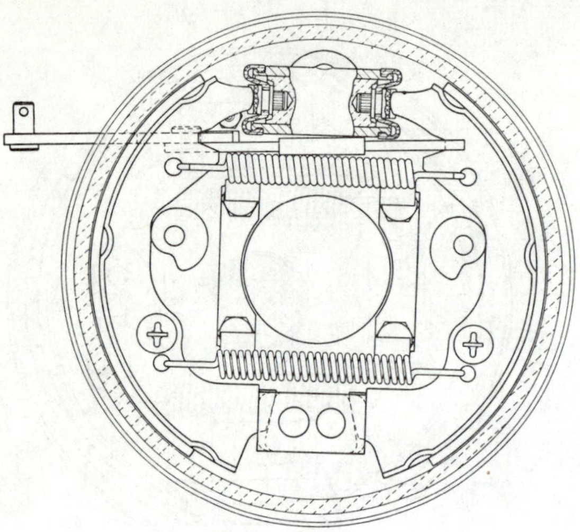

FIG 10:5 **Section view of right side rear brake assembly (500 Station Wagon)**

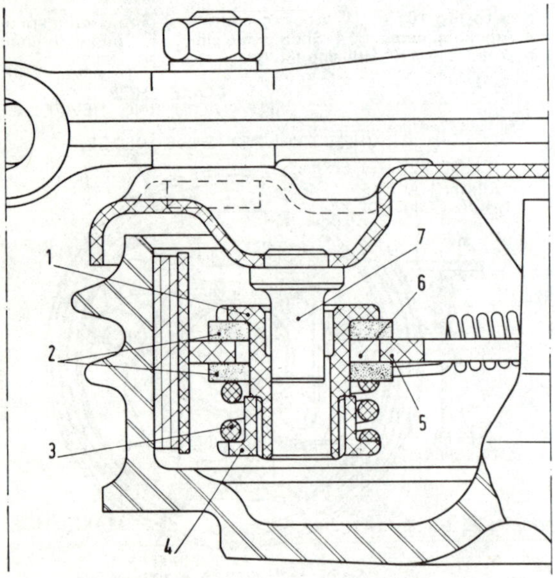

FIG 10:6 Sectional view of a self-adjusting device for automatic brake shoe-to-drum clearance take-up (500 Sedan)

Key to Fig 10:6 1 Pin 2 Friction washers 3 Load spring 4 Bushing 5 Shoe 6 Self-adjustment slot 7 Stud

2 Make a note of the location of the shoe return springs and gently ease the shoes away from the backplate (see **FIG 10:4**).

3 Disconnect the hydraulic line from the rear of the wheel cylinder and also the shoe operating lever return spring, the pin, washer and clevis from the lever so releasing the handbrake inner operating cable.

4 Remove the two cylinder retaining bolts and lift away the hydraulic cylinder.

Brake shoe linings:

Refer to **Section 10:3.**

Brake drums:

Refer to **Section 10:3.**

Reassembly of rear brakes:

This is the reverse procedure to dismantling. Ensure that the pull-off springs are correctly fitted to the holes in the webs of the brake shoes and that the shoes register in the slotted ends of the pistons and the side mounting plate.

Carefully retract the position of the brake shoes and ease the drum towards the hub ensuring that the four bolt holes line up correctly. Replace the four bolts together with their spring washers, reconnect the hand brake cable. Refit road wheel and wheel trim.

10:5 Master cylinder

Operation:

Hydraulic fluid is admitted to the master cylinder through hole 8 (see **FIG 10:7**), it seeps through the gap between the valve carrier ring 17 and the master cylinder dowel and flows through the valve carrier ring holes 15 so reaching the hydraulic lines, therefore filling the system with fluid. When the brake pedal is depressed the plunger is moved forwards by the pushrod 12. This forward action of the plunger 9 and valve carrier 17 brings the valve 16 to rest against the valve front face. The forward movement is continued so causing the valve ring 16 to pass over the compensation hole 5 and cutting off communication with the fluid reservoirs. From this point compression of the hydraulic fluid commences.

Hydraulic fluid acting on the front and inner faces of the valve enables perfect valve sealing even under high operation pressures. When the pressure reaches the fluid in the wheel cylinders (see **FIG 10:8**), it forces the plungers 3 apart and through the plungers stems so operating the brake shoes.

After releasing the brake pedal, the combined action of the brake shoe and master cylinder plunger return springs sends the fluid back to the master cylinder and all parts resume their original position. The connection between the hydraulic system and the reservoir is restored.

As there are no conventional valves fitted in the master cylinder and the communication orifice between the system and the reservoir is amply dimensioned the bleeding operation is very straightforward.

Master cylinder removal:

1 Disconnect the stoplight cables from the pressure operated switch.

2 Using a tapered wood plug of suitable size blank the hole in the brake fluid reservoir.

3 Screw out the four front and rear cylinder brake fluid delivery line connections at the master cylinder.

4 Remove the two master cylinder retaining nuts and spring washers and carefully ease the hydraulic cylinder from the body.

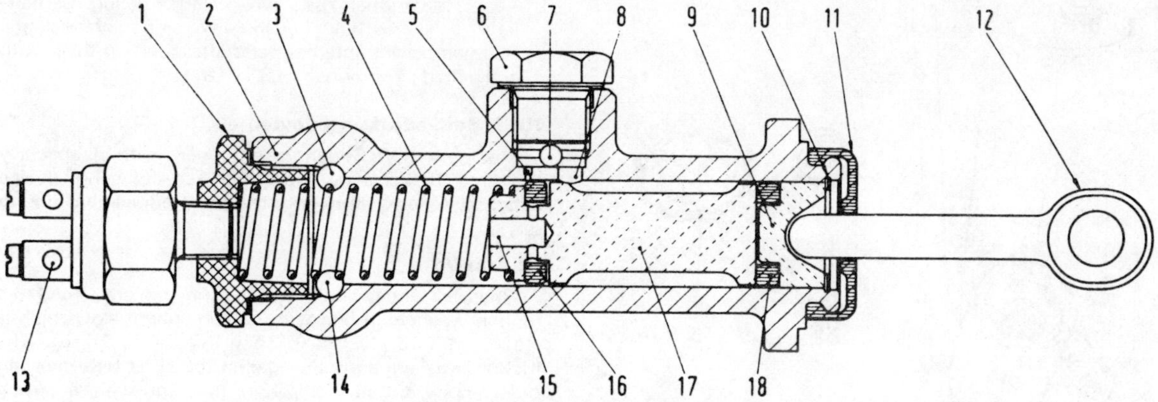

FIG 10:7 Master cylinder section

Key to Fig 10:7 1 Plug and spring seat 2 Body 3 Front wheel brake line duct 4 Plunger return spring 5 Compensating hole 6 Plug 7 Supply duct 8 Fluid inlet hole 9 Plunger 10 Plunger snap ring 11 Boot 12 Pushrod 13 Terminal, stoplight switch 14 Rear wheel brake line duct 15 Holes in floating ring carrier for fluid passage 16 Valve 17 Valve carrier 18 Valve 19 and 20 Connection and line from brake fluid reservoir 21 and 22 Lines and connections for front wheel brakes 23 and 24 Lines and connection for rear wheel brakes

Dismantling master cylinder:

1 Refer to **FIG 10:7** and remove the plunger and rubber boot from the cylinder body.
2 Using a pair of circlip pliers remove the plunger circlip.
3 Carefully slide off from the inside of the cylinder body the plunger, plunger seal, valve ring carrier, valve ring and the reaction spring.
4 Remove the stoplight pressure operated switch.
5 Remove the cylinder body stop plug and upper plug.
6 Carefully inspect the master cylinder inner surface and plunger outer surface to ensure that they have a mirror-like finish and that the play between the two parts is not excessive. Any roughness present on the cylinder inner surface may be very carefully removed using a fine oil stone. Great care must be taken when removing any roughness so that the diameter of the cylinder is not altered otherwise a hydraulic fluid leak could result. If there is any doubt the cylinder body must be renewed. Inspect the plunger return spring to ensure that it shows no sign of weakness or cracking.

Master cylinder reassembly:

1 Clean all the rubber parts in methylated spirits or correct hydraulic fluid. Any solvents used to clean metal parts must be completely dried off.
2 Renew all rubber seals when reassembling, particularly if there have been any signs of leakage. Reassemble the internal parts after wetting them with brake fluid as shown in **FIG 10:7.**

Refitting the master cylinder:

Carefully locate the master cylinder flange to the body panel ensuring that the pushrod 12 (see **FIG 10:7**) correctly locates in the plunger 9. Secure the master cylinder flange using the two nuts and spring washers. Refit the hydraulic pipes.

Remove the tapered wooden plug from the reservoir and bleed the system as described in **Section 10:10.**

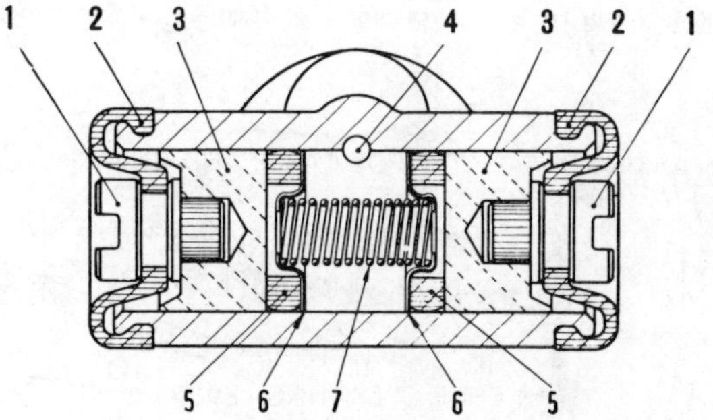

FIG 10:8 Wheel cylinder section

Key to Fig 10:8 1 Shoe actuating stems 2 Boot 3 Plungers 4 Fluid inlet hole 5 Seal rings 6 and 7 Spring thrust cups and plunger reaction spring

Apply the brakes hard for several minutes and inspect the master cylinder and hydraulic connections for leaks.

10:6 Wheel cylinder operation

Hydraulic pressure from the master cylinder reaches the fluid in the wheel cylinders by hydraulic pipes and it forces the plungers 3 (see **FIG 10:8**) apart and through the plungers the brake shoes operate. In the wheel cylinders the sealing rings 5 are axially compressed by the cup 6 under the action of the spring 7. The rings are under the radial and axial action of hydraulic pressure so that their sealing efficiency is increased as the hydraulic pressure increases.

Checking wheel cylinders:

Once the wheel cylinders have been removed from the brake backplate as previously described remove the rubber boots 2 (see **FIG 10:8**) on the ends of the cylinder. The plungers, brake shoe stems and sealing rings will be pushed out due to normal spring expansion. Remove the spring thrust cups and plunger reaction spring.

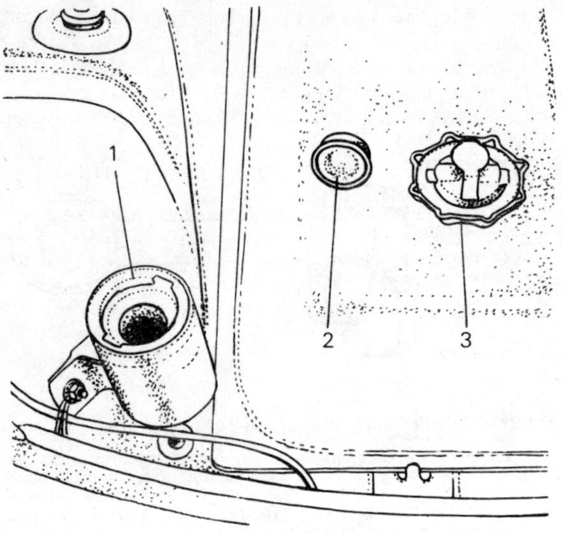

FIG 10:9 Brake fluid reservoir

Key to Fig 10:9 1 Reservoir 2 Strainer 3 Cap, vented

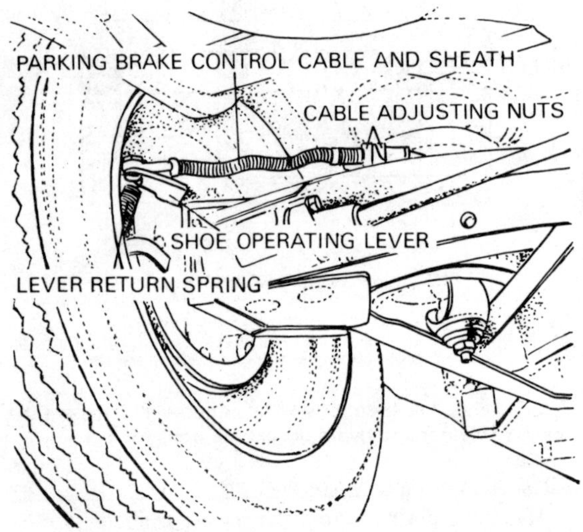

FIG 10:10 Parking brake control and adjusting mechanism at lefthand side rear wheel

Check that the dowel and plunger surfaces have a mirror finish and that there are no signs of any rough spots which may be removed by using a fine grain oil stone providing that the diameter is not affected. Fit new parts if necessary. Check also the reaction spring for weakness or signs of cracks and also the thrust washers for distortion. Fit new parts as necessary.

Reassembling wheel cylinders:

1 Clean all the rubber parts in methylated spirits or correct hydraulic fluid. Any solvents used to clean metal parts must be completely dried off.

2 Renew all rubber seals when reassembling, particularly if there have been any signs of leakage. Reassemble the internal parts after wetting them with brake fluid as shown in **FIG 10:8.**

10:7 Self-adjusting device

The new 500 Sedan is equipped with a specially designed brake shoe clearance self-adjusting device which eliminates all need for manual adjustment during service.

Operation:

On either side face of the brake shoe rim are placed two friction washers in line with an adjustment slot which is machined into the brake shoe (see **FIG 10:6**). The friction washers are held against the shoe by a pin and bush screw together through the slot with a strong spring in between. The hollow pin fits onto the stud in the brake housing flange. A clearance of .0315 inch between the pin hole and stud permits the necessary movement of the shoes to ensure proper braking under normal operating conditions.

When the shoe clearance adjustment is no longer correct, the braking action will overcome the resistance of the friction washers and drag along the shoes into contact with the drum. Once the brake pedal has been released, the action of the return springs will be weaker and the friction of the adjustment washers on the shoes and so the shoes will remain in the new position taken up. As further wear of the linings occurs the shoes will again automatically be repositioned by the device.

Inspection and assembly:

During normal brake overhaul all the components of the self-adjusting device should be thoroughly checked and any parts badly worn or damaged must be renewed. Before reassembly it is advisable to check the spring rating using Fiat tester A.11493 by compressing the spring to a height of .374 inch which should give a corresponding load reading of 97 $\pm$ 4.9 lb. To reassemble the device after testing proceed as follows:

1 Place the pin of the self-adjusting device on support A.54002/2 and insert first the friction washer followed by the shoe, the second friction washer, the load spring and the bushings.

2 Fit wrench A.54002/1 onto the support and by exerting a slight pressure to overcome the spring load fully tighten the bush onto the pin. Lock the pin and bushing using a centre punch.

3 Install the shoes onto the brake housing flange and hook up the two return springs. Move the shoes outwards as far as they will go and release them. Check that during the return of the shoes the friction washers have stayed in their new position.

10:8 Removing a flexible hose

Never try to release a flexible hose by turning the ends with a spanner. The correct procedure is as follows:

Unscrew the metal pipeline union nut from its connection with the hose. Hold the adjacent hexagon on the hose with a spanner and remove the locknut which secures the hose to the brackets. The hose can now be turned without twisting the flexible part, by using a spanner on the hexagon at the other end.

10:9 Brake fluid reservoir

The reservoir is located in the front compartment to the right of the fuel tank as shown in **FIG 10:9.** Should it be necessary to detach the fluid outlet line from the reservoir the outlet hole must be blanked off using a tapered wooden peg of suitable length so that the cap may be replaced to prevent the ingress of foreign matter into the reservoir and the absorbtion of moisture, oil or petrol vapours which would alter the properties of the hydraulic fluid.

A special filter is fitted into the top of the reservoir through which all fluid used for topping-up the reservoir must pass to ensure utmost inner cleanliness of the hydraulic system.

10:10 Bleeding the system

This is not a routine maintenance operation and is only necessary if air has entered the hydraulic system because parts have been dismantled or because the fluid level in the reservoir has dropped so low that air has been drawn into the main feed pipe to the master cylinders.

1 Fill the reservoir with Fiat 'Blue Label' hydraulic fluid. During the bleeding operation fluid will be used and constant topping-up of the supply reservoir will be needed. If this is not done it is possible for air to enter the master cylinder main feed pipe which will nullify the operation and necessitate a fresh start.

2 Attach a length of rubber or plastic tubing to the bleeder screw on the rear wheel cylinder furthermost from the master cylinder. Immerse the free end of the tube in a small volume of hydraulic brake fluid in a clean jar.

3 Open the bleed screw one turn and get a second operator to press down slowly on the brake pedal. After a full stroke let the pedal return without assistance, pause a moment and repeat the down stroke. At first there will be air bubbles issuing from the bleed tube, but when fluid alone is injected, hold the pedal firmly down on the floor panel and tighten the bleed screw. Repeat this operation on the other rear brake and then repeat the operation on the two front brakes.

4 On completion, top-up the fluid in the reservoir to the correct level. Discard all dirty fluid. If fluid is perfectly clean, let it stand for twenty four hours to become clear of air bubbles before using it again.

10:11 Hand parking brake

Normally with the new 500 Sedan model automatic brake adjusting device, adjustment of the rear brakes will take up excessive handbrake travel.

If there is excessive travel on the handbrake of the Station Wagon model even after the rear brakes have been manually adjusted, suspect worn brake shoe linings or stretched handbrake cables. Examine the linings and fit replacement shoes if necessary. Check the action of the hand parking brake again and if there is still too much travel before the brakes are applied it is permissible to take up as follows:

1 It is essential to ensure that the rear shoes are correctly adjusted as described in **Section 10:2.**

2 Apply the hand parking brake lever until the pall engages with the ratchet at the second notch.

3 Jack up the rear of the vehicle and place on firmly based stands.

4 Locate the cable adjusting nuts as shown in **FIG 10:10** and adjust these until it is just possible to turn the road wheels by heavy hand pressure. It is important that both wheels offer the same resistance to turning to obtain correctly balanced braking.

5 Return the lever to the OFF position and check that both wheels are quite free to rotate. If a brake tends to bind, remove the brake drum and hub unit and check the brake shoe pull-off spring is correctly fitted and that the lever return spring and operating lever are functioning correctly. Also check for suspected seizure of the wheel cylinder. When the fault has been rectified refit the hub and drum. Readjust and recheck.

Removing the hand parking brake cable:

1 Chock the front wheels and release the handbrake. Raise the rear of the vehicle and place on firmly based stands.

2 Remove the pin and slide the clevis pin from the underside of the lever so releasing the cable sheave and cable from the lever.

3 Slacken the bolt and slide off the outer cable retaining bracket located on the underside of the floor.

4 Remove the shoe operating lever return springs, the pin, washer and clevis pin from the lever so releasing the inner operating cable. Lift away from the underside of the vehicle.

5 Reassembly is the reverse procedure to removal. Ensure that the cable is well lubricated and finally readjust as previously described.

10:12 Fault diagnosis

(a) 'Spongy' pedal

1 Leak in the system
2 Worn master cylinder
3 Leaking wheel cylinders
4 Air in the system
5 Gaps between shoes and underside of linings

(b) Excessive pedal movement

1 Check 1 and 4 in (a)
2 Excessive lining wear
3 Very low fluid level in supply reservoir
4 Too much free movement of pedal

(c) Brakes grab or pull to one side

1 Brake backplate loose
2 Scored, cracked or distorted drum
3 High spots on drum
4 Unbalanced shoe adjustment
5 Wet or oily linings
6 Worn or loose rear spring fixings
7 Front suspension or rear suspension anchorages loose
8 Worn steering connections
9 Mixed linings of different grades
10 Uneven tyre pressure
11 Broken shoe return springs
12 Seized handbrake cable

CHAPTER 11

THE ELECTRICAL EQUIPMENT

11:1 Description

All models covered by this manual have 12 volts electrical systems in which the negative battery terminal is earthed. There are three units in the regulator box to control the charging circuit; a cut-out, a current regulator and a voltage regulator. These are adjustable but it must be stressed that accurate moving coil meters are required when checking or altering the settings. Cheap and unreliable instruments will make accurate adjustments impossible.

There are wiring diagrams in Technical Data at the end of this manual to enable those with electrical experience to trace and correct wiring faults.

For the U.K. Market the headlamps are of the double filament dipping renewable bulb type with adjustments for individual beam settings.

The battery is located in the front compartment forward of the petrol tank and the fuses to the rear of the petrol tank.

Detailed instructions for servicing the electrical equipment will be found in this chapter, but it must be pointed out that it is not sensible to try to repair that which is seriously defective, electrically or mechanically. Such equipment should be replaced by new units which can be obtained on an exchange basis.

11:2 The battery

This of the 12-volt lead/acid type and has to meet heavy demands for current particularly in the winter. To maintain the performance of the battery at its maximum it is essential to carry out the following operations.

Keep the top of the battery and surrounding parts dry and clean, as dampness can cause leakage between the securing clamps and the negative terminal. Clean off any corrosion from the metal parts of the battery mounting with diluted ammonia and paint them with an anti-sulphuric paint. If the terminal posts are corroded, remove the cables and clean with diluted ammonia. Smear the posts with petroleum jelly before remaking the connections and fit the terminals securely. High electrical resistance due to corrosion at the terminal posts is often responsible for lack of sufficient current to operate the starter motor.

Ensure that the filler plugs are in good condition and show no signs of cracks. This may cause leakage of electrolyte and consequent corrosion. Test the condition of the cells after topping-up the electrolyte level with distilled water to just above the tops of the separators as shown in **FIG 11:2. Never add neat acid. If it is necessary to make a new electrolyte due to loss by spillage add sulphuric acid to the distilled water. It is highly dangerous to add water to acid.**

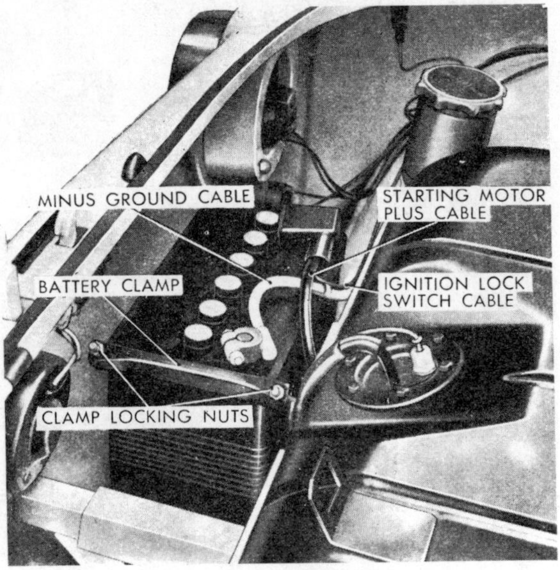

FIG 11:1 Battery location

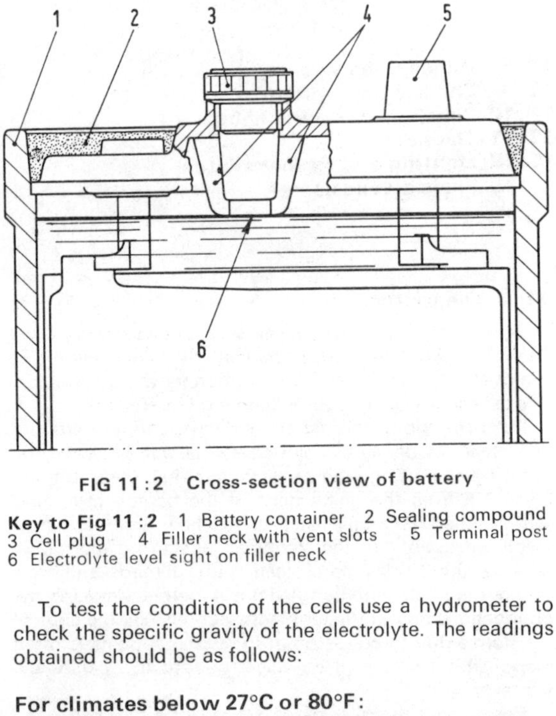

FIG 11:2 Cross-section view of battery

Key to Fig 11:2 1 Battery container 2 Sealing compound 3 Cell plug 4 Filler neck with vent slots 5 Terminal post 6 Electrolyte level sight on filler neck

To test the condition of the cells use a hydrometer to check the specific gravity of the electrolyte. The readings obtained should be as follows:

For climates below 27°C or 80°F:

Cell fully charged	Specific gravity 1.270 to 1.290
Cell half-discharged	Specific gravity 1.190 to 1.210
Cell discharged	Specific gravity 1.110 to 1.130

For climates above 27°C or 80°F:

Cell fully charged	Specific gravity 1.210 to 1.230
Cell half-discharged	Specific gravity 1.130 to 1.150
Cell discharged	Specific gravity 1.050 to 1.070

These figures are given assuming an electrolyte temperature of 16°C or 60°F. If the temperature of the electrolyte exceeds this, add .002 to the readings for each 3°C or 5°F rise in temperature. Subtract .002 if it drops below 16°C or 60°F.

All six cells should read approximately the same. If one differs radically from the rest it may be due to an internal fault or to spillage or leakage of the electrolyte.

If the battery is in a low state of charge take the car for a long daylight run or connect it to an external battery charger set at an output of 4 amps until it gases freely. When putting the battery on a charger, remove the vent plugs and ensure that no naked lights are in the vicinity. If the battery is to stand unused for long periods give a freshening up charge every month. It will deteriorate rapidly if it is left in a discharged state.

11:3 The generator

An exploded view of the generator is shown in **FIG 11:3.**

Testing when generator is not charging:

1 Check that drive belt slip is not the cause of the trouble. Tension should be such that the belt can be deflected about $\frac{13}{32}$ inch under a 22 lb pressure as shown in **FIG 1:49.** To adjust the drive belt tension remove the three nuts B, **FIG 1:49,** on the generator pulley and this will split the pulley into two parts between which are placed spacer rings. The tension of the belt is increased or decreased by either reducing or increasing the number of spacers. Place the spacer rings removed from between the pulley halves on the pulley outer face so that the rings may be reinserted when fitting a new belt. Tighten the three nuts to a torque wrench setting of 14.5 lb ft. Care must be taken not to over-tighten the belt or excessive loading will be placed on the generator bearings causing excessive bearing wear and noisy operation.

2 Check the generator connections. Generator terminal 51 must be connected to the generator regulator terminal 51 and the generator terminal 67 to the regulator terminal 67. Switch off all lights and accessories and disconnect the cables from the generator terminals 67 and 51. Connect the two terminals with a short length of wire. Run the engine at normal idling speed and clip the negative lead of a 0–20 volt moving coil meter to one generator terminal and the other lead to a good earth on the generator body. Gradually increase the engine speed up to about 1000 rev/min. The voltmeter reading should rise steadily and without signs of fluctuation, but do not let it reach 20 volts and do not race the engine in an attempt to increase the reading.

3 If there is no reading check the brush gear. If the reading is about half to one volt the field winding may be faulty. If approximately four to five volts the armature may be faulty.

4 If the generator is in good order leave the temporary link in position between the terminals and restore the original connections correctly. Remove the terminal 51 from the regulator and connect the voltmeter between this lead and a good earth on the car. Run the engine as before. The reading should be the same as that measured directly on the generator. No reading

indicates a break in the cable from the generator to regulator. Repeat the test on terminal 67. Finally, remove the temporary link from the generator. If the readings are correct, test the regulator as described in **Section 11 : 5**.

Removing generator:

1 Disconnect the leads from the generator.
2 Remove the drive belt as previously described.
3 Release the rear mounting bracket at the side of the power unit.
4 Remove the air cooling ducting from around the fan and generator area and lift away the unit.
5 Release the blower from the end of the armature shaft and finally, the mounting bolts from the air ducting.

Dismantling generator:

1 Release the pulley self-locking nut and slide the pulley off the armature shaft.
2 Remove the two Woodruff keys on armature shaft.
3 Unscrew the two through bolt nuts and pull out the bolts.
4 Partially remove the commutator end head to the point where the brushes are still seating on the commutator. Using a piece of hooked wire relieve the load of the springs on the brushes by arranging the spring ends on the brush sides. The brushes will be locked in their holders and cannot be chipped by striking against the armature shaft during the commutator end head removal.
5 Gently ease the commutator and fan end heads apart and slide out the armature.

Servicing brushes:

Lift the brushes up in the boxes and hold them in that position by letting each brush spring bear on the side of its brush. Fit the commutator end bracket over the commutator end of the armature shaft and release the brushes by hooking up the springs using a thin screw driver. Hold back each spring in turn and move the brush by pulling gently on the flexible connector. If the brush moves sluggishly remove it and polish the sides using a smooth file. Before this operation is actually carried out it is suggested that the brush is marked before removal so that it is replaced in its original working position.

The minimum permissible length of a brush is $\frac{9}{32}$ inch, so renew any that are less than this figure. Test the brush springs using a spring tension scale. New springs should have a tension of 1.3 to 1.6 lb. In service this value could fall slightly before performance is affected. Always bed in new brushes by wrapping fine sandpaper round the commutator, pressing down on the brush and rotating the commutator under it, or draw the paper too and fro. If new brushes are fitted always fit genuine Fiat replacements.

Servicing the commutator:

A commutator in good condition should be smooth and free from pitting or signs of the segments burning. Clean with a rag moistened in petrol. If necessary, polish using a fine glasspaper whilst rotating the armature. **Never use emerycloth.**

If the commutator is badly worn it may be skimmed using a centre lathe. Use a high rotational speed and take a light cut using a sharp tool. Remove only enough metal to clean up the commutator face and then polish with fine glasspaper. To undercut the insulation between the segments, it is suggested that a hacksaw blade is ground on its sides until it is the thickness of the insulation and carefully work between each pair of segments until the insulation has been cut to a depth of .0394 inch below the surface.

A thorough visual inspection may determine the cause of armature failure. Breaks in armature windings cause burnt commutator segments. Short-circuited windings are discoloured by overheating, with badly burnt commutator segments.

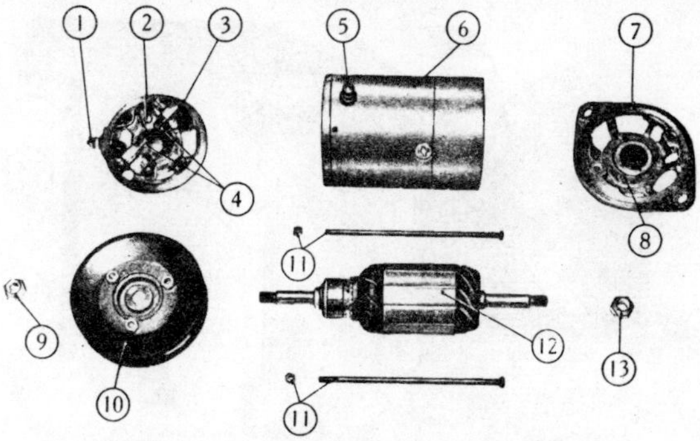

FIG 11 : 3 Components of generator

Key to Fig 11 : 3 1 Terminal 51 2 Bearing outer ring retainment terminal nut 3 Commutator end head 4 Brushes 5 Terminal 67 6 Frame 7 Blower end head 8 Bearing retainer nuts and screws 9 Pulley retainment nut 10 Pulley 11 Head mounting tie rods and nuts 12 Armature 13 Blower retainment nut

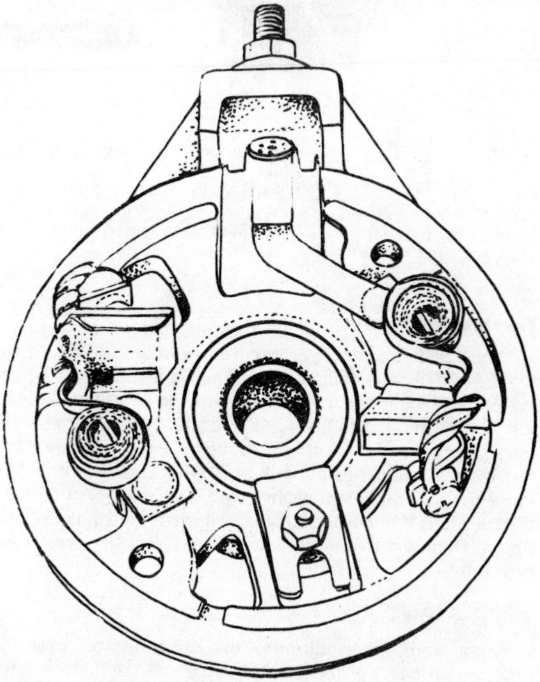

FIG 11 : 4 Commutator end head of generator DSV 90.12.16.3 S

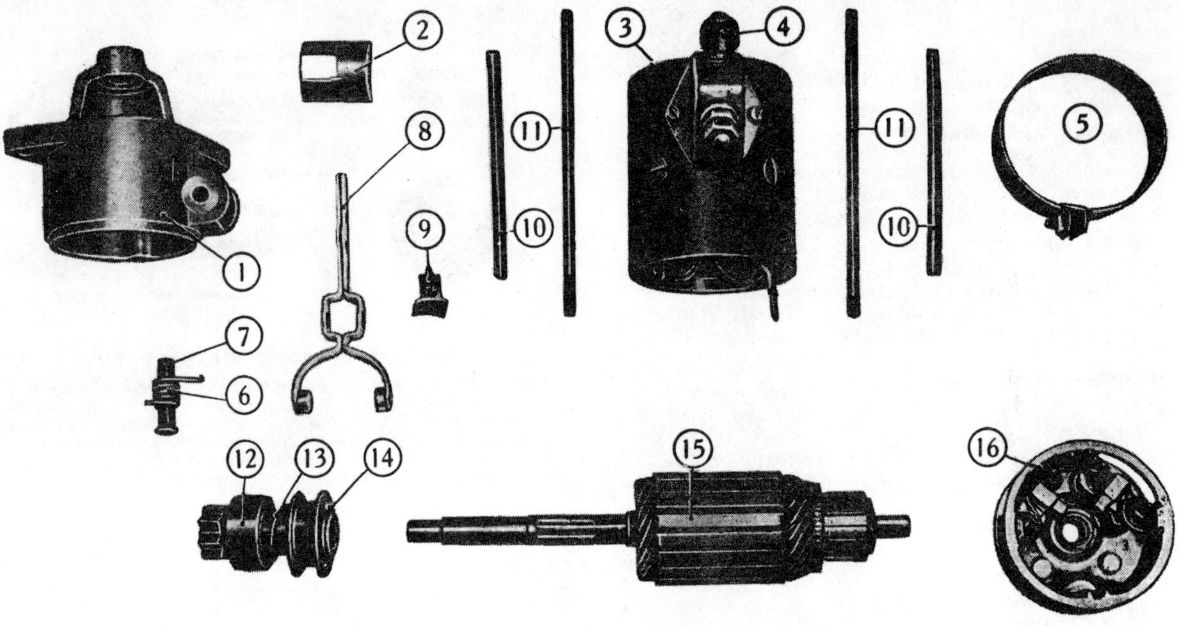

FIG 11:5 Components of starter

Key to Fig 11:5 1 Drive end head 2 Head shield 3 Frame 4 Switch 5 Commutator cover band 6 and 7 Pin and spring for lever 8 8 Starting engagement lever 9 Head shield 10 and 11 Head fixing tie rods and tubes 12 Pinion, complete 13 Starting engagement spring 14 Drive unit sleeve and free wheel hub 15 Armature 16 Commutator end head

Testing field coils:

When tested with an ohmmeter the reading should be 8+.1—.3 ohms. Failing an ohmmeter use a 12-volt supply and connect it in series with an ammeter across the field terminal and the yoke or body. The meter should read approximately 2 amps. If there is no reading the field coil winding has a break in it. If the reading is much more than 2 amps or the ohmmeter records at much less than 8 ohms it shows that field coil insulation has broken down. Renewal of the field coils is a specialist operation best left to a service station.

The armature:

Apart from reconditioning the commutator, there is little which can be done to the armature itself. Never try to straighten a bent shaft and do not machine the armature core. Armature windings are tested with equipment normally not available to the car owner. The only check for a suspected faulty armature which the owner can do is to substitute an armature which is known to be satisfactory.

Generator bearings:

1 Commutator end head bearings. Remove the ballbearing outer race stop bracket mounting screw and nut, ease out the stop brackets and the ballbearings.
2 Fan end head bearing. Remove the ballbearing retainer mounting screw nuts and ease out the retainers and the seals. Using a suitably sized drift remove the ballbearing.

Reassembly is the reverse procedure to dismantling in both cases.

Reassembly and refitting the generator:

This is the reverse procedure to dismantling. The following points should however be noted.

1 The commutator end head ballbearing outer race stop bracket mounting screw nut must be tightened to a torque wrench setting of .80 lb ft.
2 The pulley and fan-to-generator armature shaft self-locking nuts must be tightened to a torque wrench setting of 14.5 lb ft.
3 To assemble the commutator end bracket to the yoke, partially withdraw the brushes and trap them in this position by letting the springs bear on the sides of the brushes. Fit the bracket to the armature shaft and when it is about ½ inch from the yoke face, lift the springs using a thin screwdriver or a piece of hooked wire and this will let the brushes drop onto the commutator. Check that the springs now bear correctly on the tops of the brushes and push the bracket fully home.
4 Pack all ballbearings with Fiat Jota 3 grease or an equivalent grade grease.

11:4 The starter motor

Operation:

When operating the starter hand lever through a flexible coupling a lever is operated (see **FIG 11:5**) which controls the pinion engagement with the flywheel. As the lever completes its movement it closes the starter switch contacts. The starter motor rotates driving the pinion along into mesh with the ring gear. As soon as the engine fires the starter hand lever must be released which will open the starter switch contacts so stopping the starter motor and the pinion will return under the action of a spring to a neutral position.

Should the hand lever not be immediately released once the engine has fired damage will be caused to the armature.

Tests for a starter which does not operate:

Check the condition of the battery and particularly the connections to the terminals and to earth. If the battery is charged, switch on the lights and operate the starter hand lever control. If the lights go dim but the starter does not operate it shows that current is reaching the starter motor. The probability is that the pinion of the starter shaft is jammed in mesh due to dirty pinion splines or a broken spring. To release the pinion engage a low gear with the ignition switched off and rock the vehicle backwards and forwards which should allow the pinion to be disengaged from the flywheel ring gear. If it proves impossible to free a jammed pinion the starter motor must be removed for examination and repair.

If the lamps do not go dim, check the starter switch and also check the connection between the battery and the starter switch to ensure that they are tight and making good electrical connection. If the starter motor still does not work it should be removed from the power unit for inspection.

Removing the starter:

To remove the starter motor from the power unit proceed as follows:

1 Disconnect the positive terminal from the battery post.
2 Release the hand lever control cable from the starter motor engagement lever.
3 Disconnect the battery cable terminal from the starter motor switch.
4 Remove the two retaining nuts and washers holding the starter motor to body to the transmission bell-housing and gently ease backwards and lift away the starter motor.

Examining the commutator and brush gear:

Refer to **FIG 11:5** and remove the coverband 5. Hold back each spring in turn and pull gently on the flexible connection to the brush. If the brush does not move freely remove it from its holder and polish the sides using a fine file. Mark the brushes so that they will be replaced in their original positions. If the brushes are so worn that they no longer bear onto the commutator, or the brush connector has become exposed on the running face, the brushes must be renewed.

If the commutator is blackened it should be cleaned by turning it against a petrol-moistened cloth. With the brushes and commutator overhauled hold the body of the starter motor in a vice and connect it with thick cables to a 12 volt battery. One cable should go to the starter switch terminal and the other to the body of the starter. The starter should run at high speed. If it does not, it must be dismantled for further examination and testing.

Dismantling the starter:

To dismantle the starter proceed as follows:

1 Remove the coverband 5 (see **FIG 11:5**) and hold back the brush springs and take out the brushes.
2 Remove the starter switch by releasing the two mounting screws and lift away the switch.
3 Remove the commutator end head 16, slide off the armature assembly from the drive unit and from the pole shoes.
4 Release the engagement lever pin 6 and spring 7 from the lever operating bracket on the drive end head. Lift away the lever and withdraw the pinion assembly complete which is shown in **FIG 11:5**.

Servicing the brushes

Test the brush springs with a balance, the correct tension is 2.5 to 2.9 lb. according to the wear of the brushes. Fit a new spring if the tension is low.

The lash of the brushes depends on the type of service in which the vehicle is being used. In normal circumstances even when the starter is being used frequently, the brushes should last more than 18,000 miles. If the wear is found to be abnormal it will probably be found that the commutator is either damaged or excessively worn. Only Fiat replacement brushes must be used.

Testing the field coils:

Use a 12 volt bulb in one lead of a 12 volt battery. Connect one lead to the brush connection joint to the coil field and the other to the field coil current supply lead. If the bulb does not light there is a break in the field coil windings. This is not a complete test as it is still possible for a coil to be earthed. Check this by moving the lead from the brush connection and holding it on a clean metal surface on the yoke or body. If the bulb lights it shows that the field coils are earthed.

The only sure way of curing faulty field coils is to take the starter motor to a service station.

Examining the armature:

The armature shaft may be bent due to the starter being operated whilst the engine is operating. Do not try to straighten a bent shaft or machine the armature core to obtain the correct clearance.

The starter may run at very high speeds if it is engaged while the engine is running, this may cause the copper wires to lift from the commutator. This could be a reason for failure.

Starter bearings:

Bearing bushes are of the porous bronzed type and must not be reamed after fitting. Worn bearings should be withdrawn by screwing a tap into them and pulling on the tap. New bushes must be immersed in engine oil for approximately twenty four hours before fitting. Press them into place using a suitably sized drift which has a spigot the length of the bearing and the diameter of the starter shaft. When this is withdrawn after fitting, the bore of the bush should be correct to size.

The pinion drive:

This unit is shown in **FIG 11:5.** The chief sources of trouble are a dirty unit or a broken starting engagement

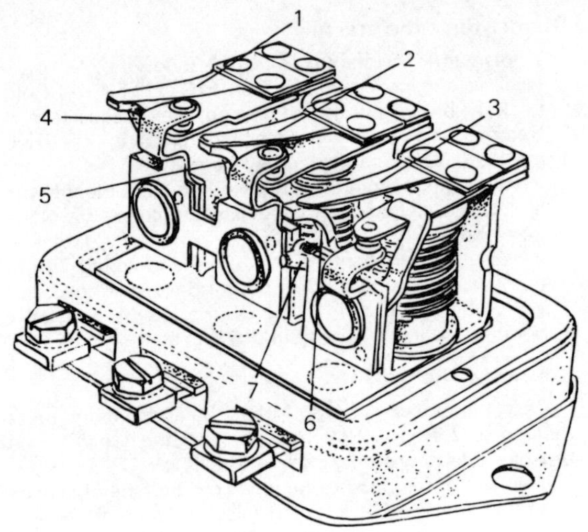

FIG 11 : 6 Regulator assembly GN 1.12.16

Key to Fig 11 : 6 1 Voltage regulator adjusting spring 2 Current regulator adjusting spring 3 Cutout adjusting spring 4 Voltage regulator adjustment arm 5 Current regulator adjustment arm 6 Cutout adjustment blade spring 7 Soldering of cutout shunt and series winding

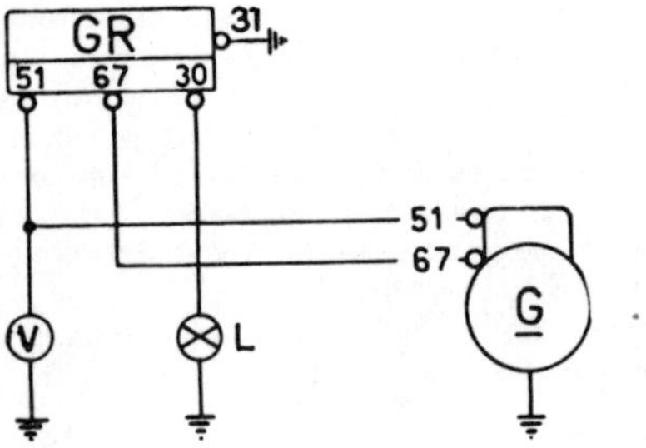

FIG 11 : 7 Wiring diagram for checking the cutout closing voltage

Key to Fig 11 : 7 **GR** Regulator GN 1.12.16 **G** Generator FIAT DSV 90.12.16.3 S **V** Voltmeter, 20 V scale (0.5% accuracy) **L** 12 V, 3 to 5 W bulb

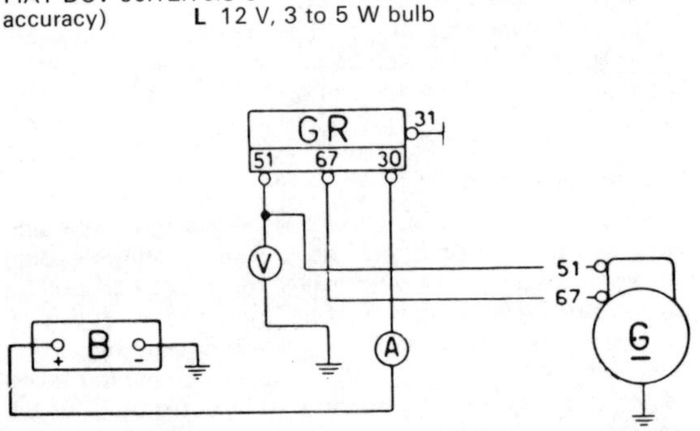

FIG 11 : 8 Wiring diagram for checking the reverse current of cutout

Key to Fig 11 : 8 **GR** Regulator GN 1.12.16 **G** Generator FIAT DSV 90.12.16.3 S **B** Battery, 50 Ah, fully charged **A** Ammeter, asymmetrical scale 10-0-15 A **V** Voltmeter, 20 V scale (0.5% accuracy)

spring 13. Should any defect be found then the pinion assembly must be renewed as one complete unit. After examining to ensure that there are no defects thoroughly clean using petrol but do not use any lubricant as this will cause dirt to adhere to the running surfaces and this is often the cause for a sticking drive.

Reassembling and refitting the starter:

In both cases this is a simple reversal of the dismantling procedure.

11 : 5 The control box:

Description:

The generator regulator fitted to the new 500 model consists of three separate units; voltage regulator, current regulator, cut-out relay (see **FIG 11 : 6**).

The voltage regulator and current regulator relays comprise a U-shaped body one of whose arms is bent to form a flange, whilst the other adjustment arm provides a stop for the hinge spring. The U-shaped body is secured to the frame by the core threaded shank and carries, on the flanged end, an armature supported by a hinge spring which comprises a steel leaf and bi-metal leaf overimposed in the current regulator and bi-metal leaf in the voltage regulator. The armature carries the movable contact.

Fixed contacts of both voltage and current regulators are mounted on two blade springs which are secured to a single bracket rivetted to the U-shaped adjustment arm. The design of the two fixed contacts carrier blade springs is such as to permit the adjustment of the contact position by suitably bending the blade springs. The cut-out is similar in design to the other two relays as shown in **FIG 11 : 6**. Again the hinge spring is bi-metallic as in the voltage regulator.

All the armatures are provided with blade springs, so that the tension may be adjusted to the required setting value. This adjustment is obtained by bending the adjustment arms.

The voltage regulator coil comprises a fine wire winding with a great number of turns, shunt connected to the generator.

The cut-out coil comprises a fine wire winding with a great number of turns shunt connected to the generator, and of a winding comprising a few turns of heavy gauge wire, which is connected in series with the generator charge circuit (cut-out series winding).

The current regulator coil comprises a few turns of heavy gauge wire which is series connected with the generator charge circuit.

The generator regulator base has three terminals to which the various cables are connected.

No. 51 – connection to generator positive terminal.
No. 67 – connection to generator field winding.
No. 30 – connection to electrical accessories.

The regulator cover is secured to the base with a rubber gasket placed in between which seals the unit against the ingress of moisture or dust.

A regulation resistor is fitted under the base and is secured to the voltage regulator and current regulator relay core threaded shanks.

Checking cut-out:

1 Closing voltage:

This test should be carried out at a temperature of 25°± 10°C and the regulator should be connected to a generator test bed as shown in **FIG 11 : 7.** The unit should be operated under no load conditions for between 15-18 minutes with the cover installed and with a voltage of between 16.5 volts for an initial operating temperature of 15–20°C or 15 volts for an initial operating temperature of 20–35°C. This will enable thermal stabilization of the unit to be obtained so that the temperature of both the cut-out shunt windings and the bymetallic springs increase due to the heat developed by the windings and reaches the normal operating setting.

Once thermal stabilization has been obtained the generator should be restarted and the speed gradually increased so that immediately the test lamp starts to glow the voltmeter reading may be taken. This will be the value of the cut-out contact closing voltage.

2 Reverse current:

This check should be carried out at a temperature range of between 25°± 10°C and it is recommended that it is performed as soon as possible after the closing voltage test so that the thermal stabilization remains unaltered. Connect the regulator as shown in **FIG 11 : 8** and gradually speed up the generator to 4500 rev/min for approximately 5 minutes. Ensure that the voltmeter reads at least 14.5 volts and then gradually reduce the generator speed carefully watching the movement of the ammeter needle which should at first indicate a charging current and then gradually move to zero and then to the other side of the scale to indicate reverse current value. If the generator speed is reduced further the reverse current reading will increase to a given value and then suddenly fall to zero which will indicate that the cut-out contact has opened. This limit indicates the maximum reverse current value which should not, under any circumstances, exceed 16 amps.

During this test, to obtain the maximum reverse current possible the reduction in generator speed must not take more than 10 seconds otherwise the battery voltage will drop excessively.

Checking voltage regulator:

This test should be carried out with the regulator under half load and at a temperature of 50°± 3°C. Connect the regulator as shown in **FIG 11 : 9** and operate the regulator for approximately 30 minutes by supplying a current half that of regulated current which is 16± 5 amp. Once the regulator has been brought to the required temperature stop the generator and start it again, gradually increasing the speed to a maximum of 4500 rev/min. Adjust the rheostat for a generator output corresponding to half load current of 8± 2 amps. When this generator output has been set the voltage should be 14.2± .3 volts.

Checking current regulator:

Leave the regulator connected as shown in **FIG 11 : 10** and this test must be carried out immediately after testing the half load regulated voltage of the voltage regulator when connected to a battery. Check that the ammeter fitted will accommodate a 40 amp deflection which if not a

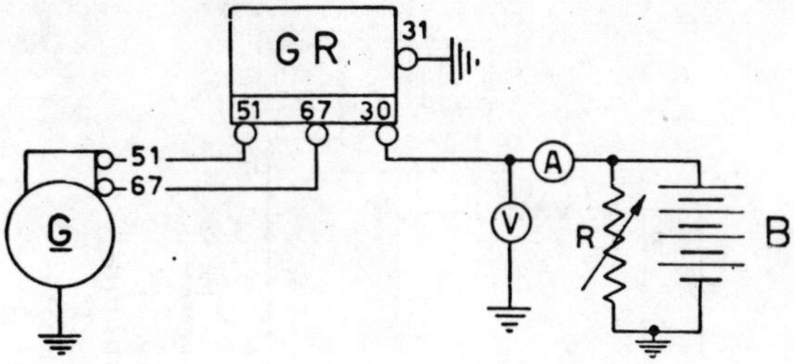

FIG 11 : 9 Wiring diagram for checking the current and voltage regulators

Key to Fig 11 : 9 **GR** Regulator GN 1.12.16 **G** Generator FIAT D 90.12.16.3 **V** Voltmeter, 20 V scale (0.5% accuracy) **A** Ammeter, 20 A scale (to check voltage regulator) and 40 A scale (to check current regulator) **R** Rheostat, 25 A. 3 Ω, **B** Battery, 50 Ah, fully charged

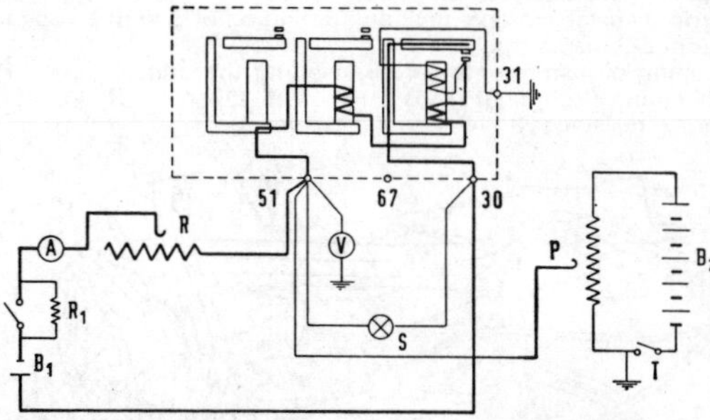

FIG 11 : 10 Wiring diagram for setting the cut-out relay

Key to Fig 11 : 10 **B_1** 2 V battery **B_2** 20 V battery **A** Ammeter, 20 A scale (1% accuracy) **V** Voltmeter, 20 V scale (0.5% accuracy), directly connected to terminals 31–51 **P** Potentiometer for voltage adjustment, having such a capacity that the current draw of the cut-out shunt winding does not cause sensible variations in the voltage readings (voltmeter under no load) **S** Test lamp, with 2 V, 3 W bulb, to signal opening and closing of contacts **R** Rheostat, 4 Ω, 12 A **R_1** Voltage drop resistor, suitable to allow turning on of A with T_1 open and cut-out contacts open
Setting of instruments before inserting the unit: **P** At minimum (voltmeter reads zero) **T** Open **R** All inserted (max. resistance) **T** Open

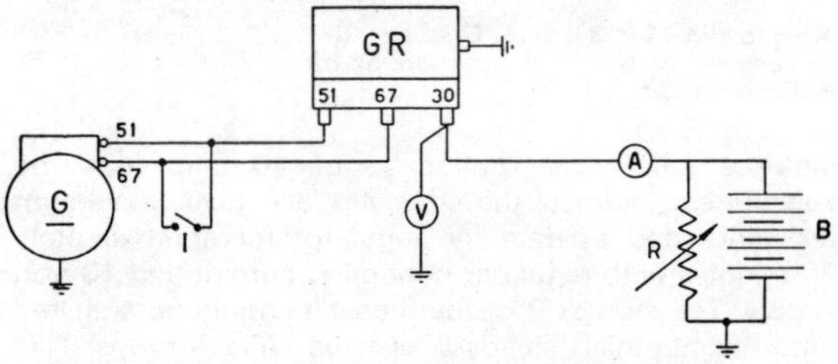

FIG 11 : 11 Wiring diagram for setting the voltage and current regulators

Key to Fig 11 : 11 **GR** Regulator assembly GN 1.12.16 **G** Generator D 90.12.16.3 **V** Voltmeter, 20 V scale (0.5% accuracy) **A** Ammeter, 20 Amp. scale (for voltage regulator), or 40 Amp. scale (for current regulator) **R** Rheostat, 25 Amps., 3 Ohms **B** 50 Amp/h battery, fully charged **I** Switch

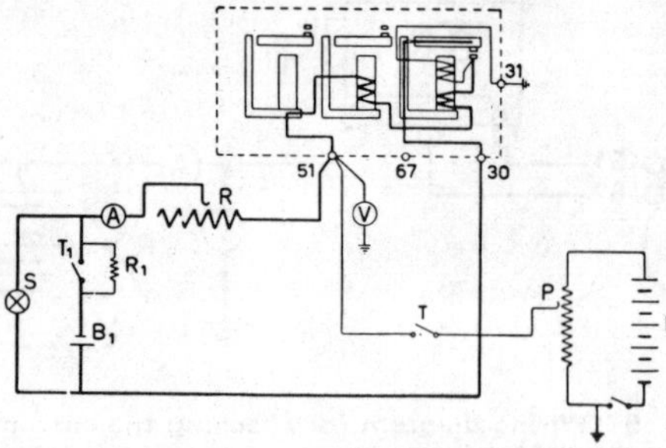

FIG 11:12 Wiring diagram for setting the cutout relay

Key to Fig 11:12 **B_1** 2 V battery **B_2** 20 V battery **A** Ammeter, 15 A scale (1% accuracy) **V** Voltmeter, 20 V scale (0.5% accuracy), directly connected to terminals 31-51 **P** Potentiometer for voltage adjustment, having such a capacity that the current draw of the cutout shunt winding does not cause sensible variations in the voltage readings (voltmeter under no load) **S** Test lamp, with 2 V, 3 W bulb, to signal opening and closing of contacts **R** Rheostat, 4 , 12 A **R_1** Voltage drop rheostat, suitable to allow turning on of S with T_1 open and cutout contacts open
Setting of instruments before inserting the unit: **P** At minimum (Voltmeter reads zero) **T** Open **R** All inserted (max. resistance) **T_1** Open

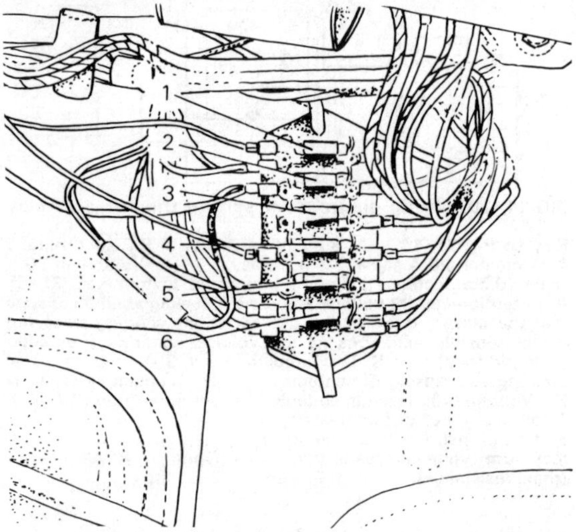

FIG 11:13 Location of electrical system fuses

Key to Fig 11:13 1 Fuse No. 30.2 2 Fuse No. 30.3 3 Fuse No. 56.b1 4 Fuse No. 56.b2 5 Fuse No. 15.54 6 Fuse No. 30

meter a fuller scale deflection of 40 amp must be substituted. Adjust the rheostat to give maximum resistance and operate the regulator for approximately 30 minutes with regulator controlled current and 13 volt supply. The resistor R of the rheostat should be adjusted until the current is steady whilst the voltage drops. This will indicate that the unit has reached normal operating temperature. Stop the generator, restart it and speed up gradually to 4500 rev/min. Check that the regulated current value corresponds to the specified value of 16± .5 amps. By continually reducing the resistance the current should remain constant. The voltage however should decrease to as low as 12 volts.

Cut-out relay adjustment:

Ascertain the type of regulator fitted and then wire to the test unit as shown in **FIG 11:10** or **FIG 11:12.** Before the unit is assembled to the test bed the instruments should be set as follows:

P – at minimum so that voltmeter reads zero.
T – open.
R – all inserted giving maximum resistance.
T_1 – open.

1 Contact closing voltage:

This test should be carried out at an ambient temperature of 25°± 10°C. Close the switch T and stabilize the regulator thermally by feeding current into it for approximately 15 to 18 minutes at 16.5 volts which is obtained by adjusting P for initial regulator operating temperatures of between 15°–20°C or at 15 volts for initial operating temperatures of 20°–35°C. Once the stabilizing of the regulator has been completed bring the voltage to 12.6± .2 volts by adjusting P. Adjust the load on the setting spring by bending the relevant arm until the pilot light S is extinguished. Reset P to minimum and again increase the voltage by P and check that the pilot lamp is extinguished at the specified voltage.

2 Reverse current:

This test must be carried out at a temperature of 25°± 10°C and it is recommended that it is carried out as soon as possible after the closing voltage test so as to maintain minimum regulator thermal stability. With the switch T closed bring the voltage to 14.5 volts by operating P. The contacts of the cut-out should be closed and the pilot lamp S off. Close T_1 and increase the reverse current by means of the rheostat R and check that the pilot lamp S glows as the contacts part. The opening may also be unsteady which will be indicated by a slight buzz from the unit. Check the value of the ammeter of the reverse current causing the opening of the contacts and this should not exceed 16 amps. If the reading is unstable or S lights up at the recommended limit reset the reverse current to the minimum value and repeat the test once more. Finally open the switches T and T_1 and again adjust rheostat R and P to the minimum settings.

Voltage regulator adjustment:

This test should be carried out at a temperature of 50°± 3°C. Connect the unit as shown in **FIG 11:11** and load the voltage regulator adjusting springs by bending the relevant arm. With the unit at the required test temperature close 1 start the generator and stabilize the regulator thermally by feeding a current for 30 minutes at 15 volts, which is obtained by adjusting the generator speed. The generator should then be stopped, I opened and the generator restarted and gradually speeded up to 4500 rev/min. The voltage regulator spring load adjustment should be set by suitably bending the relevant adjusting arm and by rheostat R so as to have a voltage of 14.2± .3 volts and a half load current of 8± 2 amps. Finally check the steadiness and accuracy of the voltage regulator setting by stopping the generator and restarting after approximately 2 minutes and gradually speeding up to 4500 rev/min.

Current regulator adjustment:

This test should be carried out immediately after adjusting the voltage regulator using the same wiring diagram (**FIG 11:11**) and instruments except the ammeter which should have a full scale deflection of 40 amps. With the regulator at the required temperature close I and start the generator and set its speed at rheostat R for a 13 volt output and 16$\pm$.5 amp output. Allow the unit to operate to the set conditions for 30 minutes with the regulator at its test temperature and then stop the generator and open I. Gradually speed up the generator to maximum speed of 4500 rev/min and adjust the current regulator to setting spring by bending the spring tab and operating rheostat R in order that the regulated current and voltage are respectively 16$\pm$.5 amps and 13 volts. Finally check the regulated current for stability and accurate setting by stopping the generator and repeating the test.

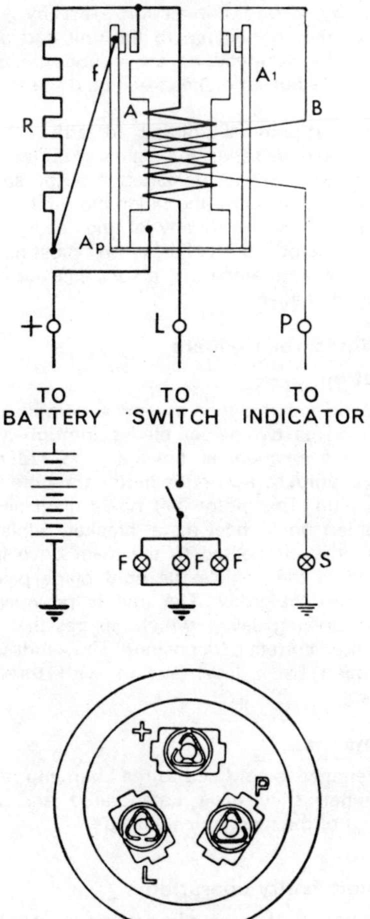

FIG 11:14 (Top) flasher unit operation diagram, for bench testing; (bottom) flasher unit contacts side view

Fig 11:14 **A** Series winding **Ap** Main armature **A_1** Auxiliary armature **B** Auxiliary winding **F** Front and rear parking and direction indicator lamps **L** and **P** Terminals **R** Additional resistor **S** Pilot lamp **f** Hot wire

Regulator resistance:

If it is found that the voltage and/or current regulator settings have altered considerably the trouble may be found in an open circuit in the regulating resistance or due to an alteration in the value of the resistance windings. Inspect the resistor to make sure that the wire is neither broken nor disconnected from the terminals and that no coils are shorted or have their insulation damaged. To check the value of the resistance insert a piece of thick paper between the current and voltage regulator contacts and take a reading across terminals 51 and 67. If a different value is found the resistance must be renewed by removing the 2 nuts together with the lockwashers. A damaged or suspect resistor must not be repaired but must be replaced with a new one.

Regulator sealing:

After the regulator has been checked and adjusted as necessary close the assembly in a warm condition ensuring first that the rubber gasket is correctly located. This eliminates any moisture which may be deposited on the windings and prevents the formation of moisture occurring when the cover is refitted onto a cold unit. If any moisture is trapped in the unit, during operation when the unit is warm moisture will evaporate and deposit on the armatures thus causing oxidization of the contacts.

11:6 Fuses

The location of the fuse unit is shown in **FIG 11:15** where it can be seen located behind the fuel tank. The electrical system is protected by six 8 amp fuses located in the fuse box.

Before replacing a burnt fuse look for the cause of blowing. Reference to the wiring diagrams at the rear of this manual will be found most useful. Below is given a table showing the protected and unprotected electrical circuits.

Fuses—fig 384	*Controlled circuits*
1 Fuse No. 30/2	Right headlamp high beam – Left front parking light with indicator – Right rear parking light.
2 Fuse No. 30/3	Left headlamp high beam with indicator – Right front parking light – Left rear parking light – Number plate light.
3 Fuse No. 56/b 1	Left headlamp low beam.
4 Fuse No. 56/b 2	Right headlamp low beam.
5 Fuse No. 15/54	Winking direction indicators with pilot light – Instrument cluster light – Stoplight.
6 Fuse No. 30	Horn – Windshield wiper – Rear view mirror light.

11:7 Flasher unit

The flashing light directional indicator system uses the higher wattage filament (20 W) of the front parking lamps, and at the rear the 20 watt bulb of parking, direction indicator and stop lamps, and the 2.5 watt bulb of both side direction indicators. The system comprises a directional signal switch, a flasher unit, the front, side and rear lamps and 2.5 watt pilot light. The directional signal switch is connected to the flasher unit and three

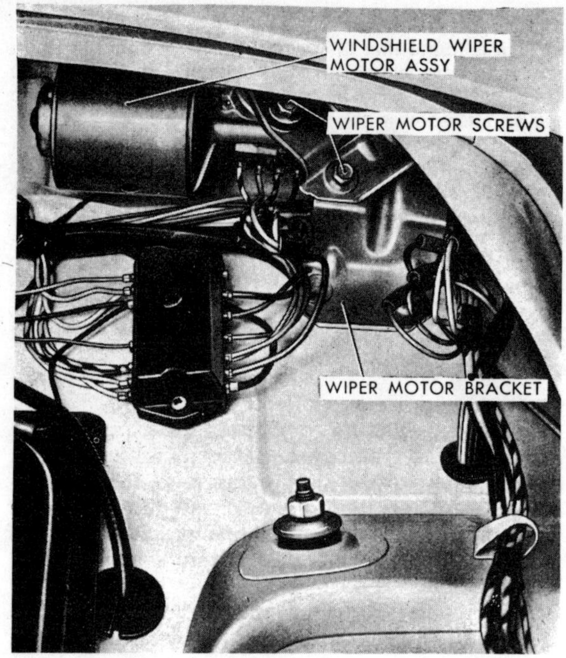

FIG 11 : 15 **Arrangement of windshield wiper unit on vehicle**

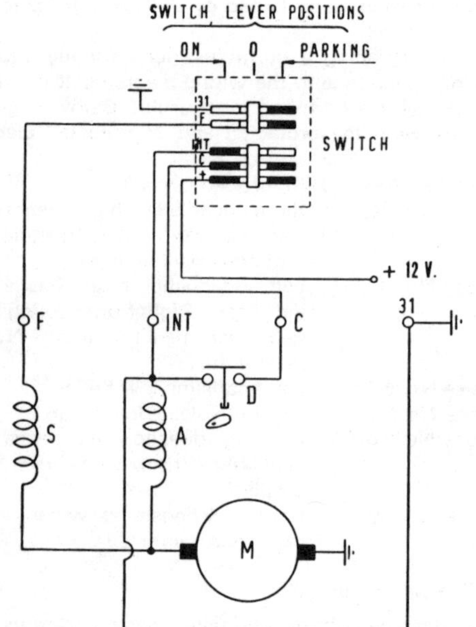

FIG 11 : 16 **Windshield wiper wiring diagram**

Key to Fig 11 : 16 **A** Series winding **B** Shunt winding **D** Switch **M** Motor **S** Additional winding **F** INT C = Terminals

signal lamp pairs. The flasher unit connections are in **FIG 11 : 14** and is of the hot wire type.

Faulty operation of flashers:

In cases of trouble check the bulb for broken filaments. Refer to the wiring diagrams in Technical Data and check all flasher circuit cables and connections. Check the appropriate fuse. Switch on the ignition and check with a voltmeter between flasher unit positive terminal and earth to see if battery voltage is present. Connect together flasher unit positive terminal and L and operate the direction indicator switch. If the flasher lamps now light, the flasher unit is defective and must be renewed. It is not possible to dismantle and repair a faulty flasher unit. Before removing make a note of the connections so that they will be replaced correctly when the new unit is being installed.

Before making the connections it is advisable to check the circuits to ensure that the new flasher unit is not damaged by wrong connection. Test by joining the cables normally connected to the unit and operate the switch. If the connections are wrong the appropriate fuse will blow but no damage will be done to the flasher unit.

Never insert terminal L directly to earth without having first connected in series the bulbs specified, otherwise the flasher unit will be damaged. For the same reason terminal L must never be shorted to ground nor must there by any short circuits in any of the leads from the L terminal to the bulbs. The flasher unit must never receive blows of any kind since it is a very delicate component and easily damaged.

11 : 8 Windscreen wipers

Description:

The windscreen wiper assembly comprises a motor unit that drives two wiper blades through a reduction gearing and mechanical linkage. The reduction gear includes a worm screw on the motor armature shaft and a helical pinion. The motor, left blade pivot and linkages are mounted on a sheet metal bracket, whilst the right blade pivot is connected to the main drive link. When assembled to the vehicle the right blade pivot is fixed directly onto the body. The unit is provided with an automatic parking device which ensures that the blades return to their correct park position. The windscreen wiper is controlled by a lever switch with three separate positions.

Maintenance:

Maintenance is confined to the changing of the wiper blades when they have deteriorated and occasional lubricating of the mechanical linkage.

Wiper unit faulty operation:

1 It is important that the wiper unit assembly is correctly fitted to the body otherwise distortion of the wiper mounting bracket can occur which will cause abnormal stresses on the pivot and linkages resulting in irregular and difficult blade sweep.

2 If the blades keep on sweeping at a reduced speed although the switch lever has been pressed to the

parking position the trouble will be found in the sliding sector which fails to open the switch D (see **FIG 11 :16**). Check by removing the four motor cover mounting screws and uncover the sliding sector. If possible suitably bend the sector to bring it against into contact with the rod tip of switch D.

3 If the automatic parking of the blades does not occur when the switch lever is fully depressed to the parking position but immediately stops when the switch is operated the cause of the trouble is that the switch D is not closing and consequently no current is flowing between the terminals C and INT. This will probably be due to dirt lodged between the movable contact and the fixed contacts of switch D. Thoroughly wash the components with petrol and if necessary reface the contacts using a very fine file.

4 Should the motor unit be noisy in operation although still operating reliably the noise is probably due to the reduction gear operation, whereby the pinion and worm are excessively worn or a tooth chipped. The motor unit must be renewed as motor unit parts are not available in service.

5 If the switch lever is pushed upwards to the 'on' position or depressed downwards to the Parking position and the wiper is still inoperative thoroughly check all terminal connections for tightness and cables for damage which if all appear to be correct the failure of the wiper to operate indicates an internal fault of the motor unit which should be repaired or renewed as necessary.

Removal and refitting the motor:

Remove the wiper arms and the electrical connections to the motor. Dismantling is a straightforward operation providing that as all items are removed so they are inspected and a note made of their locations. However, reassembly requires more care and the following procedure should be adopted.

1 Mount the wiper unit onto the body by fully tightening the nuts fixing the pivots onto which the arms are fitted. Ensure that the rubber sealing bushes between the pivots and body are correctly assembled to prevent water ingress. Slightly lubricate with glycerine.

2 Secure the mounting bracket lower edge to the body by means of the special square bracket. It is important not to distort the mounting bracket and ease of assembly is ensured by elongated holes in the square bracket. By suitable adjustment the linkages will not be subjected to distortion or abnormal stresses during operation.

3 Fit the motor unit to the mounting bracket tightening the screws and reassemble the main link to the pivot lever. Ensure that the locking of the fastener on the pivot lever is secure so that it does not become loose during operation.

4 Remake all the electrical connections and run the motor for a short time whilst checking all the switch positions including the automatic parking. It is at this position that the wiper blades and arms are assembled to the wiper mechanism.

5 Onto the pivots, install the shims, snap ring, wiper arm, plain washer and lockwasher. Fully tighten the nuts with the wiper arms in the parked position which is to the left when looking at the windshield.

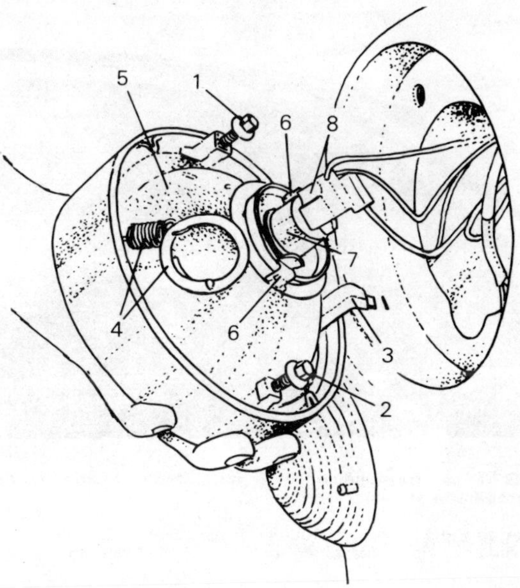

FIG 11 :17 Headlamp removal

Key to Fig 11 :17 1 Screw for vertical beam adjustment 2 Screw for horizontal beam adjustment 3 Headlamp locating hook 4 Headlamp retaining ring and spring 5 Lamp unit 6 Bulb spring retainers 7 Bulb 8 Junction block

6 Ensure that the wiper arms can be tilted 100 deg. downwards without striking against the cowl or front compartment lid. Also ensure that the blade pressure on the glass is 10.6 to 12.3 oz.

11 :9 The lighting system

Description:

The lighting system comprises two headlights with double filament bulbs of 45 watts for main beam and 40 watts for dip. Headlight control is operated through the outer light switch below the steering wheel after the toggle switch at the centre of the instrument panel has been operated.

A double filament bulb for the front parking and direction indicator lights is located below the headlights. The bulb is of 5 watt rating for the parking lights and 20 watts for the direction indicator lights.

Two side direction indicator lamps are fitted with 2.5 watt festoon bulbs. The rear number plate is illuminated by a 5 watt bulb operated from the main lighting circuit.

Two three purpose rear light units are fitted to accommodate the parking, direction indicator and brake light units and are provided with a one single filament 20 watt bulb for the direction indicator and one double filament bulb of 5 watt rating for the parking circuit and 20 watt for stoplights.

Headlamp removal:

The headlamp may be removed from the front panel by slightly depressing the lens and rotating the unit counterclockwise through 15 deg. Replacement of the

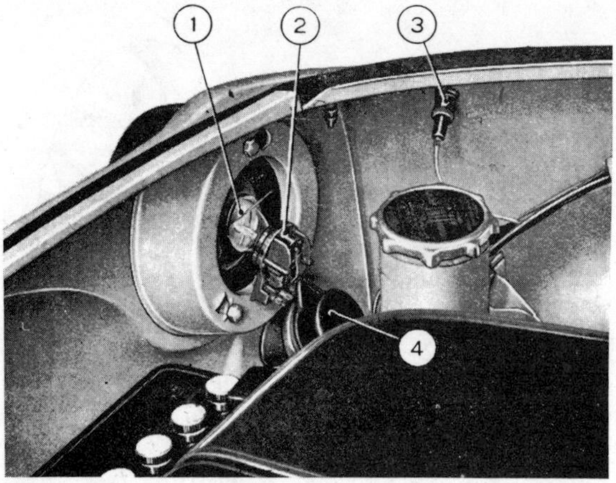

FIG 11:18 Replacement of bulb from inside front compartment

Key to Fig 11:18 1 Double-filament bulb 2 Bulbholder 2 Side direction indicator light 4 Bulbholder shield

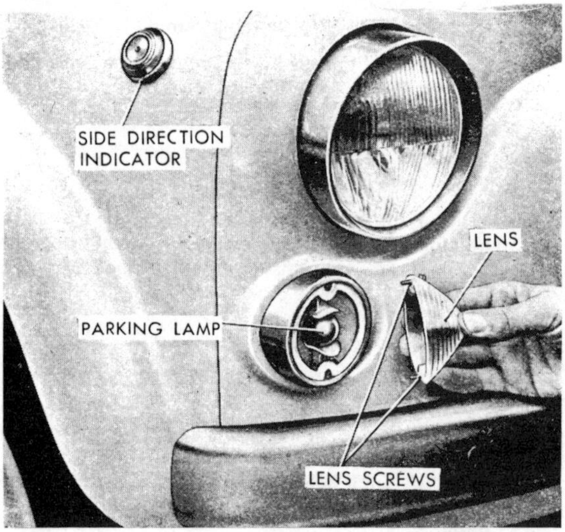

FIG 11:19 Disassembling front parking and direction indicator lamp

bulb is achieved from inside the front compartment by pulling down the upper lug of the rubber protection cap at the rear of the headlight unit and freeing the bulb holder. Pull up the bulb holder to reflector fastener spring and pull out the bulb holder complete and replace the bulb as necessary.

Beam setting:

Accurate setting is best left to a service station equipped with the necessary equipment. The main beams must be set parallel to the road surface or in accordance with local regulations. Adjustment is made by turning the top screw 1 as indicated in **FIG 11:17** for the vertical setting and the lower screws 2.

Front parking and direction indicator lamp:

To replace the double filament (5/20W), release the screws securing the lens to the lamp casing as shown in **FIG 11:19** and remove the bulb from its bayonet holder.

Rear parking, direction indicator, stop lamps and reflector lens:

To renew any of the two bulbs remove the two screws securing the lens to the lamp casing as shown in **FIG 11:20.** Bulbs are fixed by bayonet couplings.

Side direction indicator lamps:

To replace the 2.5W festoon bulb slide off the bulb holder from the rubber socket located as shown in **FIG 11:19.** The bulb is secured by a bayonet coupling.

Number plate lamp:

To replace the bayonet coupled 5W bulb remove the lens and light cap mounting screws as shown in **FIG 11:21.**

Lamps give insufficient light:

Test the state of charge of the battery and recharge if it is necessary from an independent supply. Check the setting of the lamps. If the bulbs have darkened through age fit new ones.

Lamps burn out frequently:

If this is accompanied by a need for frequent topping-up of the battery and high hydrometer readings, check the charging rate with an ammeter when the car is running. This should be around 3 to 4 amps. A reading in excess of this calls for adjustment of the regulator.

Lamps light when switched on but gradually fade:

Check the battery as it is incapable of supplying current for any length of time.

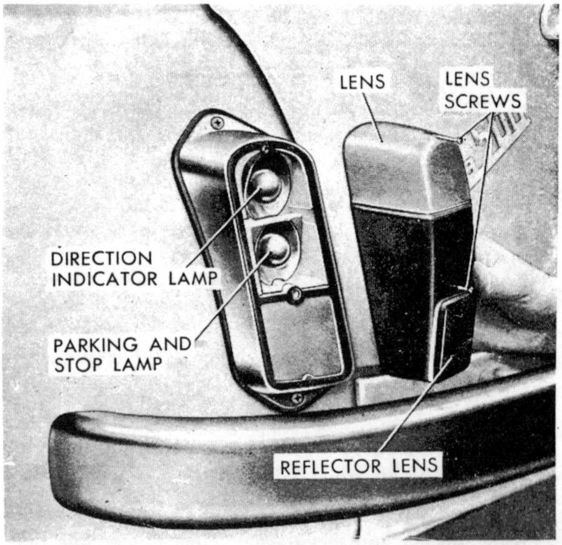

FIG 11:20 Disassembling tail parking, stop, direction indicator lamp and reflector lens

Lamp brilliance varies with the speed of the car:

Check the condition of the battery. Examine the battery connections. Make sure they are tight and renew faulty cables.

11:10 Panel and warning lights:

All the gauges are clustered in a single instrument mounted on the dashboard above the steering column. Incorporated in this cluster is the parking light pilot light, generator charge indicator, fuel reserve supply indicator, low oil pressure indicator, and the speedometer with mileage recorder.

The parking lamp indicator glows green when the ignition lock switch key is in either position 1 or 2 once the toggle switch on the instrument panel has been operated.

The generator charge indicator shows red only when the ignition is turned on. It should be extinguished when the generator output is sufficient for battery charge (12.6 ± 0.2 volts) with the engine running at a speed of 1100 rev/min and the headlights switched off.

The fuel reserve supply indicator shows red only when the ignition is turned on and the amount of fuel in the petrol tank has dropped to approximately .8 to 1.1 Imp. gallons.

The low oil pressure indicator shows red only when the ignition is turned on and should be extinguished when the oil pressure reaches 7.1 to 21.3 lb/sq in, and opens the sending unit contacts. Once the engine is at normal operating temperature but at a speed below 1000 rev/min the indicator might light up even the pressure is under control and with normal operation.

All the bulbs fitted to the above described units are of the tubular 2.5W type and to renew a bulb extract the bulb holder from the rear of the instrument cluster and release the bulb which is attached by a normal bayonet coupling.

Fuel reserve supply indicator sender unit:

The fuel reserve supply indicator should be checked for correct indication by allowing the fuel tank to empty and then inserting .8 to 1.1 Imp. gallons at which stage the light should extinguish. Any failure to do so should be checked as follows:

1 Ensure that the indicator bulb operates correctly.
2 Check for complete circuit between the sender unit and the indicator bulb.
3 If the sender unit float bracket is distorted the bulb will indicate a reserve supply of fuel greater or smaller than specified. The bracket should be adjusted to give correct indication of fuel level.
4 The sender unit could have been inadvertantly damaged in which case the unit must be renewed.

11:11 The horn

The horn circuit comprises the horn, push button at the centre of the steering wheel and normal earth return electrical circuit through the car body. One terminal is connected to the battery whilst the other to the push button on the steering wheel which when the button is depressed the circuit will be closed so causing the horn to operate.

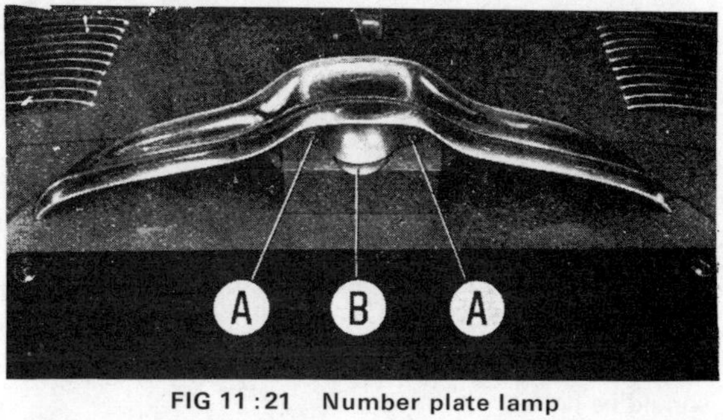

FIG 11:21 Number plate lamp

Key to Fig 11:21 **A** Lens and light cap mounting screws **B** Lens

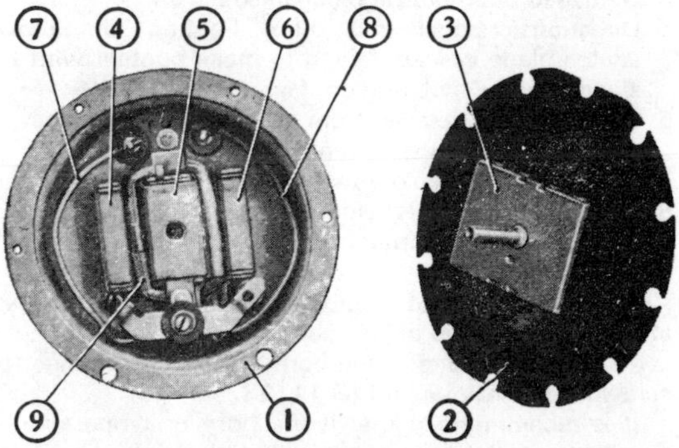

FIG 11:22 Horn (opened)

Key to Fig 11:22 1 Body 2 Diaphragm 3 Armature 4, 5, 6 Core 7 Cable: terminal-condenser-stationary contact 8 Cable: terminal-magnetizing coil end 9 Magnetizing coil

FIG 11:23 Horn sound adjustment. Obtained by adjusting the armature air gap

Before removing an apparently faulty horn check the wiring and connections. Check that the mounting bolts are tight and that the horn does not foul any adjacent part.

Removal and installation:

This is a straightforward operation and the only precaution to be taken is to ensure that the rubber gasket bonded to the horn body does not become detached. If the horn is renewed, before installing the new horn bond the rubber gasket to the new unit with adhesive in the same position as was on the original horn unit fitted.

Should the horn fail to operate the following points should be noted.

1 Damaged horn.
2 Broken connection between battery and horn.
3 Broken connection between horn and push button on steering wheel.
4 Damaged push button mechanism.
5 Directional signal and outer lighting changeover switch blade contact failing to make contact with the steering wheel hub ring contact.
6 Current lead displaced from the horn blade contact on the directional signal and outer lighting switch.
7 Distorted or broken diaphragm in horn.
8 Connections or inner windings broken or burnt.
9 Electro-magnet contact points dirty or excessively worn.

The contacts may be adjusted by the adjusting screw after the points have been cleaned and refaced.

To adjust the tone of the horn use a ring spanner and screwdriver as shown in **FIG 11:23.**

It is recommended that if the horn unit operation is unreliable a new unit should be fitted rather than the original one repaired.

11:12 Lighting and flasher switch

Description:

The two switches provide a directional signal switch which automatically returns to the rest position once a turn has been negotiated and the steering wheel is brought back to the straight-ahead position. The change over switch controls the outer lights and the headlights flasher. The complete unit is located under the steering wheel on the steering column.

Switch unit removal:

1 Carefully pry off the horn push button at the steering wheel centre using a fine blade screwdriver.
2 Disconnect the positive terminal of the battery.
3 Disconnect the plug in contact in the steering wheel hub.
4 Unscrew the steering wheel retaining nut from the inner column and remove the steering wheel from the shaft.
5 Slacken the bolts securing the steering column support to the body.
6 Remove the plug in contacts from the switch unit ensuring that their correct location is noted for re-assembly.
7 Remove the switch unit from the steering column.

Switch unit installation:

This is the reverse procedure to dismantling. It is advisable after installation to check that the steering wheel when in the straight-ahead position and the directional signal switch lever in neutral, the reference index on the outer face of the directional signal switch drum is in line with the index on the steering wheel hub. This will ensure correct sequence of operation.

11:13 Fault diagnosis

(a) Battery discharged

1 Lighting circuit shorted
2 Terminals loose or dirty
3 Generator not charging
4 Regulator or cut-out units not working properly
5 Battery internally defective

(b) Insufficient charging current

1 Loose or corroded battery terminals
2 Generator driving belt slipping

(c) Battery will not hold a charge

1 Low electrolyte level
2 Battery plates sulphated
3 Electrolyte leakage from cracked casing or top sealing compound
4 Plate separators ineffective

(d) Battery overcharged

1 Voltage regulator needs adjusting

(e) Generator output low or nil

1 Belt broken or slipping
2 Regulator unit out of adjustment
3 Worn bearings, loose pole pieces
4 Commutator worn, burned or shorted
5 Armature shaft bent or worn
6 Insulation proud between commutator segments
7 Brushes sticking, springs weak or broken
8 Field coil wires shorted, broken or burned

(f) Starter motor lacks power or will not operate

1 Battery discharged, loose cable connections
2 Starter pinion jammed in mesh with flywheel gear
3 Starter switch faulty
4 Brushes worn or sticking, heads detached or shorting
5 Commutator dirty or worn
6 Starter shaft bent
7 Engine abnormally stiff

(g) Starter motor inoperative

1 Check 1 in (f)
2 Armature or field coils faulty

(h) Starter motor rough or noisy

1 Mounting bolts loose
2 Damaged pinion or flywheel gear teeth

(i) Lamps inoperative or erratic

1 Battery low, bulbs burned out
2 Faulty earthing of lamps or battery
3 Lighting switch faulty, loose or broken wiring connections

(j) Wiper motor sluggish, taking high current

1 Faulty armature
2 Bearings out of alignment
3 Commutator dirty or short-circuited

(k) Wiper motor operated but does not drive arms

1 Gearbox components worn

CHAPTER 12

THE BODYWORK

12:1 Bodywork finish

Large scale repairs to body panels are best left to expert panel beaters. Even small dents can be tricky, as too much hammering will stretch the metal and make things worse instead of better. Filling minor dents and scratches is probably the best method of restoring the surface. The touching up of paintwork is well within the powers of most car owners, particularly as self-spraying cans of paint in the correct colours are now readily available. It must be remembered, however, that paint changes colour with age and it is better to spray a whole wing rather than try to touch up a small area.

Before spraying it is essential to remove all traces of wax polish with white spirit. More drastic treatment is required if silicone polishes have been applied. Use a primer surfacer or paste stopper according to the amount of filling required, and when it is dry, rub it down with 400 grade Wet or Dry paper until the surface is smooth and flush with the surrounding area. Spend time on getting the best finish as this will control the final effect. Apply the retouching paint, keeping it wet in the centre and light and dry round the edges. After a few hours of drying, use a cutting compound to remove the dry spray and finish with liquid polish.

12:2 Interior and chrome cleaning

The cloth upholstery of the seating and the rear compartment lining must be regularly cleaned to ensure long life and preserve its attractive appearance. Any dust or dirt that is blown into the car will settle on the upholstery and will tend to wear the cloth causing an unsightly appearance. It is recommended that the dust is wiped off using either a vacuum cleaner or a stiff brush. To remove ordinary soiling of the upholstery cloth proceed as follows:

1 Using luke warm water and a neutral soap and a piece of clean cloth wipe over the upholstery in the direction of the nap.

2 Repeat the operation using a clean damp cloth and warm water but no soap.

3 Allow the upholstery cloth to dry, use a stiff brush against the direction of the upholstery nap to restore its original fluffy look.

To obtain best results, any stains must be removed as soon as possible otherwise as time passes they will become more difficult, if not impossible to remove. Certain stains require specific solvents and the instructions must be strictly adhered to.

FIG 12:1 Detail of right door (early type). Upper arrow points to vent wing lock handle. Lower arrow points to window regulator handle

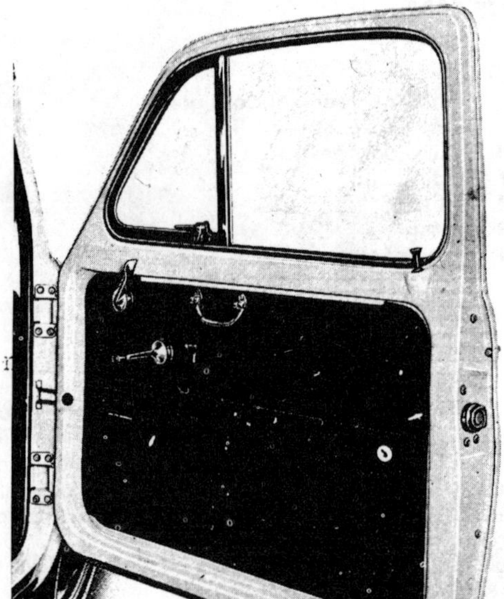

FIG 12:2 Sedan right side door (later type). Front-hinged. Door latch is of the triple acting type

Cleaning imitation leather:

To keep the imitation leather clean wash in luke warm water and a neutral soap applied with a soft cloth. Wipe clean with a clean moistened cloth with no trace of soap and finally rub with a clean dry cloth until the original lustre is restored.

The usual reason for imitation leather to lose its softness or lustre is usually attributed to unsuitable cleaners being used.

Chrome plated parts:

To ensure long life from the chrome plated parts these should be periodically washed using a cloth dampened with petrol and dried with a soft cloth. Rub with a cloth moistened in clean oil especially around the edges of the components and finally rub using a clean dry cloth until all traces of oil have been apparently removed.

Glass panels:

The glass panels must be cleaned with a chamois leather or rag. Take care that no abrasive material is allowed to be rubbed onto the glass otherwise it will be scratched.

12:3 Door trim and accessories

The two opening doors have welded upper and lower hinge halves being joined by a fulcrum pin to the other half of the hinge which is welded onto the body. Upon reassembly of a hinge the fulcrum pins must be fitted with the ball head uppermost.

Check strap:

To limit the door opening, a rubber check strap is fixed by four self-tapping screws of which two are located on the door and two on the body. When a check strap is being fitted the following points should be noted:

1 Always use sealing compound on the check strap mounting holes to ensure a moisture tight joint.
2 Insert the screws in the plates and in the strap.
3 Always place a washer on each screw between the body and the check strap, and also the door and check strap. Tighten the screws fully.

Weather strip:

A one-piece moulded weather strip is fitted to the door aperture and fixed by a special adhesive. Should the weather strip become detached or a new one requiring to be fitted proceed as follows:

1 Remove the old weather strip as necessary and thoroughly clean the door opening flange with petrol, remove any rust spots and touch in the paint work.
2 Clean the new weather strips of their preservative or the original from road dirt using petrol and thoroughly wipe clean.
3 Apply a coat of adhesive using a brush to the side to be attached to the body. Allow to dry for the recommended period of time and position the weather strip on the door opening flange ensuring that it is not distorted. The joint should be on the bottom side of the rear end of the door opening. Apply a heavy pressure on the weather strip starting from the centre and working towards the ends.

Two rubber lining strips are located on the door flange and these should be attached using the same procedure detailed above.

Ensure that the bonding of the rubber weather strips to both the door opening flange and the door panel is thoroughly dry before the door is closed, otherwise this could be the cause of subsequent water ingress.

Inner panels:

Imitation leather-lined masonite trim panels are fitted to all versions of the 'new 500' models. The panels are secured in the housing below the door window by means of four stiff clips located at the top and seven spring clips located at the bottom equally spaced around the panel border. The fasteners are located in holes in the door framework inner flange. The door framework has a plate which should be bent downwards onto the trim panel once it has been installed. This will ensure correct seating of the trim panel in the door housing.

When the door trim panel is being reassembled ensure that the tarred felt pad is cemented correctly on the door inner flange so that any water that may seep in through to the door interior from the window rubber weather strips may be kept away from the trim panel which would otherwise cause distortion and rapid deterioration.

12:4 Door handles and locks

The doors are provided with locks which are operated by handles either from inside or outside the vehicle. The driver's side door handle is provided with a key locking handle.

Removal of the lock is a straightforward operation but upon reassembly the following procedure should be followed:

1 Mount the handle assembly from the outside and insert the washer onto the stud. Screw in the nut several turns to allow correct handle-to-lock mating on final fitting.
2 Arrange the locking handle dog so that it is horizontally positioned and tighten the mounting nut.
3 Mount the lock to the door panel and secure with three screws and washers.
4 Fit the plate with the two rubber guide blocks fastening by the two screws.

Striker plates are fitted with shim adjustment to the door pillars and are secured by three screws.

12:5 Removing window regulator and door glass

Window regulator:

Description:

The window regulator unit is of the lever and gear control type which transmits crank movement to the lifting lever using high ratio gears. When the operating handle is rotated it rotates a pinion mounted on its shaft which is in mesh with a gear on the hub of which is mounted a second pinion that meshes with the lever toothed sector (refer to **FIG 12:3**). At the end of the lever a pin fitting locates in a guide rail mounted on the bottom of the glass. When the crank is rotated in one or other direction the glass is either lifted or lowered.

Regulator removal:

1 Depress the door lining panel so that the crank key may be located. Remove the key and the crank handle.
2 Using a wide blade screwdriver prise off the trim panel by inserting the blade between the panel and the door frame taking care not to scratch the door paint.
3 Remove the intermediate protection lining.

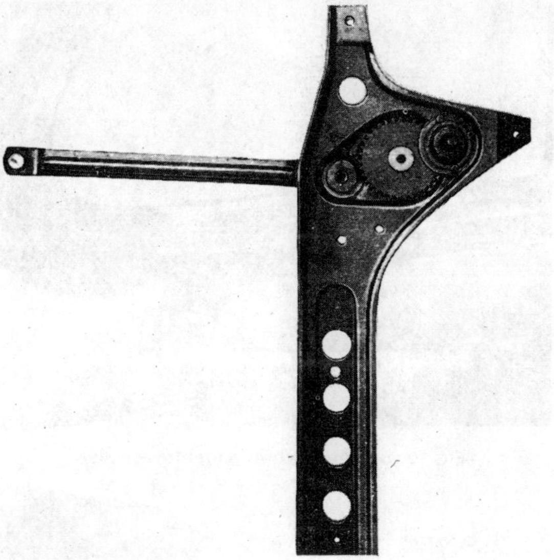

FIG 12:3 Lefthand side door window regulator, viewed from car interior

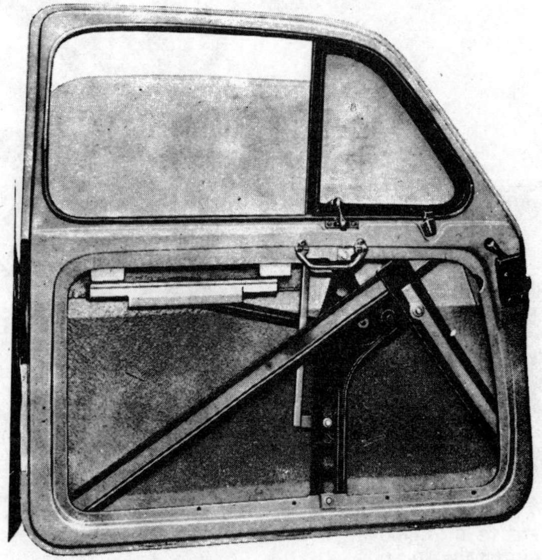

FIG 12:4 Location of window regulator in lefthand side door panel housing

4 Release the screws securing the window regulator to to the door. Carefully taut the regulator so as to disengage the lever pin from the guide on the bottom of the glass and lift away the regulator assembly.

Regulator reassembly:

To ensure satisfactory regulator operation carefully lubricate the gears and the lever pin guide and also ensure that the glass slides freely in its channels. To

FIG 12:5 Ventilation panel lower pivot

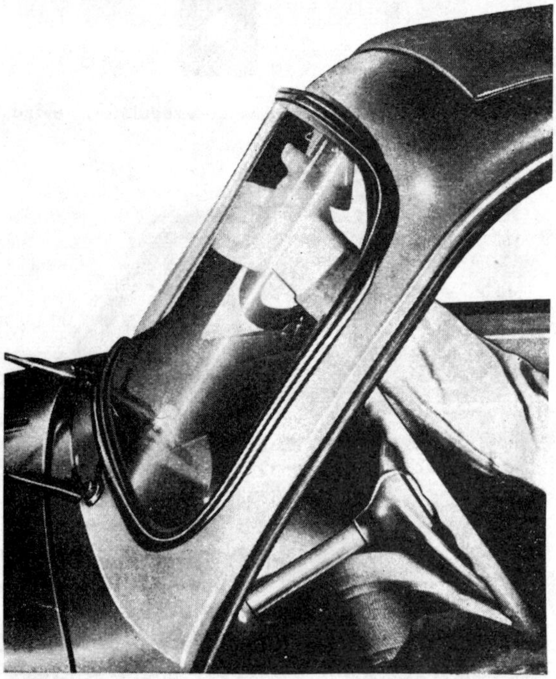

FIG 12:6 Removal of windshield glass. Simply press out as shown

reassemble the regulator to the door is the reverse procedure to dismantling. The following points should however, be noted:

1 Before the lining is refitted to the door panel ensure that the regulator operates correctly. Ensure that the glass moves up and down in its channels without excessive efforts required on the crank handle.
2 Once the lining is glued into place ensure that it adheres evenly on the door so that the window regulator operation is not interfered with at a later date due to the lining becoming detached.

Door window drop glass and weather strip:

Description:

The door windows are fitted with swivelling front glass ventilators and a drop rear glass pane. The 'new 500' convertible is equipped with stationary type window rear glass which is secured to the door panel by means of two brackets and screws together with spring washers and nuts.

Removal of door glass:

To remove the door window drop glass proceed as previously described for removing the regulator assembly, and then ease forward the front glass guide and then carefully lift away the glass.

Reassembly:

1 Fit Fiat No. 16 clips equally spaced all along the door window flange.
2 Install the glass runway by inserting it in the rear and upper side of the window groove. The runway is fastened in place by the spring clips.
3 Install the glass runway, complete with the fabric lining and secure it to the regulator frame on the top side using self-tapping screws and on the bottom side with the bracket, screw, plain washer and spring washer.
4 Secure the gear type window regulator to the door panel using the three screws, three plain washers and three toothed washers.
5 Refit the window rubber weather strips which are lined with fabric on both inner faces that touch the glass pane. Lock the weather strips in place with the Fiat clips.
6 Replace the metal joint cap.
7 Fit and correctly locate the drop glass complete with lower rubber weather strip, metal channel and run plate for sliding travel of window regulator arm.

FIG 12:7 Positioning the windshield after tilting wiper blades

8 Refit the intermediate protection lining ensuring that it is properly located and well glued. Refit the door lining panel, key and crank handle.

Door ventilator:

The door ventilator comprises the glass, weather strip placed between the glass and chromium plated frame, the chromium plated frame together with pin and bracket for upper and lower hinging, frame control handle and lining.

To remove the ventilator glass first drill the upper pivot pin using a portable electric drill and release the nut and locknut from the lower pivot bracket. Carefully lift away the glass.

Reassembly:

To reassemble the ventilator glass proceed as follows:

1 Coat the outer edge of the glass on which the chrome plated frame must be installed with a 50% solution of petrol and oil to ensure that the glass can be easily inserted into the frame.
2 Install the lock handle which is secured to the frame by means of a screw sunk into the handle body and two corrugated spring washers placed between the frame and the handle.
3 Before installing the ventilator pane on the door panel ensure that the metal channel in the front post flanges at the pane base are firmly located in place and fit the rubber weather strip arranging it carefully in its seating. The weather strip is secured by clips located on the metal channels.
4 Refit the handle striker plate and secure it to the door channel by means of two self-tapping screws.
5 Insert the lower ventilator swivel on the door panel to welded bracket. Fit the spring and secure ventilator assembly through the nut, locknut and plain washer so that it can be freely adjusted to any position without undue effort.
6 Fit the chrome cover on the lower ventilator swivel. Refit the upper ventilator swivel in the door panel brackets and clench it using a hammer and a suitably sized drift against a firm metal block. This will ensure correct ventilator movement.

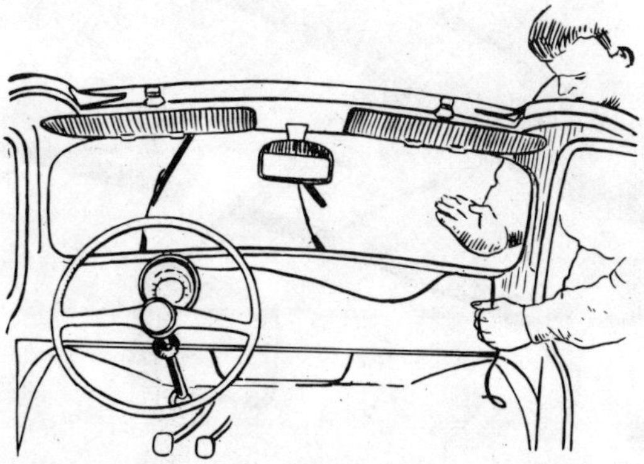

FIG 12:8 Adapting windshield weatherstrip. Simply pull the draw-cord

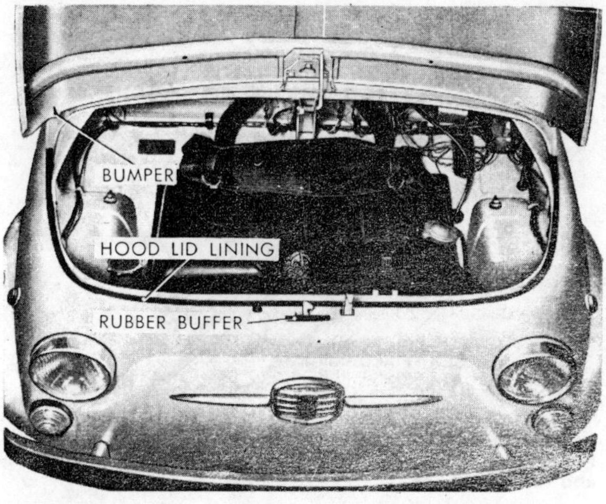

FIG 12:9 Front compartment lid lining and rubber buffers

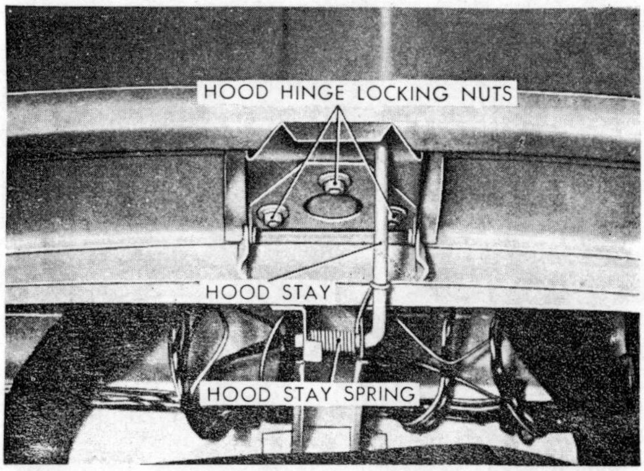

FIG 12:10 Close-up view of hood lid hinge and stay

12:6 Removing windshield glass

Removal:

To remove the windshield glass carefully push from the interior of the car against the glass and with the assistance of a second operator carefully ease the glass away from the glass aperture.

Reassembly:

1 Fit the weather strip onto the glass.
2 Insert a draw cord completely around the weather strip outer lip. Ensure that the cord ends come to the centre of the lower edge of the glass as shown in **FIG 12:6.**
3 Press the windshield assembly against the body opening from the outside as shown in **FIG 12:7** and then carefully pull the cord ends from the inside so the overlap of the weatherstrip will locate over the body opening lip.
4 Carefully replace the rear view mirror bulb cable between the weather strip lip and the body panel from

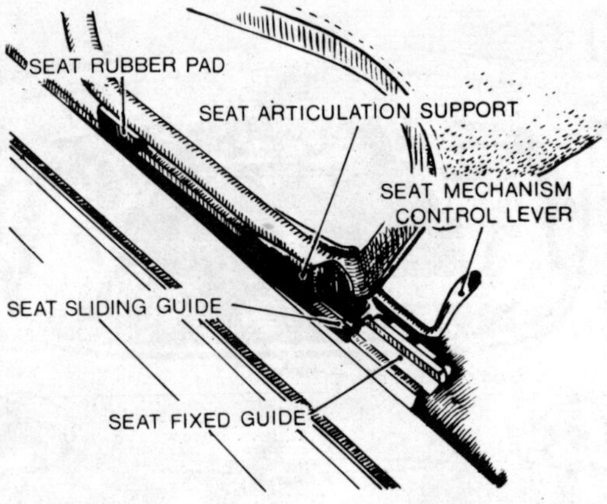

FIG 12:11 Sedan front seat, with removable cushion and reclining back

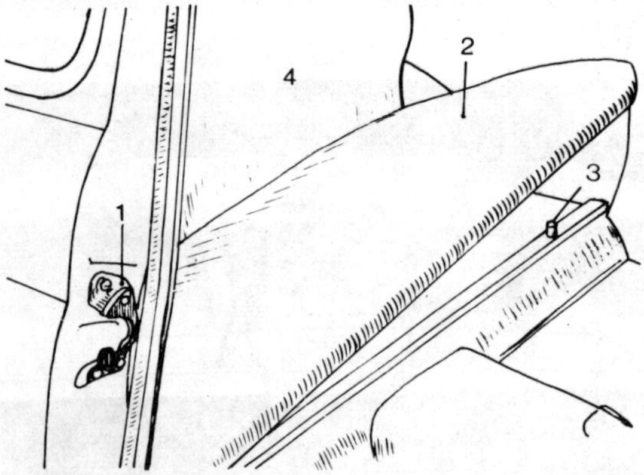

FIG 12:12 Sedan rear seat with removable cushion and reclining back

Key to Fig 12:12 1 Striker plate for triple acting door latch 2 Seat cushion 3 Dowels (two) for seat cushion location 4 Seat back

the rear view mirror to the righthand side of the dashboard.

5 Using a special compound sealing gun inject sealer between weather strip outer lip and body.

12:7 Removing rear side windows

The rear quarter glass panes are located to the body using the weather strips. To remove the glass simply push outwards ensuring that a second operator is ready to catch the glass as the weather strip becomes detached from the body.

To reassemble the glass pane proceed as directed for refitting the front windshield. Finally seal as previously described using sealing compound.

12:8 Removing rear window glass

The rear window glass is removed and replaced in the same manner as described in **Section 12:6** for the removal and replacement of the windshield glass. Ensure that the weather strip inner groove is thoroughly filled using correct sealing compound.

12:9 Front compartment lid

The front compartment lid is hinged at the centre with the lower half of the hinge welded to the body upper crossmember. The hinge upper half is secured to the lower half by nuts and washers which are screwed onto the lid studs. The compartment lid is kept closed by a catch as shown in **FIG 12:9** with an additional safety hook to avoid accidental opening.

The catch release mechanism is controlled by a handle which is located under the lefthand side of the instrument panel and connected to the lock by means of a bowden cable. The cable is arranged inside the front compartment and the inner wire passes through a bracket and secured to the catch. A return spring is fitted onto the catch, the latter pivoting on a locked pin.

A specially shaped weather strip is arranged on the front and side flange of the front compartment opening. To refit and renew the weather strip ensure that all the old bonding compound is removed using a stiff brush. Spread fresh adhesive to the body shell and carefully locate and press home the weather strip.

Six rubber bumpers are press fitted into the body shell and at both ends of the front compartment lid to ensure correct location and freedom of rattles.

12:10 Engine compartment lid

The opening and closing movement of the lid is controlled by a locking handle. The lid opens downwards and pivots on two lower hinges. The hinge pin is welded onto the lid and its socket is welded to the body rear lower crossmember. To remove the engine compartment lid proceed as follows:

1 Remove the number plate lamp cable terminal.
2 Unhook the check strap by manipulating the retaining cross piece.
3 Release the righthand pin self-locking nut and exert a slight pressure on the righthand side of the lid so pushing it towards the left.

Reassembly is the reverse procedure to dismantling.

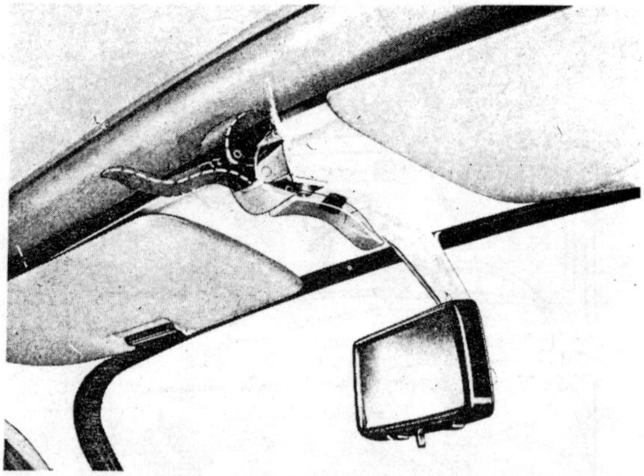

FIG 12:13 Centre catch of Sedan and Station Wagon folding top. Dotted lines show the folding top control handle in open position

12:11 Folding top

The folding top assembly comprises the following items:

1 Imitation leather top with vinylite back window.
2 Front end frame complete with two handles and catches. A movable bow which slides on the frame guide rails.
3 Three stiffening bows fixed by chrome plated buttons and tipped with rubber blocks.
4 Front mouldings for top mounting on frame.
5 Rear moulding on top mounting engine cooling air intake body panel.
6 Retaining strap for the roller stop.

The removal of the folding top is straightforward but care should be taken on reassembly to the vehicle and the following points should be noted:

1 The top rear moulding is secured by ten screws consisting of six self-tapping screws and four standard screws which are located as follows:
(a) One long self-tapping screw at each end.
(b) Two standard screws at centre.
(c) Two standard screws next to the long screws.
(d) Four self-tapping screws, two on each side between the standard screws.
These screws also secure the upper end of the engine air intake panel to body.
2 Having fixed the rear moulding spread the top across the opening. Ensure the pivoting bow is located between the second and third stiffening bows. Using special screws fix the frame rails to the upper inner ends of the body side panels.

12:12 Sunroof

The 'new 500' sunroof model differs from the convertible model in the arrangement of the top. The sunroof comprises a rear metal panel and a front imitation leather covering which acts as a collapsible top.

The weather strip surrounded back window is located on the rear metal panel and the following items are cemented in place; plastic lining, foam rubber strip at upper front end, and two rubber welts located on the sides to prevent water ingress.

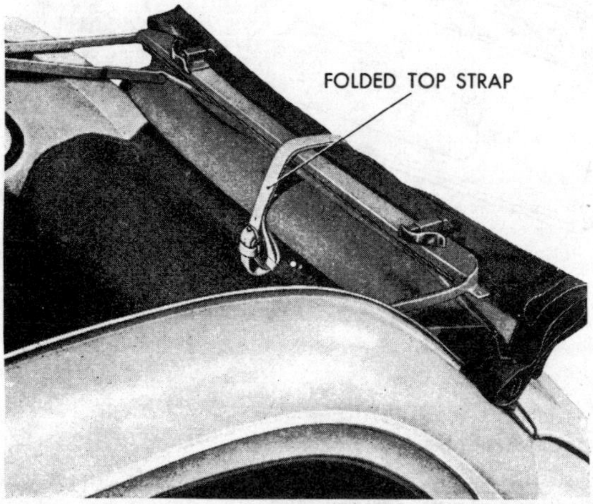

FIG 12:14 Folded top retaining strap

FIG 12:15 Arrangement of rolled top. This should be done carefully to prevent damaging the vinylite back window. Roll must never obstruct engine air intake slots

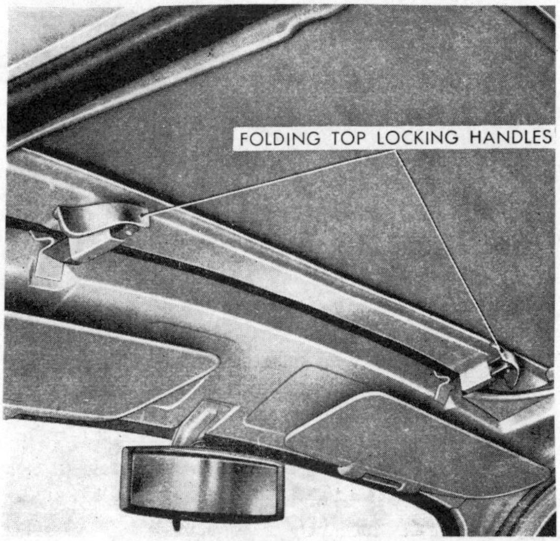

FIG 12:16 Sun Roof top in locked position

The rear metal panel is secured to the body shell by means of four screws, four plain washers and four spring washers and at the rear by means of nine self-tapping screws which provide a mounting for the engine air intake grill and gutter.

The collapsible top comprises the following items:

1 Imitation leather lining.
2 Metal frame with a front crossmember onto which the control handles and top front latch strikers are fitted. A movable bow riveted to the top lining and fitted with rubber pads which rest on the top of the body.
3 Front moulding for the top lining mounting onto the framing crossmember.

FIG 12:17 Sun Roof top in unlatched position

4 Rear moulding for the top lining mounting onto the rear metal panel.
5 Top lining retaining strap which is secured to the front end of the rear metal panel using a bridge bracket.
6 Bracket for strap which hooks up the top lining when in the folded position.

Dismantling and reassembly is a straightforward operation providing that careful note is made of the location of all screws that are removed. To reassemble it is suggested that the rear metal panel is mounted on the body shell first. The collapsible top assembly is then positioned and secured to the rear metal panel using eight rivets. The top covering should be stretched to the closed position and secured to both framing side arms to the body shell wells using the special screws.

12:13 Seats

Front seats:

The front bucket seats comprise a one-piece tubular frame covered with imitation leather or cloth padded cushion and back rest. A number of rubber straps are hooked across the frame under the cushion and in a sheath covering on the seat back.

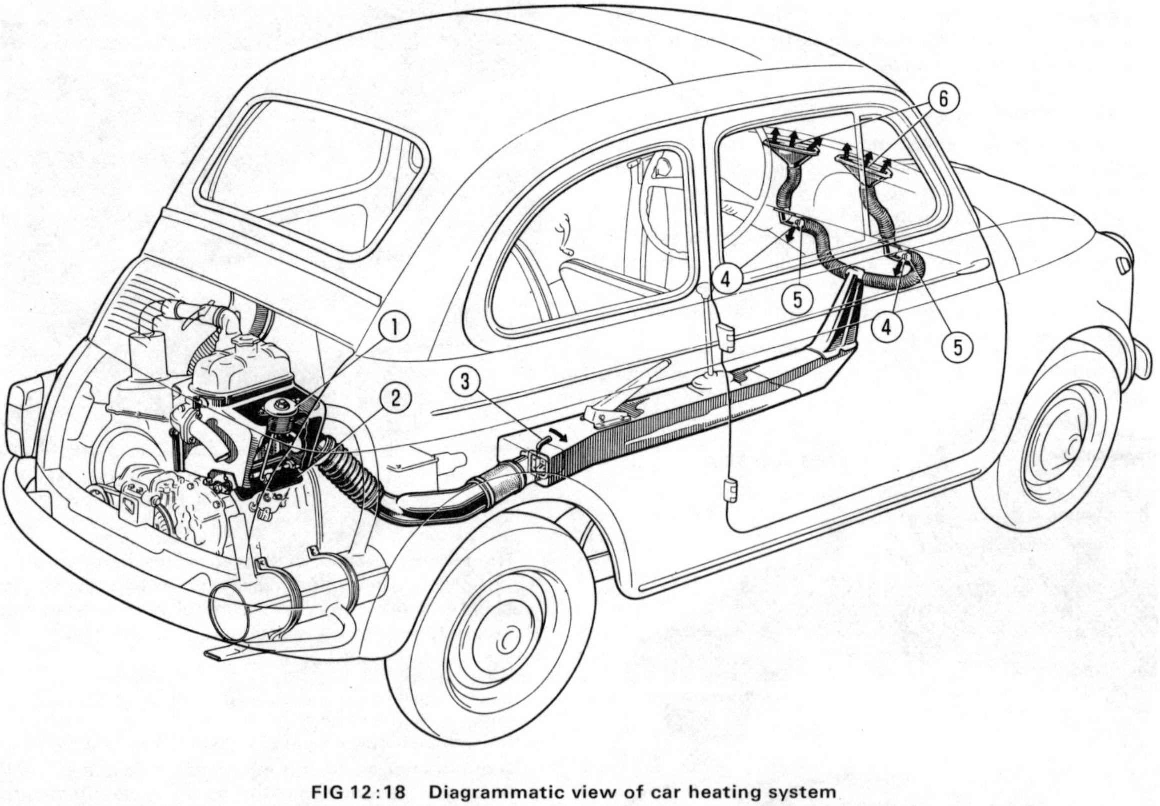

FIG 12:18 Diagrammatic view of car heating system

Key to Fig 12:18 1 Thermostat controlling shutter 2 Shutter, engine cooling air outlet 3 Lever, heater hand control 4 Warm air outlet slots 5 Demister valve control knobs 6 Windshield demister diffusers
NOTE—The car may be also equipped, optionally, with a heating booster as shown in **FIG 12:19**

The bottom of the front seat frame ends are provided with sliding guides which run in guide rails attached to the floor. The sliding guides are pivoted on the frame tubes to allow for forward tilting of the seats giving better access to the rear compartment. Two rubber pads provide cushioning of the seat frame on the guide rails as shown in **FIG 12:11.** The control lever for seat adjustment is fitted in the frame righthand tube to permit unlocking of the seats so that they may be adjusted to individual drivers requirements.

Rear seats (Sedan):

The rear seat comprises of a foam rubber cushion and back. The seat back is cemented to the rear floor and body shell bulkhead. The rear seat lining is of fabric and imitation leather. The seat lining is held in place by four self-tapping screws, two of which secure the floor below the back window and two the lining at the base of the back rest. Included with the seat assembly is a masonite floor which is fitted below the rear window.

Rear Seat (Station Wagon):

The rear seat back rest is pivoted at the base of its frame so that it can be folded down to form a load platform surface. In the upright position it is retained in place by two brackets mounted on either side of the body below the side windows.

12:14 Interior heater

Description:

Interior heating is accomplished by recirculation of warm air from the engine cooling system through engine cowling. Referring to **FIG 12:18** a hose conveys warmed air from the engine cowling to the centre tunnel floor where warm air flows out through two slots being cut on the windshield delivery hoses. Air admission can be adjusted by turning the control lever to the right which operates the tunnel throttle valve at the rear seat.

The heating system may be fitted with a booster which comprises a casing on the front exhaust pipe being connected to the engine cowling and the warmed air passage tunnel. Warm air flowing to the car interior is heated to higher temperature than that from the standard version of heater (see **FIG 12:19**).

Windshield demisting:

As will be seen from **FIG 12:18,** two air hoses with throttle valves for air flow control are relayed from a casing in front of the centre of the floor tunnel. Flexible hoses are connected to two air defuses which are located on the instrument panel and parallel to the windshield glass. When the throttle valves 5 (see **FIG 12:18**) are operated through the two control knobs, warmed air is directed onto the windshield glass so preventing misting, frosting or icing in adverse weather conditions.

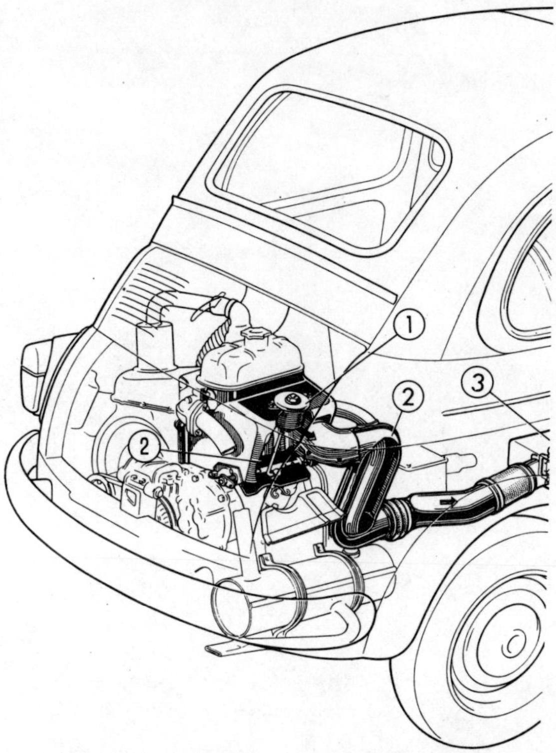

FIG 12:19 Diagram of booster

Key to Fig 12:19 1 Thermostat controlling shutter 2 Car interior heater booster 3 Hand control unit

Inspection:

Ensure that the lever, the lever spring and butterfly valve hinge are not distorted. Check that the ducting to the tunnel as well as the upper and lower hoses are airtight which if not, should be renewed.

APPENDIX

TECHNICAL DATA

WIRING DIAGRAMS

HINTS ON MAINTENANCE AND OVERHAUL

GLOSSARY OF TERMS

INDEX

TECHNICAL DATA

Dimensions are in inches unless otherwise stated

ENGINE

Cylinders and crankcase:

Cylinder barrel diameter:	
Model 500 Class A	2.5984 to 2.5988
Class B	2.5988 to 2.5992
Class C	2.5992 to 2.5996
Model 500 Sports, 500D, 500 (110F), 500L, Sedan, Station wagon Class A	2.6535 to 2.6539
Class B	2.6539 to 2.6543
Class C	2.5643 to 2.6547
Camshaft seat diameter:	
Timing gear end	1.6939 to 1.6954
Flywheel end	.8669 to .8682
Valve tappet crankcase seat diameter	.8670 to .8662

Connecting rods, bearing inserts, bushings:

Connecting rod bearing bore diameter ...	1.8555 to 1.8560
Connecting rod small end bushing bore diameter	.8637 to .8650
Standard con rod bearing half thickness	.0604 to .0675
Replacement connecting rod bearing half undersize range	.0100 to .0200 .0300 to .0400
Connecting rod small end bushing O.D.	.8661 to .8673
Connecting rod small end bushing I.D. (bushing in place)	.7874 to .7876
Piston pin, small end bushing fit:	
assembly clearance	.00020 to .00083
wear limit	.0020
Small end bushing-to-bushing bore	.0011 to .0036 pinch fit at all times
Con rod bearing half-to-con rod journal fit:	
assembly clearance	.00043 to .00240
wear limit	.0059
Maximum misalignment of connecting rod axes: $4\frac{59}{64}$ inch apart from rod centreline	± .0020
Weight tolerance in the same set of connecting rods	± .1 oz

Pistons, piston pins, piston rings:

Standard piston diameter, square to pin axis:	
Model 500 at skirt top Class A	2.5953 to 2.5957
Class B	2.5957 to 2.5961
Class C	2.5961 to 2.5965
at skirt bottom Class A	2.5972 to 2.5976
Class B	2.5976 to 2.5980
Class C	2.5980 to 2.5984
Model 500 Sports, 500D, 500 (110F), 500L, Sedan, Station wagon at skirt top Class A ...	2.6496 to 2.6500
Class B ...	2.6500 to 2.6504
Class C ...	2.6504 to 2.6508
at skirt bottom Class A ...	2.6516 to 2.6520
Class B ...	2.6520 to 2.6524
Class C ...	2.6524 to 2.6528
Piston pin bore diameter	.7868 to .7870
Piston ring groove height 1st groove	.0823 to .0829
2nd groove	.0823 to .0829
3rd groove	.0819 to .0825
4th groove	.1577 to .1583

Piston pin diameter, standard	.7872 to .7870
Replacement piston pin oversizes	.0079
Piston ring thickness:	
First compression ring and second and third oil rings	.0783 to .0779
Fourth radial-slotted oil ring	.1550 to .1540
Piston-to-cylinder barrel fit, measured square to pin axis:	
Model 500:	
At skirt top — assembly clearance ...	.0028 to .0035
wear limit	.0098
at skirt bottom — assembly clearance ...	.0008 to .0016
wear limit	.0059
Model 500 Sports, 500D, 500 (110F), 500L, Sedan, Station wagon	
At skirt top — assembly clearance ...	.0035 to .0043
wear limit	.0098
At skirt bottom — assembly clearance ...	.0016 to .0024
wear limit	.0079
Piston pin-to-pin boss fit	0 to .0004 pinch fit at all times
Piston ring-to-groove land fit (vertically):	
First compression ring and second oil ring:	
assembly clearance	.0039 to .0050
wear limit	.0079
Third oil ring:	
assembly clearance	.0035 to .0046
wear limit	.0059
Fourth radial-slotted oil ring:	
assembly clearance	.0027 to .0043
wear limit	.0059
Gap of piston rings in cylinder barrel:	
First, second and third rings:	
assembly clearance	.0098 to .0138
wear limit	.0197
Fourth ring	Touch fit at all times
Piston oversize range (Model 500 only)	.0079, .0157 to .0236
Piston ring oversize range (Model 500 only):	
First, second and third rings	.0079, .0157 to .0236
Fourth ring	.0157

Crankshaft, main bearing inserts:

Con rod journal diameter, standard	1.7328 to 1.7336
Main bearing journal diameter, standard	2.1260 to 2.1248
I.D. of standard main bearings in supporting members, camshaft and flywheel ends ...	2.1268 to 2.1274
Undersize range of main bearings in supporting members, camshaft and flywheel ends ...	.0079 to .0157 to .0236, .0315 to .0394
Main bearing-to-bearing journal fit:	
assembly clearance	.00079 to .00256
wear limit	.0039
Crankshaft end play	.0118 to .0173

Cylinder head, valves, guides, springs:

Valve guide cylinder head seat diameter	.5118 to .5125
Valve guide O.D.	.5139 to .5413
Valve guide I.D., valves in head	.3158 to .3165
Valve guide-to-cylinder head fit	.00134 to .00244 pinch fit at all times

Valve stem diameter:	
Intake and exhaust, Model 500 and intake, Model 500 Sports, 500D, 500 (110F), 500L, Station wagon	.3144 to .3150
Exhaust, Model 500 Sports, 500D, 500 (110F), 500L, Station wagon	.3136 to .3142
Valve-to-valve guide fit:	
Assembly clearance:	
Intake and exhaust, Model 500 and intake, Model 500 Sports, 500D, 500 (110F), 500L,	.00087 to .00217
Station wagon exhaust, Model 500 Sports ...	.00165 to .00295
Wear limit:	
500D, 500 (110F), 500L, Station wagon ...	.0059
Valve seat angle	45 deg. ± 5′
Valve face angle	45 deg. 30′ ± 5′
Valve head diameter—Face bottom end:	
Model 500 intake	1.1811
exhaust	1.0630
Model 500 Sports, 500D, 500 (110F), 500L, Station wagon intake	1.2598
exhaust	1.1024
Maximum run-out of valve turning on stem, with dial plunger on centre of outside face	.00079
Valve seat height	.0551
Valve seat smaller diameter:	
Model 500 intake I.D.	.9055
O.D.	1.1020 to 1.1029
exhaust I.D.	1.0236
O.D.	1.2200 to 1.2211
Model 500 Sports, 500D, 500 (110F), 500L, Station Wagon intake I.D.	.9449
O.D.	1.1414 to 1.1422
exhaust I.D.	1.1024
O.D.	1.2594 to 1.2604
Valve spring I.D.:	
Model 500	.7321
Model 500 Sports, 500D, 500 (110F), 500L, Station wagon	.7598
Free spring height:	
Model 500	1.8898
Model 500 Sports, 500D, 500 (110F), 500L, Station wagon	2.2519
Spring height under 46.3 lb of load (valves closed)	
Model 500	1.4370
Spring height under 52 lb of load (valves closed)	
Model 500 Sports, 500D, 500 (110F), 500L, Station wagon	1.5945
Spring height under 80.5 lb of load (valves open)	
Model 500	1.1024
Spring height under 78.5 lb of load (valves open)	
Model 500 Sports, 500D, 500 (110F), 500L, Station wagon	1.2598
Axial lift of valves:	
Model 500 intake	.3260
exhaust	.3244
Model 500 Sports, 500D, 500 (110F), 500L, Station wagon: intake and exhaust	.3602

Minimum load for spring height of 1.4370 Model 500	37.5 lb
Minimum load for spring height of 1.5945 inch Model 500 Sports, 500D, 500 (110F), 500L, Station wagon	43 lb

Camshaft and camshaft seats:

Camshaft journal diameter:	
Timing gear end	1.6919 to 1.6929
Flywheel end	.8653 to .8661
Camshaft seat diameter:	
Timing gear end	1.6939 to 1.6954
Flywheel end	.8669 to .8682
Camshaft journal-to-seat fit clearance:	
Timing gear end	.00098 to .0035
Flywheel end	.00079 to .0029

Tappets, rocker arms, rocker arm shaft and supports:

Valve tappet crankcase seat diameter	.8662 to .8670
Valve tappet O.D., standard	.8660 to .8652
Valve tappet oversize range	.00197 to .00394
Valve tappet-to-tappet seat fit:	
assembly clearance	.00028 to .00169
wear limit	.00315
Rocker arm shaft support bore diameter	.7089 to .7096
Rocker arm shaft diameter	.7087 to .7082
Rocker arm shaft support-to-rocker arm shaft fit:	
assembly clearance	.00020 to .00138
wear limit	.0039
Rocker arm bore diameter	.7093 to .7104
Rocker arm-to-rocker shaft fit:	
assembly clearance	.00063 to .00217
wear limit	.0059

Valve gear data

Inlet:	
Opens, BTDC:	
500, 500D, 500 (110F), 500L, Station wagon	9 deg.
500 Sports	25 deg.
Closes, ABDC:	
500, 500D, 500 (110F), 500L, Station wagon	70 deg.
500 Sports	51 deg.
Exhaust:	
Opens, BBDC:	
500, 500D, 500 (110F), 500L, Station wagon	50 deg.
500 Sports	64 deg.
Closes, ATDC:	
500, 500D, 500 (110F), 500L, Station wagon	19 deg.
500 Sports	12 deg.
These data are referred to the following rocker arm-to-valve stem adjustment clearances:	
Model 500 intake	.0177
exhaust...	.0150
Model 500 Sports, 500D, 500 (110F), 500L, Station wagon—intake and exhaust ...	.0154
Final tappet operation clearance, with cold engine, for both intake and exhaust valves:	.0059

NOTE: Up to engine No. 033069, from engine No. 033074 to No. 033308, from engine No. 033377 to No. 033384 and from engine No. 033431 to No. 033434, valve gear data, as referred to .0177 rocker arm-to-valve stem adjustment clearance, were as follows:

Intake	opens, BTDC	20 deg.
	closes, ABDC	50 deg.
Exhaust	opens, BBDC	50 deg.
	closes, ATDC	20 deg.

Final tappet operation clearance, cold engine:

Intake and exhaust ... ... .0039

CARBURETTER SETTING DATA

	Weber 26.IMB.1 New 500	*Weber 26.IMB.3 Sports*
Throat diameter	1.0236	1.0236
Primary Venturi diameter	.8268	.8661
Main jet diameter	.0441	.0433
Idling jet diameter	.0177	.0177
Choke jet diameter	.0354 F 5	.0354 F 5
Main air jet diameter	.0925	.0925
Needle seat (dampened) diameter	.0492	.0492

	Weber 26.IMB.4 500D, 500L, 500 (110F)	*Weber 26.OC Station wagon*
Body barrel bore	1.024	1.024
Choke tube	.827	.787
Main jet	.044	.041
Idling jet	.018	.018
Starting jet	.035	.031
Air correction jet	.093	.083
Needle valve (cushioned)	.049	.049
Emulsion tube		
Float level	.276	.295

IGNITION

Ignition distributor:

	500	*500 Sports*
Static advance	10 deg.	10 deg.
Centrifugal advance	18 deg at 3000 rev/min	12 deg. at 4600 rev/min
Breaker contact pressure	16.8 ± 1.8 oz	
Contact gaps	.0185 to .0209	
Condenser capacity at 50-100 Hz ...	0.15 to 0.20 μF	
Cam carrier shaft felt and oiler lubricant ...	FIAT VS oil	

Ignition coil:

Primary winding ohmic resistance at 20° ± 5°C	3.2 ohms
Secondary winding ohmic resistance at 20° ± 5°C	5000 ± 100 ohms
Ground insulation resistance at 500 V dc	50 M ohms

Spark plugs:

Thread, metric	14 x 1,25 M	
Code	CW 225 N	CW 250 A
Electrode gap	.0197 to .0236	

500D, 500 (110F), 500L, Sedan and Station wagon:

Ignition distributor:

Static advance ... ... 10 deg.

Centrifugal advance:

500D, 500 (110F), 500L, Sedan ... ... 18 deg.

500 Station wagon ... ... 28 deg.

Breaker contact pressure	16.8 ± 1.8 oz
Contact gap	.0185 to .0209
Condenser capacity at 50-100 Hz	0.15 to 0.20 μF
Cam carrier shaft felt and oiler lubricant	Engine oil

Ignition coil:

Primary winding ohmic resistance at $20° \pm 5°$C, not below	3.2 ohms
Secondary winding ohmic resistance at $20° \pm 5°$C	5000 ± 100 ohms
Ground insulation resistance at 500 V dc, not below	50 M ohms

Spark plugs:

Thread diameter and pitch, metric	14 x 1.25 M
Type:	
500D, 500 (110F), 500L, Sedan	Marelli CW 225 N
500 Station wagon	Marelli CW 260 N
	Champion L 7
Point gap Marelli	.0197 to .0236
Champion	.0236 to .0276

CLUTCH

'New 500':

Type	Single plate, working dry
Driven plate with facings of	Ferodo
Facing O.D.	5.51
Facing I.D.	3.78
Clutch springs:	
Wire diameter	.1102
Spring O.D.	.9134
Number of working coils	6
Total number of coils	$7\frac{1}{2}$
Free length	1.6417
Seated length	.9646
Corresponding load	51.80 ± 2.65 lb
Minimum load	43 lb
Lever carrier ring springs:	
Wire diameter	.0394
Spring O.D.	.3740
Number of working coils	$10\frac{1}{2}$
Length, taut spring under $1.1 \pm .11$ lb	.7677
Mounting length	1.1811
Corresponding load	$4.85 \pm .44$ lb
Pedal free travel	$1\frac{3}{8}$ to $1\frac{9}{16}$
Clearance between centre lobes of fixture A.62038 and lever carrier ring	.0039
Driven plate facing maximum permissible out-of-true	.0059 to 0.118
Clearance between clutch shaft and clutch hub splines:	
Longitudinally	.0020 to .0039
Crosswise	.0059 to .0118

500D Sedan, 500 Station wagon:

Type	Single plate, working dry
Driven plate with facings of	Ferodo
Facing O.D.	5.51 (140 mm)
Facing I.D.	3.78 (96 mm)
Clutch pressure springs:	
Wire diameter	.1142
Spring O.D.	.9213
Number of working turns	$5\frac{3}{4}$

Total number of turns	$7\frac{1}{4}$
Free length	1.5945
Seated length	.9646
Corresponding load	57.3 ± 2.6 lb
Minimum load	48.5 lb
Lever carrier ring springs:	
Wire diameter	.0394
Spring O.D.	.3740
Number of working turns	$10\frac{1}{2}$
Free length	.7677
Seated length	1.1811
Corresponding load	$4.8 \pm .4$ lb
Pedal free travel	$1\frac{3}{8}$ to $1\frac{9}{16}$

500 Sedan 110F and L, Station wagon:

Type	Single plate, dry
Throwout mechanism	Diaphragm spring
Driven plate	With friction linings
Lining O.D.	6.102
Lining I.D.	4.488
Runout of driven plate linings	.0098 to .0157
Clutch pedal free travel, corresponding to a clearance of .059 between friction ring and throwout sleeve	to $1\frac{3}{16}$
Clutch release flange travel, corresponding to a pressure plate distance of .071	.315

GEARBOX DIFFERENTIAL

'New 500' all models, Station wagon:

Speeds	4 forward and reverse	
Primary shaft	Integral with 1st, 3rd, 4th and reverse speeds drive gear cluster	
Bearings	Two	
Type	Ball	
Layshaft	Integral with final drive pinion	
Bearings front	Ball type, double row	
rear	Cylindrical roller	
Type of gears:		
Drive, 2nd, 3rd, 4th speed	Helical, constant mesh	
Driven, 2nd, 3rd, 4th speed	With dogs for quick engagement	
Drive and driven, 1st and reverse	Straight spur gears	
	Up to Engine No. 173486	*From Engine No. 173487*
Gear ratios:		
1st gear	3.27 to 1	3.70 to 1
2nd gear	2.06 to 1	2.06 to 1
3rd gear	1.30 to 1	1.30 to 1
4th gear	0.87 to 1	0.87 to 1
Reverse	4.13 to 1	5.14 to 1
Spiral bevel final drive gear ratio:		
500	8 to 41	
500 Sports	8 to 39	
Ratio to wheels:	*500*	*500 Sports*
1st gear	16.77 to 1	15.95 to 1
2nd gear	10.59 to 1	10.07 to 1
3rd gear	6.66 to 1	6.33 to 1
4th gear	4.48 to 1	4.26 to 1
Reverse	21.18 to 1	20.15 to 1

Differential case bearing	2
Type	Taper roller
Adjustment	By adjusters
Rotation torque	1.01 ± .07 ft lb
Final drive pinion and ring gear (mated):	
Backlash	.0031 to .0047
Adjustment	By shims
Pinion shim thickness	.0039 to .0059

STEERING

'New 500' all models:

Steering gear type	Worm screw and roller
Ratio	26 to 2
Worm screw bearings	Taper roller
Linkages	With relay lever
Side track rods	Adjustable by threaded ends
Intermediate rod	With incorporated ends
Sector shaft bushing	Bronze
Worm screw bearing adjustment	Through threaded sleeve adjuster
Worm screw-to-sector lash adjustment	Through sector shaft eccentric bushing rotation
Sector shaft bushing I.D....	.7874 to .7882
Sector shaft diameter	.7874 to .7866
Sector shaft-to-sector shaft bushing assembly clearance	.00000 to .00165
Turning radius	14 ft 1 in
Wheel steering angles: inner wheel	33 deg.
outer wheel	25 deg. 40 ft
Steering wheel turns (lock to lock)	3.05
Front wheel toe-in (fully laden car)	.0000 to .0787
Front track	44.09
Wheelbase, 'New 500' models	62.54
500 Station wagon	76.38

FRONT SUSPENSION

'New 500', all models:

Leaf spring	1
Leaves	1 main and 4 auxiliary
Sag, with set spring	1.1023 ± .1181 under a 297.6 lb load
Bushes for connection to kingpin housing ...	Estendblock
Connection to body bottom	By 2 supports with rubber pads
Position of spring to tighten the nut of pin for connection to kingpin housing	Static load setting
Swinging arms	2 (4 half-arms)
Connection to body	By pin and rubber bushes
Position of arm and of pin hole axes for pin nut tightening	On the same plane
Kingpin housings:	
Connection to leaf spring and to swinging arm ...	By estendblock
Kingpin angle	6 deg.
Caster	9 deg. ± 1 deg.
Caster adjustment	By shims .0197
Position of kingpin housing with respect to swinging arm plane for tightening the pin nut	95 deg.
Steering knuckles:	
	By packing rings: thkss .0977 to .098

Steering knuckle-to-kingpin housing play adjustment	*Oversize rates:* .002, .004, .006, .008, .010, .012 *Undersize rates:* .002 to .004
Geometry:	
Camber	1 deg. ± 20 ft
Camber adjustment	By shims .02 thk
Toe-in: Sedan	.0 to .0787
Station wagon	.0 to .04
Toe-in adjustment	By adjustable sleeves on track rods
Bearing lubrication	FIAT MR grease
Hydraulic shock absorbers	2
Type	Telescopic
Diameter (outer cylinder)	1.063
Fluid	FIAT S.A.1 oil
Capacity	.112 Imp. qts.

REAR SUSPENSION

'New 500':		
Swinging arms:		
Connection to body	By estendblocks	
Adjustment	Shims	
Position of arm for tightening of nuts to mounting pins on body	Wheels vertical	
Coil springs:		
Free height	8.70	
Height under a 904 ± 44 lb load	5.94	
Height under a 1268 ± 64 lb load	4.24	
Solid height	3.67	
Deflection rate	.3034 in/100 lb	
Wheel hubs:		
Roller bearing adjustment	By resilient spacer	
Bearing rotation torque, below	.36 ft lb	
Wheel alignment: toed-in (identical for both rear wheels)	0 deg. 10 ft (—10 ft, + 15 ft)	
Bearing lubrication	FIAT MR grease	
Shock absorbers	Two	
Type	Hydraulic, telescopic	
Diameter (inner cylinder)	1.063	
Fluid grade	FIAT S.A.1 oil	
Capacity	.088 Imp. qts.	
500D Sedan, 500 Station wagon:		
Swinging arms:		
Connection to underbody...	By estendblocks	
Adjustment	Shims	
Position of arm for tightening nuts to mounting pins on underbody	Wheels vertical	
Coil springs:	*500D*	*500 Station wagon*
Free height	8.70	8.74
Height under 904 ± 44 lb of load	5.94	–
Height under 1102 ± 55 lb of load	–	6.38
Height under 1268 ± 64 lb of load	4.24	–
Height under 1631 ± 82 lb of load	–	5.24
Solid height	3.67	4.09
Deflection rate	.3034 in/100 lb	.2132 in/100 lb

Wheel hubs:

Roller bearing adjustment	By resilient spacer
Bearing rotation torque, not above	.36 ft lb (5 kgcm)
Wheel alignment: toe-in (identical for both rear wheels)	0 deg. 10 ft (—10 ft, + 15 ft.)
Bearing lubrication	FIAT MR grease
Shock absorbers	Two
Type	Hydraulic, telescopic
Diameter (working cylinder)	1.063 (27 mm)
Fluid grade	FIAT S.A.1 oil
Capacity	.088 Imp. qts. – .104 U.S. qts. (100 ± 5 cc – 0.090 kg)

500 Sedan (110F), 500 Station wagon:
Coil spring data:
Sedan:

Free height	8.62
Height under a load of 904 ± 44 lb	5.83
Height under a load of 1268 ± 64 lb	4.72
Solid height	3.66
Deflection rate	.3034/100 lb

Station wagon:

Free height	8.66
Height under a load of 1102 ± 55 lb	6.30
Height under a load of 1631 ± 82 lb	5.20
Solid height	4.09
Deflection rate	.2132/100 lb

BRAKES

'New 500', all models:

Type	Hydraulic, self-centring, expanding-shoe
Drum: diameter	6.702 to 6.712
maximum diameter oversize allowance...	.0394
Linings:	
Type of bonding	Permafuse
Width	1.181
Length (developed)	7.09
Thickness...	.1654 to .1772
Shoe-to-drum clearance: All Sedan models ...	Take-up self-adjusting device
Station wagon ...	.0098 by adjusting cams
Self-adjustment device springs:	
Wire diameter	.142
Inner diameter	.720
Working coils	1
Total No. of coils	2½
Height	.484
Height, seated	.374
Corresponding load	97 ± 4.9 lb
Master cylinder diameter	3/4
Wheel cylinder diameter	3/4
Master cylinder plunger-to-pushrod clearance ...	.0197
Pedal free travel	.0984
Brake fluid:	
Type	FIAT special blue label brake fluid (or equivalent non-mineral grade)
Quantity	.232 Imp. qts.

Hand parking brake:

Type	Lever-controlled mechanical expansion of rear wheel brake shoes
Control	By hand lever on centre floor tunnel
Cable adjustment	By stretchers located on swinging arms, behind brake housing flange

WHEELS AND TYRES

Disc Wheels, with rim, size	$3\frac{1}{2}$ x 12	
Tyres:		
All Sedan models:		
Ceat	125-12 DR 52-4 ply	
Pirelli	125-12 Rolle 4 P.R.	
Pirelli	125-12 Sempione	
Michelin	125-12-4 P.R.	
Station wagon:		
Ceat	125-12 DR 52-6 P.R.	
Pirelli	125-12 Rolle 6 P.R.	
Pirelli	125-12 C-SDS	
Tyre pressures:		
'New 500' Sedan:	*Front*	*Rear*
Low load	17.1 psi	22.8 psi
Full load	17.1 psi	26.3 psi
500D and 500L, Sedan:		
	Front	*Rear*
Low load	17.1 psi	22.8 psi
Full load	17.1 psi	25.6 psi
500 (110F) Sedan:	*Front*	*Rear*
Low load	18.5	22.8
Full load	18.5	27.0
Station wagon:	*Front*	*Rear*
Low load	17.1 psi	27.0 psi
High load	17.1 psi	29.9 psi

GENERATOR AND REGULATOR

Up to Engine Number 056195, 'New 500':

Generator:

Type	R 90-180/12-2500 Spec.
Nominal tension	12 Volts
Maximum continued operation output	180 watts
Maximum steady current output (ammeter limit)	13 amps
Poles	2
Field winding	Shunt
Regulator	Separate
Cutting-in speed (20°C)	1300-1380 rev/min
Speed at which generator reaches maximum continued operation output (tension: nominal; temperature: (20°C)	2250-2400 rev/min
Maximum steady speed	7500 rev/min
Rotation, viewed from commutator end	Clockwise
Engine-to-generator drive ratio (with new belt)	1.74
Pole shoes I.D.	2.3192 to 2.3259
Armature outside diameter	2.2814 to 2.2834

Lubrication:

Ballbearings	FIAT Jota 3 Grease

A/4-180/12 Regulator:

Cut-out relay:

Feed voltage for thermal stabilization:		
Regulator initial	(15°-20°C) ...	16.5 V
Operating temperature	(20°-35°C) ...	15 V
Closing voltage	...	12.6 ± 0.2 V
Voltage-contact stroke variation: below	...	1 V/mm
Reverse current: up to and not above	...	10 amps
Air gap (closed contacts)	...	.0138
Point gap...	...	.0177 ± .0023

Voltage regulator:

Battery ...	50 A/h
Half-load current ...	6.5 ± 0.5 amps
Setting voltage after thermal stabilization in oven at (50° ± 3°C) for 30 minutes, half-load on battery	14.5 ± 0.3 V
Feed voltage for thermal stabilization ...	15 V
Air gap ...	.0391 to .0437

Current regulator:

Regulated current on battery ...	13 ± 0.5 amps
Air gap ...	.0391 to .0437

Regulating resistor ... 105 ± 3 ohms

From Engine Number 056196, 'New 500':

Generator:

Type ...	DSV 90/12/16/3 S
Nominal tension ...	12 volts
Maximum continued operation output (ammeter limit) ...	16 amperes
Maximum current output ...	22 amperes
Maximum steady power ...	230 watts
Maximum power ...	320 watts
Initial charging speed at 12 volts (20°C) ...	1710 to 1850 rev/min (*) 1710 to 1790 rev/min (**)
16 A. maximum output delivery speed (20°C) ...	2550 to 2800 rev/min (*) 2550 to 2700 rev/min (**)
22 A. maximum output delivery speed (20°C) ...	3050 to 3200
Maximum steady speed ...	9000 rev/min
Rotation, drive end ...	Clockwise
Poles ...	2
Field winding ...	Shunt
Regulator, separate ...	FIAT GN 1/12/16
Drive ratio (new belt) engine-to-generator ...	1.74
Pole shoe I.D. ...	2.2952 to 2.2991

Lubrication:

Ballbearings ...	FIAT Jota 3 Grease

(*) Refers to generators with armature package disc teeth .1732 (4,4 mm) in length (early type)

(**) Refers to generators with armature disc teeth .1969 (5 mm) in length

GN 1/12/16 regulator:

Cut-out relay:

Feed voltage for thermal stabilization:		
Regulator initial	(15°-20°C) ...	16.5 V
Operating temperature	(20°-35°C) ...	15 V
Closing voltage	...	12.6 ± 0.2 V
Voltage-contact stroke variation: below	...	1 V/min
Reverse current: up to and not above	...	16 amps
Air gap (closed contacts)	...	.0138
Point gap...	...	.0177 ± .0023

Voltage regulator:

Battery	50 A/h
Half-load current	8 ± 2 amps
Setting voltage after thermal stabilization in oven at 122° ± 5°F (50° ± 3°C) for 30 minutes, half-load on battery	14.2 ± 0.3 V
Feed voltage for thermal stabilization	15 V
Air gap	.0391 to .0437

Current regulator:

Regulated current on battery	16 ± 0.5 amps
Voltage for regulated current inspection	13 V
Air gap	.0391 to .0437
Regulating resistor	105 ± 3 ohms

500D, 500F and 500L Sedan, Station wagon:

Generator:

Type: Sedan	DSV 90/12/16/3 S
Station wagon	D 90/12/16/3 F
Nominal tension	12 volts
Maximum continued operation output (ammeter limit)	16 amperes
Maximum current output	22 amperes
Maximum steady power	230 watts
Maximum power	320 watts
Initial charging speed at 12 volts (20°C)	1710 to 1860 rev/min (*) 1710 to 1790 rev/min (**)
16 A. maximum output delivery speed (20°C) ...	2550 to 2800 rev/min (*) 2550 to 2700 rev/min (**)
22 A. maximum output delivery speed (20°C) ...	3050 to 3200
Maximum steady speed	9000 rev/min
Rotation, drive end	Clockwise
Pole shoes	2
Field winding	Shunt
Regulator, separate	FIAT GN 2/12/16
Drive ratio (new belt), engine-to-generator ...	1.74
Pole shoe I.D.	2.2952 to 2.2991

Lubrication:

Ballbearing, drive end head	FIAT MR 3 Grease

(*) Refers to generators with armature package disc teeth .1732 (4.4 mm) in length (early type)

(**) Refers to generators with armature package disc teeth .1969 (5 mm) in length

GN 2/12/16 regulator:

Cut-out relay:

Feed voltage for thermal stabilization:	
Regulator initial 59°-68°F (15°-20°C)	16.5 V
Operating temperature 68°-95°F (20°-35°C)	15 V
Closing voltage	12.6 ± 0.2 V
Voltage-contact stroke variation: below	1 V/mm
Reverse current: not above	16 amps
Air gap (closed contacts)	.0138 (0.35 mm)
Point gap	.0177 ± .0023 (0.45 ± 0.06 mm)

Voltage regulator:

Battery	50 A/h
Half-load current	8 ± 0.5 amps
Setting voltage after thermal stabilization in oven at 122° ± 5°F (50° ± 3°C) for 30 minutes, half-load on battery	14.2 ± 0.3 V
Feed voltage for thermal stabilization	15 V
Air gap	.0391 to .0437 (0.99 to 1.11 mm)

Current regulator:	
Regulated current on battery	16 ± 1 amps
Voltage for regulated current inspection	13 V
Air gap	.0391 to .0437 (0.99 to 1.11 mm)
Regulating resistor	85 ± ohms
Additional resistor, serially connected to voltage regulator	17 ± 1 ojms

STARTER MOTOR

'New 500' all models:	
Type	B 76-0,5/12 S
Voltage	12 V
Nominal power	0.5 kW
Rotation (pinion end)	Counterclockwise
Pole shoes	4
Field winding	In series
Engagement	By free wheel
Mechanical data:	
Pole shoes I.D.	2.0697 to 2.0768 in (52,57 to 52,75 mm)
Armature diameter	2.0394 to 2.0412 in (51,80 to 51,85 mm)
Mechanical characteristics test:	
Load of spring on new brushes	2.5 to 2.9 lb (1,15 to 1,30 kg)
Armature shaft axial play	.0059 to .0256 (0,15 to 0,65 mm)
Mica undercut depth, up to and not above ...	.04 (1 mm)
Lubrication:	
Drive unit splines...	FIAT Jota 2/M grease
Sleeve-to-engagement lever surfaces	FIAT Jota 2/M grease

ELECTRICAL ACCESSORIES

Low oil pressure indicator	Red light
Signals when engine oil pressure is less than ...	7.1 to 21.3 psi
Generator charge indicator	Red light
Signals when:	
Generator voltage is less than	12.6 V
Engine speed, below	1100 rev/min
Car speed in 4th gear, below	14.3 mile/hr
Fuel reserve supply indicator	Red light
Signals when the fuel tank is below	.8 to 1.1 Imp. galls.
Direction indicators pilot light:	
Number of cycles per minute of flasher unit with a nominal load of 42.5 W:	
At a nominal tension of 12 V and 20°C ...	85 ± 8
At a tension 1.25 times the nominal one (15 V) at 40°C, not above	110
At a tension 0.8 times the nominal one (9.5 V) and at 20°C, not below	45
Windshield wiper unit	Crank gear type
Sweeps per minute	50 to 60
Motor unit bench test data:	
Feed voltage	14 V
Stall torque	.43 lb ft
Stator overheating temperature, not above ...	50°C
Speed, when warm, not above	60 rev/min
Current draw, not above	1.8 amps

Starting torque (with locked shaft), warm, at 14 V, not below ... ... 5 lb ft
Wiper blade pressure on windshield ... ... 10.6 to 12.3 oz
Wiper arm tilting angle ... ... 100°
Fuses, six... ... ... 8 amps

LIGHTING SYSTEM

Description	*Type*	*Wattage (12 Volts)*
Headlamps: high beam	Globular, double filament	45
low beam		40
Front lamps: direction indicators	Globular, double filament	20
parking lights		5
Tail lamps: stop lights	Globular, double filament	20
parking lights		5
direction indicators	Globular	20
Side direction indicators	Tubular	3
Number plate lamp	Globular	5
Courtesy light	Cylindrical	5
Interior light (S.W. only)	Cylindrical	5
Instrument cluster light	Tubular	3
Direction indicators pilot light		
Generator charge indicator		
Low oil pressure indicator		
Fuel reserve supply indicator		
Parking light indicator		
High beam indicator		

CAPACITIES

'New 500', 500D Sedan, Station wagon—early:

Unit	*Quantity Imp. units*	*Fill-in*
Fuel tank	4.6 gals.	Petrol: 83 Oct. Rat., 92 Oct. Rat. (Sports) (Res. Method)
Oil pan (¹)	1.54 qts.	FIAT oil (³)
Gearbox and differential	.97 qts.	FIAT W.90.M oil (SAE 90 EP)
Steering gear	.105 qts.	
Hydraulic brake circuit	.194 qts.	FIAT blue label brake fluid for hydraulic brakes
Hydraulic shock absorbers:		
Front, each	.112 qts.	FIAT SAI oil
Rear, each	.088 qts.	FIAT SAI oil
Windshield washer bag	(²)	Mixture of water and cleaner

(¹) Total capacity of oil pan, lines, oil filter and crankshaft: 1.859 Imp. qts. for Model 500D and 2.06 Imp. qts. for 500 Station wagon. The amount shown in the table is the requirement for periodical oil changes.
(²) 1.32 Imp. pts. of pure water with 0.6 oz solution in summer or with 1.2 oz solution in winter.
(³) Recommended oil grades:

Lowest anticipated outdoor temperature	**FIAT Service MS (*) Oil** *Supplement 1 oils which fill MS sequence requirements*	**FIAT Multigrade Oil (*)**
Below —15°C (5°F) (minimum)	**VS 10 W** (SAE 10 W)	—
Between 0° and —15°C (32° to 5°F) (minimum)	**VS 20 W** (SAE 20 W)	**10 W-30**
Above 0°C (minimum)	**VS 30** (SAE 30)	**20 W-40**
Above 30° C (average)	**VS 40** (SAE 40)	

(*) **Warning**: above FIAT oils are of the detergent type: do not top up with oils of different grade or make. When changing to a detergent oil, flush the engine thoroughly.

CAUTION: Starting from engine No. 200784 the total capacity of oil pan, lines, oil filter and crankshaft is 2.64 GB qts. The capacity of the oil pan for periodical oil changes is 2.20 Imp. qts.

500 (110F), 500L Sedan, Station wagon—late:

Unit	*Quantity Imp. units*	*Fill-in*
Fuel tank	4.84 gals.	Petrol: 83 Oct. Rat., 92 Oct. Rat. (Sports)
Oil sump (1)	2.20 qts.	FIAT oil (3)
Transmission and differential ...	.97 qts.	FIAT W.90.M oil (SAE 90 EP)
Steering gear	.105 qts.	
Hydraulic brake circuit... ...	.194 qts.	FIAT blue label brake fluid
Hydraulic shock absorbers — front, each	.112 qts.	FIAT SAI oil
Hydraulic shock absorbers — rear, each	.096 qts.	
Windshield washer bag ...	.88 qts.	Mixture of water and FIAT D.P/1 fluid (2)

(1) Total capacity of oil sump, lines, oil filter and crankshaft: 2.38 G.B. qts. – 2.86 U.S. qts. (2.4 kg). The amount shown in the table is the requirement for periodical oil changes.

(2) In summer add 30 cc to each litre of water; in winter, for temperatures down to 14°F (—10°C) use a 50% solution of D.P/ fluid. For temperatures below 14°F (—10°C) fill with D.P/1 fluid undiluted.

(3) Recommended oil grades:

Outdoor temperature	**FIAT Unigrade oil**	**FIAT Multigrade oil**
	Detergent oils with low ash content, type MS, level MIL-L-2104B (*)	
Below —15°C (5°F) minimum ...	**VS 10 W** (SAE 10 W)	–
Between —15°C (5°F) and 0°C (32°F) minimum	**VS 20 W** (SAE 20 W)	**10 W 30**
Above 0°C (32°F) minimum:		
Below 35°C (95°F) maximum ...	**VS 30** (SAE 30)	**20 W 40**
Above 35°C (95°F) maximum ...	**VS 40** (SAE 40)	

(*) **Warning:** do not top up with oils of different grade or make.

TORQUE WRENCH SETTINGS

Dimensions are in lb ft unless otherwise stated

Engine:	
Main bearing support-to-crankcase screw ...	15.2
Flywheel-to-crankshaft screw	23.1
Connecting rod bearing cap screw self-locking nut	23.9
Rocker arm support-to-cylinder head stud nut ...	15.2
Cylinder head-to-crankcase stud nut	23.9
Cylinder head-to-crankcase stud cap nut ...	23.9
Driven gear-to-crankshaft screw	6.5
Generator and fan drive pulley hub screw ...	108.5
Drive pulley cover screw	5.8
Fan-to-generator self-locking nut	25.3
Pulley-to-generator self-locking nut	14.5
Commutator end bearing cup stop clamp screw nut (Engine 100 D.000)	.8
Exhaust silencer-to-cylinder head screw (Engine 120.000)	18.1
Spark plugs	18.1 to 21.7
Gearbox, differential:	
Clutch mounting screws	5.8 to 7.2
Primary shaft gear nut	18.1 to 25.3
Layshaft gear nut...	28.9 to 36.2
Ring gear-to-differential case screw	23.1
Differential bearing housing-to-gearbox casing nut	13.0
Gearbox casing and support-to-engine nut	27.5
Gearbox differential support assembly-to-engine nut	18.1 to 21.7
Axle shaft sleeve-to-flexible joint screw ...	20.3

Differential roller bearing rotation torque (not break-away)	1.01 ± 0.07
Final drive pinion-to-gear backlash	.0031 to .0047
Front suspension:	
Front swinging arm-to-body mounting pin rubber bushing nut	28.9 to 36.2
Leaf spring-to-body nut	28.9
Kingpin housing-to-swinging arm nut	39.8 to 43.4
Brake housing flange-to-steering knuckle nut ...	14.5
Leaf spring-to-kingpin housing nut	28.9
Swinging arm-to-body nut	28.9
Bearing-on-steering knuckle nut...	21.7
Wheel-to-hub screw	32.5 to 39.8
Rear suspension:	
Swinging arm pin-to-underbody nut	43.4 to 50.6
Swinging arm support-to-underbody screw ...	28.9 to 36.2
Hub and brake housing flange-to-swinging arm nut	43.4
Flexible joint-to-rear wheel shaft nut	See text
Axle shaft sleeve-to-flexible joint screw	20.3 lb ft
Wheel-to-hub screw:	
Model 'New 500' Sedan	32.5 to 39.8
500 Station wagon	43.4 to 50.6
Rear wheel bearing rotation torque, not above ...	0.36
Steering:	
Pitman arm-to-sector shaft nut	72.3 to 79.6
Idler arm pin nut (*)	39.8 to 43.4 (see text)
Steering gear-to-body nut and relay lever support nut	14.5 to 18.1
Tie rod ball pin nut	18.1 to 21.7
Steering wheel nut	28.9 to 36.2
Brakes:	
Brake housing flange-to-steering knuckle nut ...	14.5
Brake housing flange-to-swinging arm nut ...	43.4

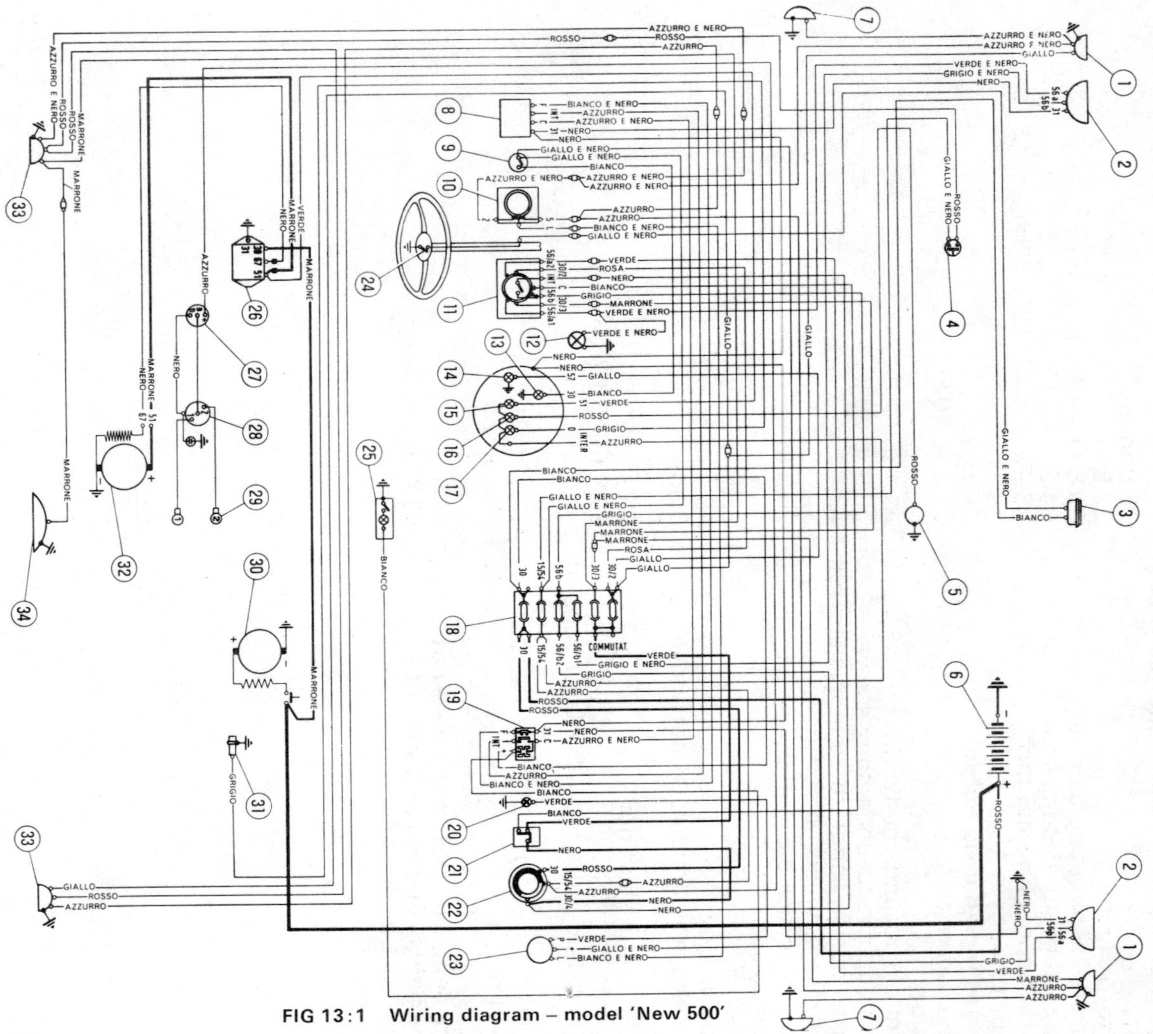

FIG 13:1 Wiring diagram – model 'New 500'

Key to Fig 13:1 1 Front parking and direction indicator lamps 2 Headlamps (high and low beams) 3 Horn 4 Stoplights pressure-operated switch 5 Fuel reserve supply indicator sending unit 6 Battery 7 Side direction indicator lamps 8 Windshield wiper motor 9 Panel light switch 10 Directional signal lever switch 11 External lighting changeover lever switch 12 Height beam indicator 13 Panel light 14 Parking lights indicator 15 Generator charge indicator 16 Fuel reserve supply indicator 17 Low oil pressure indicator 18 Fuses 19 Windshield wiper 3-position switch 20 Direction indicator pilot light 21 External light switch 22 Ignition lock switch 23 Flasher unit, direction indicators 24 Horn button 25 Rear view mirror light 26 Generator regulator 27 Ignition coil 28 Ignition distributor 29 Spark plugs 30 Starter motor 31 Low oil pressure indicator sending unit 32 Generator 33 Rear parking, stop and direction indicator lamps 34 Number plate lamp

NOTE–Mark — means that the cable is provided with numbered strip or ferrule

Key to cable colours Azzurro = Blue Bianco = White Giallo = Yellow Grigio = Grey Marrone = Brown Nero = Black Rosa = Rosy Rosso = Red Verde = Green Azzurro e nero = Black and blue Bianco e nero = Black and white Giallo e nero = Black and yellow Verde e nero = Black and green Grigio e nero = Black and grey Commutat. = switch INT-Inter = Switch

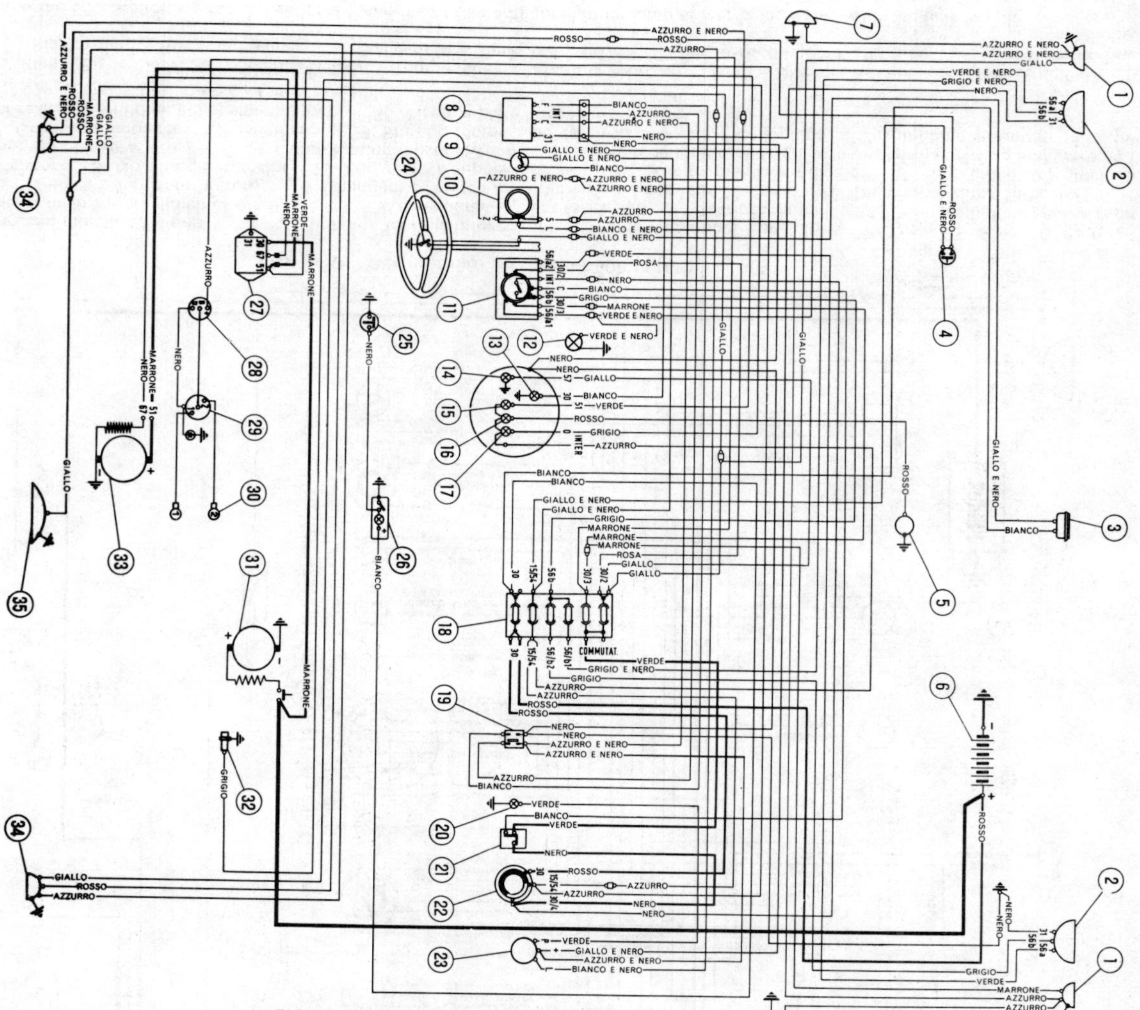

FIG 13:2 Wiring diagram, model 500D

Key to Fig 13:2 1 Front parking and direction indicator lamps 2 Headlamps (high and low beams) 3 Horn 4 Stoplight pressure-operated switch 5 Fuel reserve supply indicator sending unit 6 Battery 7 Side direction indicators 8 Windshield wiper motor 9 Panel light switch 10 Direction indicator switch 11 Outer lighting changeover switch 12 High beam indicator 13 Panel light 14 Parking light indicator 15 Generator charge indicator 16 Fuel reserve supply indicator 17 Low oil pressure indicator 18 Fuses 19 Windshield wiper switch 20 Direction indicator pilot light 21 Outer lighting master switch 22 Key type switch for ignition and warning lights 23 Flasher unit (direction indicators) 24 Horn button 25 Jam-type switch on driver's side door pillar, for light 26 26 Rear view mirror light 27 Generator regulator 28 Ignition coil 29 Ignition distributor 30 Spark plugs 31 Starter motor 32 Low oil pressure indicator sending unit 33 Generator 34 Rear parking, stop and direction indicator lamps 35 Number plate lamp

NOTE– Mark — means that the cable is provided with numbered strip or ferrule

Key to cable colours Azzurro = Blue Bianco = White Giallo = Yellow Grigio = Grey Marrone = Brown Nero = Black Rosa = Pink Rosso = Red Verde = Green
INT-INTER = Switch

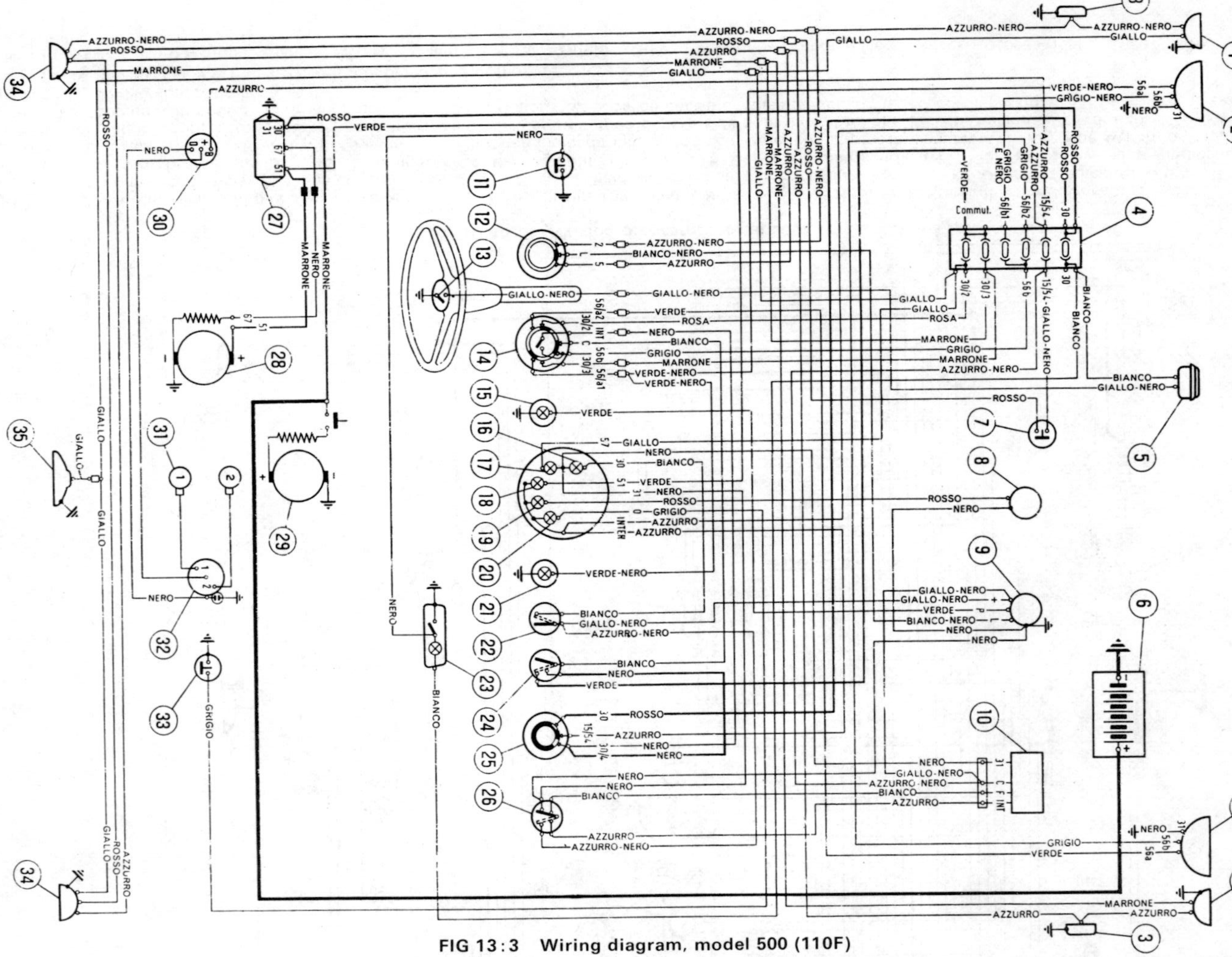

FIG 13:3 Wiring diagram, model 500 (110F)

Key to Fig 13:3 1 Front parking and directional signal lights 2 High and low beam headlights 3 Side directional signal lights 4 Fuses 5 Horn 6 Battery 7 Stoplight pressure-operated switch 8 Fuel reserve supply indicator sending unit 9 Directional signal flasher unit 10 Wiper motor 11 Courtesy light jam switch on driver's side door pillar 12 Directional signal switch 13 Horn button 14 Changeover switch for outer lighting and light flashes 15 Directional signal indicator 16 Instrument cluster light 17 Parking light indicator 18 No-charge indicator 19 Fuel reserve supply indicator 20 Low oil pressure indicator 21 High beam indicator 22 Instrument cluster light switch 23 Map light in rear view mirror 24 Outer lighting master switch 25 Key type ignition switch, also energizing starting and warning lights circuits 26 Windshield wiper switch 27 Generator regulator 28 Generator 29 Starting motor 30 Ignition coil 31 Spark plugs 32 Ignition distributor 33 Low oil pressure indicator sending unit 34 Rear tail, stop and directional signal lights 35 Licence plate light

NOTE—Mark — means that the cable is provided with numbered strip or ferrule

Key to cable colours Azzurro = Blue Bianco = White Giallo = Yellow Grigio = Grey Marrone = Brown Nero = Black Rosa = Pink Rosso = Red Verde = Green Azzurro-nero = Black and blue Bianco-nero = Black and white Giallo-nero = Black and yellow Grigio-nero = Black and grey Verde-nero = Black and green Commut.-INT. = Switch

NOTE – The wiring diagram covering the 500 Station wagon differs for the presence of an additional inner lamp at rear being wired with the fuse No. 30

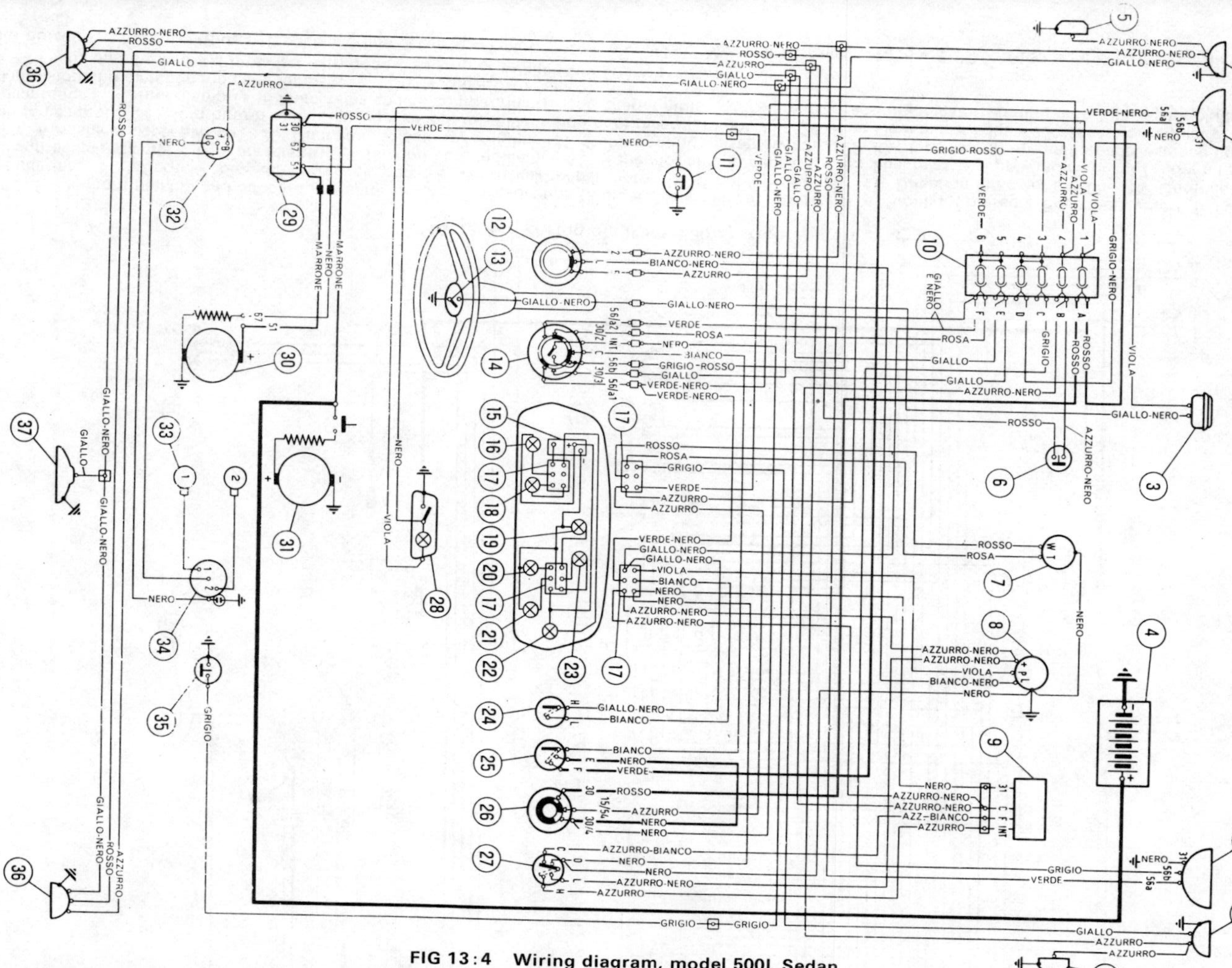

FIG 13:4 Wiring diagram, model 500L Sedan

Key to Fig 13:4 1 Front parking and direction lights 2 High and low beam headlamps 3 Horn 4 Battery 5 Side direction indicators 6 Stoplight hydraulic switch 7 Fuel gauge sending unit 8 Direction indicator flasher 9 Windshield wiper motor 10 Fuses 11 Push button switch on driver's side door for light 12 Changeover switch for direction indicators 13 Horn push button 14 Changeover switch for outside lights and signal flasher 15 Fuel gauges 16 Low fuel indicator (red light) 17 Electric cable connections 18 No-charge indicator (red light) 19 Direction indicator repeater (green light) 20 Parking light indicator (green light) 21 Headlamp high beam indicator (blue light) 22 Low oil pressure warning light (red) 23 Instrument cluster light 24 Instrument cluster light switch 25 Outside light switch 26 Ignition switch controlling other circuits 27 Windshield wiper switch 28 Interior light, built-in rear view mirror 29 Generator regulator 30 Generator 31 Starting motor 32 Ignition coil 33 Spark plugs 34 Ignition distributor 35 Low oil pressure indicator sending unit 36 Rear parking, stop and direction lights 37 Number plate light
NOTE—Mark — means that the cable has a numbered sheath or tube

Key to cable colours Azzurro = Blue Bianco = White Giallo = Yellow Grigio = Grey Marrone = Brown Nero = Black Rosa = Pink Rosso = Red Verde = Green
INT-INTER = Switch

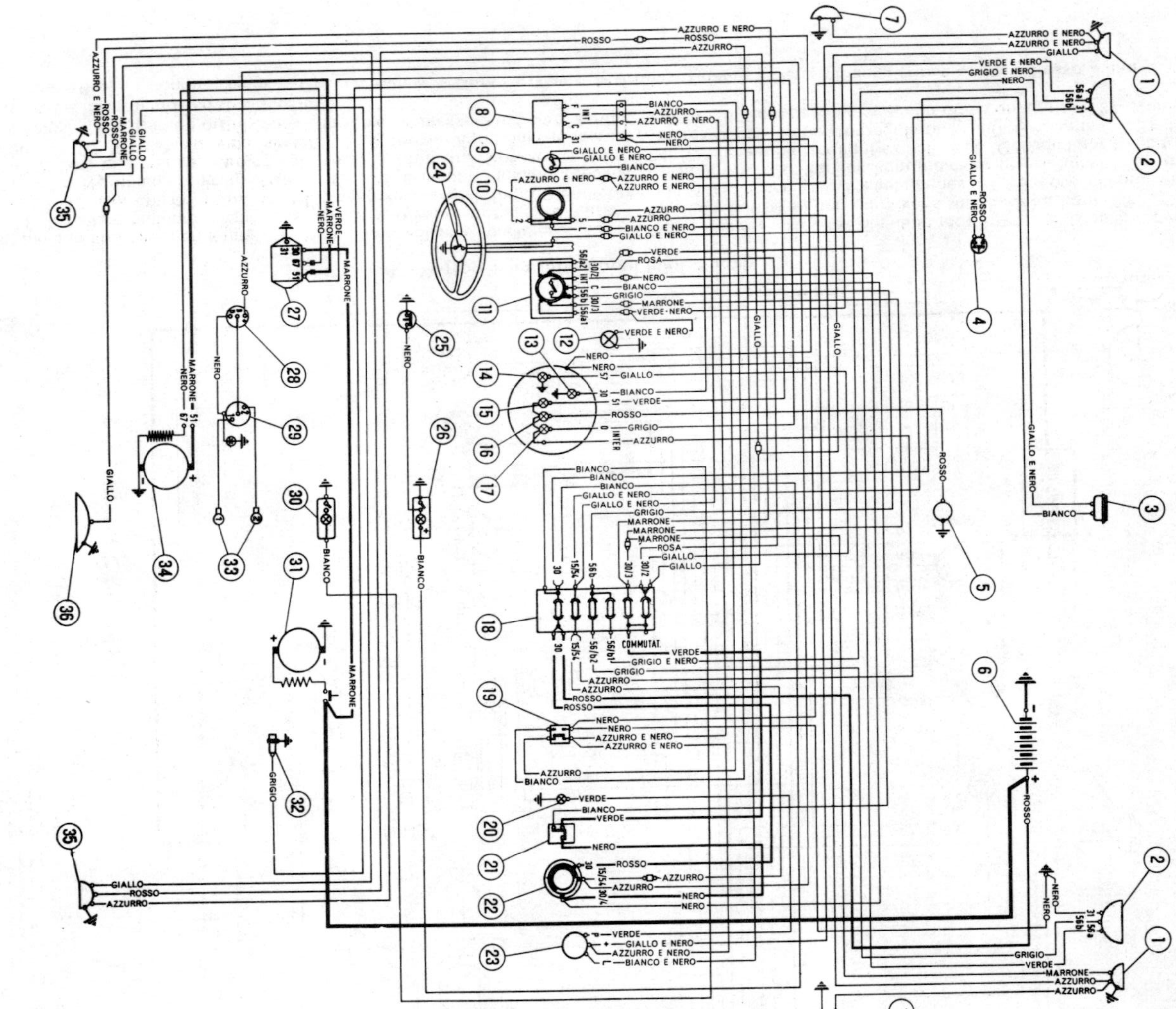

FIG 13:5 Wiring diagram, 500 Station wagon

Key to Fig 13:5 1 Front parking and direction indicator lamps 2 Headlamps (high and low beams) 3 Horn 4 Stoplight pressure-operated switch 5 Fuel reserve supply indicator sending unit 6 Battery 7 Side direction indicators 8 Windshield wiper motor 9 Panel light switch 10 Direction indicator switch 11 Outer lighting changeover switch 12 High beam indicator 13 Panel light 14 Parking light indicator 15 Generator charge indicator 16 Fuel reserve supply indicator 17 Low oil pressure indicator 18 Fuses 19 Windshield wiper switch 20 Direction indicator pilot light 21 Outer lighting master switch 22 Key type switch for ignition and warning lights 23 Flasher unit (direction indicators) 24 Horn button 25 Jam-type switch on driver's side door pillar, for light 26 26 Rear view mirror light 27 Generator regulator 28 Ignition coil 29 Ignition distributor 30 Inner lamp (also illuminates engine compartment) 31 Starter motor 32 Low oil pressure indicator sending unit 33 Spark plugs 34 Generator 35 Rear parking, stop and direction indicator lamps 36 Number plate lamp

NOTE—Mark — means that the cable is provided with numbered strip or ferrule

Key to cable colours Azzurro = Blue Bianco = White Giallo = Yellow Grigio = Grey Marrone = Brown Nero = Black Rosa = Pink Rosso = Red Verde = Green INT-INTER = Switch

HINTS ON MAINTENANCE AND OVERHAUL

There are few things more rewarding than the restoration of a car to its original peak of efficiency and smooth performance. The following notes are intended to help the owner to reach that state of perfection. Providing that he possesses the basic manual skills he should have no difficulty in performing most of the operations detailed in this manual. It must be stressed, however, that highly-skilled work which entails the use of expensive special tools and gauging equipment ought to be entrusted to the experts who have such equipment.

Problems

The chief problems which may face an operator are:

1 External dirt.
2 Difficulty in undoing tight fixings.
3 Dismantling unfamiliar mechanisms.
4 Deciding in what respect parts are defective.
5 Confusion about the correct order for reassembly.
6 Adjusting running clearances.
7 Final tuning.

Practical suggestions to solve the problems

1 Use newspaper instead of rag for preliminary cleaning. Having removed most of the dirt, continue with a brush and paraffin. Progressive cleaning is best done with two containers, using the second one for those parts which are almost clean. Finish off with clean petrol. This will dry, eliminating the use of rag which may leave clogging fibres behind. Do not dismantle anything until the outside has been cleaned, particularly round joints which will be separated. This ensures that gritty dirt cannot fall inside. Be careful not to wash dirt into holes. Plug them first, but do not use matchsticks, as these may break off short. If dirt can enter, blank off all orifices in parts which will be dismantled for some time, but be sure that the material used cannot be pushed into a place where it would be difficult to remove. This applies, for example, to the plugging of water passages in the top face of a cylinder block.

2 It is not advisable to hammer on the end of a screw thread, but if it must be done, first screw on a nut so that it is flush with the end. This applies particularly to the removal of cotters. Nuts and bolts seem to 'grow' together, especially in exhaust systems. If penetrating oil does not work, try plenty of heat, but be careful of starting a fire. Asbestos sheet or cloth is useful to isolate heat.

Tight bushes or pieces of tail-pipe rusted into a silencer can be removed by splitting them with an open-ended hacksaw. Tight screws can be started by hammering on the end of an all-metal screwdriver. Many tight fixings will yield to the judicious use of a hammer, but it must be a soft-faced hammer if damage to surfaces is to be avoided. This treatment is very useful when trying to part tapered fixings such as those of a steering ball-joint pin in a steering arm. Distortion of the arm is prevented by holding a heavy block of steel on the opposite side of the boss.

Straightening bent parts, especially those in suspension and steering systems, must be done with caution, as cracking might eventually lead to failure.

3 It often happens that an owner is baffled when trying to dismantle an unfamiliar piece of equipment. So many modern devices are pressed together or assembled by spinning-over flanges, that they must be sawn apart. The intention is that the whole assembly must be renewed. However, parts which appear to be in one piece to the naked eye, may reveal close-fitting joint lines when inspected with a magnifying glass, and this may provide the necessary clue to dismantling.

Be very careful when dismantling mechanisms which may come apart suddenly. Work on a sheet of paper which will catch everything as it falls, and drape a piece of cloth over the device if springs are likely to fly in all directions. Mark everything which might be reassembled in the wrong position, scratching a line across joint faces before parting them, and using scratched symbols where necessary. A sequence of tiny dots from a centre punch are also useful to identify the position of apparently identical parts, but be quite sure that any marks will not weaken the part or damage working surfaces. **Springs and torsion bars, for instance, must never be scratched or marked.** Store parts which look alike in the correct order for reassembly. Never rely upon memory to assist in the assembly of complicated mechanisms, especially when they will be dismantled for a long time. Make notes, draw diagrams, and put labels on detached wires.

4 Rust stains may indicate unlubricated wear. This can sometimes be seen round the outside edge of a bearing cup in a universal joint.

Look for bright rubbing marks on parts which normally should not make heavy contact. These might prove that something is bent or running out of truth. For example, there might be bright marks on one side of a piston, at the top near the ring grooves, and others at the bottom of the skirt on the other side. This could well be the clue to a bent connecting rod.

Test parts for wear, especially ball- and roller bearings, by first washing them free from lubricants. Accurate checks are best made with expensive tools like micrometers, but much can be done by getting the right 'feel' with a pair of calipers or a vernier gauge, especially if the latter has jaws for both inside and outside measurements. Sometimes it is possible to make quite accurate dimensional checks by using something of known diameter, like a twist drill shank, to set the calipers or vernier gauge.

The clearance between parts can often be measured by bolting them together with a tiny piece of lead wire or cored solder in between. This will be flattened to the dimension of the clearance. Such a method is very handy when trying to shim a housing which locates a bearing endwise, as it does in some hubs and gearboxes. Alternatively, use a proprietary material like 'Plastigage'.

Sometimes joint faces leak persistently, even after gasket renewal. The fault will then be traceable to distortion, to dirt or to burrs. The last-named can be found by rubbing a smooth flat file over the faces, spanning opposite surfaces if possible, so that the file is kept flat. This will remove burrs without damaging the joint faces. Studs which are screwed into soft metal frequently raise burrs at the point of entry. A quick cure for this is to chamfer the edge of the hole in the part which fits over the stud.

Always check a replacement part with the original one before it is fitted.

5 If parts are not marked, and the order for reassembly is not known, a little detective work will help. Look for marks which are due to wear to see if they can be mated. Joint faces may not be identical due to manufacturing errors, and parts which overlap may be stained, giving a clue to the correct position. Most fixings leave identifying marks especially if they were painted over on assembly. It is then easier to decide whether a nut for instance has a plain, a spring, or a shakeproof washer under it. All running surfaces become 'bedded' together after long spells of work and tiny imperfections on one part will be found to have left corresponding marks on the other. This is particularly true of shafts and bearings and even a score on a cylinder wall will show on the piston.

6 Checking end float or rocker clearances by feeler gauge may not always give accurate results because of wear. For instance, the rocker tip which bears on a valve stem may be deeply pitted, in which case the feeler will simply be bridging a depression. Thrust washers may also wear depressions in opposing faces to make accurate measurement difficult. End float is then easier to check by using a dial gauge.

It is common practice to adjust end play in bearing assemblies, like front hubs with taper rollers, by doing up the axle nut until the hub becomes stiff to turn and then backing it off a little. **Do not use this method with ballbearing hubs as the assembly is often pre-loaded by tightening the axle nut to its fullest extent**. If the splitpin hole will not line up, file the base of the nut a little.

Steering assemblies often wear in the straight-ahead position. If any part is adjusted, make sure that it remains free when moved from lock to lock. Do not be surprised if an assembly like a steering gearbox, which is known to be carefully adjusted outside the car, becomes stiff when it is bolted in place. This will be due to distortion of the case by the pull of the mounting bolts, particularly if the mounting points are not all touching together. This problem may be met in other equipment and is cured by careful attention to the alignment of mounting points.

7 When a spanner is stamped with a size and A/F it means that the dimension is the width between the jaws and has no connection with ANF, which is the designation for the American National Fine thread. Coarse threads like Whitworth are rarely used on cars to-day except for studs which screw into soft aluminium or cast iron. For this reason it might be found that the top end of a cylinder head stud has a fine thread and the lower end a coarse thread to screw into the cylinder block. If the car has mainly UNF threads then it is likely that any coarse threads will be UNC, which are not the same as Whitworth. Small sizes have the same number of threads in Whitworth and UNC, but in the $\frac{1}{2}$ inch size for example, there are twelve threads to the inch in the former and thirteen in the latter.

8 **It is useless to tune an engine which has not reached its normal running temperature.** In the same way, the tune of an engine which is stiff after a rebore will be different when the engine is again running free. Remember too, that rocker clearances on pushrod operated valve gear will change when the cylinder head nuts are tightened after an initial period of running with a new head gasket.

Trouble may not always be due to what seems the obvious cause. Ignition, carburation and mechanical condition are interdependent and spitting back through the carburetter, which might be attributed to a weak mixture, can be caused by a sticking inlet valve.

For one final hint on tuning, never adjust more than one thing at a time or it will be impossible to tell which adjustment produced the desired result.

GLOSSARY OF TERMS

AF	Across flats of nut or bolt head. Width between spanner jaws.
Allen key	Wrench of hexagonal bar used to turn socket-head screws.
Ambient temperature	Surrounding temperature.
ANF	American National Fine screw thread.
Annulus	Ring-like space
Armature	Of generator or starter motor—part which revolves in a magnetic field. Of a solenoid—plunger which is pulled into a hollow magnet.
Asymmetrical	Not quite symmetrical.
AVC	Automatic voltage control.
Axial	Something belonging to, or revolving round, an axis.
BA	British Association screw thread. Frequently used for small screws associated with electrical equipment.
Backlash	Play between parts, e.g. between teeth of meshing gears.
Balance lever	A cross-lever which divides a central push or pull equally between two rods or cables attached to the outer ends.
Banjo axle	Hollow rear axle casing with large-diameter housing to accommodate the drive gears.
Bendix pinion	Self-engaging drive on starter motor shaft.
Bevel pinion	Small gear with sloping teeth on side face. Meshes with another gear at an angle to it, (usually a right-angle).
bhp	Brake horse power.
bmep	Brake mean effective pressure. Average pressure on piston during working stroke.
BSF	British Standard Fine screw thread. Now almost superseded by UNF on cars.
BSP	British Standard Pipe screw thread. A fine thread for pipe work. Can be parallel or tapered. Size indicates bore of thick-walled pipe, not top of thread diameter.
BSW	British Standard Whitworth screw thread. A coarse thread no longer used on cars.
Bypass	Oil filter—one which cleans a small volume of oil from the pump and returns it to the sump.
Camber	Angle at which a wheel is tilted from the vertical.
Capacitor	Modern term for electrical condenser. Chiefly used in ignition distributor.
Castellated nut	Top face slotted across to take a locking splitpin
Castor	Angle at which the kingpin or swivel pin is tilted when viewed from the side.
Clevis	A U-shaped fork much used in brake cable connections.
Clockwise	Like onward rotation of clock hands when viewing face of object.
Collet	Collar, often split and located in a groove in a shaft, e.g. on a valve stem.
Commutator	Rotating segmented current distributor between armature windings and brushes in a generator or motor.
Condenser	See 'Capacitor'.
Core plug	Thin metal discs blanking off manufacturing holes in castings. See 'Welch plug'.
Crown wheel	Large gear with ring of teeth at shallow angle to one face. Typically meshes with bevel pinion in rear axle.
'C' spanner	Like a 'C' with an extended handle. The top hook engages in slots round the periphery of a part.
CVC	Constant voltage control.
Damper	Latest term for shock-absorber. Used in suspension systems to damp out spring oscillations.
Depression	The lowering of atmospheric pressure, e.g. in the inlet manifold and carburetter.
Dowel	Close-fitting peg, tube or bolt which accurately locates holes in mating parts.
Drag link	Rod connecting steering gearbox arm to nearest road wheel.
Dry liner	Thin tube pressed into bored-out engine cylinder.
Dry sump	Does not store main oil supply, which is pumped into a separate tank.
Dynamo	Original term for 'Generator'.
Electrode	Terminal point in electrical circuit, e.g. sparking plug points.
Electrolyte	In car batteries, a solution of sulphuric acid and distilled water.
End float	Or end thrust. Free endwise movement of a part, e.g. shafts and parts mounted on shafts.
EP	Extreme-pressure lubricants for arduous duties, e.g. between the teeth of rear axle gears.
Fade	Of brakes. Reduced efficiency due to heat.
Field coils	Stationary windings to produce magnetism in generators or motors.
Fillets	Narrow finishing strips usually applied to interior bodywork.

First motion shaft Input shaft from clutch into gearbox.

Fullflow An oil filter which cleans all the oil all the time unless the element is clogged, when relief valve opens.

Gear pump For oil. Pumps it round between the outer teeth of two meshing gears and a close-fitting casing.

Generator Latest term for 'Dynamo'. Produces electricity from rotating energy.

Grommet A ring of protective or sealing material.

Halfshaft One of a pair transmitting power from the differential gearing to the rear wheel hubs.

h.c. High compression ratio in an engine combustion chamber.

Helical Spiral, as in a valve spring. Helical gear—a thin section of teeth in a spiral form.

Hot spot Warms mixture from carburetter on its way to engine. Ususally provided by clamping inlet and exhaust manifolds together.

HT High tension electricity. Produced by coil for sparking plugs.

Hydrometer Used to test Specific Gravity of battery electrolyte. Withdraws sample to lift graduated scale.

Hypoid bevel gears Small bevel pinion meshing below centre line of crownwheel in rear axle. Gives lower propeller shaft line.

Idler Passes on movement, e.g. a gear between input and output gears. Transmits track rod movement to side rods in steering gear.

i.f.s. Independent front suspension.

Impeller Of a water pump. Centrifugal fan rotating to stimulate flow.

Journals Those parts of a shaft which are in contact with the bearings.

Kerosene Paraffin.

Kingpin Main vertical pin. Typically carries front stub axle and road wheel.

Laminations Leaves, as in a suspension spring.

Layshaft Often called the second motion shaft. A cluster of gears driven by the input or first motion shaft in a gearbox.

lb ft Value of torque or twisting effort. Pull of ten pounds at a radius of one foot equals ten lb ft.

lb/sq in Pounds per square inch.

l.c. Low compression ratio in engine combustion chamber.

Little-end The small end of a connecting rod. Takes the gudgeon pin.

l.s. The leading shoe in a brake. Tries to wedge into drum, so increasing the braking effect.

LT Low tension electricity, usually battery rating in cars.

Mandrel Axle or cylindrical rod used for centring purposes.

Manifold A pipe with several branches.

Needle rollers Bearing rollers which are many times longer than their diameter.

Oil bath A reservoir which lubricates working parts by immersion. In air filters, a separate oil supply for wetting a wire-mesh element.

Oil wetted In air filters, the wetting of a wire mesh element by dipping in oil and allowing to drain.

Overlap Period during which the inlet and exhaust valves are open simultaneously.

Panhard rod One which is connected between a fixed point and an axle to restrict sideways movement.

Pawl Pivoted lever catching in teeth of a ratchet wheel to prevent reverse rotation.

Peg spanner One with two spaced pegs which engage in holes in a part which must be rotated.

Pendant pedals Pedal levers which are pivoted at the top.

Phillips screwdriver Fluted blade with a cross-point to engage the crossed slots in a special screw head.

Pinion Usually the smaller of two gears, originally a spur gear.

Piston-type damper Damping pistons work in cylinders in a housing fixed to chassis. Pistons reciprocated by linkage to suspension system.

Pre-loading Built-in end pressure on ball- or roller-bearings. Pressure is not due to working loads.

Radial Like rays or spokes in a wheel.

Radius rod Pivoted arm restraining a moving part to make it travel in an arc.

Ratchet Toothed wheel or rack which can move in one direction only, return being prevented by a pawl.

Recessed-head screw Crossed slots in head need special (Phillips) screwdriver.

Ring gear Ring of gear teeth attached to flywheel. Starter pinion engages with it.

Run-out Amount by which a rotating part is out of truth.

SAE Society of Automobile Engineers.

Semi-floating axle Outer end of rear axle halfshaft is carried on bearing inside axle casing. Wheel hub secured to end of shaft.

Servo Additional power applied to a control, often by vacuum, e.g. vacuum-servo for powerful brake operation.

Setscrew Hexagon-headed screw with shank threaded for entire length.

Shackle Coupling link. Two parallel pins connected by side plates to control the moving end of a leaf spring.

Shell bearing Thin steel tube lined with anti-friction metal. Used in halves for main bearings and big-end bearings.

Silentbloc bearing Rubber bush bonded to inner and outer metal sleeves. Permits small rotational movements.

Socket-head screw Deep screw head with central hexagonal socket. Turned by hexagonal Allen key.

Solenoid Coil of wire which becomes a magnet when electric current passes. Will draw in a soft iron plunger.

Spur gear One with straight teeth.

Stator tube Stationary tube inside moving steering column to carry horn and indicator wiring.

Stub axle Short projecting axle fixed at one end only.

Tachometer Instrument which shows rotational speed, usually in revolutions per minute.

TDC Top dead centre when piston is at top of its travel. BTDC and ATDC indicate before and after top dead centre.

Thermostat Automatic device for regulating temperature.

Third motion shaft Output shaft of gearbox carrying gears which mesh with those on the layshaft.

Three-quarter floating axle Inner end of axle shaft splined to differential side gear, outer end flanged and bolted to hub. Hub runs on bearing mounted on outside of axle casing.

Thrust bearing or washer Reduces friction caused by end thrust of shafts or rotating parts.

Torque Twisting effort, see 'lb ft'.

Track rod Bar across vehicle which connects both steering arms together.

t.s. Trailing shoe in brake. Has tendency to be pushed away from drum.

U.J. Universal joint in propeller shaft or drive shaft.

UNF Unified National Fine screw thread.

Vacuum-servo Gives extra power, particularly for brake operation by using the partial vacuum in the inlet manifold.

Venturi A smooth specially-shaped throat in a tube which increases the speed of air or fluid passing through it.

Vernier A small graduated scale used to obtain fractional readings of a coarser scale.

Welch plug A domed thin-metal disc which is partially flattened to make it lock in a machined recess. Much used as a core plug in castings like cylinder blocks.

Wet liner Renewable cylinder barrel with sealing rings at each end. Is surrounded by engine coolant.

Wet sump The usual form, consisting of a pan beneath the crankcase which holds all the lubricating oil.

INDEX

THE AUTOBOOK SERIES OF WORKSHOP MANUALS

Make	*Author*	*Title*
ALFA ROMEO		
1600 Giulia TI 1961–67	Ball	Alfa Romeo Giulia 1962–71 Autobook
1600 Giulia Sprint 1962–68	Ball	Alfa Romeo Giulia 1962–71 Autobook
1600 Giulia Spider 1962–68	Ball	Alfa Romeo Giulia 1962–71 Autobook
1600 Giulia Super 1965–70	Ball	Alfa Romeo Giulia 1962–71 Autobook
1750 Giulia Saloon 1968–71	Ball	Alfa Romeo Giulia 1962–71 Autobook
1750 Giulia Spider 1968–71	Ball	Alfa Romeo Giulia 1962–71 Autobook
1750 Giulia Coupé 1968–71	Ball	Alfa Romeo Giulia 1962–71 Autobook
ASTON MARTIN		
All models 1921–58	Coram	Aston Martin 1921–58 Autobook
AUDI		
Auto Union Audi 100	Ball	Audi 100 1969–71 Autobook
Audi 100 1969–71	Ball	Audi 100 1969–71 Autobook
Audi 100 S 1969–71	Ball	Audi 100 1969–71 Autobook
Audi 100 LS 1969–71	Ball	Audi 100 1969–71 Autobook
AUSTIN		
A30 1951–56	Ball	Austin A30, A35, A40 Autobook
A35 1956–62	Ball	Austin A30, A35, A40 Autobook
A40 Farina 1957–67	Ball	Austin A30, A35, A40 Autobook
A40 Cambridge 1954–57	Ball	BMC Autobook Three
A50 Cambridge 1954–57	Ball	BMC Autobook Three
A55 Cambridge Mk 1 1957–58	Ball	BMC Autobook Three
A55 Cambridge Mk 2 1958–61	Ball	Austin A55 Mk 2, A60 1958–69 Autobook
A60 Cambridge 1961–69	Ball	Austin A55 Mk 2, A60 1958–69 Autobook
A99 1959–61	Ball	Austin A99, A110 1959–68 Autobook
A110 1961–68	Ball	Austin A99, A110 1959–68 Autobook
Mini 1959–71	Ball	Mini 1959–71 Autobook
Mini Clubman 1969–71	Ball	Mini 1959–71 Autobook
Mini Cooper 1961–70	Ball	Mini Cooper 1961–70 Autobook
Mini Cooper S 1963–70	Ball	Mini Cooper 1961–70 Autobook
1100 Mk 1 1963–67	Ball	1100 Mk 1 1962–67 Autobook
1100 Mk 2 1968–70	Ball	1100 Mk 2, 1300 Mk 1, 2, America 1968–71 Autobook
1300 Mk 1, 2 1968–71	Ball	1100 Mk 2, 1300 Mk 1, 2, America 1968–71 Autobook
America 1968–71	Ball	1100 Mk 2, 1300 Mk 1, 2, America 1968–71 Autobook
1800 Mk 1, 2 1964–71	Ball	1800 1964–71 Autobook
1800 S 1969–71	Ball	1800 1964–71 Autobook
Maxi 1500 1969–71	Ball	Austin Maxi 1969–71 Autobook
Maxi 1750 1970–71	Ball	Austin Maxi 1969–71 Autobook
AUSTIN HEALEY		
100/6 1955–59	Ball	Austin Healey 100/6, 3000 1956–68 Autobook
Sprite 1958–71	Ball	Sprite, Midget 1958–71 Autobook
3000 Mk 1, 2, 3 1959–68	Ball	Austin Healey 100/6, 3000 1956–68 Autobook
BEDFORD		
CA Mk 1 and 2 1957–64	Ball	Vauxhall Victor 1, 2 FB 1957–64 Autobook
Beagle HA 1964–66	Ball	Vauxhall Viva HA 1964–66 Autobook
BMW		
1600 1966–70	Ball	BMW 1600 1966–70 Autobook
1600–2 1966–70	Ball	BMW 1600 1966–70 Autobook
1600TI 1966–70	Ball	BMW 1600 1966–70 Autobook
1800 1964–70	Ball	BMW 1800 1964–70 Autobook
1800TI 1964–67	Ball	BMW 1800 1964–70 Autobook
2000 1966–70	Ball	BMW 2000, 2002 1966–70 Autobook

Make	*Author*	*Title*
2000A 1966–70	Ball	BMW 2000, 2002 1966–70 Autobook
2000TI 1966–70	Ball	BMW 2000, 2002 1966–70 Autobook
2000CS 1967–70	Ball	BMW 2000, 2002 1966–70 Autobook
2000CA 1967–70	Ball	BMW 2000, 2002 1966–70 Autobook
2002 1968–70	Ball	BMW 2000, 2002 1966–70 Autobook
CITROEN		
DS19 1955–65	Ball	Citroen DS19, ID19 1955–66 Autobook
ID19 1956–66	Ball	Citroen DS19, ID19 1955–66 Autobook
COMMER		
Cob Series 1, 2, 3 1956–65	Ball	Hillman Minx 1 to 5 1956–65 Autobook
Imp Vans 1963–68	Smith	Hillman Imp 1963–68 Autobook
Imp Vans 1969–71	Ball	Hillman Imp 1969–71 Autobook
DAIMLER		
Daimler Sovereign 2.8, 4.2 litre 1970–72	Ball	Jaguar XJ6 1968–72 Autobook
DE DION BOUTON		
One-cylinder 1899–1907	Mercredy	De Dion Bouton Autobook One
Two-cylinder 1903–1907	Mercredy	De Dion Bouton Autobook One
Four-cylinder 1905–1907	Mercredy	De Dion Bouton Autobook One
DATSUN		
1200 B 110 1970–72	Ball	Datsun 1200 1970–72 Autobook
1200 KB 110 1970–72	Ball	Datsun 1200 1970–72 Autobook
1300 1968–70	Ball	Datsun 1300, 1600 1968–70 Autobook
1600 1968–70	Ball	Datsun 1300, 1600 1968–70 Autobook
240Z HLS 1970–71	Ball	Datsun 240Z Sport 1970–71 Autobook
240Z HS 1970–71	Ball	Datsun 240Z Sport 1970–71 Autobook
FIAT		
500 1957–61	Ball	Fiat 500 1957–69 Autobook
500D 1960–65	Ball	Fiat 500 1957–69 Autobook
500F 1965–69	Ball	Fiat 500 1957–69 Autobook
500L 1968–69	Ball	Fiat 500 1957–69 Autobook
600 633 cc 1955–61	Ball	Fiat 600, 600D 1955–69 Autobook
600D 767 cc 1960–69	Ball	Fiat 600, 600D 1955–69 Autobook
850 1964–71	Ball	Fiat 850 1964–71 Autobook
850S 1964–71	Ball	Fiat 850 1964–71 Autobook
850S Coupé 1965–68	Ball	Fiat 850 1964–71 Autobook
850S Special 1968–71	Ball	Fiat 850 1964–71 Autobook
850S Spyder 1965–68	Ball	Fiat 850 1964–71 Autobook
850 Sport 903 cc 1968–71	Ball	Fiat 850 1964–71 Autobook
1300 1961–66	Ball	Fiat 1300, 1500 1961–67 Autobook
1500 1961–67	Ball	Fiat 1300, 1500 1961–67 Autobook
124A 1966–71	Ball	Fiat 124 1966–71 Autobook
124AF 1967–71	Ball	Fiat 124 1966–71 Autobook
124 Special 1969–71	Ball	Fiat 124 1966–71 Autobook
124 Spyder 1966–70	Ball	Fiat 124 Sport 1966–70 Autobook
124 Coupé 1967–69	Ball	Fiat 124 Sport 1966–70 Autobook
FORD		
Anglia 100E 1953–59	Ball	Ford Anglia Prefect 100E Autobook
Anglia 105E 1959–67	Smith	Ford Anglia 105E, Prefect 107E 1959–67 Autobook
Anglia Super 123E 1962–67	Smith	Ford Anglia 105E, Prefect 107E 1959–67 Autobook
Capri 109E 1962	Smith	Ford Classic, Capri 1961–64 Autobook
Capri 116E 1962–64	Smith	Ford Classic, Capri 1961–64 Autobook
Capri 1300, 1300GT 1968–71	Ball	Ford Capri 1300, 1600 1968–71 Autobook
Capri 1600, 1600GT 1968–71	Ball	Ford Capri 1300, 1600 1968–71 Autobook
Capri 2000 GT 1969–71	Ball	Ford Capri 2000 GT, 3000 GT 1969–71 Autobook

Make	Author	Title
Capri 3000 GT 1969–71	Ball	Ford Capri 2000 GT, 3000 GT 1969–71 Autobook
Capri 3000 E 1969–71	Ball	Ford Capri 2000 GT, 3000 GT 1969–71 Autobook
Classic 109E 1961–62	Smith	Ford Classic, Capri 1961–64 Autobook
Classic 116E 1962–63	Smith	Ford Classic, Capri 1961–64 Autobook
Consul Mk 1 1950–56	Ball	Ford Consul, Zephyr, Zodiac 1, 2 1950–62 Autobook
Consul Mk 2 1956–62	Ball	Ford Consul, Zephyr, Zodiac 1, 2 1950–62 Autobook
Corsair Straight Four 1963–65	Ball	Ford Corsair Straight Four 1963–65 Autobook
Corsair Straight Four GT 1963–65	Ball	Ford Corsair Straight Four 1963–65 Autobook
Corsair V4 3004E 1965–68	Smith	Ford Corsair V4 1965–68 Autobook
Corsair V4 GT 1965–66	Smith	Ford Corsair V4 1965–68 Autobook
Corsair V4 1663 cc 1969–70	Ball	Ford Corsair V4 1969–70 Autobook
Corsair 2000, 2000E 1966–68	Smith	Ford Corsair V4 1965–68 Autobook
Corsair 2000, 2000E 1969–70	Ball	Ford Corsair V4 1969–70 Autobook
Cortina 113E 1962–66	Smith	Ford Cortina 1962–66 Autobook
Cortina Super 118E 1963–66	Smith	Ford Cortina 1962–66 Autobook
Cortina Lotus 125E 1963–66	Smith	Ford Cortina 1962–66 Autobook
Cortina GT 118E 1963–66	Smith	Ford Cortina 1962–66 Autobook
Cortina 1300 1967–68	Smith	Ford Cortina 1967–68 Autobook
Cortina 1300 1969–70	Ball	Ford Cortina 1969–70 Autobook
Cortina 1500 1967–68	Smith	Ford Cortina 1967–68 Autobook
Cortina 1600 (including Lotus) 1967–68 ..	Smith	Ford Cortina 1967–68 Autobook
Cortina 1600 1969–70	Ball	Ford Cortina 1969–70 Autobook
Cortina 1600 OHC Mk 3, GT 1971–72 ..	Ball	Ford Cortina 1600 GT, 2000, OHC, Mk 3 1971–72 Autobook
Cortina 2000 OHC HC Mk 3 1971–72 ..	Ball	Ford Cortina 1600 GT, 2000, OHC, Mk 3 1971–72 Autobook
Escort 100E 1955–59	Ball	Ford Anglia Prefect 100E Autobook
Escort 1100 1967–71	Ball	Ford Escort 1967–71 Autobook
Escort 1300 1967–71	Ball	Ford Escort 1967–71 Autobook
Executive 1966–71	Ball	Ford Zephyr V4, V6, Zodiac 1966–71 Autobook
Prefect 100E 1954–59	Ball	Ford Anglia Prefect 100E Autobook
Prefect 107E 1959–61	Smith	Ford Anglia 105E, Prefect 107E 1959–67 Autobook
Popular 100E 1959–62	Ball	Ford Anglia Prefect 100E Autobook
Squire 100E 1955–59	Ball	Ford Anglia Prefect 100E Autobook
Taunus 1300 OHC LC and HC 1971–72 ..	Ball	Ford Cortina 1600 GT, 2000, OHC, Mk 3, 1971–72 Autobook
Taunus 1600 OHC GT 1971–72	Ball	Ford Cortina 1600 GT, 2000, OHC, Mk 3 1971–72 Autobook
Zephyr Mk 1 1950–56	Ball	Ford Consul, Zephyr, Zodiac 1, 2 1950–62 Autobook
Zephyr Mk 2 1956–62	Ball	Ford Consul, Zephyr, Zodiac 1, 2 1950–62 Autobook
Zephyr 4 Mk 3 1962–66	Ball	Ford Zephyr, Zodiac Mk 3 1962–66 Autobook
Zephyr 6 Mk 3 1962–66	Ball	Ford Zephyr, Zodiac Mk 3 1962–66 Autobook
Zodiac Mk 3 1962–66	Ball	Ford Zephyr, Zodiac Mk 3 1962–66 Autobook
Zodiac Mk 1 1953–56	Ball	Ford Consul, Zephyr, Zodiac 1, 2 1950–62 Autobook
Zodiac Mk 2 1956–62	Ball	Ford Consul, Zephyr, Zodiac 1, 2 1950–62 Autobook
Zephyr V4 2 litre 1966–71	Ball	Ford Zephyr V4, V6, Zodiac 1966–71 Autobook
Zephyr V6 2.5 litre 1966–71	Ball	Ford Zephyr V4, V6, Zodiac 1966–71 Autobook
Zodiac V6 3 litre 1966–71	Ball	Ford Zephyr V4, V6, Zodiac 1966–71 Autobook

HILLMAN

Avenger, 1970–71	Ball	Hillman Avenger 1970–71 Autobook
Avenger, GT 1970–71	Ball	Hillman Avenger 1970–71 Autobook
Hunter, GT 1966–71	Ball	Hillman Hunter 1966–71 Autobook
Minx series 1, 2, 3 1956–59	Ball	Hillman Minx 1 to 5 1956–65 Autobook
Minx series 3A, 3B, 3C 1959–63	Ball	Hillman Minx 1 to 5 1956–65 Autobook
Minx series 5 1963–65	Ball	Hillman Minx 1 to 5 1956–65 Autobook
Minx series 6 1965–67	Ball	Hillman Minx 1965–67 Autobook
New Minx 1500, 1725 1966–70	Ball	Hillman Minx 1966–70 Autobook
Imp 1963–68	Smith	Hillman Imp 1963–68 Autobook
Imp 1969–71	Ball	Hillman Imp 1969–71 Autobook

Make	*Author*	*Title*
Husky series 1, 2, 3 1958–65	Ball	Hillman Minx 1 to 5 1956–65 Autobook
Husky Estate 1969–71	Ball	Hillman Imp 1969–71 Autobook
Super Minx Mk 1, 2, 3 1961–65	Ball	Hillman Super Minx 1961–65 Autobook
Super Minx Mk 4 1965–67	Ball	Hillman Minx 1965–67 Autobook
HUMBER		
Sceptre Mk 1 1963–65	Ball	Hillman Super Minx 1961–65 Autobook
Sceptre Mk 2 1965–67	Ball	Hillman Minx 1965–67 Autobook
Sceptre 1967–71	Ball	Hillman Hunter 1966–71 Autobook
JAGUAR		
XK 120 1948–54	Ball	Jaguar XK 120, 140, 150 Mk 7, 8, 9 1948–61 Autobook
XK 140 1954–57	Ball	Jaguar XK 120, 140, 150 Mk 7, 8, 9 1948–61 Autobook
XK 150 1957–61	Ball	Jaguar XK 120, 140, 150 Mk 7, 8, 9 1948–61 Autobook
XK 150S 1959–61	Ball	Jaguar XK 120, 140, 150 Mk 7, 8, 9 1948–61 Autobook
Mk 7, 7M, 8, 9 1950–61	Ball	Jaguar XK 120, 140, 150 Mk 7, 8, 9 1948–61 Autobook
2.4 Mk 1, 2 1955–67	Ball	Jaguar 2.4, 3.4, 3.8 Mk 1, 2 1955–69 Autobook
3.4 Mk 1, 2 1957–67	Ball	Jaguar 2.4, 3.4, 3.8 Mk 1, 2 1955–69 Autobook
3.8 Mk 2 1959–67	Ball	Jaguar 2.4, 3.4, 3.8 Mk 1, 2 1955–69 Autobook
240 1967–69	Ball	Jaguar 2.4, 3.4, 3.8 Mk 1, 2 1955–69 Autobook
340 1967–69	Ball	Jaguar 2.4, 3.4, 3.8 Mk 1, 2 1955–69 Autobook
E Type 3.8 1961–65	Ball	Jaguar E Type 1961–70 Autobook
E Type 4.2 1964–69	Ball	Jaguar E Type 1961–70 Autobook
E Type 4.2 2+2 1966–70	Ball	Jaguar E Type 1961–70 Autobook
E Type 4.2 Series 2 1969–70	Ball	Jaguar E Type 1961–70 Autobook
S Type 3.4 1963–68	Ball	Jaguar S Type and 420 1963–68 Autobook
S Type 3.8 1963–68	Ball	Jaguar S Type and 420 1963–68 Autobook
420 1963–68	Ball	Jaguar S Type and 420 1963–68 Autobook
XJ6 2.8 litre 1968–72	Ball	Jaguar XJ6 1968–72 Autobook
XJ6 4.2 litre 1968–72	Ball	Jaguar XJ6 1968–72 Autobook
JOWETT		
Javelin PA 1947–49	Mitchell	Jowett Javelin Jupiter 1947–53 Autobook
Javelin PB 1949–50	Mitchell	Jowett Javelin Jupiter 1947–53 Autobook
Javelin PC 1950–51	Mitchell	Jowett Javelin Jupiter 1947–53 Autobook
Javelin PD 1951–52	Mitchell	Jowett Javelin Jupiter 1947–53 Autobook
Javelin PE 1952–53	Mitchell	Jowett Javelin Jupiter 1947–53 Autobook
Jupiter Mk 1 SA 1949–52	Mitchell	Jowett Javelin Jupiter 1947–53 Autobook
Jupiter Mk 1A SC 1952–53	Mitchell	Jowett Javelin Jupiter 1947–53 Autobook
LANDROVER		
Series 1 1948–58	Ball	Landrover 1, 2 1948–61 Autobook
Series 2 1997 cc 1959–61	Ball	Landrover 1, 2 1948–61 Autobook
Series 2 2052 cc 1959–61	Ball	Landrover 1, 2 1948–61 Autobook
Series 2 2286 cc 1959–61	Ball	Landrover 2, 2A 1959–71 Autobook
Series 2A 2286 cc 1961–71	Ball	Landrover 2, 2A 1959–71 Autobook
Series 2A 2625 cc 1967–71	Ball	Landrover 2, 2A 1959–71 Autobook
MG		
TA 1936–39	Ball	MG TA to TF 1936–55 Autobook
TB 1939	Ball	MG TA to TF 1936–55 Autobook
TC 1945–49	Ball	MG TA to TF 1936–55 Autobook
TD 1950–53	Ball	MG TA to TF 1936–55 Autobook
TF 1953–54	Ball	MG TA to TF 1936–55 Autobook
TF 1500 1954–55	Ball	MG TA to TF 1936–55 Autobook
Midget 1961–71	Ball	Sprite, Midget 1958–71 Autobook
Magnette ZA, ZB 1955–59	Ball	BMC Autobook Three
MGA 1500, 1600 1955–62	Ball	MGA, MGB 1955–68 Autobook
MGA Twin Cam 1958–60	Ball	MGA, MGB 1955–68 Autobook

Make	Author	Title
MGB 1962–68	Ball	MGA, MGB 1955–68 Autobook
MGB 1969–71	Ball	MG MGB 1969–71 Autobook
1100 Mk 1 1962–67	Ball	1100 Mk 1 1962–67 Autobook
1100 Mk 2 1968	Ball	1100 Mk 2, 1300 Mk 1, 2, America 1968–71 Autobook
1300 Mk 1, 2 1968–71	Ball	1100 Mk 2, 1300 Mk 1, 2, America 1968–71 Autobook
MERCEDES-BENZ		
190B 1959–61	Ball	Mercedes-Benz 190 B, C, 200 1959–68 Autobook
190C 1961–65	Ball	Mercedes-Benz 190 B, C, 200 1959–68 Autobook
200 1965–68	Ball	Mercedes-Benz 190 B, C, 200 1959–68 Autobook
220B 1959–65	Ball	Mercedes-Benz 220 1959–65 Autobook
220SB 1959–65	Ball	Mercedes-Benz 220 1959–65 Autobook
220SEB 1959–65	Ball	Mercedes-Benz 220 1959–65 Autobook
220SEBC 1961–65	Ball	Mercedes-Benz 220 1959–65 Autobook
230 1965–67	Ball	Mercedes-Benz 230 1963–68 Autobook
230 S 1965–68	Ball	Mercedes-Benz 230 1963–68 Autobook
230 SL 1963–67	Ball	Mercedes-Benz 230 1963–68 Autobook
250 S 1965–68	Ball	Mercedes-Benz 250 1965–67 Autobook
250 SE 1965–67	Ball	Mercedes-Benz 250 1965–67 Autobook
250 SE BC 1965–67	Ball	Mercedes-Benz 250 1965–67 Autobook
250 SL 1967	Ball	Mercedes-Benz 250 1965–67 Autobook
MORGAN		
Four wheelers 1936–69	Clarke	Morgan 1936–69 Autobook
MORRIS		
Oxford 2. 3 1954–59	Ball	BMC Autobook Three
Oxford 5, 6 1959–70	Ball	Morris Oxford 5, 6 1959–70 Autobook
Marina 1.3, 1.3 TC 1971–72	Ball	Morris Marina 1971–72 Autobook
Marina 1.8, 1.8 TC 1971–72	Ball	Morris Marina 1971–72 Autobook
Minor series 2 1952–56	Ball	Morris Minor 1952–71 Autobook
Minor 1000 1957–71	Ball	Morris Minor 1952–71 Autobook
Mini 1959–71	Ball	Mini 1959–71 Autobook
Mini Clubman 1969–71	Ball	Mini 1959–71 Autobook
Minor series 2 1952–56	Ball	Morris Minor 1952–71 Autobook
Minor 1000 1957–71	Ball	Morris Minor 1952–71 Autobook
Mini Cooper 1961–70	Ball	Mini Cooper 1961–70 Autobook
Mini Cooper S 1963–70	Ball	Mini Cooper 1961–70 Autobook
1100 Mk 1 1962–67	Ball	1100 Mk 1 1962–67 Autobook
1100 Mk 2 1968–70	Ball	1100 Mk 2, 1300 Mk 1, 2, America 1968–71 Autobook
1300 Mk 1, 2 1968–71	Ball	1100 Mk 2, 1300 Mk 1, 2, America 1968–71 Autobook
1800 Mk 1, 2 1966–71	Ball	1800 1964–71 Autobook
1800 S 1968–71	Ball	1800 1964–71 Autobook
NSU		
Prinz 1000 L, LS 1963–67	Ball	NSU 1000 1963–70 Autobook
Prinz TT, TTS 1965–70	Ball	NSU 1000 1963–70 Autobook
1000 C 1967–70	Ball	NSU 1000 1963–70 Autobook
TYP 110 1966–67	Ball	NSU 1000 1963–70 Autobook
110 SC 1967	Ball	NSU 1000 1963–70 Autobook
1200, C, TT 1967–70	Ball	NSU 1000 1963–70 Autobook
OPEL		
Kadett 993 cc 1962–65	Ball	Opel Kadett, Olympia 993 cc and 1078 cc 1962–71 Autobook
Kadett 1078 cc 1965–71	Ball	Opel Kadett, Olympia 993 cc and 1078 cc 1962–71 Autobook
Kadett 1492 cc 1967–71	Ball	Opel Kadett, Olympia 1492 cc, 1698 cc and 1897 cc 1967–71 Autobook
Kadett 1698 cc 1967–70	Ball	Opel Kadett, Olympia 1492 cc, 1698 cc and 1897 cc 1967–71 Autobook

Make	*Author*	*Title*
Kadett 1897 cc 1967–71	Ball	Opel Kadett, Olympia 1492 cc, 1698 cc and 1897 cc 1967–71 Autobook
Olympia 1078 cc 1967–70	Ball	Opel Kadett, Olympia 993 cc and 1078 cc 1962–71 Autobook
Olympia 1492 cc 1967–70	Ball	Opel Kadett, Olympia 1492 cc, 1698 cc and 1897 cc 1967–71 Autobook
Olympia 1698 cc 1967–70	Ball	Opel Kadett, Olympia 1492 cc, 1698 cc and 1897 cc 1967–71 Autobook
Olympia 1897 cc 1967–70	Ball	Opel Kadett, Olympia 1492 cc, 1698 cc and 1897 cc 1967–71 Autobook
Rekord C 1.5, 1.7, 1.9 1966–70	Ball	Opel Rekord C 1966–70 Autobook
PEUGEOT		
404 1960–69	Ball	Peugeot 404 1960–69 Autobook
504 1968–70 (incl. fuel injection)	Ball	Peugeot 504 1968–70 Autobook
PLYMOUTH		
Cricket 1971	Ball	Hillman Avenger 1970–71 Autobook
PORSCHE		
356A 1957–59	Ball	Porsche 356A, 356B, 356C 1957–65 Autobook
356B 1959–63	Ball	Porsche 356A, 356B, 356C 1957–65 Autobook
356C 1963–65	Ball	Porsche 356A, 356B, 356C 1957–65 Autobook
911 1964–67	Ball	Porsche 911 1964–69 Autobook
911L 1967–68	Ball	Porsche 911 1964–69 Autobook
911S 1966–69	Ball	Porsche 911 1964–69 Autobook
911T 1967–69	Ball	Porsche 911 1964–69 Autobook
911E 1968–69	Ball	Porsche 911 1964–69 Autobook
912 1582 cc 1965–69	Ball	Porsche 912 1965–69 Autobook
RELIANT		
Regal Coupé 1952–56	Ball	Reliant Regal 1952–70 Autobook
Regal Mk 3, 4, 5, 6 1957–62	Ball	Reliant Regal 1952–70 Autobook
Regal 3/25 1962–68	Ball	Reliant Regal 1952–70 Autobook
Regal 3/30 1968–70	Ball	Reliant Regal 1952–70 Autobook
5 cwt, Super, Supervan 1956–70	Ball	Reliant Regal 1952–70 Autobook
RENAULT		
R4L 748 cc, 845 cc 1961–65	Ball	Renault R4, R4L, 4 1961–70 Autobook
R4 845 cc 1962–66	Ball	Renault R4, R4L, 4 1961–70 Autobook
4 845 cc 1966–70	Ball	Renault R4, R4L, 4 1961–70 Autobook
6 1968–70	Ball	Renault 6 1968–70 Autobook
R8 956 cc 1962–65	Ball	Renault 8, 10, 1100 1962–70 Autobook
8 956 cc, 1108 cc 1965–70	Ball	Renault 8, 10, 1100 1962–70 Autobook
8S 1108 cc, 1968–70	Ball	Renault 8, 10, 1100 1962–70 Autobook
1100 1108 cc 1964–69	Ball	Renault 8, 10, 1100 1962–70 Autobook
R10 1108 cc 1967–69	Ball	Renault 8, 10, 1100 1962–70 Autobook
10 1289 cc 1969–70	Ball	Renault 8, 10, 1100 1962–70 Autobook
Dauphine (R1090) 1957–64	Ball	Renault Dauphine Floride 1957–67 Autobook
Gordini Models (R1091 and R1095) 1959–67	Ball	Renault Dauphine Floride 1957–67 Autobook
Floride (R1092) 1959–63	Ball	Renault Dauphine Floride 1957–67 Autobook
16 1470 cc 1965–71	Ball	Renault R16 1965–71 Autobook
16TS 1968–71	Ball	Renault R16 1965–71 Autobook
16TL 1970–71	Ball	Renault R16 1965–71 Autobook
12L 1969–71	Ball	Renault 12 1969–71 Autobook
12TL 1969–71	Ball	Renault 12 1969–71 Autobook

Make	Author	Title
RILEY		
1.5 1957–65	Ball	BMC Autobook Three
Elf Mk 1, 2, 3 1961–69	Ball	Mini 1959–71 Autobook
1100 Mk 1 1965–67	Ball	1100 Mk 1 1962–67 Autobook
1100 Mk 2 1968	Ball	1100 Mk 2, 1300 Mk 1, 2 America 1968–71 Autobook
1300 Mk 1, 2 1968–69	Ball	1100 Mk 2, 1300 Mk 1, 2 America 1968–71 Autobook
ROVER		
60 1953–59	Ball	Rover 60–110 1953–64 Autobook
75 1954–59	Ball	Rover 60–110 1953–64 Autobook
80 1959–62	Ball	Rover 60–110 1953–64 Autobook
90 1954–59	Ball	Rover 60–110 1953–64 Autobook
95 1962–64	Ball	Rover 60–110 1953–64 Autobook
100 1959–62	Ball	Rover 60–110 1953–64 Autobook
105R 1957–58	Ball	Rover 60–110 1953–64 Autobook
105S 1957–59	Ball	Rover 60–110 1953–64 Autobook
110 1962–64	Ball	Rover 60–110 1953–64 Autobook
2000 SC 1963–71	Ball	Rover 2000 1963–71 Autobook
2000 TC 1963–71	Ball	Rover 2000 1963–71 Autobook
3 litre Saloon Mk 1, 1A 1958–62	Ball	Rover 3 litre 1958–67 Autobook
3 litre Saloon Mk 2, 3 1962–67	Ball	Rover 3 litre 1958–67 Autobook
3 litre Coupé 1965–67	Ball	Rover 3 litre 1958–67 Autobook
3500, 3500S 1968–70	Ball	Rover 3500, 3500S 1968–70 Autobook
SAAB		
95, 96 1960–64	Ball	Saab 95, 96 Sport 1960–68 Autobook
95(5), 96(5) 1964–68	Ball	Saab 95, 96 Sport 1960–68 Autobook
Sport 1962–66	Ball	Saab 95, 96 Sport 1960–68 Autobook
Monte Carlo 1965–66	Ball	Saab 95, 96 Sport 1960–68 Autobook
99 1969–70	Ball	Saab 99 1969–70 Autobook
SIMCA		
1000 1961–65	Ball	Simca 1000 1961–71 Autobook
1000 Special 1962–63	Ball	Simca 1000 1961–71 Autobook
1000 GL 1964–71	Ball	Simca 1000 1961–71 Autobook
1000 GLS 1964–69	Ball	Simca 1000 1961–71 Autobook
1000 GLA 1965–69	Ball	Simca 1000 1961–71 Autobook
1000 LS 1965–71	Ball	Simca 1000 1961–71 Autobook
1000 L 1966–68	Ball	Simca 1000 1961–71 Autobook
1000 Special 1968–71	Ball	Simca 1000 1961–71 Autobook
1100 LS 1967–70	Ball	Simca 1100 1967–70 Autobook
1100 GL, GLS 1967–70	Ball	Simca 1100 1967–70 Autobook
1204 1970	Ball	Simca 1100 1967–70 Autobook
1300 GL 1963–65	Ball	Simca 1300, 1301, 1500, 1501 1963–71 Autobook
1300 LS 1965–66	Ball	Simca 1300, 1301, 1500, 1501 1963–71 Autobook
1301 GL 1966–71	Ball	Simca 1300, 1301, 1500, 1501 1963–71 Autobook
1301 LS 1966–68	Ball	Simca 1300, 1301, 1500, 1501 1963–71 Autobook
1500 L 1963–65	Ball	Simca 1300, 1301, 1500, 1501 1963–71 Autobook
1500 GL 1965–66	Ball	Simca 1300, 1301, 1500, 1501 1963–71 Autobook
1500 GLS 1965–66	Ball	Simca 1300, 1301, 1500, 1501 1963–71 Autobook
1501 GL 1966–70	Ball	Simca 1300, 1301, 1500, 1501 1963–71 Autobook
1501 GLS 1966–68	Ball	Simca 1300, 1301, 1500, 1501 1963–71 Autobook
1501 GLS 1970–71	Ball	Simca 1300, 1301, 1500, 1501 1963–71 Autobook
1501 Special 1968–71	Ball	Simca 1300, 1301, 1500, 1501 1963–71 Autobook
SINGER		
Chamois 1964–68	Smith	Hillman Imp 1963–68 Autobook
Chamois 1969–70	Ball	Hillman Imp 1969–71 Autobook
Chamois Sport 1964–68	Smith	Hillman Imp 1963–68 Autobook
Chamois Sport 1969–70	Ball	Hillman Imp 1969–71 Autobook
Gazelle series 2A 1958	Ball	Hillman Minx 1 to 5 1956–65 Autobook
Gazelle 3, 3A, 3B, 3C 1958–63	Ball	Hillman Minx 1 to 5 1956–65 Autobook

Make	*Author*	*Title*
Gazelle series 5 1963–65	Ball	Hillman Minx 1 to 5 1956–65 Autobook
Gazelle series 6 1965–67	Ball	Hillman Minx 1965–67 Autobook
New Gazelle 1500, 1725 1966–70	Ball	Hillman Minx 1966–70 Autobook
Vogue Mk 1 to 3 1961–65	Ball	Hillman Super Minx 1961–65 Autobook
Vogue series 4 1965–67	Ball	Hillman Minx 1965–67 Autobook
New Vogue 1966–70	Ball	Hillman Hunter 1966–71 Autobook
SKODA		
440, 445, 450 1957–69	Skoda	Skoda Autobook One
SUNBEAM		
Alpine series 1, 2, 3, 4 1959–65	Ball	Sunbeam Rapie Alpine 1955–65 Autobook
Alpine series 5 1965–67	Ball	Hillman Minx 1965–67 Autobook
Alpine 1969–71	Ball	Hillman Hunter 1966–71 Autobook
Arrow 1969–71	Ball	Hillman Hunter 1966–71 Autobook
Rapier series 1, 2, 3, 3A, 4 1955–65	Ball	Sunbeam Rapier Alpine 1955–65 Autobook
Rapier series 5 1965–67	Ball	Hillman Minx 1965–67 Autobook
Rapier H.120 1967–71	Ball	Hillman Hunter 1966–71 Autobook
Imp Sport 1963–68	Smith	Hillman Imp 1963–68 Autobook
Imp Sport 1969–71	Ball	Hillman Imp 1969–71 Autobook
Stilletto 1967–68	Smith	Hillman Imp 1963–68 Autobook
Stilletto 1969–71	Ball	Hillman Imp 1969–71 Autobook
1250 1970–71	Ball	Hillman Avenger 1970–71 Autobook
1500 1970–71	Ball	Hillman Avenger 1970–71 Autobook
TOYOTA		
Corolla 1100 1967–70	Ball	Toyota Corolla 1100 1967–70 Autobook
Corolla 1100 De luxe 1967–70	Ball	Toyota Corolla 1100 1967–70 Autobook
Corolla 1100 Automatic 1968–69	Ball	Toyota Corolla 1100 1967–70 Autobook
Corona 1500 Mk 1 1965–70	Ball	Toyota Corolla 1500 Mk 1 1965–70 Autobook
Corona 1900 Mk 2 1969–71	Ball	Toyota Corona 1900 Mk 2 1969–71 Autobook
TRIUMPH		
TR2 1952–55	Ball	Triumph TR2, TR3, TR3A 1952–62 Autobook
TR3, TR3A 1955–62	Ball	Triumph TR2, TR3, TR3A 1952–62 Autobook
TR4, TR4A 1961–67	Ball	Triumph TR4, TR4A 1961–67 Autobook
TR5 1967–69	Ball	Triumph TR5, TR250, TR6 1967–70 Autobook
TR6 1969–70	Ball	Triumph TR5, TR250, TR6 1967–70 Autobook
TR250 1967–69	Ball	Triumph TR5, TR250, TR6 1967–70 Autobook
1300 1965–71	Ball	Triumph 1300, 1500 1965–71 Autobook
1300TC 1967–71	Ball	Triumph 1300, 1500 1965–71 Autobook
1500 1970–71	Ball	Triumph 1300, 1500 1965–71 Autobook
2000 Mk 1 1963–69	Ball	Triumph 2000 Mk 1, 2.5 PI Mk 1 1963–69 Autobook
2000 Mk 2 1969–71	Ball	Triumph 2000 Mk 2, 2.5 PI Mk 2 1969–71 Autobook
2.5 PI Mk 1 1963–69	Ball	Triumph 2000 Mk 1, 2.5 PI Mk 1 1963–69 Autobook
2.5 PI Mk 2 1969–71	Ball	Triumph 2000 Mk 2, 2.5 PI Mk 2 1969–71 Autobook
Herald 948 1959–64	Smith	Triumph Herald 1959–68 Autobook
Herald 1200 1961–68	Smith	Triumph Herald 1959–68 Autobook
Herald 1200 1969–70	Ball	Triumph Herald 1969–71 Autobook
Herald 12/50 1963–67	Smith	Triumph Herald 1959–68 Autobook
Herald 13/60 1967–68	Smith	Triumph Herald 1959–68 Autobook
Herald 13/60 1969–71	Ball	Triumph Herald 1969–71 Autobook
Spitfire 1962–68	Smith	Triumph Spitfire Vitesse 1962–68 Autobook
Spitfire Mk 3 1969–70	Ball	Triumph Spitfire Mk 3 1969–70 Autobook
Vitesse 1600 and 2 litre 1962–68	Smith	Triumph Spitfire Vitesse 1962–68 Autobook
Vitesse 2 litre 1969–70	Ball	Triumph GT6, Vitesse 2 litre 1969–70 Autobook
GT Six 2 litre 1966–68	Smith	Triumph Spitfire Vitesse 1962–68 Autobook
GT Six 1969–70	Ball	Triumph GT6, Vitesse 2 litre 1969–70 Autobook

Make	Author	Title
VANDEN PLAS		
3 litre 1959–64	Ball	Austin A99, A110 1959–68 Autobook
1100 Mk 1 1963–67	Ball	1100 Mk 1 1962–67 Autobook
1100 Mk 2 1968	Ball	1100 Mk 2, 1300 Mk 1, 2 America 1968–71 Autobook
1300 Mk 1, 2 1968–71	Ball	1100 Mk 2, 1300 Mk 1, 2 America 1968–71 Autobook
VAUXHALL		
Victor 1 1957–59	Ball	Vauxhall Victor 1, 2 FB 1957–64 Autobook
Victor 2 1959–61	Ball	Vauxhall Victor 1, 2 FB 1957–64 Autobook
Victor FB 1961–64	Ball	Vauxhall Victor 1, 2 FB 1957–64 Autobook
VX4/90 FBH 1961–64	Ball	Vauxhall Victor 1, 2 FB 1957–64 Autobook
Victor FC 101 1964–67	Ball	Vauxhall Victor 101 1964–67 Autobook
VX 4/90 FCH 1964–67	Ball	Vauxhall Victor 101 1964–67 Autobook
Victor FD 1599 cc 1967–71	Ball	Vauxhall Victor FD 1600, 2000 1967–71 Autobook
Victor FD 1975 cc 1967–71	Ball	Vauxhall Victor FD 1600, 2000 1967–71 Autobook
VX 4/90 1969–71	Ball	Vauxhall Victor FD 1600, 2000 1967–71 Autobook
Velox, Cresta PA 1957–62	Ball	Vauxhall Velox Cresta 1957–70 Autobook
Velox, Cresta PB 1962–65	Ball	Vauxhall Velox Cresta 1957–70 Autobook
Cresta PC 1965–70	Ball	Vauxhall Velox Cresta 1957–70 Autobook
Viscount 1966–70	Ball	Vauxhall Velox Cresta 1957–70 Autobook
Viva HA (including 90) 1964–66	Ball	Vauxhall Viva HA 1964–66 Autobook
Viva HB (including 90 and SL90) 1966–70	Ball	Vauxhall Viva HB 1966–70 Autobook
Viva HC 1159 cc 1971	Ball	Vauxhall Viva HC, Firenza 1971 Autobook
Viva HC SL 1159 cc 1971	Ball	Vauxhall Viva HC, Firenza 1971 Autobook
Firenza 1159 cc 1971	Ball	Vauxhall Viva HC, Firenza 1971 Autobook
Firenza SL 1159 cc 1971	Ball	Vauxhall Viva HC, Firenza 1971 Autobook
VOLKSWAGEN		
1200 Beetle 1954–67	Ball	Volkswagen Beetle 1954–67 Autobook
1200 Beetle 1968–71	Ball	Volkswagen Beetle 1968–71 Autobook
1200 Karmann Ghia 1955–65	Ball	Volkswagen Beetle 1954–67 Autobook
1200 Transporter 1954–64	Ball	Volkswagen Transporter 1954–67 Autobook
1300 Beetle 1965–67	Ball	Volkswagen Beetle 1954–67 Autobook
1300 Beetle 1968–71	Ball	Volkswagen Beetle 1968–71 Autobook
1300 Karmann Ghia 1965–66	Ball	Volkswagen Beetle 1954–67 Autobook
1500 Beetle 1966–67	Ball	Volkswagen Beetle 1954–67 Autobook
1500 Beetle 1968–70	Ball	Volkswagen Beetle 1968–71 Autobook
1500 1961–65	Ball	Volkswagen 1500 1961–66 Autobook
1500N 1963–65	Ball	Volkswagen 1500 1961–66 Autobook
1500S 1963–65	Ball	Volkswagen 1500 1961–66 Autobook
1500A 1965–66	Ball	Volkswagen 1500 1961–66 Autobook
1500 Karmann Ghia 1966–67	Ball	Volkswagen Beetle 1954–67 Autobook
1500 Transporter 1963–67	Ball	Volkswagen Transporter 1954–67 Autobook
1500 Karmann Ghia 1968–70	Ball	Volkswagen Beetle 1968–71 Autobook
1600 TL 1965–70	Ball	Volkswagen 1600 Fastback 1965–70 Autobook
1600 Variant 1965–66	Ball	Volkswagen 1600 Fastback 1965–70 Autobook
1600 L 1966–67	Ball	Volkswagen 1600 Fastback 1966–70 Autobook
1600 Variant L 1966–70	Ball	Volkswagen 1600 Fastback 1965–70 Autobook
1600 T 1968–70	Ball	Volkswagen 1600 Fastback 1965–70 Autobook
1600 TA 1969–70	Ball	Volkswagen 1600 Fastback 1965–70 Autobook
1600 Variant A, M	Ball	Volkswagen 1600 Fastback 1965–70 Autobook
1600 Karmann Ghia	Ball	Volkswagen 1600 Fastback 1965–70 Autobook
Delivery Van 1600 1968–71	Ball	Volkswagen Transporter 1968–71 Autobook
Pick-up 1600 1968–71	Ball	Volkswagen Transporter 1968–71 Autobook
Kombi 1600 1968–71	Ball	Volkswagen Transporter 1968–71 Autobook
Micro-Bus 1600 1968–71	Ball	Volkswagen Transporter 1968–71 Autobook

Make	Author	Title
VOLVO		
121, 131, 221 1962–68	Ball	Volvo P120 1961–68 Autobook
122, 132, 222 1961–68	Ball	Volvo P120 1961–68 Autobook
123 GT 1967–68	Ball	Volvo P120 1961–68 Autobook
142, 142S 1967–69	Ball	Volvo 140 1966–70 Autobook
144, 144S 1966–70	Ball	Volvo 140 1966–70 Autobook
145, 145S 1968–70	Ball	Volvo 140 1966–70 Autobook
P 1800 1961–63	Ball	Volvo 1800 1961–71 Autobook
1800S 1963–69	Ball	Volvo 1800 1961–71 Autobook
1800E 1969–71	Ball	Volvo 1800 1961–71 Autobook
WOLSELEY		
1500 1959–65	Ball	BMC Autobook Three
15/50 1956–58	Ball	BMC Autobook Three
6/99 1959–61	Ball	Austin A99, A110 1959–68 Autobook
6/110 1961–68	Ball	Austin A99, A110 1959–68 Autobook
Hornet Mk 1, 2, 3 1961–71	Ball	Mini 1959–71 Autobook
1100 Mk 1 1965–67	Ball	1100 Mk 1 1962–67 Autobook
1100 Mk 2 1968	Ball	1100 Mk 2, 1300 Mk 1, 2 America 1968–71 Autobook
1300 Mk 1, 2 1968–71	Ball	1100 Mk 2, 1300 Mk 1, 2 America 1968–71 Autobook
18/85 Mk 1, 2 1967–71	Ball	1800 1964–71 Autobook
18/85 S 1969–71	Ball	1800 1964–71 Autobook

NOTES

NOTES

NOTES

NOTES